P9-CAY-112

# The
# Psychoanalytic
# Study
# of the Child

## VOLUME FORTY-EIGHT

*Founding Editors*
ANNA FREUD, LL.D., D.SC.
HEINZ HARTMANN, M.D.
ERNST KRIS, Ph.D.

*Managing Editor*
ALBERT J. SOLNIT, M.D.

*Editors*
ALBERT J. SOLNIT, M.D.
PETER B. NEUBAUER, M.D.
SAMUEL ABRAMS, M.D.
A. SCOTT DOWLING, M.D.

*Associate Editor*
LOTTIE M. NEWMAN

*Editorial Board*

Samuel Abrams, M.D.
A. Scott Dowling, M.D.
Herbert Gaskill, M.D.
Hansi Kennedy, Dip. Psych.
Anton O. Kris, M.D.

Peter B. Neubauer, M.D.
Lottie M. Newman
Samuel Ritvo, M.D.
Albert J. Solnit, M.D.
Robert L. Tyson, M.D.

Kindly submit seven copies of new manuscripts to

Albert J. Solnit, M.D.
Yale Child Study Center
P.O. Box 3333
New Haven, CT 06510

# The Psychoanalytic Study of the Child

VOLUME FORTY-EIGHT

*New Haven and London*
*Yale University Press*
*1993*

Copyright © 1993 by Albert J. Solnit, Peter B. Neubauer,
Samuel Abrams, and A. Scott Dowling.
All rights reserved. This book may not be
reproduced, in whole or in part, including illustrations, in any form
(beyond that copying permitted by Sections 107
and 108 of the U.S. Copyright Laws and except by
reviewers for the public press), without
written permission from the publishers.

Designed by Sally Harris
and set in Baskerville type.
Printed in the United States of America by
Vail-Ballou Press, Inc., Binghamton, N.Y.

Library of Congress catalog card number: 45-11304
International standard book number: 0-300-05780-6
A catalogue record for this book is available from the British Library.

The paper in this book meets the guidelines for
permanence and durability of the Committee on
Production Guidelines for Book Longevity of the
Council on Library Resources.

2   4   6   8   10   9   7   5   3   1

*This volume is dedicated to our beloved, distinguished colleague and friend, Lottie M. Newman, who died at the age of seventy-three following the complications of an automobile accident. Shortly before the fatal accident, in her usual masterful way, she had completed the editing and organization of this volume in her capacity as Associate Editor. Born in Vienna, Lottie Maury Newman had been associated in a major way with* The Psychoanalytic Study of the Child *for more than forty years, having served from 1950 to 1970 as Chief Editor of International Universities Press, the previous publisher of the* Study. *She worked closely with Anna Freud for many years and became her literary executor. She was a founding member of the Sigmund Freud Archives and in 1984 received the Distinguished Contributor Award of the American Psychoanalytic Association. Her lasting legacy is evident in the legions of older and younger analysts with whom she worked. Her zestful, expert collaboration has contributed to improved scholarship and style throughout psychoanalytic literature.*

# Contents

# TRIBUTE TO
# GEORGE S. MORAN

# How People Get Better

## SAMUEL ABRAMS, M.D.

MY INTRODUCTION IS INTENDED TO SERVE TWO FUNCTIONS. ONE IS TO establish some continuity with past meetings; the second is to propose an outline for engaging this one.

This year's topic is how people get better. It can be usefully approached within a framework bordered by five linked issues.

1. Being well;
2. Becoming sick;
3. Getting better;
4. The vehicle for getting better;
5. Actualizing the vehicle.

In psychoanalysis we know these issues respectively as:

1. The concept of normality;
2. The theories of pathogenesis;
3. The mechanism of therapeutic action;
4. The therapeutic process;
5. The treatment relationship or contract.

In past meetings we have dealt with some of these issues, but our focus this weekend is upon the fourth of these five, the therapeutic process, the vehicle for conveying therapeutic action. However, as we have long since discovered, each issue is so inextricably linked with the others that it is not ever possible to discuss any one in isolation. It is regrettable that this is true because the psychoanalytic theories of normal mind, pathogenesis, treatment action, process, and contract are vast, complex, ambiguous, and even controversial regions.

It was not always the case. Contrast the contemporary turbulence with the elegant simplicity with which these five issues were addressed

Clinical Professor, Department of Psychiatry, New York University School of Medicine.
Introduction to the Thirteenth International Scientific Colloquium at the Anna Freud Centre on the subject of "Therapeutic Process in Child and Adult Psychoanalysis," November 1, 1991.

in the 1890s. One hundred years ago, Freud viewed mind as rising and falling titres of mental energies. He understood pathogenesis as the accumulation of libidinal excesses arising from childhood seduction. Therapeutic action, therefore, necessitated the discharge of the unwelcome resident cathectic abscess. The treatment process was conceptualized as marshaling the strangulated affect and opening the sluices to motility. To actualize the process, doctor and patient, unambiguously oriented toward relief of symptoms, deployed their contractual duties. The doctor applied hypnosis and forehead pressure to bring the libidinal affect to a head, while the patient compliantly revived reminiscences and emoted.

For a brief time, Freud was persuaded that his hypotheses accounted completely for his observations. He understood all five issues: being well, becoming sick, getting better, why it happened, and how to do it. Built into the doing was a conviction that he knew what was wrong and that his patient did not know and could not know. That conviction shaped the nature of his initial therapeutic contract and lent further leverage to the authoritative power required to marshal the affect. In truth, this first therapeutic process relied more on the doctor's certainty and the patient's faith than on any cathectic liberation. Fortunately, in time, Freud recognized that this was so and turned from the solace that conviction brings to the discomforts of the actual ambiguities in the clinical situation. In doing so, he became a psychoanalyst.

Those initial theories have grown considerably in the past 100 years. Some are more mature than others and one or two have an adolescent restlessness about them, as if they are not quite sure what they are. All are complex, somewhat enigmatic, and controversial. Many analysts believe that there is much more of value embedded somewhere within those growing complexities if only we had a way of teasing it out. This weekend, we intend to give it a try.

We have chosen what might seem to be an unusual approach. One would imagine that attempting to conceptualize and comprehend the therapeutic process would be difficult enough to do were we to concentrate upon adults or children alone. Yet, we have elected to proceed with our study by contrasting and comparing *both* children and adults, in the hope that by making the topic more difficult, we will somehow make it easier. It would seem a foolhardy premise, were it not for the fact that just such an approach has proven so successful here at the Centre in so many prior colloquia.

What can we glean from our 100-year-old theories?

*Being well, or the concept of the normal mind.* Mind has grown up to be much more than states of equilibria governed by the pleasure principle. It has long since been established that it is more useful to view the mind in terms of a variety of developing schematic configurations. In general, for very practical reasons, analysts often prefer to tie such schemas to central dynamic issues and to derivatives of the object inter-action system. Freud himself pioneered such a tactic when he noted that the normal tripartite mind is a precipitate of the expected infantile neurosis and later Klein described the normal paranoid and depressive positions. However, some analysts, particularly those inspired by infant observational and longitudinal studies, add to these pragmatic per-spectives the examination of nonconflictual determinants of structure formation, variations in ego equipment, and the impact of emerging developmental organizations. For this second group, the mind has grown from its economic, dynamic, and structural bases to a program synthesized out of drives, the object-interaction system, and equip-ment pulled together in a sequence of progressive, hierarchically or-dered, developmental organizations. Some therapists balk at such com-plexities. Do we need all of that? They wonder if we can securely find our clinical way in such a conceptual maze. Perhaps, they add, it is better to remain focused on dynamics and object relations in order to do more even if it means knowing less. The two papers prepared in advance for this colloquium brush against these questions and may come up with somewhat different answers.

*What about growth in our understanding of pathogenesis?* Our categories of disorders have grown along with our concept of mind. Not unexpec-tedly, clinicians who link normal development to expected dynamic or interactive determinants, also prefer to classify disorders in terms of dynamic and interactive pathogens. This yields such comforting slo-gans as "Neuroses are oedipal," "Narcissistic disturbances reflect un-empathic mothering," and "Depression is aggression turned against the self." On the other hand, there are some clinicians who lean toward descriptive categories while evaluating patients, categories that are not immediately linked to an expectable pathogenic source. They argue that such an approach leaves open the possibility of discovering some-thing entirely unexpected, e.g., other dynamics, equipmental failures, or developmental deviations. We are likely to encounter these dispa-rate preferences in the papers and in the discussions they will evoke.

*The theory of therapeutic action,* getting better, has had a vibrant growth. The cure is no longer conceptualized merely as discharge; rather, for most analysts it entails a fresh putting together, a new inte-gration. The results of the putting together are sometimes new struc-tures or new insights and even new ways of knowing. While analysts generally agree that therapeutic action is a new integration, they often disagree about what they prefer to see integrated in their patients. Those who are more concerned with changes in the unconscious ego and superego incline themselves a bit more toward accessing drive-derived fantasies and resolving intrapsychic conflicts; those who are focused upon changes in the representations of the self and others are usually more tilted toward addressing the consequences of the actu-alities of past experiences. I emphasize that I speak of inclinations rather than absolute polarities.

In addition to a new integration of past pathogens, there seem to be other ways of getting better, e.g., buttressing defenses, learning more felicitous adaptive strategies, feeling loved, having faith, identifica-tions, and, especially with children, finding experiences that can acti-vate developmental processes. Physicians tell us that when treating a disease, mixing different prescriptions sometimes poses risks. Do our different modes of therapeutic action always readily harmonize with one another? Or can we safely do a little of this and a little of that without violating the overall treatment program?

What about our central focus, *the vehicle that conveys the treatment action, therapeutic process*? Most analysts accept the proposition that for a new integration to take place, it is necessary to acquire access to the origins of the unrecognized infantile pathogens. Our stance and tech-nique, therefore, are designed to promote regression and induce the calling up of the unsettled conflicts and disordered relationships and the ushering of them into the treatment relationship. Our theory de-clares that once so revived and consolidated in the transference, the hitherto unconscious elements can be "analyzed," "worked through," and finally be put together by the patient in a new way. The fundamen-tal components of the therapeutic process most familiar to all of us, therefore, are the revived past, the transference, the action of new integration, and the resistance encountered to each step.

None of these highly prized components are free of controversy. For example, while the revived past highlights the "there and then," some adult analysts and many child analysts insist on the importance of the "here and now." Furthermore, most child analysts, because they are so aware of the developmental dimension, also oblige themselves to at-tend to the "yet to be." How difficult is it to maintain a stance that coordinates the "there and then," the "here and now," and the "yet to be"? Does the fostering of one time zone impair the activation of an-other? Or can we move freely through past, present, and future like Marley's ghost?

A second prized component of the treatment process is the *trans-ference*, a beleaguered word. What is that overly burdened term to include? Is regressive revival limited to what was, or is it also to include what was not or what might have been? Is transference old object alone or also real object, externalized object, projected object, mirrored object, idealized object as well as some conglomerate? These are painfully complex questions, but some child analysts complicate them further. They declare that an analyst can sometimes be therapeutically more useful as a new object for emerging developmental organizations than as a past object for conflict resolution. They wonder if such a therapy should be called psychoanalysis. We have been assured by Freud that any treatment that attends to the transference and to the resistance deserves the designation psychoanalysis. Regrettably, Freud offered that assurance at a time when there was considerably more agreement as to what those terms mean than exists today. Transferences to whom? Resistances to what? It will not be possible to avoid confronting the enigmatic features of such terms this weekend.

The third component of the therapeutic process is the active putting together, the curative comprehension, the integration itself. Who does it and how does it happen? Are the analyst's interpretations the act of putting together or do they merely facilitate differentiation? Is comprehension a *resolution* of past conflicts or a *curtailment* of past pathogenic objects? Furthermore, how much does effective comprehension lean on the integrity of the integrative capacities? Sadly, as the reading of the papers prepared for this meeting suggests, such capacities are not always unfettered. Child analysts recognize that the equipment of integration itself is often limited, sometimes because of immaturity, sometimes because of some innate defect, and everyone knows that integration can be impaired by inhibition. How do we distinguish neurotic inhibition from inherent limitation when we face obstacles in the patient's new putting together?

The last of our five sequential issues is the *treatment relationship*, the implicit contract that informs the activities needed to actualize the therapeutic process.

In the 1890s, the treatment contract was sealed once authority shook hands with compliance. In the 1990s the contract has changed in the direction of a more cooperative enterprise, entailing greater equality. One hundred years ago Freud pictured himself as the detached "incisive" surgeon. His metaphors gradually changed. He became a fertile inseminating male in one, a knowledgeable traveling companion in another. Our current metaphors have grown in numbers and complexity. Child analysts find themselves swept up in images of parenting and educating as ways of promoting development and this "developmental" focus has gripped many adult analysts as well. Other clinicians are wrapped in symbols implying corrective care or intimate partnerships. A study of such images should enrich our understanding of how our view of the treatment contract informs the ways we launch and maintain the therapeutic process. The data we have been provided with for the colloquium offer us some opportunity to discuss such influences.

To summarize this proposed framework:

Therapeutic process contains orientation, stance, transference, resistance, and conveys treatment action. It is a concept influenced by models of the normal mind and theories of pathogenesis. It is initiated and sustained by a treatment contract which shapes its form and direction.

At the outset I said that one of the functions of my introduction was to offer an outline to engage the topic. I recognize that my introduction also contains an unannounced function. In preparing it, I unwittingly changed the title of the weekend's colloquium from "Therapeutic Process in Child and Adult Psychoanalysis" to "Therapeutic Process*es* in the Psychoanalytic Treatment of Adults and Children." I blame my uncustomary presumptuousness to the influence of a study group sponsored by the Psychoanalytic Research and Development Fund, of which I am a member. Over recent months the group has come to recognize the value of differentiating *processes* rather than hunting for *the* process. The processes approach is predicated upon the belief that psychoanalysis provides the foundation for understanding a variety of vehicles for getting better rather than just a single one, each an inventive application of some of our fundamental facts and theories. In the next day or two we may be tempted to channel our discussion into determining which of these different vehicles deserves the special designation *psychoanalytic;* if we yield to that temptation our weekend is likely to be transformed into a complex legal battle over the rights of ownership. Let us defer the courtroom drama for another forum where I will be more than willing to present my own brief. For now, we have before us descriptions of several patients who got better. Our time will be better spent if we attempt to establish criteria for separating the different ways each got better. This will focus our attention upon different therapeutic actions and the appropriate vehicles for conveying them.

# The Roles of Mental Representations and Mental Processes in Therapeutic Action

PETER FONAGY, PH.D.,
GEORGE S. MORAN, PH.D.,
ROSE EDGCUMBE, B.A., M.S.,
HANSI KENNEDY, DIP. PSYCH.,
and MARY TARGET, M.Sc.

*In this paper we describe two models of the psychoanalytic treatment of mental disturbance. The first describes the mechanism by which the patient is helped to recover threatening ideas and feelings which have been repudiated or distorted as a result of conflict and defense. The second points to the therapeutic effects of engaging previously inhibited mental processes within the psychoanalytic encounter. The two forms of therapeutic action imply two distinct means available to the individual to deal with psychological conflict. They highlight different aspects of the psychoanalytic process and technique in child and adult psychoanalysis.*

THIS PAPER PRESENTS A DEVELOPMENTAL VIEW OF THERAPEUTIC ACTION in psychoanalysis. We start with the assumption that therapeutic action must be considered, first and foremost, in terms of the mechanisms

This paper is the product of the work of the Research Group on the Efficacy of Child Psychoanalysis, which has received considerable intellectual stimulation and support from Professors Donald Cohen and Alan Kazdin of Yale University. The authors are also indebted to Professor Joseph Sandler for his illuminating comments on an earlier draft. This is an extended version of a paper presented at the 13th International Colloquium at the Anna Freud Centre, November, 1991. Tragically, George Moran died shortly after completing his work on this paper. The authors wish to dedicate it to his memory. The authors also wish to express their gratitude to therapists Pat Radford, Sheila Melzak, and Ava Bry for additional case material.

which underlie psychic change. We go on to delineate two schematic models to highlight distinct aspects of curative factors in the psychoanalytic treatment of mental disturbance. The first, which we call the *representational model,* focuses on the mental mechanisms involved in the recovery of threatening ideas and feelings and the consequent reorganization of mental structures commonly invoked in explanations of psychoanalytic process. The second model, the *mental process model,* attempts to explore new ground opened up by the psychoanalytic treatment of seriously disturbed patients. It may help to explain how and why psychoanalysis benefits those whose pathology resides within the ego, and has been described in the past under headings such as ego deficit, ego restriction or developmental pathology. It draws attention to the therapeutic effects of engaging previously inhibited mental processes in the here-and-now of the psychoanalytic encounter.

The two models of therapeutic action imply two distinct, potentially pathological, means available to the individual to deal with psychological conflict. The purpose of differentiating two models is not formally to distinguish one group of patients from another, nor do we expect them necessarily to overlap with categories within a psychiatric nosology. Nor are we aiming to put forward a new metapsychology to add to or to replace existing points of view. However, models may have heuristic value in the context of therapeutic action and psychic change, especially in explaining differences in patients' rate of psychic change and in the techniques employed to bring about change.

At the focal point of psychoanalytic formulations concerning therapeutic action are changes in the internal organization of feelings, beliefs, and ideas (mental contents), brought about through interpretive work and other aspects of the psychoanalytic situation. In the first part of this paper we elaborate a framework for conceptualizing therapeutic action as reorganization of mental structures, making extensive use of the construct of mental representations. This may help toward clarifying how the changes in mental structure within individual sessions accumulate to bring about the kinds of outcome we expect from the entire psychoanalytic process (Compton, 1988, cited in Weinshel, 1990; De Witt et al., 1990).

### THE REPRESENTATIONAL MODEL

Two principal propositions seem to us to be shared by many psychoanalytic formulations of therapeutic action; namely, that (1) pathology is associated with the persistence of developmentally primitive mental structures, and (2) psychoanalysis exerts its mutative influence through a process of reorganization and integration of repudiated unconscious mental structures with developmentally higher order conscious ones. The most comprehensive formulation based on these assumptions is the "schematic model" proposed by Abrams (1980, 1987, 1988, 1990). We would like next to restate this model within a framework which enables us to elaborate some of the ways that the psychoanalytic process acts upon mental representations and contributes to the psychic changes we observe in our patients.

Mental representation is a theoretical construct that psychoanalysts may use to understand and explain the inner world of patients (Sandler and Rosenblatt, 1962; Jacobson, 1964). It is axiomatic that human thought and action must involve a "representational system." Formulation of therapeutic action in terms of changes in mental representation does not replace formulations based on structural theory or object relations; instead, it aims to describe the same set of phenomena, merely at a different level of abstraction. Analysis of psychic change at the level of the modifications of mental representations, however, may serve to highlight certain qualitative differences in the psychic mechanisms of therapeutic action which may represent different aspects of the analytic process.

It is misleading to use representation in the sense of a symbol that "stands for" some external reality. Rather, mental representations are better conceived of as patterns of mental activation, as links between the component features of representations.[1] They not only store our past experience but also guide our perception and influence our experience of our external and internal worlds.

Objects are "represented" in the sense that we construct mental models which integrate numerous attributes into a single system. Connections between attributes may be based on experience or the activation of attributes by wishes, fantasies, fears, or other affective structures with the capacity to distort the internal organization of mental life. Objects may be represented in numerous ways as person schemas,

---

1. Our use of the concept of mental representation includes the notion that representations are stored as "networks" of "nodes" spread across the brain (Rumelhart and McClelland, 1986). In essence a representation is a pattern of activation within such a hypothetical neural net. As a new representation is created, the strength of connections between a set of such nodes (also referred to as features or components) is altered. A single node or feature may be active or inactive. Its activity is a function of the state of other nodes in the system to which it is connected. The undoubted power of this model of mental representation lies in the inherent property of such networks to extract and represent the "invariants," the most commonly repeated co-occurring aspects, of object or relationship representations. In our view, representations are the common pathway through which all therapeutic agents of change act.

as representations of frequently encountered patterns of relation-ships, as assumptions of functions frequently associated with the ob-ject, as representations of typical interpersonal interactions, and so on.

Mental representation may be considered a dynamic (motivationally relevant) construct insofar as it is inextricably linked to emotional ex-perience.[2] The motivational properties of drive states and intrapsychic conflicts at the level of psychic structure are experienced in terms of both conscious and unconscious, positive and negative, emotional states (Sandler, 1972).

We will now present a clinical example which illustrates therapeutic action and the analytic process readily conceived of in terms of the representational model. The example illustrates the way in which un-conscious mental representations are subjected to analytic scrutiny and undergo reorganization within the microcosm of a single session.

CASE ILLUSTRATION

On his sixth birthday, to everyone's surprise, Sam announced that he was "the unhappiest person in the world."[3] During the assessment 7-year-old Sam told me that *everything* had been bad since he was 6. I was forced to agree that "things" were not good for Sam. At 6, he was still sleeping in the same bed as his mother. He had not yet given up the bottle, and he "insisted" on keeping a wide strand of his hair waist-length at the back. Notwithstanding his remarkable intelligence (he tested at 151 IQ on the WPPSI), his school performance was average, and his teachers' reports indicated that he was withdrawn and passive at school and bullied, even though he was taller than the rest of his class.

Sam's family history was his greatest burden. His mother Priscilla, a beautiful, petite 30-year-old woman of Swedish descent with a childlike appearance and frankly infantile diction, was herself deprived of a loving childhood. Her mother died in childbirth; her father, a Circuit Judge, never remarried; yet she had no recollection of individual housekeepers who would have looked after her. She had an abortion before having Sam at the age of 25. Sam's father, Peter, was in the process of a painful divorce when he had his brief affair with her. After

2. Emotional experience is constructed out of mental representations. The separa-tion of thinking and affect may only be possible at the level of common parlance, based on and restricted to phenomenal experience. Mental representations are imbued with affective content in the sense that affective valuations are associated with all types of representational content (beliefs, expectations, associations, wishes, desires).

3. This case was treated by Peter Fonagy (whose report this is) and was supervised by Anne-Marie Sandler. The authors would like to express their gratitude for her valuable contributions to the clinical understanding of the case.

Sam's birth, he remarried and started a third family, although he kept in contact with Sam and his mother during Sam's earliest years. Priscilla had no qualifications, no private means, but a curious expectation of a right to assistance reminiscent of the values of past centuries.

Fred was the provider. He had known Priscilla for at least 10 years. The relationship may once have been sexual, but this ended many years before Sam's father made his brief appearance. In fact, even at the time of the pregnancy, the three of them often holidayed together and Sam's mother invited Fred to be present at the birth together with Sam's father, an offer which Fred uncharacteristically was able to de-cline. Fred was a somewhat ineffectual, indecisive, sadly unsuccessful man. He bought a house with Sam's mother because of his fondness for Sam. He fulfilled the role of a substitute father with affection, yet strangely he had his own children, both Sam's juniors by several years, by a girlfriend whom he visited briefly at weekends, braving Priscilla's at times fierce protests. He was clearly wary of her; an attitude which he unequivocally revealed when, in a telephone conversation with me, he said, "Well, as Priscilla isn't here, I don't mind telling you that Sam has been a great deal better since you have been seeing him."

Sam's relationship with his mother was a complex one. Evidently in one way he was her pride and joy, "her little cavalier." She had the capacity to provide him with overt affection and physical comfort albeit in a highly seductive manner. On the other hand, she was a woman who suffered from chronic depression. She had frequent rages with Sam and walked out of the house leaving Fred to cope with the entire daily routine at the expense of his business commitments. Her sentimental concern for Sam was combined with total ruthlessness, verging on cruelty. On one occasion when the analyst saw both Priscilla and Fred for their regular monthly meeting, she said she was fed up with Sam for taking up room in *her* bed and for his lack of respect for *her* privacy. Fred timidly suggested that Sam might consider Priscilla's bedroom his own, since after all he slept there every night. She said that that was nonsense, he knew perfectly well that his bedroom was two floors down (where nobody else slept); after all, he had slept there once before, two years ago, for part of the night. She went on to suggest, without a hint of irony, that the best method for dealing with the problem might be to lock Sam in his room and let him cry, if necessary all night, until he became accustomed to his new home.

Priscilla's insensitivity to Sam's concerns was such that she refused to accept the suggestion of the diagnostician that Sam's "sadness" on his sixth birthday might have been linked to his father's departure for Canada with his new family just before Sam turned 6.

Sam was in analysis for nearly three years. I came to understand how heavily his burden of having to affirm his mother's existence and provide a route out of her depression sat on him and impeded the growth of his sense of identity and self-esteem. In the first year he was frequently babyish. He dribbled, he asked me to feed him, and he smelled everything; but his infantile role protected him from the humiliation and terror he feared in his relationship with his mother.

I was struck by his play with tiny, almost invisible specks of dust and fluff. He called them "cars," pushed them round the table, "parked" them overnight, and eagerly looked for them at the beginning of the next session. He was visibly relieved when I explained that I understood that Sam sometimes wished to be as small as the cars so that he could go unnoticed, but also could get inside people and things, because inside it would feel safe and protected. He told me that his ambition was to grow into a 6-month-old baby girl. I suggested that as a baby he would be protected by me and his mother, and then secretly he could keep a tiny part of what *was* Sam.

To illustrate the issues associated with therapeutic action, it may be profitable to look at material from a session in the second year of analysis. One Friday Sam behaved very strangely. He was unsettled, he did not want to get involved with anything. He quickly abandoned games he had started, but spent a considerable time climbing up onto the table and jumping off onto the carpet. I did not understand his mood, and wondered aloud if perhaps the long weekend (there was a Bank Holiday coming up) felt to Sam like the gap into which he was jumping from the table. Sam replied, "I am jumping into the unknown." At this stage I did not know to what he was referring, but I detected his anxiety and wondered whether Sam was practicing for something that seemed frightening. He said, "Maybe." To my surprise, when Fred came to collect him and I said good-bye to Sam with my usual "See you," he again replied, "Maybe." Fred was also surprised and said, "What do you mean? I know that it is half-term, but you are coming on Tuesday as usual. that is what we agreed with Dr. Fonagy." Sam had thus prepared me for the message from his mother which was left on the answer-phone on Sunday night. She had decided not to bring Sam on Tuesday, despite our agreement that Sam would come to analysis during the half-term break as I had been away for a few days some weeks before. I was to discover later that Sam had been given quite a different impression by his mother.

On Wednesday Sam arrived on time. I saw him from the top of the staircase. Unusually, he did not kiss his mother good-bye, but shut the door very carefully behind him and came up the staircase much more slowly than usual. I greeted him and he responded by smiling and swinging his head cheerfully from side to side, but I had a sense that Sam was pretending. He sat down at the table, laid his head on it, stuck his fingers in his ears, and started "making a concert" (making a concert is what he and I called his humming, usually a popular classical theme, when he was not too keen to hear what I had to say). I said, "Sam, I wonder what it is that you think I am going to say, that you don't feel like listening to?" He replied crossly, "You are going to say that I am angry that you were not here yesterday! I am not angry and that's that!" He then changed his voice from the angry tone of the previous exchange to a "sleepy" voice, "I am very *sleepy* and *tired*. Very, very *tired*. So *tired* that I can't keep my eyes open."

He said, "We had our hair cut." He smiled for a moment, then with considerable vehemence he added, "I will *kill* the man who cut so much off. He cut off two and a half inches or two centimeters or even two millimeters." His voice trailed off into uncertainty. He then told me about the holiday that had been arranged in Tunis for the summer. His mother and the mother of a friend of his were planning to take their children together. He described the hotel and seemed particularly excited about the swimming pool. He looked out of the window to point out how big the pool was. "It is as big as the gap between the houses over there and the houses over there," pointing to the two rows of houses separated by about 50 meters of garden. I remarked, "You know, Sam, sometimes very small changes like the two days we missed yesterday and the Bank Holiday can feel like very big gaps, even if they are not the summer holiday, and I think that you feel cross because your house and my house felt like they were a very great distance from one another over the past few days." He was *tired* and *sleepy*. He decided that he wanted to sleep on the table. He climbed on the table and grabbed the cushion from the chair. He lay down and pretended to sleep. He told me that he wanted to take a rest and to "think." I should let him think and not disturb him all the time. I talked to him in psychoanalese and was always wrong. He sounded like Greta Garbo saying that she wanted to be alone. I remained silent and Sam went on to tell me how hard *he* had worked on Sunday. It was a long and complicated story, but the gist of it was that he had helped Fred to send out a flyer about a new product.

I commented, "It is very hard for you. It makes you feel very bad about yourself to think that I didn't see you on Tuesday because I was too *tired* and I didn't want to work. I just wanted to take a rest and it didn't matter how much it would upset you." He sat up on the table sharply and retorted, "I didn't think that. Mummy said that you didn't want to see me because you were probably tired." Then sitting on the table, dangling his feet over the edge, he showed me a new game which he called Dead Fingers. He leaned on the palm of his left hand and with his right hand pulled up his fingers in turn letting them slap back on the table. For a few minutes he seemed absorbed in the game. I did not understand the game and so stayed silent. From time to time he would change the order in which he picked up the fingers. There seemed to be a predetermined counting sequence which he apparently kept getting wrong. He said, "I am confused which dead finger is next."

As I looked a little bit more closely at what Sam was doing, I realized that each time Sam went round the five fingers he would pass one by without picking it up. I commented, "I think I know how terribly confusing and frightening it is when you feel that you may be forgotten or overlooked by someone too tired or too sad to count on. You wonder if I know that being left out can feel almost like being dead inside—a bit like feeling very, very tired." He responded by picking up two "dead" fingers and letting them slap down with a painful thump. I continued, "It's frightening that not only do you feel dead-tired inside, but somehow I am sad-tired or dead-tired too: so tired that it's not safe to do anything else with me but sleep."

He stopped the game and sat back in his chair. He told me that he had had a dream about Emil and the Detectives. Sam did not often tell dreams, so I listened attentively to a somewhat muddled narrative. "Emil had money stolen in a bus by a wicked man when he fell asleep and Emil had many friends. And there were four evil men and they all ganged up against him. And Emil and the boys discovered all the money from the bank. They found the bank robbery money, and Emil's money." Then he told me about being frightened of robbers who are in the cupboard at the top of the stairs at home, and how Fred was not there on Saturday night to take him to the loo past the robbers. He then turned to me and asked, as if it was the most obvious sequence, "How old are you?" I replied, "You know Sam, when Mummy is sad or tired, it feels very good to have a man around, a friend like Fred or me. But today you feel very let down by me, as sometimes you do with Mummy. And of course you feel angry, but then it feels as if you have no friends and there is nowhere to keep your special things safe."

When I said this, Sam cheered up and wanted to play "hangman," in which one player attempts to identify a word by guessing its letters. The first word turned out to be FEET, but not before I was almost "hanged" because Sam cheated and said that there was no F in the word. The nearly hanged figure was filled in with black pencil at the end of the game and then Sam smudged it, covering the whole paper. "It looks horrid," he commented, sounding satisfied, but then looked glum again. He dreamily pushed the smudged piece of paper around the table with his index finger. I said, "Showing me how horrid and horrible you feel when I am not available makes you frightened that I might do something evil like rob you of something." He remarked in a childlike voice, "Naughty Dr. Fonagy," and pushed the piece of paper off the table, looked up, and smiled.

Not looking the least bit tired, Sam ran over to his box and suggested that we should play family trees again. We went over the whole three generational diagram, naming everyone. Sam said, "I have understood something. There are three families. There is Priscilla's family, Fred-Dad's family, and Peter's family. But Fred-Dad's family and Peter's family are *not* really families because they have other children." Then listening for the noises in the house, "How many children do you have?" I replied, "I think I now understand better why you feel *so* angry when we don't meet. You feel so easily that Fred and Peter have real families with other children who are loved, while in your family there is only you and Priscilla and when she is too tired you feel cheated and cross." He replied, "If you have babies, then they require a lot of attention." At the same time he dribbled but quickly wiped up his saliva with the sleeve of his jumper. I continued, "When you are a baby you hope that Mummy and I will concentrate only on you. But if you are a 7-year-old with short hair and angry feelings, you fear that we will get tired and won't have time for you." He said, as if explaining something rather obvious, "There are three kinds of tiredness." There is, it seems, sad-tired which is when he lies on the table putting his feet at the far end and his head near where the analyst is sitting. There is tired-tired when he has his feet at the analyst's end, and there is happy-tired and then he sleeps on the carpet. I replied that I thought we understood that when Sam wanted me to help with what was happening inside his head, then he wanted his head to be near his analyst, so that he could look into it to see why Sam was feeling sad, just like today. He said, "Exactly."

COMMENT

In the vignette of Sam we can see how repudiated mental representations are verbalized by the analyst and transformed and reintegrated into Sam's representations of self and object. These representations are more enduring than representations of the individual experiences which gave rise to them. They become organizing mental representations by virtue of the frequency with which they occur, and they may be seen as embodying "prototype" representations of the self, the object, or the interaction between the two. Sam's representation of himself in relation to his mother as a 6-month-old baby girl was an example of such a prototype which was enacted in the analysis in his dribbling, smelling things, and requests to be fed. His was a pathological solution to a conflict about what kind of relationship he could safely have with his depressed and unavailable mother and abandoning father-analyst. Aspects of these representations were taken up in the interpretations at different times in the course of the analysis and in the session reported in detail: his wish to be protected (not abandoned); his confusion in the face of mother's withdrawal; his wish to be small enough to get "inside" where it is safe; also to be helpless and incapable as a defense against his anger and retaliatory castration anxieties; his fear that his masculine protest has driven his objects away.

The session with Sam reveals in his sleepiness a mental representation of the depressed mother whom he fears he has either damaged or caused to lose interest in him, and it is clear that these unconscious fantasies have come to characterize the transference. The painfulness of the affect associated with this idea causes the representation to be distorted, displaced from mother to self, and from self to analyst in the transference. The interpretation of the transference allowed Sam to clarify his confusion about what his mother had told him. Then in the dead finger game he elaborated further upon the mental representation of interactions between self and other which threatened attack and counterattack (e.g., death and castration). Once this was verbalized, he went on to tell a story which demonstrated a related repressed mental representation of his anger with his father and his wish to rob him; together with the hangman game, a derivative of the same set of representations, the analyst was able to interpret Sam's fear that it was his own badness that turned his world nasty. His anger to his love objects turns his mental representation of them into dangerous people. The interpretations served to relieve his conflict and freed him to use his more mature, 7-year-old intellect in speaking of the reality of his three families, trying to understand it; he also indicated his transference fear of exclusion from the analyst's family. The effect of the interpretation was to allow Sam to voice in the transference his disappointment at not having a reliable father, siblings, or an extended family. To combat his anxieties deriving from his angry wishes and other painful affects, Sam sought safety in enactments of the fantasy of being a baby girl. When the defensive nature of these fantasies was addressed, Sam turned detective and he used his very considerable intelligence to tease out the meanings of his own tiredness and, in working through the transference, the meaning of his mother's inaccessibility.

When the analyst, for the second time, verbalized Sam's representation of the analyst as vulnerable, manifested in Sam's expectation that his anger made the analyst leave him, Sam's reply in word and action confirmed that in his perception the safe solution was to remain a baby. After the analyst spelled out this representation, Sam further illustrated the liberating effect of such interventions on a patient's mental capacity. The analyst's intervention gave Sam the opportunity to recast his old mental representations and develop new, more differentiated models. He could explain his own tiredness as "sad-tired," which required the analyst's intervention, and distinguished it from two forms of normal tiredness, which did not require analytic aid. He demonstrated not only how, in this way, more advanced representations became accessible, but also how his mental capacities, his intellect and capacity for self-observation could be readily reactivated through being helped to understand the pathological aspects of his more infantile, conflict-bound mental representations.

This session was representative of numerous similar sessions in the second year of Sam's analysis. We chose this period to illustrate therapeutic action on the mental mechanisms mediating psychic change. It also corresponds with Sam's improved functioning at home and at school. Most importantly, soon after this session he took up residence in his own room and initiated a number of activities with boys of his own age. This work also coincided with a dramatic improvement in Sam's school performance, and this was in part determined by a stronger identification with the interest in mathematics and science which he shared with his stepfather.

#### THERAPEUTIC ACTION AND MENTAL REPRESENTATIONS

We can identify three mechanisms of therapeutic action through changes in mental representations: integration, elaboration, and the genesis of new representational structures.

*Integration*

The first aspect of therapeutic action concerns the enhancing effect of interpretations on the integrity of mental representations. We conceive of mental representations as being either partially or fully activated, depending on the proportion of the features defining it that are active concurrently. Each activation of the representation strengthens the links between the features in such a way that subsequent partial activation is more likely to lead to the activation of the entire representation. The internal cohesion or integration of the representation will thus improve with repeated activation.

For example, we saw that Sam was unconsciously angry and hurt following two missed sessions. As he began to talk of distances and gaps, his associative links allowed the analyst to identify in an affectively meaningful way Sam's perception of the analyst as being too far away to be accessible. Thus this partially activated representation of the analyst influences associations and play. But the analyst has to "spell out" the idea, often in several guises, for the patient to be able to begin to integrate the idea into his current thinking. As a mental representation is brought from a preconscious to a conscious state, a transformation takes place which enhances the internal coherence and boundaries of components of the representation, a process which may be labeled integration. This consolidation of a representation in consciousness by such interventions is the most common form of therapeutic action in the psychoanalytic situation. Such work has the effect of further delineating mental representations, and allows them to be more readily called upon in different contexts.

While some components of representations need to be made explicit and coherent, others are so tightly integrated that they become fully activated even from very partial cues. This was the case for Sam's representation of the depressed maternal object. The mere repetition of a particular pattern of activation establishes powerful links between features, leading to a very highly integrated representation. Because of the strong links between its features such representations are very readily activated and impose themselves on a wide variety of experiences. Mental representations thus have the potential to aggregate experience, and the strongest representations need not correspond to actual occurrences. Sam's representation of his mother lying down, claiming to be tired, which he enacted in the session, may or may not correspond to a memory of her retreating to her bed and expressing a wish to die. Nevertheless, the features of passivity, inaccessibility, the expression of hopelessness, and seeking attention may have been the underlying invariants of Sam's experience with her across many different situations, leading to this powerful, highly integrated representation. We regard changes to such representational prototypes as the hallmark of psychoanalytic therapeutic action and success.

*Elaboration*

Elaboration establishes relationships among mental representations and creates the kind of network of relations that is basic to the process of understanding. "Understanding" an idea may amount to placing that idea in appropriate relation to the family of ideas which articulate with it.

Sam was frightened that he felt deprived by his analyst of the sessions that rightly belonged to him. The existing links in his system of meanings led him to believe that someone who stole was evil. His wish to punish the analyst conflicted with his need for help, expressed in his associations to Fred's absence on Saturday night. The perception of the analyst as evil was also worrying for Sam because it fitted poorly with his other representations of him as kindly and helpful. He expressed his confusion about the analyst's identity in his apparently arbitrary comment, "How old are you?" The therapeutic action of the interpretations, evident in his emotional response, was in helping Sam integrate the isolated idea of an evil analyst into his representational system by *elaborating* his mental representations: "You feel angry and want to punish me at this time because you feel I have taken something away." (And by implication: "This does not mean that you feel like this all the time.")

In our view, the majority of interpretive work in psychoanalysis has the primary aim of the making of new links between representational structures so that the influence of more *primitive* mental structure is curtailed. The process of elaborating well-integrated representations will then define larger representational units, which in their turn will need to be *bounded* and integrated. The idea that one may experience intensely angry and loving feelings toward the same person was one such representation for Sam, which needed considerable further reworking in the analysis before it became a sufficiently stable idea for him to use it reliably in understanding his ambivalence.

## The Genesis of New Representational Structures

The integration of poorly articulated representations and the elaboration of relationships between representations within a system combine over time to facilitate the child's unique contributions to the therapeutic process. The distinction Sam made between sad-tired and fatigue constituted the creation of a new mental structure. Using this, he could take account of a certain category of experience which previously had left him confused and frightened, namely, his mother's depressive withdrawal.

Interpretation does not create the new structures. Interpretation identifies the reason why particular internal or external experiences were difficult or dangerous; once such dangers are addressed and elaborated in the context of other experiences, it then becomes possible for the patient himself to initiate the change in his mental representational system to accommodate the previously unacceptable experience.

The psychoanalytic situation enables the patient to create the new mental representation. In particular, working within the transference enhances the potential of the therapeutic situation to present the patient directly with novel affective experiences and thus maximize the opportunity to bring about a self-initiated change in psychic structure. Sam's opportunity to develop a representational structure to accommodate his reaction to his mother's depression was initiated by the analyst's attention to Sam's constructions concerning the analyst's absence over the weekend.

*Summary of the Representational Model*

We described three ways whereby developmentally primitive mental representations are, so to speak, assimilated into higher-order mental organizations. Through enhancement of the integrity of mental organizations, elaboration of their connections with other systems, and the creation of new representations of both internal and external states, the representational system is restructured. This takes place in such a way that previously isolated, unintegrated, incompatible representations cease to be pathogens. In this framework pathogenic parts of the dynamic unconscious are seen as a distinct set of mental representations which are, in some important way, incompatible with evolving mental structures. The representational model assumes that therapeutic action comprises the harmonization of mental representations through interpretation, and through the patient's natural capacity to achieve increasingly sophisticated constructions concerning experience.

In the representational model the process of change is a result of the modification of unconscious mental representations as part of the interpretive work as well as the more generalized aspects of the analytic encounter. The perception of the analyst as one with empathy (Emde, 1990) or healing intention (Stone, 1961) may bring about changes in object representations through the same mechanisms of change as interpretations. Regardless of the agent of change, therapeutic action mediated through changes in mental representations will be relatively rapid and self-evident.

To give an example, a somewhat narcissistic young man who presented with sexual problems and anxieties about the superficial quality of his relationships with women spent the first year of his analysis describing in some depth and with some sophistication his rivalrous and ambivalent feelings about his father, whom he greatly admired. During this time his problems with women remained unchanged. The analyst deliberately waited 18 months before pointing out that, although the patient was talking of his complex feelings toward his father, he had never *once* mentioned his mother in the analysis. This recognition shook the patient, and over subsequent sessions he began to recall his feelings of having been neglected and ignored by her and linked this to his anxiety about being abandoned by any woman he intensely desired. Gradually, his terrifying perception of women as in total control of life and death was integrated in his conscious feelings and his behavior toward them changed. His potency problems disappeared and he established a deep friendship with a junior colleague whom he later married.

Representational changes of this kind are readily evident to patient and analyst alike. They usually last, and can at times be dramatic in terms of sudden realizations and consequent reconstructions. We should point out that we only see psychic change of this form as rapid or readily apparent relative to the second model of change we are about to discuss. Mostly, the modification of unconscious mental representation is strongly resisted by patients, and whatever change is achieved is hard won.

## THE MENTAL PROCESS MODEL

There are patients who, unlike Sam, do not respond in anticipated ways to interpretations addressing aspects of mental representations. In such cases the analyst may, for example, be deprived of the familiar signs of resistance following accurate interpretations of conflict. Such situations have led us in the past to postulate ego deficits to account for the patient's apparent inability to regress under the influence of the analysis, and thereby expose repudiated thoughts and feelings with his capacity for self-observation intact. A major shortcoming of the concept of ego deficit is that it carries with it no account of how it came to characterize the patient's personality, although formulations employing this term frequently suggest some deprivation in the child's early environment.

In these cases psychoanalysis does not work by the removal of repression and other distortions of mental representations. In fact, at times it may appear that the analytic process cannot be established. A 27-year-old male patient was treated at the Anna Freud Centre for severe depression, violent antisocial behavior, alcohol abuse, and overwhelming anxieties about a sense of himself as empty (Fonagy, 1991). During the early years of treatment, progress was slow because of his remarkable inability to comprehend what the analyst was attempting to do. His associations lacked depth, resonance, and evocativeness. He could not make comprehensible what was going on in his mind and responded to the severe helplessness this caused him to feel by abusive behavior and a totally derogatory attitude to his analyst. Initially he could not benefit from more than the simplest verbalizations of affect at the moment he felt it, because he could not conceive of himself as a person with various feelings and thoughts in the past and the present. In dreams and fantasies he frequently represented people as photographs without faces, robots, corpses, etc., all sharing the common characteristic of a lack of mental capacity. Eventually, after many years of treatment, this patient began to improve and established a productive transference. He became able to reflect upon his infantile perception of his sexually abusive father as harboring malicious thoughts about him, and of his mother as voluntarily emptying her mind, providing vacuous parenting and thus passively perpetuating the abuse. The all-encompassing nature of such a patient's resistance and its apparent imperviousness to interpretation indicates something other than neurotic pathology and requires a treatment process qualitatively different from that involving the interpretation of defense and conflict alone.

Both child and adult analysts have increasingly drawn attention to a group of patients with whom therapeutic action appears not to conform to the concepts used in traditional psychoanalysis. Analysts working with such patients have noted that interpretation of conflict and defense is insufficient and does not lead to psychic change. They have advocated modifications of technique to address developmental deviations, impairments or deficits, and underlying structural deficiencies (Kohut, 1977; A. Freud, 1974; Bene, 1977; Edgcumbe, 1984). These modifications go beyond the representational model of therapeutic action outlined in the previous section. Alternative models of therapeutic action govern the treatment of borderline personality organizations (Kernberg, 1980), or narcissistic personality disorders (Kohut, 1977), and a wide range of developmental disorders. These emphasize such factors as the real transactions between the patient and the analyst as a curative experience, and the early mother-child relationship as the most appropriate analogue for the analytic encounter (e.g., Balint, 1949; Gitelson, 1962; Klauber, 1972). Developmental processes are invoked by those who link therapeutic action to the holding environment (Winnicott, 1965; Modell, 1976), separation-individuation (Masterson, 1976; Stolorow and Lachmann, 1978), a sense of union with the primary object (Loewald, 1960, 1973, 1979), social referencing (Viederman, 1991), empathy (Emde, 1990), or other aspects of developmental processes (Goodman, 1977; Settlage et al., 1980; Schlessinger and Robbins, 1983; Blatt and Behrends, 1987).

Abrams (1990) has called into question the assumption of a parallel between the psychoanalytic process and processes of development. He points to the tendency to blur the difference between normal infants and pathological adults in developmental terms. Abrams argues that such developmental analogies ignore the obvious and powerful biological constraints placed on development by an inherent timetable (phases) and progressive transformation. An examination of the similarities and differences between developmental sequences in psychoanalysis and infancy easily reveals fundamental discrepancies. On the other hand, a judicious metaphorical comparison between developmental processes as they occur during infancy and childhood and derivatives of these processes as they occur in psychoanalysis may be a useful exercise. Emde (1990), for example, explicitly points to a biologically based mental process which has the potential to stimulate development throughout the life-span. No analyst works with an expectation that his patient's treatment will follow a strict sequence of developmental phases. It seems important to emphasize, however, that in these contexts development is used as a metaphor to denote as yet unspecified psychological processes.

In the previous section we explored the therapeutic action of psychoanalysis upon object relationships, defenses, the sense of self, and other critical constructs in the context of the changes to mental representations. Mental representations cannot be separated from the *psychological processes* which generate and organize them. Just as it is necessary to think of light in terms of both particles and waves, one cannot conceive of mental life other than in terms of both mental representations and the mental processes which create and operate upon them. Mental representations are best thought of as the products of mental processes. If a mental representation is a tune, the mental process is the violin from which it originates. Thus a fantasy (a mental representation) is the product of the mental process of fantasizing.

The distinction between mental representation and process, long accepted in philosophy of mind and cognitive science, may also be put to good use in dynamic accounts of psychological disturbance. It is implicit in psychoanalytic theory that psychic processes are as vulnerable to the vicissitudes of conflict as mental representations. Segal (1978), for example, illustrated how thinking puts a limit on the omnipotence of fantasy and can therefore be despised and fervently resisted. Anna Freud (1965) discussed the way in which specific lines of mental development may be *inhibited* or abandoned in the face of hostile or simply unfacilitating environments.

We chose the *inhibition of mental processes* as a suitable framework to study therapeutic action with so-called "difficult" patients because it offers a convenient way to ask important questions concerning *how* the patient's impaired ego functioning may become the focus of therapeutic action. We tried to contrast two complementary modes of therapeutic action, and to elaborate the distinction made by Anna Freud between the mutative effects of interpretation per se and what she called the by-products of analysis from which the child also benefits. In using the term *inhibition of mental processes,* we are describing the situation in which *a whole class or category of mental representations appears to be absent from a patient's mental functioning.* We assume that the situation comes about as a primitive attempt by the individual to protect his mental functioning from specific, extremely painful, mental representations, which occurred as a result of using a particular mental process. In such cases the mental representations which generate unpleasure are too central to be isolated from the core of the representational system which may become part of consciousness. The child therefore disengages or inhibits the entire mental process that creates that class of mental representations. For example, in an earlier paper (Fonagy and Moran, 1991), we described a boy, David, who in the face of abuse by his parents appeared to have excluded from his mental activity *all* representations concerning the thoughts and feelings of his objects. Forgoing thought about the mental state of others may be the only means available to such a child to deal with the terror of contemplating his primary object's murderous wishes toward him.

Similarly, all of us have seen patients whose experience of their lives is concrete, totally devoid of sentiment or affect. They experience things "as they are" and (sometimes aggressively) assert their complete control over their feelings. As McDougall (1974), Sifneos (1977), and de M'Uzan (1974) have noted, such patients commonly present with somatic disorders. Psychoanalytic treatment frequently reveals early experiences of having been overwhelmed by affect (theirs and their object's) at a time when the capacity to bar from access to consciousness specific affect-laden representations was not yet available. Prior to the development of more sophisticated ego defenses the child was only able to prevent the devastation of unmanageable feelings by disengaging or inhibiting some of the crucial mental processes which play a part in the generation and recognition of affect.[4]

4. In their early stages of evolution, all mental processes are vulnerable to the influence of the balance between pleasure and unpleasure contained within the mental representations upon which they act. In later development, mental processes, as all procedural knowledge, occur automatically and nonexperientially and only under exceptional circumstances will it come under inhibition permanently. Earlier in development, however, the child can only prevent painful mental experiences arising by inhibiting the mental process itself.

We are just beginning to enumerate mental processes pertinent to psychoanalytic models of psychological disturbance; as yet we lack sufficient information even to allow us to specify those mental processes which account for particular psychological capacities. It is largely through the psychoanalytic study of psychological disturbance that the precise nature of the malfunctioning of mental processes will eventually be ascertained. For example, formulations such as those we have presented about David are at present only a little way beyond restatements of the observed phenomena, but they may help toward denoting classes of mental processes which subserve a function notable by its absence in the clinical material.

The curtailment of a mental process has more drastic consequences for psychic functioning than the repudiation or defensive distortion of specific representational structures. The absence of psychological functions may *descriptively* be thought of as deficits or ego restrictions. The term *deficit,* however, is inaccurate insofar as it fails to denote the causal relationships between intrapsychic conflict and certain types of mental function. In the present context, failures of mental process are invariably seen as defensive in purpose because their inhibition, stunting, or distortion serves an economic function whereby the individual is able to avoid specific classes of painful, conflictual, mental representations. We hold such dynamic and economic considerations to be relevant even in cases where constitutional factors make a person vulnerable to the inhibition of particular mental functions.

Both mental representational and mental process aspects of pathology have to be conceptually distinguished from developmental pathologies based on constitutional or biological deficit.[5] As regards the latter, epidemiological and biological evidence strongly suggests that the absence of a psychic process is not apparent but real; no interpretive work can bring about a reactivation. This is not to say that psychoanalytic work with such individuals will not be beneficial in improving their adaptation to an impaired psychic state, as has been shown, for example, in the work of Cohen (1991) with children with Gilles de la Tourette's syndrome.

The value of the concept of inhibition of mental processes relative to

5. Although we view this conceptual distinction as important, in practice we anticipate great difficulty in distinguishing between the three levels of pathology proposed. It is likely that constitutional vulnerability of a mental process will increase the likelihood of conflict-related inhibition. Further, the failure of mental function consequent upon constitutional or conflict-related inhibition of mental processes may well increase the child's vulnerability to psychopathology associated with distortions to mental representations.

that of ego deficit is clearest in the context of therapeutic action. Formulations solely in terms of ego deficits do not readily lend themselves
to explanations of how slow yet significant shifts in ego functioning can
nevertheless come about in the course of successful psychoanalytic
treatments of patients suffering from such so-called deficits. While the
term "developmental help" has been useful to describe this aspect of
our work with children (e.g., Kennedy and Moran, 1991), it does not
sufficiently clarify what the "help" consists of, or what "development"
means in the context of adult psychoanalysis. The notion of unutilized,
inhibited mental processes offers a preferable conceptual bridge between psychoanalytic work with children and adults and makes clear
that "developmental help" does not imply gratification or education,
but true psychoanalytic work.

### CHILD CLINICAL VIGNETTES

We intend to provide three illustrations of the way in which inhibition
of mental processes may be seen as underpinning some serious forms
of psychological disturbance, and how the psychoanalytic process may
bring about the freeing up of a mental process. Children with narcissistic character disturbance will not only have substantial difficulties in
comparing their own performance with that of others, but they also
may well have difficulties in integrating their actions, thoughts, and
affects in the service of creating a coherent mental representation of
themselves.[6] When mental processes responsible for elaborating an
integrated image of the self have been inhibited, the patient's self-
image will be distorted. Thus, it may alternate between a derogated
and an omnipotent representation.

Some children with extreme forms of narcissistic disturbance beginning at an early age may show abnormal development in both their
object relationships and their thought processes, so that they combine
egocentric, need-satisfying relationships with omnipotent thinking,
lack of reality testing, and projection. Inhibition of mental processes is
manifest in their inability to be aware of the real motives, feelings, and
attitudes of external objects, and in their belief that they control people
and events by wishing and fantasizing. This means that, at best, they

6. Omnipotent representation of the self may sometimes, but not invariably, arise in
this way. An equally plausible mechanism to account for such a representation of the self,
not involving inhibition of mental processes, is a defense against the internalization of
the intermittent denigratory appraisal of a primary object, for example, an alcoholic
father. The analyst may distinguish between these possibilities in terms of the readiness
with which the patient's arrogant behavior responds to the analyst's interpretations of the
patient's mental pain in the face of a derogated self-image.

persistently misunderstand other people and events and are bewildered when things do not go as they expect. At worst, it means that they may become quite out of touch with the real world, retreating into fantasy, or fly into rages at the slightest threat to their belief in their own omnipotence, or become terrified at minor mishaps since they do not distinguish these from major catastrophes, and hold themselves responsible for everything that happens.

When Robert entered nursery school at age 3 1/2, he was found to be intellectually precocious, and his speech had an oddly adult quality. However, his control over impulses and feelings was poor; he was restless, tense, distractible, and easily overexcited. He seemed to enjoy teasing and interfering with other children, and often frightened them with his threats and physical attacks. At the same time he was prone to overwhelming anxieties associated with great apparent confusion. He frequently went into screaming panics for no observable reason and he was mistrustful of the teachers.

It was soon clear that much of Robert's behavior represented reactions to and identifications with his mother. Following his parents' separation when he was 6 months old, he lived alone with her in a one-room flat. She was a very disturbed woman who reacted to Robert on the basis of her own needs, not his, and who could not bear his feelings not coinciding with hers. In her mind Robert was completely identified with his father, whom she saw as a dishonest, sexually promiscuous, murderous psychopath. Her view of her husband was as distorted by her own projections as was her view of her son. Her terror that Robert would become antisocial or criminal made her berate him constantly for being "bad." She would see him in this way as soon as he failed to comply instantly and absolutely with her wishes. For example, he would be "bad" for not abandoning his play immediately when she called him for a meal or for bedtime. If, however, anyone else criticized Robert, she defended him with the ferocity of a tigress, raging at the teachers and blaming the trouble on other badly brought-up children or on antagonistic adults. She usually spoke in a loud, hoarse voice, sometimes lost her temper and hit Robert quite viciously, and repeatedly threatened to send him away. She was also sexually seductive, allowing him to see her naked and share her bed, and encouraging much kissing and cuddling. She denied, however, that he was ever sexually curious or excited, in spite of evidence such as his frequent erections and attempts to look under the skirts of little girls.

In his therapy, much of the work centered on his fears of punishment and rejection for his "bad" sexual and aggressive wishes. It proved particularly important for the therapist to help Robert under-

stand the distinction between neurotic anxiety resulting from projection of "bad" sexual wishes and realistic anxiety about his mother's
behavior.

The abilities to adopt the viewpoint of another and to model aspects
of oneself on aspects of another are normal mental processes which
may have abnormal outcomes if the relevant viewpoints and aspects of
the object are abnormal. Robert began to divulge an identification with
his mother's view of him as murderous and dangerous. This made the
process of creating an accurate and stable representation of himself a
highly dangerous one which Robert seemed willing to forgo. In other
words, the abnormality of the object's perception of him resulted in
Robert developing painfully distorted representations of himself and
his object, so that processes which created and made use of these representations became associated with mounting unpleasure. In Robert's
case, as he conformed more and more to his mother's view of him as
hostile, dangerous, and perhaps even murderous, we see increasing
distortions in the processes of self-organization. These gradually led to
a stunting of his capacity to integrate actions, thoughts, and affects in
creating a coherent mental representation of the self, and to elaborate
an integrated image of himself. He thus became less and less able to
safeguard the integrity of his self-image, and to maintain a distinct self-
representation while responding appropriately to the object. His
panics were probably consequent upon episodes of identity diffusion.

The therapeutic relationship enabled Robert to rekindle his attempts to create stable, integrated representations of himself. His
mother's perception of him became a possible subject of discussion,
and at the same time his sense of the therapist's view of him also disconfirmed the unbearable germ of his self-image as murderous. His improved capacity for self-representation enhanced his functioning in
numerous areas. His reality testing was less distorted by omnipotent
thinking, which was previously essential to protect his fragile sense of
self. His aggressiveness and panics in the nursery school diminished,
but his relationships became rather distant. He became more settled
and able to concentrate, so that he could find pleasure and relief in
intellectual pursuits and manage the transition to primary school fairly
well. Robert's mother had accepted regular interviews for herself, but
they could do little more than protect his treatment for a time, and help
her to channel some of her anxiety, hostility, and seductiveness away
from Robert. His therapy was ended prematurely because he was no
longer giving trouble in school.

Inhibition of mental processes normally arises in the context of intense trauma, but this does not necessarily involve parental distur-

bance. Such inhibition does, however, require internal experience that is sufficiently intense to make a permanent distortion of a basic mental capacity adaptive in function. This was the case, for example, for Joan who had had a bone disease beginning at age 5 weeks which persisted throughout the first two years of her life. She suffered from pain which spoiled all the normal, pleasurable, physical interactions with her mother; being cuddled, washed, dressed, and fed all hurt; in addition, her mother had to help in painful and frightening medical procedures. This resulted in a deeply ingrained view of mother as attacker and of herself as hurt, damaged, and deprived. The mother in turn felt helpless and inadequate, and severe distortions of object representations were inevitable.

Because the early mother-child interactions were painful rather than pleasurable, they gave rise to severe inhibition and stunting of mental processes involved in communication and self-observation (her willingness to represent her own internal experiences or monitor her internal state). Further, the steroids which eventually cured her disease, bloated and immobilized her as a toddler. This interference with mobility restricted her capacity to discharge or control any form of aggression, excitement, or affect, especially to displace it away from mother, thus also interfering with the processes of impulse and affect control.

Joan was referred for therapy at age 11 because of her constant verbal and sometimes physical abuse of her mother, and her readiness to engage in battles over many issues of daily living, because she so easily felt slighted or unfavored and reacted with rage. She was severely withdrawn and had great difficulties in making any relationships at her school. She particularly envied the good relationship between her mother and younger sister, who had been a far easier, cuddly baby, who was actually much more rewarding for the mother.

Joan began treatment unwillingly. She appeared to have no wish to communicate with her analyst. In particular she seemed totally to lack curiosity about her inner world. She manifested no awareness of problems in herself; she had no wish for insight or self-exploration, and experienced no sense of achievement even when she reached an understanding of herself. She spent the first two years of treatment abusing and blaming her analyst. Verbalization of affect and interpretation of conflict had little impact on her, and she denigrated the analyst's attempts to think about her or make sense of her experiences. Externalization and projection were her favored defenses. She felt attacked whenever her analyst tried to address Joan's own contribution to events. She had no sense of her emotional state and would never admit to feeling worried or upset, or understood if the therapist was accurate in identifying her mental state. She would, however, fly into a rage with anyone who crossed her. Although she suffered from frequent minor illnesses such as colds and hayfever, she was unable to recognize when she was ill.

It fell to the analyst to give some meaning to Joan's rages, illnesses, and other states. She attempted to help Joan to distinguish, for example, whether she was ill or in a bad mood. At first Joan was far from grateful for such interventions. Gradually, however, her minor illnesses diminished in frequency. Prolonged experience of her analyst trying to understand and ameliorate Joan's somatic and psychic states eventually helped her to begin to develop an interest in and ideas about her intrapsychic state. At this point her conflicts about her relationship with her mother became more available for analysis in the transference. She experienced intense conflict between her strong wishes for total passive dependence on the object and an equally strong belief that she would be damaged by close contact or communication. At first the analyst had to state and restate these conflicts. As processes of representing her internal state and communicating it to her object were brought back into use, Joan was able to move to a slightly more active role in exploring her inner world.

In cases where the early environment is broadly unfacilitative, the use of most mental functions will be met by disappointment and unpleasure. In such children a very wide range of mental processes may become partially inhibited. These children may give the impression of being dull and mentally defective, but the therapeutic engagement brings about substantial change which distinguishes them from children of innately low intelligence. In such cases the therapist creates a setting in which the child can feel that it is safe to begin feeling, thinking, wishing, and imagining.

Mary, for example, came from a large, disadvantaged, disorganized family in which all the children seemed to be intellectually underfunctioning. She entered nursery school at age 3 with two of her brothers. The two boys were active and impulsive, prone to noisy tantrums, but at least fought for what they wanted. They were capable of quite strong relationships and of enthusiastic, albeit unruly involvement in activities. Mary, by contrast, was passive, prone to whining rather than tantrums, never knew what she wanted to do, and easily lost interest in activities. She could neither compete for attention nor hold on to her possessions. She looked, and apparently felt, neglected and unlovable. She was often dirty and smelly and had a runny nose. Unlike her brothers, she did not form a strong attachment to particular adults in the nursery school, nor did she seek out other children to play with;

instead she indiscriminately wanted to sit in the lap of any available adult.

When she was aged 4, a therapist began working with her, not expecting her to be able to use classical analysis. The therapist was struck by Mary's incapacity to show an interest, express a need, or indicate a wish. She could initiate nothing herself, she was reluctant to envision anything she wanted, she could only wait for it (whatever it was) to be provided for her. She constructed no expectation, had no image of a desired outcome, and could therefore experience no disappointment. The analyst, in order to counteract the profound inhibition upon the elaboration of wishful fantasies, decided to search for and selectively to gratify transference wishes. Mary could be helped to distinguish her wishes and began to feel safer in expressing them. Correspondingly, she began to experience feelings of frustration, anger, sadness, and eventually even guilt and shame. Now it became possible for patient and therapist to explore together why she so dreaded the object's failure to comply with her wishes, and how she felt annihilated by any lack of response to her.

As the analytic delineation of Mary's chaotic inner world proceeded, recognizable conflicts and defenses emerged, and their effect on her development could be traced. Mary's difficulties, like those of her brothers, involved the organization and control of impulses, wishes, and affective states. But her attempts to deal with overwhelming affects by the primitive defense of inhibiting many aspects of mental function restricted numerous aspects of her psychic development such as object relations, self-organization, self-monitoring, and self-evaluation. In other words, her environment made her feel that using virtually any mode of mental functioning was unsafe. The early stage of the intervention, its intensity and its coupling with the facilitating environment of the nursery school made it possible to reverse the widespread inhibition and to revive and develop the potential for full mental functioning. Mary's consistent disowning of wishes and her renunciation of aspirations had initially rendered the nursery teachers powerless to mobilize active and progressive forces within her. But this changed as her therapy enabled her to represent these wishes and aspirations and to link them to her self-representation. It was an important moment when Mary's sense of identity and her growing awareness that she might be able to feel good about herself reached a point where she could formulate the question to her therapist, "How do I be proud of myself?"

Thus, even severe and widespread inhibition of mental processes may be successfully tackled in child analysis. Technique in such cases includes the identification of the cause for this maladaptive tendency within the developmental process, and its correction through appropriate interpretive and other therapeutic interventions. The developmental pull of childhood facilitates therapeutic action and the reestablishment of functioning mental processes becomes a major problem only if the adverse environmental pressure persists in unmodifiable ways.

The situation is totally different in cases where the mental processes remain inhibited throughout childhood and inadequate mental functioning is encountered in adult psychoanalysis. In the remaining part of this paper we will give a clinical illustration of an adult patient who benefited substantially from psychoanalytic help, yet whose psychological changes (at least on the surface) ill fitted the representational model of change outlined in the first part of the paper. We then go on to offer a conceptual framework for therapeutic action in such cases, and consider some characteristic technical features of work with such individuals.

### ADULT CASE ILLUSTRATION

Mrs. T. had a pervasive terror of vomiting which dominated all areas of her life, and which had begun to ease after 15 years of analysis.[7] Mrs. T. recently asked, "What's gone wrong with my mind?" I have been grappling with this question for the last 15 years. It was, however, a landmark that Mrs. T. herself recognized the problem. She had certainly had no such awareness or even interest previously in the functioning of her own mind.

Outwardly Mrs. T. appeared to be an intelligent, well-organized, competent middle-class housewife, who also had a professional career, and was a committed member of her local church. Her arrival on the analytic couch was something of a surprise to both of us. She came at age 27, having been sent by a gynecologist whom she had encountered in the course of a series of investigations for a mysterious abdominal pain. But, as she was finally able to explain 8 or 9 years later, "I didn't understand why I was coming, so I just had to think of some reason to tell you." She thus introduced herself and her problems to me with the words, "I want you to talk me into having a baby." I replied that I did not talk people into things, but would talk with her to find out what she wanted.

7. Mrs. T. read an earlier draft of this paper when her permission was sought for publication. Going over the material provided an impetus for further analysis, and Mrs. T. also made some valuable corrections which are incorporated in the final draft.

Finding out what she wanted, however, immediately proved extraordinarily difficult. Mrs. T. was unable to talk about anything of importance to herself, could not follow a train of thought, and was out of touch with most of her feelings. She wanted to see me more and more often, but did not know why, seemed alarmed by most things I said to her, and could not understand how analysis works. Afraid of "falling out" with her husband, Tim, she thought she ought to try sorting out her sexual difficulties, but saw no point in talking about anything else. When I attempted to explain the importance of free association, she tried to comply, and I soon realized she had taken my remarks as instructions, but did not understand them.

For the first 5 or 6 years I was frequently in doubt whether analysis was appropriate for her. My usual analytic techniques failed to make any impression on her, and I could not arrive at a diagnosis which might have helped me to comprehend the technical difficulties; nor could the many colleagues I consulted over the years. Diagnoses ranging from hysterical and obsessional neurosis through borderline, anorectic and alexythymic to psychotic were all suggested; but though I could always see the features in her that prompted each diagnosis, none was a satisfactory fit. In the end I came to feel that it was my experience with children, and especially the ones who, at the Anna Freud Centre, receive "developmental help," that allowed me to find ways of working with her.

For as long as she could remember Mrs. T. had obeyed a dictum she attributed to her mother for dealing with upset or unpleasantness of any kind, "Don't think about it." This was one reason why, for the first year of treatment, she failed to mention her terror of vomiting. More importantly, she now suggests, it was a "secret," about which she felt ashamed and guilty. Further, it did not occur to her that anything could be done about it, so she did not think it relevant to tell an analyst. She only decided to tell me when she did because she was finding it increasingly difficult to tell me about other things without explaining about this fear.

Her childhood was largely forgotten and she at first maintained that it had been happy. She was surprised as memories began to emerge which I pointed out as unhappy experiences. There were some difficult (but not obviously traumatic) experiences in her early years; she had had many moves of home and school, and she and her mother seemed often to have been isolated, far from friends and family, and with only one another to rely on. One thing she never forgot was her mother's comment, "I hope when you have a baby it'll be as awful as you were." Her mother had told her that she had had, among other problems, eating and sleeping difficulties and constipation, and that she had refused to get out of her pushchair until she went to school. Her recollection of events, though painfully slow, began to cluster around the age of 6. Without linking the events to any one thing or to a particular emotional context, she recalled the birth of her brother, various asthma attacks, refusing to eat, and crying for her mother during her parents' absences, and getting caught and told off for playing sexual games with a little boy. Disjointed memories of her fear of vomiting also emerged; feeling sick and panicking whenever her parents went out together, being sedated with phenobarbitone; being sick in the parents' bedroom, as well as an incident in which her father threw a bowl at her and said, "Be sick then." No matter how I tried to interpret or link together aspects of this material, for many years it proved impossible to help her to make sense of them, or use them to construct a narrative of her life. Interpretations of resistance, let alone transference, proved to be a meaningless exercise for Mrs. T. This was apparent from her pervasive puzzlement about what she understood as my "strange" expectations.

I gradually began to think that much of her "forgetting" was due to some more malignant process than isolation and repression. It repeatedly happened that while trying to reply to something I said, Mrs. T. would falter and find she had forgotten what it was she was answering; or she would forget what it was she had started out to say. When I reminded her of things we had talked about in previous sessions, she often expressed surprise, having no recollection of it herself. For example, she spoke of feeling on edge with her husband, and wondered why this might be. I reminded her that two days earlier she had been very upset by his threat to leave her because of her frigidity. She had "forgotten" this. Being reminded about it allowed her to recall her husband's threat and her own upset; but she could not remember telling me about it.

So great was her difficulty in talking spontaneously, that I often acquiesced in her need, asking for more information when she gave only "headlines," reminding her of things she left unmentioned that seemed likely to be of special importance to her, telling her again about things she had "forgotten" between sessions. The analytic "Mm" was never enough to assure her of interest or help her to keep talking. She eventually explained that she thought I might be tiptoeing out of the room as her mother used to do after getting her off to sleep as a child. She would often break a silence only to ask, "Why don't you talk to me?" and the most effective response I ever made to this was an unpremeditated (and somewhat irritable), "Because I'm thinking about what you just said." She responded with a surprised, "Oh, really? I thought you were bored with me," and often subsequently referred to her pleasure and surprise at the realization that she was mistaken in assuming that silence always meant lack of interest.

She gradually revealed the effects of her fear of vomiting: an ever-increasing range of avoidances and restrictions, which puzzled her family to whom she had not confided her fear. Often when I tried to show her how she increased her terror by not sharing it or seeking comfort, she became upset, and I at first took this for anger. She was nonplussed by this idea, and it became increasingly clear to me that she simply felt frightened when I insisted on talking about ideas and feelings she would have preferred to ignore. At the same time she welcomed such acknowledgements of her inner life. The resulting conflict produced many difficult periods when she would provoke her mother or her husband into saying that she should stop treatment. She was often afraid of "falling out" with me, and frequently provoked it with toddlerlike truculence. "Won't," "Don't want to," and "Why should I?" were frequent reactions to my attempts to get her to explain further or think about things I said to her. I began to feel very strongly that the most important meaning of this battling with me was a desperate attempt not to "give in" because it would mean giving up her familiar, fragile, and restricted sense of herself.

Toward the end of the second year of treatment an episode occurred which introduced a severe regressive phase lasting two years. This followed sessions in which her childhood fears of loneliness emerged, especially that she might lose control of herself if no one was near to help. One Friday, she described an evening when she had enjoyed playing the piano, and afterward had felt like sitting on Tim's lap. He responded by wanting to make love to her and she panicked and ran away. She was concerned that he might creep up on her in bed when she was asleep, and she might not waken in time to stop him penetrating her. The following Monday, after much initial reluctance, she described how, after the Friday session, she had sat in her car crying, feeling "useless." She tried to drive off and do her shopping, but could not pull herself together. She came back but did not dare try to see me again. She finally went home and tried to ring Tim at work, but could not get him either.

She did not want to talk about it, since even talking made her feel "peculiar." She had said this before but had been unable to describe the "peculiar" feeling. This time she managed to identify that her heart was pounding, she was trembling, and felt cold. I said that sounded like fear.

She continued to be strikingly unable to distinguish her feelings. When she felt "useless," she wanted to be near me without knowing why. She would sit crying in my waiting room, would follow me around London, sit in her car outside my house at weekends, and complain that she did nothing but wait for it to be time to come to her session. At times I worried that I had provoked a breakdown I could not handle, and thoughts of the need for hospitalization crossed my mind. But elsewhere, she seemed to be coping with her job, running her home, and fulfilling her church commitments.

She seemed less like someone having a psychotic breakdown than like a frightened child. She did not create any countertransference resentment of her intrusiveness or manipulativeness, and she did not make paranoid complaints about me. The only time I became seriously alarmed about her was when she began falling asleep whenever she tried to think of conflictual things. When she did this on the couch, it was manageable, but when she did it at the wheel of her car on a motorway, it was dangerous. It was a dramatic illustration of the extremity of her retreat from thinking.

By this time there was enough evidence of oedipal and preoedipal conflicts for me to try out a range of interpretations of her regressive behavior: as an avoidance of sexual conflicts, particularly her sexual excitement in relation to me; as a fear of her aggression in the transference; as an avoidance of guilt and responsibility; as a fear of independence of her mother in the past and me in the present; as a fear of retribution if she thought about things or had strong feelings. None of this seemed to make much sense to her at this stage of the analysis, and again it felt to me that this was not resistance, it was incomprehension.

I was, however, aware of having to do her thinking for her, and thus being part of herself in the sense of supplying a missing function. She was interested, and sometimes pleased with an interpretation, e.g., that she was following me around and watching me like a jealous lover, because, "At least it's an explanation; otherwise what I'm doing seems senseless." She even seemed to prefer the explanation of a homosexual attachment to me to one about clinging like a child to her mummy, feeling it was more grown up. But she could not make anything further of it. Somewhere around the fifth or sixth year of treatment when she was already feeling less "useless," but still following me around, I came out of the hospital where I worked one day to find her running up to me. She said, "Here I am, I've found you." Taken by surprise, I said, "There's a clever girl." She went off satisfied. In the next session she recalled running in to see her father at his place of work and being told off for disturbing him—a link she had been unable to make before.

It gradually became apparent that Mrs. T. needed to exercise and expand mental processes which would allow her to think, and that she was not ready to benefit from interpretations which aimed to expand her awareness of unconscious content. For example, she recalled some occasions when her mother got in a rage and hit her, but she did not know why. Mrs. T. asked, "Is it important?" I said that it contrasted with the impression she had given me of her mother as quiet and rather timid, wanting to avoid upset and telling her it was best to forget unpleasant things; and that it might be important to know whether she had done something extreme enough to account for mother's rage, or whether something else was upsetting mother; also that it would be important to know how it made her feel. With a mixture of wonderment and admiration she asked, "How do you think of so many things? I can never think of anything!" She often made such admiring comments.

She was surprised by my wish to look for connections, and would ask, "Why do you want to connect things up all the time?" At first I mistook such comments and questions for resistance and tried to deal with them by exploring such things as: her fear of finding out about herself or her family; her reluctance to have her feelings stirred up; her resentment of my intrusion; her wish to attack me and her fear of my retaliation in kind. I even, in desperation, tried symbolic interpretations such as her wish to keep her parents separate in her mind. But it became apparent that this was not resistance in the ordinary sense of a patient summoning up defenses to prevent the emergence of specific representations. Interpretation of defense and verbalization of affect never resulted in the emergence of repressed ideas and further associative material, as it did in the analysis of Sam. All that happened was that Mrs. T. began to see the relevance of the connections I was making, and wanted to follow them up herself, but became more and more frustrated by her inability to get her own thoughts to flow.

Looking back now I realize that she had devised her own way of proceeding by asking me questions: Why is that so important? Why do you want to connect those things? Doesn't everyone want to forget unpleasant things? What do other people feel about this? I sometimes gave answers, much as one would to a small child learning about life. It was not easy for her to pluck up courage to ask questions. She dreaded the possibility that I might laugh at her, as she thought her mother used to, if she just told me about things that occurred to her. Her mother told her she used to be a chatterbox, but she only remembered herself as a silent child. I told her I wished she could be a chatterbox again now. She devised another technique, once she realized that if she mentioned things she was reluctant to face having to do, I would ask why, and start thinking of possible reasons. She began to ask me to "talk her through" what might happen, so that she could be prepared.

This technique of helping her to articulate her questions and their implications proved the most accessible route to her childhood thinking and the reasons for the inhibitions that had come to characterize her mental life. For example, she asked, "How does the baby know when to start?" Her question enabled me to uncover her infantile sexual theories. She started with the question, "How does the baby know when to start growing?" which revealed her assumption that the baby is waiting inside her. But "If you can't have a baby until you are married, how does the baby know when you are married?" and so on. In trying to understand the importance of such infantile reasoning alongside her better knowledge, it seemed that her fear of becoming pregnant was linked to the unconscious fantasy of being taken over by the infant within.[8]

We had already established important clues suggesting to me, though not necessarily to her, that her mother had found it hard to cope with her daughter's growing independence and she had experienced the child's demands as overwhelming (probably increasing after the birth of Mrs. T.'s younger brother). Such a construction allows for the inference that Mrs T. responded to what she perceived as her capacity to overwhelm her mother by a wide-ranging inhibition of the developing mental functions that produced her overpowering affects and intolerable ideas. Thus she remained helpless and childlike.

For the first 5 or 6 years I had been inclined to think that Mrs. T.'s disturbance must have started early, because of the severe inhibition of thinking, feeling, and communicating with the object. But as memories and a wide range of feelings slowly emerged, and began falling into patterns that made sense to her, I became more inclined to think that while her early experiences had left her with areas of vulnerability, she had been getting by fairly well developmentally until the events at age 6 proved more than she could cope with. At this point she retreated from being the chatterbox child who could enjoy herself, to being the silent child terrified of doing, saying, or even thinking the wrong thing. To this Mrs. T. now comments: "The trouble with telling something to you (or anybody else) is that I'm no longer in control of it, you can then think what you like about it, and I can't stop you."

The content of her conflicts is not uncommon: fear of losing control of her destructiveness and excited sexuality; and some specifically

8. More recently, she has clarified that but for the fact that pregnancy makes you sick, she would not have been unduly anxious about having a baby.

oedipal guilt and anxiety which remained unresolved. But her reaction to these conflicts went beyond neurotic symptoms or character structure, to a pervasive defensive inhibition of thinking and feeling, until she was apparently unable to distinguish even such basic feelings as sexual excitement, rage, and nausea. Her fears of self-assertion, initiative, and spontaneity led to a pervasive compliance with the wishes of the object, and an attempt to hand over responsibility to the object for her own inner life.

Her improvement is perhaps well illustrated by a small vignette from a recent session in which we tried to tackle once again her tendency to constrict her mental processes. I said, "Perhaps your need to stop us talking and thinking is like stopping your bodily and mental feelings." She said, "I'm getting upset . . . don't know what to say . . . it's so frustrating." She spoke of her fear of going on and on if she started crying, and likened it to her fear of being unable to stop vomiting if she once started. She commented, "I'm beginning to learn better ways of coping. It's in my mind I don't cope. I don't think I've ever felt the same way about it as other people do." This was when she asked, "What's gone wrong with my mind? I used to think it was something I'd grow out of, because it had to do with being a child. But I never did. There was something wrong from the start." She began trying to think of incidents, and came up with episodes from the time when she was 6 of another child being sick at school and of herself being sick, herself commenting that it was around the time of her brother's birth. I noted that she would have had many feelings to control at that time: anger at being pushed out; sadness at losing mother; fright at being sent away to stay with friends. I asked whether it was not also the time of the sexual games with the little boy (she had already recovered the memory of enjoying those games, and felt sad now that she could not enjoy sex with her husband). "Yes," she said, "so it's all come together. I know we've said this before, but it feels new somehow. Sex is the other thing that goes wrong and we don't talk about it. Perhaps one stands for the other."

It is a sobering thought that after 15 years of analysis I still find myself pleased when she is able to make such a thoughtful comment. Although objectively she now copes much better with feeling sick and with other people being sick, she maintains that her fear of vomiting feels as bad as ever. She has commented that if she lost this fear she wouldn't know herself.

### DISTURBANCES OF MENTAL PROCESSES

The distinction between representational and mental process disturbances can never be sharp, and may be regarded merely as a heuristic device to explain differences in the rate of psychic change (Fonagy and Moran, 1991). Thus even in neurotic disturbances there is some degree of inhibition of mental processes as well as distortions of representations. In adult psychoanalysis, those patients with inhibited mental processes stand out as more severely disturbed and more refractory to interpretation. In child analysis, particularly with younger children, the distinction between representational aspects of disturbance and those deriving from poorly functioning mental processes is far less clear. This is because the treatment of children occurs alongside the development of mental processes. As Abrams (1987) points out, with development "the capacities to relate, adapt, render meanings, and transform experiences into structures become more differentiated and complex" (p. 444). The case of Mrs. T. shows that we must concern ourselves with the capacities patients possess or lack to work with, to shape and transform their mental representational systems.

With the development of defense mechanisms, the child will have available mental processes with which to distort or bar from access to consciousness those mental representations associated with the experience of unpleasure. Before defense mechanisms proper are reliably established, the child is able to prevent unpleasurable mental experiences by inhibiting the evolving mental process itself, which is a more generalized, primitive defense. Some of the mental processes which Mrs. T. partially inhibited clearly involved the consideration of alternative explanations for her own thoughts and feelings. The analysis revealed that this inhibition derived from a reluctance to create links between ideas and feelings. The extent to which she avoided making links went beyond what could be accounted for in terms of the defenses of isolation and repression. Rather, it entailed the defensive maneuver of deactivating a whole class of mental functions concerned with postulating alternatives and with making links to enhance meaning.

The curtailment of a mental process has more general pathological consequences for development than does the repudiation of specific mental representations. The distortions of personality which result from inhibitions of functioning are apparent in the wide-ranging limitations on the individual's capacity for mental representation. Mrs. T. was limited in her view of herself as a wife, potential mother, and patient; there were only isolated aspects of adult functioning, none of these involving intense emotional investment, which were unaffected. She could give no account of why she was in treatment; she could not understand why her husband was dissatisfied with her; and she was perplexed by her analyst's expectations, not to mention her bewilderment when offered interpretations.

The analyst interprets conflict by addressing representations which have been warded off and appear in the material as a component of a compromise formation. The case of Sam showed how such interpretations can generate the therapeutic process. By contrast, even the most accurate interpretations of conflict and defense in the early years of Mrs. T.'s analysis led to little more than gratification that her analyst valued her enough to want to think about her. The therapeutic action in cases like that of Mrs. T. is generated by the disinhibition or *reactivation of inhibited mental functions*.[9] Although interpretations remain crucial in this respect, their function is no longer limited to the lifting of repression and altering the nature of specific mental representations. Besides their capacity to present alternative views of mental events, the process of making interpretations requires the analyst to become actively involved in the mental functioning of the patient and creates the possibility for the patient to become reciprocally involved with the working of the analyst's mind. Thus, they entail the active involvement of one individual in the representational world and mental functioning of another. The experience of mental involvement with another human being without the threat of overwhelming mental anguish was what ultimately led to the freeing up of the inhibition of Mrs. T.'s mental functioning.

In the treatment of disturbances deriving from the inhibition of mental processes, the patient's active mental involvement is elicited by the analyst's attention to the elaboration of the patient's preconscious mental content. This mental involvement, combined with interpretations of the anxieties which led the patient to curtail certain mental processes, gradually brings about a reactivation of inhibited mental processes. As this occurs slowly, the patient may become open to a gradual restructuring of distorted mental representations through further analytic work.

In the account of Mrs. T. we saw how the analyst's interpretations set the patient's mind "a challenge" to look at the working of her own mind and, in the transference, to explore her analyst's mental state. The successful engagement of the patient in trying to work out how the analyst arrives at stable constructions of the patient's subjective mental experience probably provides the route by which the patient's own mental processes may become disinhibited. Over a prolonged time period, diverse interpretations were made concerning the patient's perception of herself and her analyst. These, as she became able to think and feel, enabled her to integrate the analyst's understanding

9. We assume the functions to be present even if they are inefficient and rarely used.

into her own mental world. This, then, in greatly simplified terms, is the second form of psychic change that can be achieved through psychoanalysis. Compared to changes of mental representation, the rate and extent of such changes will normally be small.

Mrs. T. is also a good illustration of how the analyst preconsciously compensates for the patient's lack of mental capacity. The analyst's early interpretations, for example, of Mrs. T.'s sexual anxieties, assumed (erroneously as it turned out) that she was aware of and therefore might be concerned about the object's reactions. Working with Mrs. T., the analyst was forced to question many of her preconscious assumptions about the contents of her patient's mind in order to prevent herself from externalizing and attributing to the patient her own intact mental capacities. In individuals where an aspect of mental functioning is severely impaired, dealing with the implications for the transference may be considered a precondition of analytic treatment. As was sometimes the case with Mrs. T., a failure to achieve this may lead patients to treat interpretations as assaults, and analytic ideas as abusive intrusions.

In the best of situations, when the patient understands the analyst's comments, the patient's mental work recapitulates that of the analyst, albeit within the limitations set by the patient's level of development. The reactivation of mental processes consequent on the analyst's endeavor to focus on and elaborate the mental life of the patient is seen by us in this context as the primary mechanism of therapeutic action, which then permits the techniques belonging to the representational model to become more effective. Hence we view frequent and accurate interpretations of the presumed contents of the patient's mind as an essential component of successful treatment in these cases. Similarly, interpretations of the countertransference focusing on the contents of the analyst's mind may also be central to therapeutic effectiveness with such patients.

Mrs. T.'s symptoms certainly can be understood as partial expressions of repudiated mental representations. The content of her memories connected with vomiting helped the analyst to begin to understand important aspects of drive organization, anxieties, and her representation of her relationship to her objects. They may also be seen, however, as indications of her own mental functioning. Her fear of vomiting can be understood as a concrete representation of her expectation of the unimaginably destructive effects of letting out feelings and thoughts, by which both she and the object would be overwhelmed. When Mrs. T. felt sick, she became unable to think what to do to help herself; this mental inhibition was reflected in a physical inability to move. The analysis, particularly the regression in the transference, suggested that Mrs. T. was in conflict about her perception of herself as overpowering and out of control. It thus seems reasonable to speculate that as a child Mrs. T. inhibited her capacity to think about her feelings and wishes in order to avoid the disturbing representations of herself as a source of danger to herself and her mother. In this respect, her fear of vomiting can be understood as an endopsychic perception of the self as danger-ously likely to lose control over its functioning. It was only secondarily a repudiated representation of her sexual and aggressive conflicts. For this reason the analyst could not expect improvement in response to interpretations of defense and conflict about sexual and aggressive wishes alone. Rather, only when inhibited mental processes could be invoked so that conflict about using her mind could be explored and her experience of her mental functioning radically altered, could the slow movement toward symptomatic improvement begin.[10]

In child analysis there is a further way in which the analytic process facilitates the development of mental processes. In his interpretive work the analyst, sometimes unwittingly, takes for granted the opera-tion of mental processes in the child which exceed the child's capacities. In so doing, he may call upon the child to develop certain mental processes precociously, for example, the capacity to tolerate mixed feelings or ambiguity (Hodges and Edgcumbe, 1990). While this may seem inappropriate developmentally, its effects may be no more delete-rious than the assumptions underlying the so-called "conversations" which mothers carry on with their babies.

### CONCLUSION

In this paper we have drawn attention to certain qualitative differences in the therapeutic action of psychoanalysis with two aspects of psycho-logical disturbance. We distinguish between defense as manifested in the repudiation or distortion of mental representations, and as evi-denced in the inhibition of categories of mental functioning. In mak-ing this distinction, we recognize that we are proposing no more than a small step along the route established by Anna Freud, Heinz Hart-

---

10. In reading this paper, Mrs. T. thought that Sam's analysis sounded unbelievably easy. Her main overall comment on the piece about herself was: "I know there is nothing in here I haven't told you myself, or we haven't talked about. But seeing it all put together is shocking." She also commented that we had made it sound as though she is better, and this is not yet true. She pointed out that since the paper is about how much more difficult it is to treat patients like herself than "classical" analysands, we should not spoil our argument by making her sound too easy.

mann, and others who have advanced the psychology of the ego. We hope that it may prove helpful in thinking about the psychoanalytic treatment of certain serious forms of psychological disturbance in developmental terms, and place concepts such as structure building within the framework of psychic conflict and defense. Our approach brings into question the dynamic and developmental determinants of mental activities that have failed to become adequately established. Drive influences, economic factors, and all the useful perspectives that psychoanalysis offers can in this way be brought to bear on the origins of ego deficits which become manifest in the course of psychoanalytic treatment, and on how these may be alleviated through the interpretation of conflict, defense, and resistance.

## BIBLIOGRAPHY

ABRAMS, S. (1980). Therapeutic action and ways of knowing. *J. Amer. Psychoanal. Assn.*, 28:291–307.

———— (1987). The psychoanalytic process: A schematic model. *Int. J. Psychoanal.*, 68:441–452.

———— (1988). The psychoanalytic process in adults and children. *Psychoanal. Study Child*, 43:245–261.

———— (1990). The psychoanalytic process: The developmental and the integrative. *Psychoanal. Q.*, 59:650–677.

BALINT, M. (1949). Changing therapeutical aims and techniques in psychoanalysis. *Int. J. Psychoanal.*, 30:117–124.

BENE, A. (1977). The influence of deaf and dumb parents on a child's development. *Psychoanal. Study Child*, 32:175–194.

BLATT, S. J. & BEHRENDS, R. S. (1987). Internalization, separation-individuation, and the nature of therapeutic action. *Int. J. Psychoanal.*, 68:279–297.

COHEN, D. J. (1991). Tourette's syndrome. *Int. Rev. Psychoanal.*, 18:195–210.

COMPTON, A. (1988). The idea of a psychoanalytic process. In COPE-PAP, December: Reports to the Committee on Psychoanalytic Education, The Study Group on the Psychoanalytic Process, The Board of Professional Standards of the American Psychoanalytic Association.

DE M'UZAN, M. (1974). Psychodynamic mechanisms in psychosomatic symptom formation. *Psychother. & Psychosom.*, 23:103–110.

DE WITT, K. N. ET AL. (1990). Scales of psychological capacities. (Unpublished paper.)

EDGCUMBE, R. (1984). Modes of communication. *Psychoanal. Study Child*, 39:137–154.

EMDE, R. N. (1990). Mobilizing fundamental modes of development. *J. Amer. Psychoanal. Assn.*, 38:881–913.

FONAGY, P. (1991). Thinking about thinking. *Int. J. Psychoanal.*, 72:639–656.

———— & MORAN, G. S. (1991). Understanding psychic change in child analysis. *Int. J. Psychoanal.*, 72:15–22.

FREUD, A. (1965). *Normality and Pathology in Childhood.* Harmondsworth, Middx: Penguin.

———— (1974). A psychoanalytic view of developmental psychopathology. *W.*, 8:57–74.

GITELSON, M. (1962). On the curative factors in the first phase of analysis. In *Psychoanalysis: Science and Profession.* New York: Int. Univ. Press, 1973, pp. 311–341.

GOODMAN, S., ed. (1977). *Psychoanalytic Education and Research.* New York: Int. Univ. Press.

HODGES, J. & EDGCUMBE, R. (1990). Mixed feelings. *Bull. Anna Freud Centre*, 13:169–181.

JACOBSON, E. (1964). *The Self and the Object World.* New York: Int. Univ. Press.

KENNEDY, H. & MORAN, G. S. (1991). Reflections on the aims of child psychoanalysis. *Psychoanal. Study Child*, 46:181–198.

KERNBERG, O. F. (1980). Some implications of object relations theory for psychoanalytic technique. In *Psychoanalytic Explorations of Technique*, ed. H. P. Blum. New York: Int. Univ. Press, pp. 207–239.

KLAUBER, J. (1972). On the relationship of transference and interpretation in psychoanalytic therapy. *Int. J. Psychoanal.*, 53:385–391.

KOHUT, H. (1977). *The Restoration of the Self.* New York: Int. Univ. Press.

LOEWALD, H. W. (1960). On the therapeutic action of psycho-analysis. *Int. J. Psychoanal.*, 41:16–33.

———— (1973). On internalization. In *Papers on Psychoanalysis.* New Haven: Yale Univ. Press, pp. 69–86.

———— (1979). Reflections on the psychoanalytic process and its therapeutic potential. *Psychoanal. Study Child*, 34:155–167.

MCDOUGALL, J. (1974). The psychosoma and the psychoanalytic process. *Int. Rev. Psychoanal.*, 1:437–459.

MASTERSON, J. (1976). *Psychotherapy of the Borderline Adult.* New York: Brunner/Mazel.

MODELL, A. H. (1976). "The holding environment" and the therapeutic action of psychoanalysis. *J. Amer. Psychoanal. Assn.*, 24:285–307.

RUMELHART, D. E. & MCCLELLAND, J. L. (1986). *Parallel Distributed Processing*, 2 vols. Cambridge, Mass.: MIT Press.

SANDLER, J. (1972). The role of affects in psychoanalytic theory. In *From Safety to Superego.* London: Karnac, 1975.

———— & ROSENBLATT, B. (1962). The concept of the representational world. *Psychoanal. Study Child*, 17:128–145.

SCHLESSINGER, N. & ROBBINS, F. (1983). *A Developmental View of the Psychoanalytic Process.* New York: Int. Univ. Press.

SEGAL, H. (1978). On symbolism. *Int. J. Psychoanal.*, 59:315–319.

SETTLAGE, C. F., ET AL. (1980). Excerpt from the report of the preparatory commission on child analysis. *Psychoanal. Contemp. Thought*, 3:131–138.

SIFNEOS, P. E. (1977). The phenomenon of 'alexithymia.' *Psychother. Psychosom.*, 28:47–57.

STOLOROW, R. & LACHMANN, F. (1978). The developmental prestages of defenses. *Psychoanal. Q.*, 47:73–102.

STONE, L. (1961). *The Psychoanalytic Situation*. New York: Int. Univ. Press.

VIEDERMAN, M. (1991). The real person of the analyst and his role in the process of psychoanalytic cure. *J. Amer. Psychoanal. Assn.*, 39:451–489.

WEINSHEL, E. M. (1990). Further observations on the psychoanalytic process. *Psychoanal. Q.*, 59:629–649.

WINNICOTT, D. W. (1965). *The Maturational Process and the Facilitating Environment*. London: Hogarth Press.

# Play and Therapeutic Action

PHYLLIS M. COHEN, ED.D., and
ALBERT J. SOLNIT, M.D.

*Children in clinical psychoanalysis are able to resolve conflicts and move ahead developmentally. This therapeutic process is facilitated by the psychoanalyst's understanding of the child, reflected in multi-faceted and thoughtful clinical technique. We review aspects of the analyses of four developmentally deviant children who were engaged in child psychoanalysis because of ego disturbances that impaired their ability to learn. These clinical analyses are used to exemplify three intertwined processes related to the therapeutic action of child psychoanalysis: therapeutic alliance, transference, and the role of the child analyst as a real person. These processes were expressed in and were influenced by the emergence of particular types of play in which the children explored complex issues in their lives. Along with other aspects of psychoanalytic technique, including interpretation, the analyses of these four children illustrate the therapeutic meanings of play in child psychoanalysis.*

PLAY IN CHILD PSYCHOANALYSIS CONTAINS WITHIN IT MANY DIFFERENT levels of meaning and experience. However, it is possible to pull together certain general themes in play, or certain modes of playing, and to analyze them in terms of their influence on therapeutic action. In this paper we use the terms *therapeutic action* and *process* to describe and explicate the therapeutic impact of child psychoanalysis.

In particular, we focus on a mode of dramatic play which has

Phyllis M. Cohen is Associate Clinical Professor, Yale University Child Study Center. Albert J. Solnit is Sterling Professor Emeritus, Pediatrics and Psychiatry; Senior Research Scientist; and Commissioner, Department of Mental Heath, State of Connecticut.

Presented at the Anna Freud Centre Colloquium, "Therapeutic Process in Child and Adult Psychoanalysis," in London, November 1–2, 1991.

We appreciate our discussion with the study group on The Many Meanings of Play in Child Psychoanalysis, sponsored by the Psychoanalytic Research and Development Fund, and are especially appreciative of the suggestions of Matthew Cohen, M. Phil.

emerged during the psychoanalyses of four prelatency-age boys (Ritvo, 1993). This play process forces into view the relationship between therapy that emphasizes the unlocking of obstacles to development and that which emphasizes the clarification and resolution of those neurotic disorders associated with symptomatic behavior, inhibitions, depression and anxiety, or their equivalents. Both approaches are necessary to assure a sound psychoanalytic process.

In the four prelatency boys to be presented, theoretical issues concerning choice of technical approach in psychoanalytic treatment suggested a validation of a hypothesis most clearly formulated by Peter Neubauer (1987, 1993). This hypothesis is related to an overarching conviction of Anna Freud's. In numerous presentations and publications she indicated that the major criteria for terminating child psychoanalytic treatment are symptomatic relief and the resumption of progressive development. In Neubauer's formulation, children suffering from an impaired ego (i.e., from developmental deviation largely related to equipmental or endowment factors) require a technical and theoretical approach to psychoanalytic treatment that emphasizes the identification of and rechanneling of deviant developmental characteristics and lags. For the purposes of this report we do not emphasize that part of our psychoanalytic treatment of these children in which resistance, defense, and conflict are clarified, interpreted, and worked through in relieving the child's neurotic suffering.

Each of the children to be presented suffered from serious emotional difficulties with ego impairments, the most common of which was a learning disability that played a significant role in the timing of (formal schooling was about to begin) and motivation for referral for psychoanalytic treatment. Each boy's needs and family's sustained investment in psychoanalytic treatment were related to an awareness of the importance of education. This also involved helping the parents keep the teachers and school administrators informed and supportive of their student's psychoanalytic treatment.

As we present the clinical material, it is useful to keep our presumption in mind that play with a child psychoanalyst can have a development-promoting impact with a minimum of verbalization and interpretation. It is not likely to be therapeutic if such play is not with a psychoanalytic therapist who is empathic, attuned to his patient's moods and fantasies, and available as a player as well as an active psychological-emotional transference presence as the child plays out (with or without an active play role assigned by the child to the analyst) the inner drama, longings, attitudes, motives, and characteristics of his impaired development. In order to focus the relationship of therapeutic action to removing obstacles to progressive development, the case material emphasizes the play interaction more than it does the ongoing interpretation of resistance, defense, and conflict.

## CLINICAL MATERIAL

The four cases described below have some common features. All were children of academic or professional families of at least moderate means. All the children were diagnosed as having learning disabilities. The fourth child, although quite bright and an early reader, was also described by his teachers as learning disabled because of his extreme behavioral problems, impulsivity, and negativism.

All four children entered analysis between the ages of 4 and 7 and terminated between the ages of 7 and 10. The analytic treatments lasted 2 to 4 years. In the course of each of the analyses, a play world reflecting deviant, impaired development was constructed, explored, modified, and understood as the treatment progressed and was terminated. The nature and valence of the transference changed during the course of the analysis, but initially it was related to distorted relationships evoked by the child's deviant development. Over the course of treatment the transference revealed a potential for more realistic and developmentally appropriate relationships and learning behaviors.

Finally, all four cases were responsive in a sustained manner to psychoanalytic treatment in modifying and significantly reducing the obstacles to a more normal progressive development, as reflected in their inner lives and in their relationships and behavior at home and in school. The children came to be at greater ease with themselves and others, showed improvement in their academic performances, and found more pleasure and satisfaction in their experiences of both the world of inner reality and the actual world in which they lived. They could be said to have begun or resumed a progressive development with past and present obstacles having been minimized.

The four cases were previously discussed in *The Many Meanings of Play* (Cohen and Cohen, 1993).

### CASE 1: TOMMY

Tommy, at 6 years, was a confused and anxious child who was not learning. He seemed distant and withdrawn and quite puzzling to his teachers and family. Tommy's older brother was an excellent student. His parents, both academics with advanced degrees, were very attached and close to his older brother, Michael, who was outgoing and successful. But they were perplexed by Tommy and saddened by his lack of academic success. They observed that he was not learning and was not outgoing like Michael, but they could not understand why.

In the beginning of treatment Tommy appeared to be a profoundly sad and troubled child. His play consisted of telling stories with small animal and people figures. Often the themes of the stories were disconnected, repetitive, and without much development. His drawings had a listless and laborious quality. The first spark of excitement was noted when he observed and wanted to count some bottles of soda. He observed this in an unusually curious, even agitated way.

Tommy's parents had no sense of what he was experiencing. To the best of their knowledge, they thought that their son was well cared for and they truly believed that they were doing as much as they could for him. Tommy had been attending day care since he was a small child. They reported that he never showed any separation anxiety in parting. He was not tearful when he parted from his parents; neither was he ever aggressive in his manner. He was quiet, and showed no expression of affect whatsoever when he was left by his parents at day care early in the morning and when he was picked up in the evening. And yet, from what we know about Tommy, this experience was very stressful for him. In particular what was hardest was the disorientation in his sense of time. He could not understand for how long he would be left alone at day care, when his parents would come, and so on. The days would go on and on without an end in sight. He was adrift in an ocean of time, helpless, with no safe harbor within sight.

In the small treatment room (7 feet by 8 feet), Tommy's dramatic play developed around this very metaphor. In the conceptual world which we co-created, Tommy and I were two sailors on a ship at sea. It was a stormy sea with many dangers—hidden rocks, sea monsters, pirates. He was a crewman and I was assigned to be his "Matey," his friend and buddy. In our dramatic play, Tommy spoke to Matey in an (assumed) British accent—and I answered him in turn with the best imitation of a British accent I could muster. At times he designated me the role of captain; at other times he treated me as an equal. Occasionally, Tommy himself became the ship's commanding officer.

In this phase of treatment, he enacted play shipwrecks. The sea was tempestuous; it seemed impossible to control where the ship would go. Of great importance were the maps and charts which Tommy constructed, with the encouragement and aid of Matey. He depicted the sea's geography, the position of dangerous rocks, of monsters and pirates, and the whereabouts of safe harbors and ports of call. These charts—which were used in the dramatic play, quickly drawn with crayon, pen, or marker on plain white paper—were carefully stored in his private drawer from session to session. They did not seem to be objects prized in and of themselves, but seemed to be useful for the exploration of Tommy's play world. He frequently revised them, or even redrew them from scratch, for the topography of the sea was always changing and one needed to have an accurate representation of it.

In addition to the maps, another important development was the introduction of a single-lensed telescope. The telescope was not represented by a physical object, but was represented in the dramatic play by putting one's two hands together and holding them up to one's eye. In our dramatic play, the child and Matey would stand on the deck of the ship or on top of cliffs (represented by chairs and couches) and try to focus the lens to see what lay about us. This imaginary device, a prop represented by a part of the body, was elevated by me, with the consent and complicity of Tommy, to a level of critical importance in the course of the development of the conceptual world. It was used as a way of assessing our current situation and to understand what lay ahead. With the careful, assiduous employment of this powerful instrument for observation, one could safely navigate the treacherous seas and reach a safe harbor.

The intensity of his anxiety was most fully explored in this phase. Oftentimes, when the sea became stormy and there was a danger of a shipwreck, the telescope would have a sense of urgency associated with it. The waves washed over the side of the ship. The wind howled. "I can't see anything! The telescope won't focus for me!" cried the Matey. "Here, you take it!" Tommy took the telescope, put it up to his eye, and started to focus it. "What can you see? Do you know where we are?" the Matey inquired, barely able to make herself heard above the fury of the storm. Fortunately, Tommy saw where they were and was able to guide the ship to find the food, warmth, and security in a safe harbor.

Tommy discovered that he had the capacity to see around him. He learned that one of the ways of overcoming the anxiety of being abandoned and having to be alone was to look around him—not to close his eyes and see the world through a glassy-eyed stare—but to see where he was and act upon that knowledge.

Tommy and his Matey became old sea hands over time. Through their use of charts and especially the employment of the telescope, we eventually memorized the sea lanes. As the world became a more peaceful, friendlier place and the theme of "man against the sea" became less interesting for Tommy, another theme emerged inside the same play world. Until this point, at the back of my mind I held the theoretical assumption that the storms, the shipwrecks, the pirates, and so on were an expression of aggression and (denied) hatred, perhaps toward Tommy's older brother, who was the object of his parents' admiration and love. But the material which emerged at this point of the analysis suggested alternate interpretations.

More and more the dramatic play revolved around the idea of Tommy being marooned on a desert island with his Matey. Here the word "Matey" was used by Tommy primarily not as a way of expressing friendliness and the state of being my "buddy." In the context of the deepening transference at this point of the analysis, I felt it meant something more akin to the word "mate," as in lover. This suggested that the earlier torrential storms were also a representation of the fearful side of the primal scene, while the scenes on the deserted island were a way to express its more affectionate, intimate side. While before, Tommy metaphorically had to fight off his fears and anxieties, here he was able to express unchallenged affection and closeness, without the rivalry of his older brother or father. For as Erikson (1963) states, in his description of the efficacy of play therapy, "The most obvious condition is that the child has the toys and the adult for himself, and that sibling rivalry, parental nagging, or any kind of sudden interruption does not disturb the unfolding of his play intentions, whatever they may be" (p. 222). Tommy now had his Matey (mate-mother-analyst) alone, in the privacy of a secret island.

Yet another way of understanding Tommy's fantasy world, being marooned on a desert island also was associated with the earlier experience of abandonment, isolation, and loneliness. Now, however, even if marooned on a desert island, he no longer experienced the fear of abandonment, for he had his Matey with him. Through his play with the analyst, Tommy had, in a transferential sense, incorporated his mother into his own self; he had his own claim on her which had become internalized in his enhanced self-esteem.

By the time Tommy was $8\frac{1}{2}$, he had shown considerable improvement in school. His glassy-eyed stare had become more focused, and he showed signs of vitality and interest in life. He also was more outgoing and involved and more expressive of his emotions. The emotional stress and anxieties which Tommy experienced lifted; he no longer felt so disturbed or helpless in being alone and not knowing where he was. Today, about 9 years after the termination of his analysis, Tommy has met with academic success in high school and now shows promise as a playwright. Tommy has been able to use his rich and creative imagination, which we saw in his play world, and relate his own fantasies to a public audience.

When Rob started treatment, he was 6 years old. His parents were both academics. Their older son was a successful student. Rob was failing for the second year in school. He was aggressive and suffered from encopresis. He defecated in his pants at home and in the most visible, public situations. Children and teachers avoided him and were frightened by him. Rob's parents were extremely concerned. His mother, who suffered from frequent bouts of depression, dated the onset of Rob's difficulties to age 2 years when the parents went on vacation and left the children with a female family friend who at the time was quite emotionally unstable. She was sadistic and aggressive in her attempts to toilet train Rob.

Rob's play in the analysis consisted of playing basketball. He also discussed his experiences of being on the swim team. He assigned me the role of Coach. As far as this play in the analysis was concerned, there really were no other people involved—no other teammates or referees. His play was unimaginative (drill after drill and emphasis on scorekeeping). He tossed the ball into the waste basket; the only variations were from which angle and from what distance. Not infrequently there were aggressive attacks, or Rob would run out of the room, run out of the building, dart across a dangerous room or climb to the roof top.

At times he reported incidents of defecating in the swimming pool and often, preceding a session, he urinated on top of a radiator. This had the effect of making a normally (semi)concealed act more public, for the fumes from his urine would carry through the halls and up and down one or more flights of stairs. I began to understand the association of defecation with swimming, and sitting on top of a radiator was a way to link the act with his mother. The mother, symbolized by the pool's water and radiator's warmth, thus received Rob's feces—even as he made people go away from him and recreated the trauma of being abandoned and left alone.

One of my responsibilities as Coach was to track his vital statistics. The Coach was informed on all aspects of Rob's physical behavior. Central were issues of control over his body and over the bodies of others. Just like the feces which were a love object to his mother, his scoring was presented to me.

Rob himself became aware of his behavior and all of his physical "statistics" as he made the identification with Coach. He gradually lost interest in playing basketball with Coach and going swimming. Rob's great concern with his physical prowess became less pressing. Ultimately, the statistics became Rob's own concern. He took pride in being his own manager.

After three years of analysis, Rob's encopresis became more and more infrequent. It reached the point where he would never defecate in his pants at school. He did, however, occasionally continue this symptom in my office; I believed that these episodes of encopresis represented a persisting marker of the crystallization of the symptom within the transference. In the analytic situation and through the transference neurosis, Rob was most actively aware of the conflicts in trying to control his behavior. Over time, the symptom disappeared from the analytic office as well. Rob met with more success in school. After the termination of analysis I intermittently heard from Rob's parents. He developed into a solid, energetic, latency-age youngster, and his movement into puberty was not very eventful; he enjoyed his increasing autonomy; he was accepted into a fine prep school, where he had a circle of friends, including boys and girls, and played on a team.

When Rob was 14 years old, his parents went away for a weekend. He arranged to stay at the home of his friend, but chose to go home to his empty house. This revived his earlier trauma of abandonment when he was 2 years old. He thus promptly invited 30 or 40 of his "close friends" from school to have a wild party in his house. They "trashed" the house, being particularly destructive of Rob's parents' bedroom. He was abandoned, and he responded by metaphorically defecating. No one had to tell him anything, but after Rob's parents returned from their trip, Rob knew that it was time to see the analyst with whom he had overcome his problem of encopresis. After two or three months of sessions with me, he could again defer and channel his anger and was able to resume his normal relations with his parents, his environment, and his own body. Now, two years after this episode of trashing, Rob is a popular teenager interested in becoming a psychologist when he grows up. He remains interested in sports—in a positive, healthy manner, without the obsessive concern for statistics and the control of his body.

### CASE 3: BENJAMIN

From an early age, Benjamin was showing signs of having a severe learning disability. At age 4, a neurologist recommended special education placement, based on what he assessed was an organic impairment in cognitive and motor functions. The exact nature of the disorder was never clearly diagnosed. The father, a professor of education, wondered if Benjamin was perhaps autistic, as he seemed very impaired and lacked basic social skills as well. Yet at the same time, Benjamin's father identified with his son.

It became clear to me early in Benjamin's analysis that Benjamin's disabilities in learning were caused at least as much by emotional factors as by constitutional determinants. He was a very rigid, anxious boy, constantly feeling and then reliving the experience of stress caused over the most minor failures.

On the whole, Benjamin's dramatic play was uninteresting and unimaginative. He repeatedly played school. In the beginning, Benjamin played the role of the stupid student and cast the therapist as his demanding, critical teacher. His dramatic play was thus very masochistic; he was constantly punished for being unable to spell and compute successfully. Many of the learning difficulties seemed related to how he perceived his "damaged" body. It was only when the punitive analyst/teacher referred to him as Mr. Mixup Man or Mr. Opposite that he allowed himself to become the teacher and made me the damaged student. It was through this change that he allowed the analyst as criticized student to verbalize anger, disappointment, frustration, fear, loneliness, and sadness.

Benjamin now was able to take advantage of playing in a town soccer team with some success. His father, who had never played a sport, watched his child with pride. He, too, joined in the activity and became the coach for his son's team. As a result of their mutual involvement in the sport, Benjamin's father no longer felt trapped by the resonating identification he experienced through the related but differing clumsiness that he and his son shared; neither did Benjamin's own identification with his father focus on this aspect of the father's behavior and attitudes. Benjamin came to internalize the image of his father as coach. This idealized aspect of his parent helped form Benjamin's emerging ego ideal. This, along with the work in the analysis, allowed for the clarification and attenuation of a complex developmental obstacle.

### CASE 4: JASON

Jason, age 5, a precocious reader and a math whiz, tyrannized the classroom with his aggression, impulsivity, outbursts, and noncompliant behavior. He terrorized the teachers and other children. He was unresponsive to learning in school. Nobody seemed able to figure him out.

Jason's parents, hard-working architects, left him in day care for 10-hour days. When he was 2 his sister was born and his father mysteriously abandoned the family for several months. Jason's mother became depressed. Jason became confused and upset, for his father's disappearance had taught him that it was possible for either or both of his parents to disappear suddenly at any time. He was convinced that his own anger had caused his father to go away to another city.

In the play world which Jason constructed, he was in business with his therapist. My analytic office became a business office. The physical properties which were used were quite extensive—stationary, documents, models for development and marketing. Sometimes Jason and I were co-workers; at other times Jason assumed the role of boss and I was his subordinate. He would tell his employee what to do, fantasize about all his "great ideas" for a "new product," and so on. At certain moments I became a high-ranking executive, while Jason was an employee of the company. As an executive, I was expected to point out all the important "issues" and could discuss Jason's past "business failures." The fantasy world did not have a playful quality to it—its tone was very serious. Jason became angry if I was slow to respond: "Come on! What are you doing there?"

There were many businesses that emerged. The actual nature of the product changed over time. During the course of the analysis, a number of different products were discussed, modeled, and toyed with. There was one product in particular, however, which seemed to have serious economic possibilities. This was a phone-watch. With this watch, a businessman could get in touch with any of the most important people in his business at any time. "It will become absolutely necessary for every executive to own one," Jason, the businessman, said. "With a phone-watch, you can know where the most important people are all the time." For Jason, that most important person to whom he occasionally referred, by way of example, was his mother. Although he seemed determined and aggressive, Jason was actually very sensitive. Most of all he worried about the possibility of his parents disappearing, how his own actions might cause this, and what he should do in order to prevent this from happening. In order to cope with this anxiety, he put some protective space between himself and his parents, the people closest to him and most linked to his anxiety concerning abandonment. Rather than passively accepting his parents' disappearances, Jason became defensively aggressive and angry. The rage he felt at his parents for his father's disappearance and his mother's depression and then her hospitalization was eventually generalized to include nearly everyone.

Jason appeared very adultlike both in and outside of the play world he constructed. This early maturity had a defensive function. In many ways Jason remained very infantile. He enjoyed cuddling with his stuffed animals and needed a night-light at bedtime. His apparent maturity was thus part of Jason's defensive shielding—the ways in which he distanced himself from the insecurities of being a child and dependent on adults.

The internalization of the phone-watch and the process of identification which took place in the analytic process allowed Jason to cope with the insecurities aroused by his experience of being separated from his parents. This separation was both physical, as when his father left when he was 2 years old or when he was dropped off at day care, and emotional, as in the distance he experienced between himself and his mother when she was depressed. With the identification and internalization of his "product" and the play world which he created, Jason became less aggressive and troublesome; the school no longer threatened to expel him.

In many sessions the phone-watch which Jason was developing was clearly the most interesting and relevant product for Jason; it was not the last "idea for a product." Just before termination, when Jason was 8 years old, he discussed the possibilities of a paper airplane mail-order business. "We could sell do-it-yourself kits, parts, paint. If a part broke, you could send away for it and it would arrive in two days."

This time the issues of separation and specifically termination in the analysis were developed in the paper airplane mail-order business. He showed some anxiety at the prospect of termination and the resultant separation from me, just as he felt anxious around vacations. He wished to hold onto me, to keep me from disappearing. Jason offered all kinds of incentives to his business partner for not dissolving our partnership. He mentioned how, if we promoted certain airline companies in our model business, he and his "business partner" would definitely get free tickets on real airplanes—we could go any place we wanted together. The business showed an associative connection between Jason's memory of his mother's hospitalization and his fantasies concerning me after the analysis terminated. As he remembered taking an airplane when he visited his mother when she was hospitalized, having free airplane tickets meant that he could visit me any time he wanted, even after the analysis terminated.

At the time of termination Jason was no longer as aggressive; the collaboration was not as one-sided. In the end, Jason reluctantly agreed to make me a "consultant," whom he could call upon in times of need. He agreed that he could manage the day-to-day affairs of the business on his own. Both Jason and I were thus able to dissolve the business partnership, as he replaced it with the gratifications that became available in his more progressive, less deviant development.

## DISCUSSION

Our consideration of therapeutic process in child psychoanalysis, a complex theoretical and clinical area, is confined in this paper to three issues that are brought into view by the psychoanalytic study and treatment of four boys as they were moving from the oedipal to the latency period in their developmental trajectories.

The first issue is the nature of the therapeutic alliance; the second is the nature of the transference; and the third issue is the role of the child analyst as a real person, as a significant, influential adult in the growing-up experience of his analysands. These three issues are closely and inseparably tied together; their fit provides a clinical view of how to understand and be guided in the technical management of the psychoanalytic treatment of developmentally deviant children and the theoretical questions these issues raise when looked at together.

In the treatment of the four boys the analyst, when invited, was quite active in the play, feeling the seriousness of the drama as important in its own right. The analyst formed a close alliance with each of these boys in the adventures they created. She noted how the strength and intensity of the therapeutic alliance was forged in the play with minimal interpretation of unconscious feelings and conflicts. The play was the thing! Paradoxically, in the context of treating developmentally deviant children, the analyst as a new or real person gained in importance in fueling the therapeutic process, while the analyst as a transference object, never insignificant, became less central in providing therapeutic leverage. As Peter Neubauer said recently, "We strive these days to do more than just undo the repressed. For example, we also work to overcome [developmental] deviations and arrests" (Abrams, 1991).

For example, Jason's difficulty in termination could be understood in terms of the play world he created and its relation to the rest of his life. The play world was not marginalized as "child's play." Jason was serious; what he was doing was in many ways real to him. In the play world of business which Jason created, he was honing his skills as a businessman, rehearsing for his future occupation, and engaged in activities which were important to him and real in and of themselves. With a serious determination which only a young child can have, he once actually requested "development funds" from his parents to support the "research" and "test-marketing" of the phone-watch. This request apparently caused a minor crisis in the family. His parents had no idea how they should respond. They did not know if Jason was "only playing" or whether his request for money was serious and real. They felt that they could not make the decision for themselves and went to the analyst for consultation. Jason's play world was not far removed from the real world in which he lived. This is similar to the children described by Solnit (1987) and Vygotsky (1978) who were, in Vygotsky's words, "playing at reality."

In the midst of such play, the child does not sharply distinguish the play world from reality. This is not a sign of pathology, but of the intense investment in the elaboration of imagination and fantasy. Engagement in the play drama, as in the theater, is "real" for the time being. Play worlds such as Jason's seem to be very close to the border of reality. Others, such as Tommy's, are much more distal, while the majority, such as Rob's and Benjamin's, seem to be approximately intermediate in distance between the child's inner reality and the world in which he lives. This does not mean, of course, that the child cannot place boundaries around the play world. In fact, the children described sometimes did this quite clearly, in tone of voice, through setting the scene, or even by such phrases as "let's pretend."

However, when they were fully at play—in their developmental effort to reshape their worlds—they could suspend disbelief and fully allow, at least for moments, the expression of their capacities for imagination which enabled them to see themselves and their world more openly and with more opportunities to be active in practicing their "experimental" reshaping of it than in their past nonplay world. The suspension of reality testing, exercise of imagination, and playing out of hypotheses of alternating views appeared to be vital in facilitating the psychoanalytic process with these children. With the support of the child psychoanalyst, the emergence of capacities to experiment in play and to elaborate and explore the inner fantasy world becomes a development-promoting exercise for these children in confronting the distortions and inhibitions that characterize their particular developmental difficulties.

In his more general observations about play, Freud (1908) referred to an intermediate area of experience, the dialectic between reality and fantasy, that has increased significance for this discussion. He said, "Might we not say that every child at play behaves like a creative writer, in that he creates a world of his own, or, rather, re-arranges the things of his world in a new way which pleases him" (p. 143f.). In this view Freud suggested the development-promoting aspect of play for children.

As an imaginative activity which borders reality, playing with a child psychoanalyst has a therapeutic value that in the neurotic child must be translated, interpreted, and worked through to have more than transient therapeutic value. In the developmentally deviant or ego-impaired child, as in the four boys reported in this paper, the play is essential, whereas translation, interpretation, and working through are replaced in importance by how the play and the participation by the child psychoanalyst open up the obstacles to a more normative progressive development. In this context, the analyst as real or new object gains in importance as compared to the analyst as a transference object. It is not a matter of either/or but how the predominance of the former (analyst as new or real object) has a shaping influence on technique as a pathway to therapeutic leverage and action.

In each of these cases, the critical issue was how the child explored and used the analytic opportunities for playing with, or in the presence of, the adult psychoanalyst. As the analyst was observing and playing she was enabling each child to explore alternative ways of viewing himself and his world. The push for this is derived from the libidinal and aggressive drives and the maturational energies that constitute the forces that move development ahead. Within the metaphor of these play world activities, the child identifies with the analyst in tolerating change and in forgoing the familiar stickiness of the deviant developmental views and expectations associated with learning disabilities and distorted self-esteem representations. In turn, this analytic work, including the interpretation and working through of neurotic conflicts and defenses, enabled these children to use their differentiations in object relationships to promote capacities for object constancy, friendship, and identifications that can be elaborated and liberating.

## BIBLIOGRAPHY

ABRAMS, S. (1989). Therapeutic processes. *Psychoanal. Study Child*, 44:43–56.
——— (1990). The psychoanalytic process. *Psychoanal. Q.*, 59:650–677.
——— [interviewer] (1991). A conversation with Peter B. Neubauer. *Amer. Psychoanalyst*, 25(3):10.
COHEN, P. M. & COHEN, M. (1993). Conceptual worlds. In *The Many Meanings of Play*, ed. A. J. Solnit, D. J. Cohen, & P. B. Neubauer. New Haven: Yale Univ. Press, pp. 75–98.
DOWNEY, T. W. (1987). Notes on play and guilt in child psychoanalysis. *Psychoanal. Study Child*, 42:105–126.
ERIKSON, E. H. (1963). *Childhood and Society*, 2nd ed. New York: Norton.
FREUD, A. (1926). Four lectures on child analysis. *W.*, 1:3–69.
——— (1965). *Normality and Pathology in Childhood*. New York: Int. Univ. Press.

FREUD, S. (1908). Creative writers and day-dreaming. *S.E.*, 9:141–153.

HOFFER, W. (1949). Mouth, hand, and ego integration. *Psychoanal. Study Child*, 3/4:49–56.

KLEIN, M. (1932). *The Psycho-analysis of Children*. London: Hogarth Press.

——— (1961). *Narrative of a Child Analysis*. London: Hogarth Press.

KOHUT, H. (1971). *The Analysis of the Self*. New York: Int. Univ. Press.

LOEWALD, E. L. (1987). Therapeutic play in space and time. *Psychoanal. Study Child*, 42:173–192.

MORAN, G. S. (1987). Some functions of play and playfulness. *Psychoanal. Study Child*, 42:11–29.

NEUBAUER, P. B. (1987). The many meanings of play. *Psychoanal. Study Child*, 42:3–10.

——— (1993). Playing: Technical implications. In *The Many Meanings of Play*, ed. A. J. Solnit, D. J. Cohen, & P. B. Neubauer. New Haven: Yale Univ. Press, pp. 44–53.

PELLER, L. (1954). Libidinal phases, ego development and play. *Psychoanal. Study Child*, 9:178–198.

RITVO, S. (1978). The psychoanalytic process. *Psychoanal. Study Child*, 33:295–305.

——— (1993). Play and illusion. In *The Many Meanings of Play*, ed. A. J. Solnit, D. J. Cohen, & P. B. Neubauer. New Haven: Yale Univ. Press, pp. 234–251.

SANDLER, J., KENNEDY, H., & TYSON, R. L. (1980). *The Technique of Child Psycho-analysis*. Cambridge, Mass.: Harvard Univ. Press.

SOLNIT, A. J. (1987). A psychoanalytic view of play. *Psychoanal. Study Child*, 42:205–219.

TYSON, P. & TYSON, R. L. (1990). *Psychoanalytic Theories of Development*. New Haven: Yale Univ. Press.

VYGOTSKY, L. S. (1978). *Mind in Society*. Cambridge, Mass.: Harvard Univ. Press.

WINNICOTT, D. W. (1971). *Playing and Reality*. New York: Tavistock Publications.

——— (1977). *The Piggle*. New York: Int. Univ. Press.

# PSYCHOANALYTIC THEORY

# Insights into the Struggle of Creativity

## A Rereading of Anna Freud's "Beating Fantasies and Daydreams"

### RACHEL B. BLASS, M.A.

*The wish to create, the dilemmas regarding the value, source, and owner-ship of one's potential and ideas, and the threats that these involve, are explored as they emerge in a dialogue between Anna Freud and her father, embedded in Anna Freud's first paper "Beating Fantasies and Daydreams" (1922). Insight into these aspects of the struggle of cre-ativity contributes to the understanding of their relationship to writing, masochism, sublimation, and other associated psychological processes. Through the analysis of the paper the identity of the patient described is revealed to be Anna Freud herself. This sheds light on her personal development and the way in which it influenced developments in psycho-analytic thinking.*

BEATING FANTASIES AND DAYDREAMS

IN 1922 ANNA FREUD PRESENTED A PAPER TO THE VIENNESE PSYCHO-analytic Society entitled "Schlagephantasie und Tagtraum" as a re-quirement for acceptance to the society. The first part of the paper describes the evolution of beating fantasies in a girl. Making their first appearance in early childhood as "father is beating a sibling," they are transformed to a fantasy, always unconscious, that "father is beating

Department of Psychology and Student Counseling Services, Hebrew University of Jerusalem and the Kfar Shaul Mental Hospital, Jerusalem.

I am very grateful to Dr. Rivka R. Eifermann who struggled with me through the original analyses of the texts, sharing many important insights.

me," and then back to a conscious version, "A boy is being beaten by a grownup" (A. Freud, 1922, p. 139).[1] This final version of the fantasy emerges in the girl some time prior to her entering school. She also describes the processes and reactions, emotional and physical, that accompany these fantasies. Anna Freud explains the motives for the formation of the fantasy as well as the diminishment in the frequency of its appearance when the girl is somewhere between 8 and 10 years old. Oedipal love, the various forms of gratification of those sexual feelings, their regression to the anal-sadistic phase, and their repression are at the foundation of these explanations.

The second part of Anna Freud's paper discusses the relationship between these beating fantasies and certain daydreams, the first appearance of which coincided with the diminishment of the beating fantasy. The girl at that time had begun to form elaborate daydreams and stories, which instead of beatings contained interactions (we are told) primarily of a pleasant kind. The content of the daydreams and stories—"nice stories" ("schöne Geschichten") as the girl referred to them—varies. Anna Freud highlights one set of these daydreams, in which the two main protagonists are a knight of the castle, and a youth who is his prisoner. These daydreams were triggered and influenced by a story in a boy's book which the girl had come across. What Anna Freud describes as characteristic of the various scenes of this set of daydreams is that the knight's specific threats of torture, which appear in each of the daydreams, are never carried out; the daydreamed stories always end on a reconciliatory note. Anna Freud explains these daydreams as attempts to deal with the unpleasant, painful, shameful aspects of beating fantasies. But they are also a transformation of infantile masochistic fantasies to a higher level; that is, the "nice stories" represent the sublimation of the beating fantasies.

The third part examines the processes involved in putting a daydream into writing. She describes a knight daydream written by the girl and offers explanations of why it was written down and why this allowed for the expression of certain contents that could not find their way into any of the unwritten daydreams. She ultimately explains this in terms of a shift in the girl's focus from an attempt autistically to satisfy her personal needs to an attempt socially to respond to the needs of her prospective readers in the hope of satisfying her ambitious tendencies. "The written story treats all parts of the content of the daydreams as equally objective material, the selection being guided solely by regard for their suitability for representation" (p. 157). With

1. I cite mainly from Anna Freud's English version of 1974.

the writing down of this daydream the knight daydreams no longer appeared.

Anna Freud's most explicit concern is with the second part of this paper. "It was the object of this paper to examine the nature of the relationship between beating fantasies and daydreams which coexisted side by side" (p. 153). Thus the section on the evolution of the beating fantasies is presented as a preface and background to the central second part. The final section, on writing, while clearly of great interest to Anna Freud, is not announced or led up to in the course of the paper, thus giving it the appearance of being of secondary importance.

In terms of Anna Freud's explicit statements, her understanding of beating fantasies is directly derived from that of her father as he conceptualized it in "A Child Is Being Beaten" (1919). When it comes to daydreams, her understanding is initially and most directly presented as an "illustration" of a remark of Freud's which addressed the relationship between beating fantasies and daydreams (p. 138). Later Anna Freud explicitly considers her work to be an *examination* of this remark, i.e., an examination with an overtly supportive intent: "I shall attempt to demonstrate the extent to which we are justified in regarding these daydreams" along the line that Freud set forth (p. 143). Finally, the source that Anna Freud makes note of in presenting her ideas on writing is "Bernfeld's observations (1924) of the creative attempts of adolescents" (p. 156). Freud is not cited in this regard.

In this paper I put forth the view that Anna Freud's acknowledgment of her father's works as foundations for her own, but omission of it when it comes to her final point, both reflect and conceal an important dialogue between daughter and father, for the most part an unconscious one. The dialogue is complex, involving the source of her ideas and her creativity, as well as the source of her analysis. The conflictual nature of these issues may be understood through a careful reading of Anna Freud's paper. This sheds light on Anna Freud's struggle with these conflicts, her theoretical formulations, and the psychological processes involved. While these issues are addressed in recent studies of Anna Freud (Dyer, 1983; Peters, 1985; Young-Bruehl, 1988), my analysis attempts to clarify these issues and certain misunderstandings regarding them, allowing for a better appreciation of their complexity and their influence on the evolution of psychoanalytic thinking.

## Anna Freud's Dialogue with Her Father

To appreciate the nature of the dialogue between Anna Freud and her father it is necessary first to take note of the discrepancies between the explicit statements regarding the foundations and sources and those foundations and sources that become apparent from a careful comparison of the writings of Anna and Sigmund Freud.

*Sigmund Freud's Views*

In "A Child Is Being Beaten" Freud (1919) posits that the first stage of the beating fantasy, "*My father is beating the child*" (p. 185), reflects the child's early sexual longing for the father. The father is beating another child, a sibling, thus "My father [does not love this child, he] loves only me" (p. 189). This fantasy undergoes repression. Two kinds of guilt feelings are responsible for the repression. One is over the developing genital love for the father, and the other is guilt over the expression of the sadistic tendencies. In the course of the repression there is a regression of the genital strivings to the anal-sadistic phase, the sadism is transformed into masochism, and the fantasy becomes unconscious. It is then that the second phase of the beating fantasy evolves, "My father is beating me." Here the beating constitutes a punishment for the forbidden genital strivings but also a regressive substitute for them. The longings for the father are now expressed in terms of anal-aggressive (that is, sadistic) wishes for beatings from the father. The sexually exciting wishes find an outlet in masturbatory acts. When punishment and sexual love are simultaneously gratified through the redirection of anal-sadistic wishes toward oneself, we have what Freud defines (in 1919) as "the essence of masochism" (p. 189). In the third phase of the beating fantasy—"Some child is being beaten by some grownup"—beating returns to consciousness but retains, as in the second phase, the "strong and unambiguous sexual excitement attached to it, and so provides a means for masturbatory satisfaction" (p. 186). This third phase allows for masochistic gratification while neutralizing the threat to oneself as the subject of the beating. This takes place through unconscious identification with the child who is being beaten, and subsequently enhances the repression of the wish to obtain sexual genital gratification by the father. While this and preceding fantasies are to be found in individuals who do not suffer from "manifest illness" (p. 179), Freud regards its presence to be reflective of certain complications. It evolves in "children in whom the sadistic component was able for constitutional reasons to develop prematurely and in isolation" (p. 189), and in girls it points to an active "masculinity complex" (p. 191).

*Anna Freud's Views*

Anna Freud does not present a theoretical statement on beating fantasies. Rather she describes the evolution of these fantasies in a specific girl. The framework she evokes to explain the evolution is that of Freud. In the course of her description certain differences between the girl's dynamic picture and that described by Freud become apparent. While such differences could be understood in terms of the variance often encountered between the individual and the typical case, here such a proposition does not apply. Examination of the idiosyncrasies of the girl's dynamic picture reveal differences in the theoretical framework implicitly underlying the dynamics. An ambivalent awareness of this may be seen in Anna Freud's own statements.

Anna Freud writes, "In the case of our daydreamer the sense of guilt that arose in the wake of her repressed strivings for her father was at first attached less to the content of the fantasy . . . than to the autoerotic gratification which regularly occurred at its termination. For a number of years, therefore, the little girl made ever-renewed but ever-failing attempts to . . . retain the fantasy as a source of pleasure and, at the same time, to give up the sexual gratification which could not be reconciled with the demands of her ego" (p. 140). Anna Freud describes how the girl's "invariably unsuccessful attempts to separate the beating fantasy from the autoerotic gratification" were behind the gradual diminishment in the frequency of the appearance of the fantasy, inasmuch as that kind of gratification evoked "violent self-reproaches, pangs of conscience, and temporary depressed moods" (p. 141f.). In contrast to the focus on guilt over the oedipal fantasy and related sadistic tendencies found in Sigmund Freud's work, Anna Freud's understanding of the girl's repressive forces centered on guilt over autoerotic gratification, i.e., masturbation. This difference is not one of degree or emphasis, because for Freud at that time guilt about masturbation could not constitute a repressive force. Acknowledging the existence of this kind of guilt, Freud (1919) asserts that only the masturbation of early childhood truly arouses guilt; later guilt over masturbation possibly arises through its association to the earlier period. But even the early guilt, Freud stresses, is "to be connected not with the act of masturbation but with the phantasy which, although unconscious, lies at its root—that is to say, with the Oedipus complex" (p. 195). For Anna Freud, in contrast, masturbation and oedipal fantasy are two partially independent factors. The girl described could tolerate the fantasy, even enjoy it at points, but could not bear some of the feelings that arose in reaction to seeking and finding masturbatory

pleasure. Thus the specifics of the case express a latent dispute between Freud and Anna Freud over a fundamental and theoretical
aspect of the beating fantasies—the nature of the guilt responsible for
their repression.

Another latent point of dispute was the degree to which the processes involved in the evolution of the beating fantasies may be considered to be constructive. Whereas Freud had pointed to complications that these processes reflect, Anna Freud speaks of the same
processes in positive terms. For example, the turn away from the incestuous love for the father through male identification, typical in the
course of the evolution of the beating fantasies, is clearly considered
by Freud to be problematic as it involves the girl's abandonment of
the feminine role. Anna Freud, in contrast, considers the abandonment of "the difference of the sexes" and the girl's representation of
herself "as a boy" to greatly facilitate the sublimation of sensual love
(p. 153).

There are also certain differences on the descriptive level. That is,
the way in which the beating fantasy is expressed in the case Anna
Freud describes is at variance with Freud's descriptions of its expression. At one point this variance is crucial. According to Anna Freud, an
integral part of the beating fantasy is always a fantasied misdeed; unknown or indefinite, this is the reason for which the castigation is
administered. Freud has no such concern with the misdeed. Although
the nature of the misdeed and its underlying meaning remain unknown and indefinite throughout Anna Freud's paper, both her concern with it and what may be deduced regarding its content are central
to the understanding of the processes involved.

DAYDREAMS

*Sigmund Freud's Views*

Freud (1919) makes brief reference to two of his four female patients
in which "an elaborate superstructure of day-dreams, which was of
great significance for the life of the person concerned, had grown up
over the masochistic beating-phantasy" (p. 190). It would appear that
these daydreams were beating fantasies in disguise. They centered on a
hero, always male, being beaten (and at times humiliated and punished) and the result of these daydreams was "satisfied excitation, even
though the masturbatory act was abstained from" (p. 190). Freud contends that the attainment of this kind of sexual gratification without

masturbation was indeed the function of the daydream, the reason for its formation.

*Anna Freud's Views*

Anna Freud both describes the girl's daydreams and reviews and studies them. There are discrepancies between the daydreams as they are presented and Anna Freud's reviews of them. This introduces some complexity into the explication of her views. It is clear, however, that in her most explicit statement regarding the nature of the day-dreams Anna Freud posits that what is uniquely characteristic of the daydreams in contrast to the beating fantasies "rests in their solution, which in the fantasy is brought about by beating, and in the daydream by forgiveness and reconciliation" (p. 149). Here she clearly diverges from Freud. Anna Freud also notes that the daydreams are charac-terized by mounting fear and tension. While she does not consider this characteristic to be unique, but rather an essential attribute of the beating fantasies as well, her actual descriptions of the beating fanta-sies lack this attribute.

In Anna Freud's descriptions of the girl's daydreams, that is, in the raw data of the daydreams themselves (pp. 146–148), it becomes ap-parent that the central experience of the daydream is not that of reconciliation so much as one of a special kind of tension that emerges from an interweaving of threats of punishment and of feelings of relief when those threats fail to be actualized. Furthermore, while the threats are not carried out, the tension itself appears to be tortuous at times. In addition, the hero is subject to a variety of "deprivations," which, while not listed among the knight's predetermined set of tortures, appear painful and are in fact so intended. Anna Freud considers such painful contents of the daydream to be only *attempts* of the beating theme to break through, maintaining that in the daydream the execu-tion of the beating scene is as a rule forbidden. Finally, while Anna Freud openly affirms that the daydreams, like the beating fantasies, describe interactions between "strong and weak persons," this dis-tinction holds only on a very superficial level, as hidden strengths and weaknesses covertly find expression. The youth emerges at points as a person of great fortitude, and the knight as one who cannot carry out his threats and who is readily swayed by the youth. These experi-ences and characteristics are not discussed in Sigmund Freud's re-marks on daydreams. On the one hand they contradict Freud's presen-tation of the essential nature of the daydream as disguised beating fantasy by an authoritative father figure, and on the other hand they contradict Anna Freud's presentation of it as almost devoid of beating per se.

In addition, Anna Freud's concern with a misdeed that takes place in the daydream (here, too, as in relation to the beating fantasy) constitutes an important digression from Freud.

As to the feelings and experiences of the daydreamer during and following the daydreaming process, Anna Freud emphasizes the absence of sexual gratification. "We have learned that the climax of the beating fantasy is inseparably associated with the urge to obtain sexual gratification and the subsequently appearing feelings of guilt. In contrast, the climax of the nice stories is free of both" (p. 152). What characterizes the daydream is that in the place of sexual gratification and guilt aroused by the beating fantasy, the daydream arouses in its creator "various tender and affectionate stirrings" (p. 153). While at times the daydream would eventuate in sexual gratification, this could come about only on those "rare occasions" (p. 151) when the beating fantasy infiltrated the daydream. For according to Anna Freud it was only the beating fantasy, not the daydream, that was responsible for the gratification. Here Sigmund Freud's view that the daydream typically results in "satisfied excitation" is overlooked or perhaps overturned. Anna Freud's position on the function of the daydream suggests the latter.

Regarding the function of the daydream, Anna Freud states, "While the beating fantasy thus represents a return of the repressed, the nice stories on the other hand represent its sublimation. In the beating fantasy the direct sexual drives are satisfied, whereas in the nice stories the aim-inhibited drives . . . find gratification. . . . The two fantasy products can now be compared . . . the function of the beating fantasy is the disguised representation of a never-changing sensual love situation. . . . The function of the nice stories, on the other hand, is the representation of the various tender and affectionate stirrings" (p. 152f.). Here it becomes apparent that the absence of sexual gratification following daydreams is an essential component of her view that daydreams reflect the operations of higher functions, such as sublimation, that are associated with more advanced developmental phases. Thus in putting aside the sexual gratification of daydreams, Anna Freud is *opposing* Freud's most central contention regarding the daydream. For him the daydream, *like* the beating fantasy, is aimed at sexual gratification and is also equally problematic in terms of the developmental process.

Anna Freud suggests that she knows that she is directly contradicting her father's views. She states that Freud's views on beating fantasies would "suggest" ("drängt" in the German, i.e., urge) that the daydream is "nothing but a return to an earlier phase. . . . But this assertion still lacks an important link" (p. 152). It is here that she advances her view on the daydream as an act of sublimation. The contradiction is sharper than she openly states at this point. It was not only that Freud's views on beating fantasies suggest or urge that the daydream does not reflect a progressive step. This was not merely an inference from Freud. He had very directly addressed the topic. Anna Freud herself noted this earlier in her paper. She apparently could note this so long as she maintained that her ideas were merely illustrative of those of Freud. When opposing or contradicting Freud, the fact that Freud had explicitly assumed a stance is blurred. Interestingly, the blurring of this point allows for revision of Freud's actual stance. Freud indeed did not consider the daydream a progressive move, but neither did he consider it a regressive one. In fact, he noted that in one of his cases the daydreams almost reached the status of a work of art. "Inferring" that Freud would view daydreams as regressive, Anna Freud offers a possible Freudian explanation of the loving scenes depicted in the daydreams. But Freud himself did not consider the daydreams to be necessarily of a loving kind. They were only beating fantasies in disguise. In presenting a *probable* Freudian explanation of the daydream rather than the explanation of the daydream that Freud *actually* presented, Anna Freud avoids the fact that Freud did not acknowledge that the daydream was loving (rather than chastising); not only did her explanation of the phenomenon of the daydream differ from that of her father, but her *experience* of the basic nature of the phenomenon differed as well. Further evidence that greater controversy with her father underlies Anna Freud's position on daydreams and the way in which they differ from beating fantasies may be seen from the fact that her claim that "an important link" was not taken into account is only a modified version of her original claim. In the original it is "the most important link" that is missed (p. 328).

Anna Freud's understanding of the daydream leaves several points unanswered. Her conclusion that the daydream constitutes an act of sublimation is based on the absence of sexual gratification and guilt. As a rule daydreams and fantasies affect the individual in similar ways. If the content of a daydream more directly represents a repressed wish than a fantasy does, the daydream should provide more gratification and elicit more guilt. If it does not, then sublimation must have occurred. But would it not be likely to assume that the absence of these experiences is tied to basic *differences* between daydreams and fantasies? That the fantasy, experienced as real in terms of the fantasizing child, has a greater potential to arouse such experiences? Further-more, if indeed the daydream is to be considered an act of sublimation, how is it that the daydreams came to dominate the daydreamer's fan-tasy life? The compulsive and pervasive quality of the daydreaming that she describes is not congruent with an explanation in terms of sublimation. Finally, if the daydream is to be considered an act of sublimation, why is a new form of solution—what Young-Bruehl (1988, p. 107) also refers to as a sublimation—sought through the writing down of one of the daydreams and why would such writing result in the disappearance of the daydream?

### THE WRITTEN STORY

Anna Freud does not cite her father in her discussion of the processes involved in writing down a daydream, referring instead to the work of S. Bernfeld (1924). Further exploration of the ideas Anna Freud puts forth on this matter raises questions as to what determined this choice of reference and the latent interchange with Freud that these ideas contain.

Anna Freud's remarks on the transformation of a daydream into a written story are brought in the context of an attempt to "follow the further development and fate of one of these continued daydreams" (p. 154), which is put into writing. She focuses on "two important dif-ferences between the daydream and the written story." The first is "the abandonment of the individual scenes" (p. 155). "In the daydream the friendship between the strong and the weak characters had to be estab-lished over and over again in every single scene . . . the interest, which in the daydream was concentrated on specific highpoints, is in the written version divided equally among all situations and protagonists" (p. 154). The second difference is that while in "the daydream each new addition or repetition of a separate scene afforded a new opportunity for pleasurable instinctual gratification . . . [in] the written story . . . the direct pleasure gain is abandoned. While the actual writing was done in a state of happy excitement, similar to the state of daydream-ing, the finished story itself does not elicit any such excitement. A reading of it does not lend itself to obtaining daydreamlike pleasures. In this respect it had no more effect on its author than the reading of any comparable story written by another person." Anna Freud then presents the girl's explanation for writing down the daydream—the writing was "a defense against excessive preoccupation with it." After writing it down, "The daydream of the knight was in fact finished, as far as she was concerned" (p. 154f.). The daydream came to "termination" (p. 138). Anna Freud points out that "this account of her motivation still leaves many things unexplained: the very situations that owing to their overvividness are supposed to have impelled her to write down the story are not included in it, whereas others that were not part of the daydream (e.g., the actual torturing) are dwelt on extensively. The same is true with regard to the protagonists: the written story omits several figures whose individual characterization was fully executed in the daydream and instead introduces entirely new ones, such as the prisoner's father" (p. 155f.). It is at this point that Anna Freud turns to Bernfeld's work on the creative attempts of adolescents. "He remarks that the motive of writing down daydreams is not to be found in the daydream itself, but is extrinsic to it . . . that such creative endeavors are prompted by certain ambitious tendencies originating in the ego; for example, the adolescent's wish to influence others by poetry, or to gain the respect and love of others by these means" (p. 156). Applying this theory to the girl's story of the knight, Anna Freud considers the development from daydream to written story to be motivated by social ambitions of the kind Bernfeld describes. The written story is a communication which allows "regard for the personal needs of the daydreamer . . . [to be] replaced by regard for the prospective reader. The pleasure derived directly from the content of the story can be dispensed with, because the process of writing by satisfying the ambitious strivings indirectly produces pleasure in the author" (p. 156). This explains the difference in the content of the written story and all of the other daydreams: "the written story (as the inclusion of the torture scene demonstrates) can discard the restrictions imposed on the daydream in which the realization of situations stemming from the beating fantasy had been proscribed. The written story treats all parts of the content of the daydream as equally objective material, the selection being guided solely by regard for their suitability for representation. For the better she succeeds in the presentation of her material, the greater will be the effect on others and therefore also her own indirect pleasure gain" (p. 156f.). Anna Freud concludes that in writing down the daydream autistic activity is transformed into social activity and "the road that leads from . . . fantasy life back to reality" is found.

The presentation of these views raises many questions. How is it that in the comparison of the written story and daydream, the daydream is presented as a source of "pleasurable instinctual gratification," while earlier it was contended that what distinguished the daydream from the beating fantasy was the absence of such gratification? In writing "personal needs . . . are replaced by regard for the prospective reader," but are the needs of the reader essentially different from those of the writer? How is it that the needs of the reader are determined primarily by "suitability for representation" and not, as for the writer, the possibility for gratification? Is it the move from autistic to social activity that constitutes the solution, and in what sense can this solution be considered to be a sublimation (Young-Bruehl, 1988, p. 107)? If so, what is its relationship to the sublimation that Anna Freud had shortly beforehand claimed to take place in the transition from beating fantasy to daydream? And why doesn't the report of the daydream, which we know took place in the analysis prior to its being put down in writing, constitute social activity? Finally, it remains unclear how a single act of writing could result in the cessation of a whole series of daydreams. It would in fact seem more likely that having found the transformation of a daydream to a written story an appropriate form of expression, the process would often be repeated. This would be the case if the solution is of a sublimatory kind.

The answers to these questions are to be found in the nature of the dialogue that Anna Freud was carrying on with her father through the presentation of these ideas. Before I turn to that dialogue, its context must be delimited. The exploration of Anna Freud's ideas on the written story points to a new context—Freud's 1908 paper "Creative Writers and Day-dreaming." Freud had originally delivered this paper as a lecture on December 6, 1907, when Anna Freud was 12 years old, and then the following year had it published in *Die Zeit*. In the light of her interest in the topic, it is likely that Anna Freud would have chosen to study this paper carefully. This is especially so since the kind of writing that Freud focuses on in this paper is that of stories of heroism, chivalry, and rivalries between characters that are sharply divided into good and bad. In fact, Anna Freud appears at times to have been almost citing from it. For instance, in speaking of the variability of the girl's daydreams, she notes how the "setting of the story readily changed with every change in the life of the daydreamer" (p. 142). This is to be compared with Freud's comment on the topic: "they fit themselves in to the subject's shifting impressions of life, change with every change in his situation" (1908, p. 147).

Freud does not directly address Anna Freud's question of why the writer writes. This question is indeed more directly studied in Bernfeld's work. But Freud addresses the question of the nature of the pleasure experienced in and through the written story. Freud's position markedly differs from that of Anna Freud. In his comparison of the daydream and written story Freud (1908, p. 153) asserts that if the daydreamer were to communicate his daydreams to us, "he could give us no pleasure by his disclosures. . . . [They would] repel us or at least leave us cold. But when a creative writer presents his plays to us or tells us what we are inclined to take to be his personal day-dreams, we experience a great pleasure. . . . We give the name of an *incentive bonus,* or a *fore-pleasure,* to a yield of pleasure such as this . . . all the aesthetic pleasure which a creative writer affords us has the character of a fore-pleasure of this kind, and our actual enjoyment of an imaginative work proceeds from a liberation of tension in our minds. It may even be that not a little of this effect is due to the writer's enabling us thenceforward to enjoy our own day-dreams without self-reproach or shame." According to Freud, it is not the communication that allows for the change in the basic nature of the daydream. Communicated daydreams often "leave us cold." Nor is it writing that makes the difference. Other forms of communication may be equally effective. Freud's distinction is between the daydream and the artistically presented daydream. The artistically presented daydream allows the reader the experience of the pleasures that are derived from his own fantasies. That is, the creative writer evokes in the reader the experience of the original pleasure of the daydream and its underlying fantasy and thus allows for "a liberation of tensions." While not denying the possibility that the writer may be motivated by social ambitions and that these may affect the nature of his writing, it is not the social ambition that transforms the daydream but rather the attempt to evoke fantasies and liberate tensions in a nonthreatening way. This concern with gratification—gratification of a sublimated kind but nevertheless gratification—is considerably toned down in Anna Freud's paper. Her focus on "suitability for representation" and "social ambitions" contains only traces of this concern. The artist's talent to use his daydreams in a way that evokes feelings and liberates tensions—the essence and secret of his creativity, according to Freud—is replaced by Anna Freud with an ability to treat "all parts . . . of the daydream as equally objective material" and to select appropriate material that will make "an impression on others" (p. 157).

It would appear that what determined Anna Freud's focus as well as her choice of Bernfeld's paper as her reference is her interest in the girl's *wish* to create, rather than her creativity. Anna Freud's overt and primary question is why the girl needed to write down this daydream, not how and why did she become an artist, a creative writer. A concern with creativity, however, does shine through. The creative attempts of Anna Freud's little girl afford her real pleasure as her social ambitions appear to be satisfied in reality, not only in fantasy. It is this that allows her to find her way along "the road that leads from her fantasy life back to reality" (p. 157). But Anna Freud does not directly discuss this creativity of the girl. Apparently she was unsure as to whether the girl was simply elaborate and monotonous in her daydreams and a wishful, ambitious, adolescent in writing them down, or whether in fact the daydreams were "artistic" (p. 143) and her writing a work of art. The failure to cite Freud may be understood as an expression of this uncertainty, perhaps ambivalence. If the girl's written story is not an instance of creative writing, Freud's paper on creative writers is not relevant. And yet in rendering that basic paper on creative writing and daydreams irrelevant, the novelty, innovativeness, and ultimately creativity of Anna Freud's own work on the topic are highlighted. I suggest an intimate tie between the concerns of the girl as presented by Anna Freud and those of Anna Freud herself.

## ANNA FREUD'S CONCERNS

### THE MANIFEST THEMES OF THE DIALOGUE

Through the presentation of the dialogue the manifest (albeit not directly stated) theoretical differences that become apparent may be summarized as follows: Freud contends that the child is conflicted over her oedipal desires. She seeks their materialization, their gratification, and yet knows that they are forbidden. The consequent guilt will normally lead to repression, but in certain pathological conditions this will not occur. This is the case when the child continues to seek gratification through beating fantasies. The male identification that evolves in the course of the fantasy is also considered problematic. Daydreaming based on the beating fantasy allows for gratification without masturbation, but the degree to which these daydreams are a developmental advance is not at all clear. While Anna Freud thought that Freud was speaking of a regression, in terms of ideation coming closer to the gratifying source, Freud's writings do not point in that direction. They do not clearly suggest either regression or progression. Freud notes that one of the daydreams *almost* reached the status of a work of art. Had it reached such a status, the daydream could have been considered a sublimation. For according to Freud, we may speak of sublimation when there is a channeling of the sexual impulses in such a way that an aim of higher value is attained. In this process not only the artist but also those who view the work of art are allowed gratification in a nonthreatening way.

In contrast, for Anna Freud, the crux of the conflict did not reside in the oedipal fantasy. What aroused guilt and required repression was the act of masturbation. Everything that contributed toward the curbing of that behavior, including the girl's identification with the male figure, was considered progressive. The daydreaming was considered to be progressive as well. The transformation of the directly sexual impulses toward the father to affectionate ties with him that occurred within the daydreaming reflected sublimation, regardless of the artistic quality of the daydream. In addressing artistic writing Anna Freud does not focus, as Freud does, on the transformation of libidinal gratification both in the writer and reader. Writing, according to Anna Freud, allows for the *substitution* of a concern with libidinal gratification for a concern with the gratification of certain ambitious strivings.

#### UNDERLYING CONCERNS

The manifest theoretical themes only barely scrape the depths of the dialogue between Anna Freud and her father. Through analytic attunement, that is, through free-floating attention to the details and discrepancies, the nature of the specific examples, the shifts that take place, the choice of words, the tone of the communication etc., the author's underlying concerns—wishes, conflicts, defenses—begin to surface. The study of Anna Freud's paper on beating fantasies is the analytic study of a text of Anna Freud's analytic studies of several texts—those of the girl's fantasies, her daydreams, and her written story. Thus two intertwined levels of analysis as well as the analysis of the relationship of the two is required. We may, for instance, wonder about the choice of examples presented both by the girl to the analyst and by Anna Freud to her audience and readers.

#### THE MISDEED

A central concern of Anna Freud's is with a *misdeed*. What is without explicit mention added to Freud's description of the beating fantasy is the imagined misdeed for which the beating is being administered. Furthermore, the girl not only fantasies an unspecified misdeed but also commits misdeeds. First, her masturbation is experienced as a forbidden act for which she subjects herself to punishment and which (contrary to Freud's position) initiates the repression and the consequent daydreaming. Second, the creation of the story of the knight originates in a misdeed. This point has not yet been elaborated.

In introducing the girl's knight daydreams Anna Freud expands on the moment of their first appearance. The girl takes a boy's book that does not belong to her and it then becomes the basis for the extensive series of knight daydreams. While Anna Freud does not specifically refer to the reading and use of the book as a misdeed, it becomes apparent that is how she experienced it. It is emphasized that the girl's reading of the book was "accidental" and that she then "returned the book to its owner [in German "rightful owner"] and did not see it again" (p. 144). We are also told that after several attempts to distinguish the girl's daydreams from what she read fail, such attempts were abandoned by the analyst; moreover, the source of the daydream "in any event has no practical significance" (p. 145). Then why does Anna Freud go to such lengths to describe the related events? One likely solution is that Anna Freud was uncomfortable about the girl's "taking possession" of the boy's story and its character and then spinning out a tale "just as if it had been her own spontaneous fantasy product" (p. 145). In the process of appropriation the original story is "cut up into separate pieces" and is "drained of . . . content" (p. 145). In the earlier translation what we are told is that the content of the boy's story "had been dismembered and devoured by her active imagination" (1923, p. 94). Thus it would seem that Anna Freud provides us with details of "no practical significance" precisely because the source of the daydreams was of considerable significance to her. She had to explain first that the book had little effect and that even if it did have a major effect, we wouldn't be able to determine it, and in any case such major effects are of no real importance. The significance of this misdeed of misappropriation as well as of the others becomes more apparent through the examination of the central theme of misdeed that emerges in the stories of the knights.

The theme of misdeed repeatedly crops up within the knight stories. While Anna Freud asserts that their nature was left "indefinite" (p. 149) it becomes apparent that there are three major forms of misdeed: (1) The youth does not betray his secrets; (2) he strays beyond the limits of his confines; and (3) after a series of vague misdeeds he finally transgresses "a specific prohibition" (p. 147). The most prominent of the misdeeds, however, relates to the withholding of his secrets—the reason for which the youth is taken captive in the first place. While he is punished for failing to reveal his secrets, their revelation would have been an offense of equal severity, this time directed not at the knight but rather at the father of the youth. (Significantly the written story, which also emerged from the knight series of daydreams, does not contain a misdeed, the story beginning "with the prisoner's torture" [p. 154]).

Two major points come across in the context of these misdeeds. First, the youth could have avoided punishment, but he opts not to (transgresses very specific prohibitions) or does not consider the possibility of avoiding them (does not think of telling the secrets he is withholding). Second, the youth is passive and weak, even in committing his misdeeds (he "*strays* beyond the limits of his confine" [p. 146; my ital.]), but in so doing he is strong (he displays great "fortitude") and he sets the knight into action (bringing upon himself the punishment). Here light is shed on the matter of weakness and strength and "the matter of a misdeed" (p. 149)—what Anna Freud considers to be two important analogies between the beating fantasy and nice stories. The youth is not, as Anna Freud explicitly defines him, merely weak and helplessly transgressing the rules of the all-powerful knight and hence faced with punishment by him. Rather the youth possesses power as well; and weakness and strength, and crime and valor, are not to be so neatly divided. The youth chooses passively to commit the misdeed and in so doing he is strong, he supports his family and gains the admiration of the knight. The issue of the intentionality and aim of the misdeed that emerged in Anna Freud's remarks on the girl's offense—her "accidental misappropriation" of a boy's book—seems to be further (unconsciously) explored in Anna Freud's remarks on the content of the daydreams she created.

Just as the misdeeds assigned to the youth provide a context for the study of the sense of misdeed experienced by the girl, so the misdeeds latently attributed to the girl provide a context for the analysis of Anna Freud's own sense of misdeed. Her interest in the girl's misdeeds is not expressed from a "neutral" or "objective" stance. Rather in presenting the misdeeds, she reveals a latent wish to protect and exonerate the girl. The girl may have masturbated, but Anna Freud hastens to inform us that she did all she could to master these tendencies. There is also a strong need to convince the reader that in her daydreams the girl indeed did sublimate her instinctual striving in relation to her father (counter to Freud's view of daydreaming) and that her daydreaming never affected her relationship to reality. It is emphasized that "the climax of the nice stories is free of both . . . the urge to obtain sexual gratification and the subsequently appearing feelings of guilt" (p. 152). We are also told that the girl's "fantasy life, in spite of its abundance, had never come into conflict with reality" (p. 138). However, from Anna Freud's own descriptions it is clear that she was in some sense aware that this was not the case. For example, in discussing the move to the written story, Anna Freud does acknowledge that "In the daydream each new addition or repetition of a separate scene afforded a new opportunity for pleasurable gratification" (p. 154). In addition, the girl affirms that it was the obstrusiveness of the daydreams that led her to write down one of them. While the girl's reality testing was not affected, she did, nevertheless, have to employ "a defense against excessive preoccupation" with her daydreams (p. 155). Anna Freud is thus identified with the concern with misdeeds that emerges in the various characters of whom she writes.

There is, however, another fundamental level on which Anna Freud's concern with her misdeeds emerges more directly. As we have seen, Anna Freud differs with Freud on the formulation of the dynamics underlying beating fantasies, daydreams. and creative writing as well as on the nature of the phenomena that these involve. In fact, at points the positions she assumes directly challenge those of her father. But these differences and challenges are not openly acknowledged. On the contrary, Anna Freud repeatedly affirms that her work is no more than an illustration of Freud's conjectures. Her descriptions are presented almost as if they were taken directly from the writings of Freud himself. There are points at which it seems as though Anna Freud is about to step outside the confines of her father's formulations, but then this step dissipates within the assertions of agreement.[2] It is thus necessary to examine the question of what prevented Anna Freud from owning up to the basic nature of her work in relation to that of Freud, what was unacceptable to Anna Freud in her differences and challenges, what did she feel was wrong in these, i.e., what was her misdeed?

But Anna Freud had difficulty owning up to one other crucial deed—the very act of presenting the paper. The original German version of the paper, the version read to the Vienna Society, contains a brief preface that was omitted in the translations. Its first paragraph reads as follows: "Gentlemen and Ladies! I have been taking advantage of your hospitality for a number of years, but until now without making myself noticeable by any active participation, though I know from a good source that the Society usually does not tolerate such onlooking among its guests. But I believe I would have persisted in my behavior if it were not for your strict rules that anyone who applies for membership must first present something to you. Thus my wish for acceptance by the Vienna Society is the motive and at the same time the excuse for my lecture today" (1922, p. 317). In abandoning her passive form of misbehavior, Anna Freud shifts to an active form. She now excuses herself for the lecture she is about to present, placing part of the responsibility for it on the Society and its demands. Here, in regard to Anna Freud's own writing, we may more directly discern underlying concerns encountered in the girl and her daydreams: concerns with activity concealed within apparent passivity (e.g., "taking advantage"

2. The running head of the first English version may be seen as an attempt to conceal all disagreements in a blanket statement of acceptance of authority. The heading, "Beating-phantasies in a Daydream," totally dismisses Anna Freud's major argument regarding the basic distinction between beating fantasies and daydreams—according to her "the most important link" overlooked by Freud.

by being "unnoticeable"), with the mixed nature of the misdeed (the presentation is a requirement that demands an excuse), and with the question of who is the powerful one (he who sets down the strict rules or he who disregards them for a number of years).

### THE UNDERLYING STRUGGLE OF CREATIVITY

The misdeeds of the girl, of the youth of her daydreams, and of Anna Freud who writes of them both, contain a common theme. They all involve a story that is to be told; the girl, her daydreams and her history of masturbatory practice; the youth, his secrets which he must not betray; and Anna Freud, her ideas and her lecture. Telling the story is as much a misdeed as failing to do so. Were the daydreams not created and communicated, the girl would retain her forbidden sexual practice of masturbation, but the creation and the communication of the day-dreams also involve a forbidden act—the appropriation of the boy's book; taking a story created by another and forcefully making it one's own. In the case of the youth, the choice is between telling and thus betraying, or refusing to tell and thus committing a severe offense in terms of the knight. Finally, for Anna Freud, telling is offensive; it involves unacceptable disagreement with the views of her father and requires excuse, but refusing to tell is equally offensive. Passive on-looking is also unacceptable; one must present. Also common to the misdeeds is the threatening or frightening step toward freedom and independence that they involve. The girl is in a constant struggle to achieve sublimation and control of the need for masturbatory gratifica-tion of her sexual fantasies in relation to her father; the youth is seek-ing a way to step beyond the confines of the knight's territory; and Anna Freud is seeking membership, full and equal status in the Vienna Society. For Anna Freud's search for membership involves not only joining forces with Freud—illustrating his works—but also taking the dangerous step of challenging them. Conflict and guilt in relation to the figure of the father are at the center of all three of these struggles toward freedom.

In these struggles to tell and to be free, it becomes apparent that the various characters are contending with their creativity and its inherent conflicts. Are the creations one's own or are they wrongly taken from another? Are the creations true acts of creativity or merely failed at-tempts at being creative, no more than direct expressions of prohibited drives? Can one's sexual wishes for the father ever truly be transformed into a creative communication? Finally, can one choose to reveal these and other inner stories or must one constantly remain within the confines determined by the father? Anna Freud, the girl and the youth, gradually comes in contact with the fact that to be creative is to step beyond these confines. To be creative is to believe that one possesses the creative powers of the father and to be able to withstand the guilt that this arouses. It is to be able to accept one's inner fantasies directed toward the father as a source of creative potential. Once again the guilt that this arouses must be worked through.

With both revelation and retinence, creativity and its absence, equally unacceptable action is difficult. The combination of wish and guilt can be paralyzing. Anna Freud's solution, like the solution of the girl and the youth, is found in a certain form of passivity and finally in overcoming that passivity. It is here that Anna Freud's ideas on masochism assume their personal significance.

### MASOCHISM AND THE MOVE FROM PASSIVITY TO CREATIVITY

The youth of the knight story was presented as passive and at the mercy of the powerful knight, but his passive behavior also was a source of strength. He opted for the possibility of punishment and withstood the threats. It gradually becomes apparent that in his passivity, the youth evokes punishment. He brings upon himself the torments of his captor and threats of possible torture. Not only is the girl who repeatedly creates these daydreams of torture expressing masochistic fantasies, but so is the hero of her story. Beating is sought through an activating kind of passivity.

While the context differs, a similar kind of passivity may be seen in Anna Freud herself. It is her passive onlooking, a passive behavior which in many ways was satisfactory to Anna Freud, that she feels to be unacceptable to the members of the Society and a source of their demand that she present her lecture.

Passivity brings about disapproval, but this disapproval is of an active kind. It involves possible penalties, but also is a source of demand. The youth in his passivity also rekindles an active demand that he tell. Awareness of these processes sheds light on the nature of the masochistic experience that Anna Freud is describing. Masochism may emerge in the wish for beating, and beating may reflect a latent wish to be loved. But this is not the entire story. Through the examination of the details of Anna Freud's presentation, additional motives become apparent; these in part explain the specific form that this wish for love assumes. These motives are paradoxically opposed. The fantasied or daydreamed punishment is experienced both as a fitting response to the prohibited creative strivings and a wished-for stimulus to creative expression. The creative strivings cannot be acknowledged and acted upon, but if it is the powerful father figure who demands self-expression, what choice is there but to consent. In this passive and inescapable form, the youth, the girl, and Anna Freud herself can allow themselves some degree of creative self-expression outside the confines of what is experienced as the father's limits. The masochistic fantasy here described is thus in part one of having one's inner creative experience (wish, fantasy, dream, story) beaten out. This point is highlighted as we see the struggle with the conflict over creativity attain some degree of resolution through communication.

### WRITING: A STEP TOWARD THE RESOLUTION OF THE CONFLICT OF CREATIVITY

According to Anna Freud, it was the writing of the daydream that led to its termination. The act of communication, the shift to ambitious strivings, and the consequent concerns with the needs of the prospective reader, rather than self-gratification of instinctual wishes, were seen to lie behind this. I suggest that the clue to how and why the writing down of the daydream coincided with the termination of the series is to be found in what is unique to the one daydream that the girl chose to write. Anna Freud recognizes certain unique attributes but considers these to be *a result* of the fact that the story was to be written and not *what determined* its choice as the story to be written. According to Anna Freud, the fact that the story was to be written allowed for a focus on material most "suitable . . . for representation" (p. 157), and therefore, for example, the torture scenes may be directly described in the written story. However, something of the essentialness of the attributes unique to the written story is lost in this explanation. For example, relying on "suitability for representation" and the consequent possibility of introducing entirely new characters in the written story blur the meaning that in the one knight story that the girl chooses to write down, it is specifically the father of the youth who appears as a protagonist for the very first time.

The written story "began with the prisoner's torture and ended with his refusal to escape. One suspects that his voluntary choice to remain at the castle is motivated by positive feelings for the knight. All events are depicted as having occurred in the past, the story being presented in the frame of a conversation between the knight and the prisoner's father" (p. 154). This story is markedly different from the other knight stories and allows for various readings of its underlying meanings. But what is blatant are the shifts from active to passive and vice versa. The youth now actively chooses to stay despite the torture, a process which up to this point was both passive and latent. The father is actively told, whereas beforehand the dialogue with the father was implied only. Gone, however, are the attempts to escape. Structurally, this story is characterized by the shift to an active acceptance of passivity, including the notification of the father of this shift. In terms of content, the different readings may come together in the idea that what is expressed is a story of rivalry and of love. The youth informs his father that he is joining forces with his rival. He has made an active choice and now opposes his father. At the same time what is occurring is an acknowledgment of love for the father whose figure throughout the knight daydreams has been represented by the knight. The active acknowledgment of the passive state of both love and rivalry is the key to understanding why the communication of *this* story became tied to the termination of the series of daydreams. The story reflects an acceptance of the conflict over creativity. It contains both the stepping beyond and the remaining within. It recognizes the opposing forces, and suggests an impossible solution—paradoxically, the only kind possible under the circumstances.

## OBSTACLES IN THE WAY OF CREATIVITY AND THE CONCEPT OF SUBLIMATION

Anna Freud's "Beating Fantasies and Daydreams" ends on a positive note: "By renouncing her private pleasure in favor of making an impression on others, the author has accomplished an important developmental step: the transformation of an autistic activity into a social activity. We could say: she has found the road that leads from her fantasy life back to reality" (p. 157). Young-Bruehl (1988), in her very thorough and comprehensive analysis of Anna Freud's development, considered the step the girl took in writing her story to parallel the one Anna Freud took in presenting her first paper—a sublimation. "Anna Freud's paper is both a study of sublimation and an act of sublimation" (Young-Bruehl, 1988, p. 107). Assertions of this kind are, however, based on the misconception that "the girl Anna Freud portrayed began to write short stories" (p. 106).[3] Anna Freud's girl put only a single story into writing. Her explicit aim in doing so was to bring her all too obtrusive preoccupation with the knight daydream to an end, and in this she succeeded. Writing did not become a new avenue of expression

---

3. Such assertions also require that the distinction between the *daydream* as sublimation and the *written story* as sublimation be overlooked.

but rather was a means to the damming up of another one—that of daydreaming. As such this does not appear to be a sublimation. Furthermore, the shift from autistic activity to social activity that is attributed to the girl does not in itself constitute sublimation. In fact, Anna Freud, who was well-familiar with the concept and applied it to the daydreams, does not use the term when speaking of the girl's written story. Clarifying the exact nature of Anna Freud's formulation of the developmental step allows for a better understanding of what was impeding the girl. We may also gain further insight into the barriers to creativity that Anna Freud was still struggling with and why they had to be concealed by the paper's happy ending.

Two factors characterize sublimation: (1) the channeling of instinctual drives from their original sexual aim, in contrast to the damming up of those drives that occurs in repression; and (2) the higher personal and cultural value of the formations that emerge through this channeling. On the basis of the latter we may distinguish between sublimations and compromise formations such as symptoms, which also emerge from a kind of diversion of the original sexual aim of repressed impulses (Loewald, 1988).

The shift from autistic activity to social activity points to the appearance of a higher cultural aim, but we must examine whether this is indeed the case and whether concomitant with this there is a channeling of originally sexual drives. On both counts it would appear that, in terms of Anna Freud's formulation of the shift to social activity, this is not the case. In her explanation of the girl's communication, the social motives underlying the move are "ambitious strivings," the wish to make an impression on others. These narcissistic aims are not indicative of development. Moreover, it is clear that the instinctual aim underlying the daydream about to be written is not modified or desexualized; it is simply renounced. Anna Freud considers the motive for the writing of the daydream to be "extrinsic to it." The sexual aims are "*replaced* by regard for the prospective reader" (p. 156,; my ital.) rather than intrinsically transformed. In "making an impression on others" the girl renounces "her private pleasure" (p. 157).

While this is clearly not sublimation, Anna Freud had a strong interest in demonstrating that progressive development was nevertheless taking place. This might be the case were the girl's story to emerge as a true work of art, but Anna Freud does not venture to make such an assertion. This is reflected in her choice of Bernfeld's paper on creative *attempts* of nonprofessionals as a reference rather than Freud's essay on those who have already distinguished themselves as creative writers. If the girl's development is not in the area of art, perhaps it is in the fact

that she ultimately made a return "from fantasy life back to reality."
This is indeed a development. Were the girl to remain within her
overwhelming world of fantasy to the neglect of reality, then indeed the
situation would be pathological and detrimental to her well-being. But
the need to renounce libidinal gratifications, shifting instead to a concern with narcissistic ones that are expressed in her social activity,
implies that in order to maintain an adaptive relationship to reality,
harsh defensive maneuvers were required. Contact with reality and
interpersonal relatedness came at the expense of the instincts. This is
why Anna Freud's explanation of the processes behind the girl's "development" does not point to a normative progressive step. It points
rather to the heart of the girl's obstacles in her struggle toward creativity as well as to Anna Freud's need to conceal these obstacles, emphasizing instead the advances that were taking place.

   The following course of events suggests itself: the girl had wanted to
do away with the instinctual nature of her wishes toward her father that
were finding expression in her beating fantasies. The masturbation
that accompanied these fantasies was totally unacceptable to her. The
girl, as well as Anna Freud even at the time of writing the paper,
wanted to believe that she had succeeded in doing away with the unacceptable wishes and practices; that she had succeeded in transforming
them into "various tender and affectionate stirrings" (p. 153). To the
dismay of (once again) the girl as well as Anna Freud herself, it turns
out that successful sublimation does not occur. The girl admits to the
infiltration of the beating fantasy, and to being dominated by the daydreams, and proceeds to seek an alternate means to deal with them—
writing. And Anna Freud, never directly acknowledging the failure
(although she takes note of the girl's statements and actions and latently questions the higher value of the daydreams), turns to the study
of this necessary alternative. In writing, there is no longer a hope of
transformation of the instincts. From the girl's point of view, all that is
sought at this point is some peace and quiet from the pressing daydreams. What is sought is another kind of gratification, that of ambitious strivings—a substitute for the wish for instinctual gratification. It
is her hope that in this way some kind of positive development may take
place even if the instincts are not to be sublimated. But the substitute
gratification is not ongoing. The girl puts the daydream into writing
and thereby "terminates" it along with its instinctual pressure. We are
not told of the beginning of a writing career but rather how the source
of the writing, the daydream, was eliminated. It is as if the girl could not
truly allow for gratification in the social context. She could not allow for
the instinctual wishes to be transformed, nor could she even allow for
the ongoing gratification of ambitious strivings within a relationship.

Perhaps as a self-inflicted punishment for failure of her earlier attempt at sublimation, perhaps as a wish, sublimation could be envisioned only in a more direct way, only in relation to her father, and there it failed.

This formulation of the course of events allows for an understanding of some of the more confusing aspects of Anna Freud's presentation; e.g., the daydreams were both sublimations and instinctually dominating the girl's fantasy world in a way that necessitated further measures. This formulation also sheds light on the issue of masturbation and why it was so disturbing to the girl and so central to Anna Freud's understanding of the processes she was undergoing. Both the girl and Anna Freud were concerned with the necessity of actually being in a relationship with an external other. To be in relationships only in one's daydreams is to be "autistic"—"social activity" is required. For the girl as well as for Anna Freud the masturbation reflected the actualization of the internal relationship. It is a statement that the other, the father or any substitute for him, is not needed. *The relationship can be fulfilled on one's own* (Blass, 1992, p. 180). The fulfillment of this wish, over and beyond the fulfillment of the oedipal fantasy, is forbidden in the eyes of the girl and Anna Freud. Here there is a parallel of utmost importance between central dimensions of both the conflict over masturbation and the conflict over creativity. At the heart of both is wish and fear of appropriating the father's (pro)creative powers. Recognition of this parallel allows for a further understanding of the fear. Not only does the father forbid such appropriation and threaten with punishment, but full appropriation holds an inherent threat—it is to remain alone, to remain "autistic." If the actual father or a substitute for him is not needed, if the father is experienced as actually within, then there is creativity but also stagnation. The reason to express one's creativity in reality is lost.

From the theoretical standpoint the writing could not have led to the termination of the daydream; rather, with the writing there came a working through of the conflict, a partial resolution which mitigated the need for having the creativity masochistically beaten out. But the full acceptance of the creativity, allowing for the expression of its essentially libidinal origin, remained one step ahead of the girl. This is a step that Anna Freud herself begins to take in the very act of presenting this case to the Vienna Society.

## FROM ANALYSIS TO SELF-ANALYSIS

The identity of the girl was never revealed. While it has been claimed, in part on the basis of Anna Freud's explicit declarations, that she was Anna Freud's first patient (Dyer, 1983, p. 42), or that she was a patient of some other analyst who then transferred the notes to Anna Freud (Peters, 1985, p. 49), these claims are dismissed by Young-Bruehl (1988), who argues that the girl was none other than Anna Freud herself: "The exact extent to which either Sigmund Freud or Anna Freud used Anna Freud's analysis in their essays is not, finally, determinable. But it is at least clear from her various correspondences that 'Beating Fantasies and Daydreams' was modeled—in general, if not in complete detail—on her own case" (p. 104). She is referring here to Anna Freud's analysis with her father, an analysis which began in 1918 and which lasted several years. Young-Bruehl brings additional historical data in support of her contention.

My analysis of "Beating Fantasies and Daydreams" conclusively establishes that indeed the girl Anna Freud was describing was Anna Freud herself. Recognizing this allows for the further elucidation of the developmental process that Anna Freud underwent and how this process influenced her and the way both she and her father theorized. In demonstrating the identity of the girl, I rely only on the text of Anna Freud's paper. I highlight three points from the abundance of available evidence.

1. Throughout the paper there are numerous parallels between the girl and Anna Freud that go beyond what could be considered similarities or identifications. These parallels are both in form and content, in thought and affect.

2. Careful reading of "Beating Fantasies and Daydreams" reveals that it is not written clearly from the perspective of the analyst. For example, there are points at which the analyst is described as knowing what was known only to the girl. A noted instance of this is Anna Freud's descriptions of the "detailed elaborations of [the girl's] fantasy" (p. 141) despite the fact that the girl's "reference to them during the analysis were quite scanty and vague" (p. 139). Stated more explicitly, "during the analysis the girl gave only the most cursory account of the beating fantasy" (p. 143). Another noted instance emerges in Anna Freud's remarks regarding the story from the boy's book which served as the frame for the knight daydream. Anna Freud goes to great lengths to convince the audience that the contents and source of the original story cannot be known, nor, more specifically, could these be known to the analyst in the course of the analysis (p. 145). But then one may wonder how Anna Freud could make such a certain assessment. Other instances of this kind may be seen in Anna Freud's very certain statements regarding how the girl would have responded if certain interpretations had been offered her; e.g., "The daydreamer herself was quite unaware of any connection between the nice stories and the

beating fantasy, and at that time would most certainly and without hesitation have denied it" (p. 143). Similar statements may be seen to emerge from the momentary adoption of the girl's denial; e.g., "certainly, there no longer was any autoerotic activity connected with [the daydream]" (p. 143).

Not only does Anna Freud sound like the girl, but the girl, at points, sounds like Anna Freud, providing explanations surprisingly reminiscent of those which Anna Freud later formulated; e.g., "She believed that she had turned to writing at a time when the daydream of the knight was especially obtrusive . . . as a defense against excessive preoccupation with it" (p. 155).

3. The fact that the analyst could not serve as an "other." To overcome the daydream, Anna Freud tells us, the girl needed to communicate it to others. But why then was the communication of the daydreams to the analyst, which was undoubtedly occurring in the course of the analysis, not a form of communication? Why did the analyst not serve as another one whom she could hope to impress? In other respects, such as moral conduct, the analyst was described as being perceived in part by the girl as an "other," a representative of society, one from whom one must, for example, conceal inappropriate sexual practices. I contend that the reason the analyst could not serve as another in terms of communication was because he was not only the girl's analyst but also her father. It may be seen that the girl's father is, according to Anna Freud's own formulations, the only one who could not serve as such another person in this context. To hope to impress the father would not be to replace regards for personal needs for those of the prospective reader. It would not be a renouncing of her private pleasure. Rather, the kind of directing of ambitious strivings toward the father that is described would be more immediately an expression of the beating fantasy and an attempt to gain the associated gratifications. While other analysts have treated their daughters, some close to the time of Anna Freud's analysis, if one takes all the evidence together, it does not seem likely that the identity of the father-daughter dyad described in "Beating Fantasies and Daydreams" is any other than that of Sigmund and Anna Freud.

The discovery of the identity of the girl allows us a view of the continuation of her developmental process and the theoretical implications of this. The presentation of "Beating Fantasies and Daydreams" as her candidacy paper and Anna Freud's opening of a dialogue with Freud therein may now also be seen as another step in the girl's development in her struggle with creativity. In the written story Anna Freud accepted the conflict over creativity and no longer needed her masochistic maneuvers, but she could not yet allow herself to be creative. The acceptance of the libidinal origin of the creativity that this requires is begun in Anna Freud's presentation. Through the presentation Anna Freud not only *tells* her father, but she also *becomes* her father. As she reappropriates her own analysis, she goes beyond the decisive step outside her father's confines that the girl took in writing her story. She goes on to enact her conflictual masturbatory wishes. While writing of autism as developmentally inferior, something to be overcome in favor of social intercourse, Anna Freud, in effect, transforms her analysis with her father into a self-analysis. Two become one. And yet at the same time this autistic transformation is not completely concealed. The masturbatory act and its libidinal origins are ambivalently revealed. Through this revelation, through the sharing of what cannot be shared, instead of stagnation there emerges a creative piece of psychoanalytic theorizing.

A fuller integration of the libidinal origins of creativity, of the sexual source of sublimation, was not at this point possible for Anna Freud. This is apparent from the nature of her explicit remarks and formulations in the paper she presented. With time, however, this further developmental step of integration did come about. This is reflected in Anna Freud's later theoretical conceptualizations.

### Theoretical Implications of the Dialogue over Creativity

In psychoanalysis theoretical developments emerge to a large extent from the study of subjectivity and inevitably our personal experience shapes the nature of our conceptualizations. Accordingly, Anna Freud's personal experiences of beating fantasies, daydreams, and their sublimation in creative activity, as well as her interactions with Freud regarding these, influenced the way she formulated these and related phenomena and processes. From the perspective of the entire corpus of her work several fundamental effects of these influences can be discerned. In the present context I will very briefly outline two.

1. Anna Freud changed her views of sublimation. In her writings there emerges a gradual integration of the instinctual drives in the creative act. The sexual origins of the sublimatory creative act are directly acknowledged, as is the pleasurable sexual gratification that may be attained through it. This development found form in the theoretical views she put forth in her paper "Sublimation as a Factor in Upbringing" (1947). Anna Freud's focus on the sublimation of anal-sadistic drives and sexual curiosity to the neglect of the genital strivings is noteworthy. In a later step, the genital strivings are directly acknowl-

edged. In her preface to Milner's *On Not Being Able to Paint* (1957) Anna Freud reveals not only her growing contact with the maternal influences on her creativity and her understanding of these (Young-Bruehl, 1988, p. 330), but also the influence of the genital wishes directed at the father. "Readers who have personal experience of any form of creative work . . . will acknowledge willingly, although shamefacedly, the truth of her [Milner's] brilliant explanation of the confusion in the creator's (especially the author's) mind between the orgiastic feelings during creation and the value of the created" (p. 489).

2. Anna Freud downplayed aggression relative to her focus on the libidinal forces and formulated the defensive solution of identification with the aggressor. These may be traced back to Anna Freud's early emphasis on the loving aspects of beating; difficulties in analyzing feelings of hate toward father and siblings when one's analyst is also one's father; feelings of anger and disappointment with her analysis and analyst which would inevitably arise and be especially difficult to work through and which were in part resolved through identification—as may be seen in the very act of her presenting herself as her analyst. Most telling in this regard is Anna Freud's letter to Lou-Andreas Salomé of May 14, 1924, in which she speaks of her daydream as having been "pulled apart, analyzed, published, and in everyway mishandled and mistreated" (in Young-Bruehl, 1988, p. 121).

Sigmund Freud was not oblivious to Anna Freud's personal and theoretical developments and the related dialogue with him. He seems at times, in effect, to have responded to her, becoming an active party to the dialogue. The influence on his theorizing are noted as well. The following (all subsequent to Anna Freud's presentation of her paper and the initiation of a second analysis with him) are some of the results of these influences. (1) Freud shifted from a focus on masochism in women to masochism in men. While in "A Child Is Being Beaten" Freud claimed to have insufficient material regarding this masochistic fantasy in men, in "The Economic Problem of Masochism" (1924) he restricts his discussion of the related kind of masochism to men "owing to the material at my command" (p. 161). (2) Freud later contends that underlying the fantasy "a child is being beaten" is a confession of masturbation. "The child which is being beaten (or caressed) may ultimately be nothing more nor less than the clitoris itself" (Freud, 1925, p. 254). (3) Freud becomes very doubtful as to the possibility of sublimation in women. While in "A Child Is Being Beaten" he maintains that sublimation is a common form of transformation of the beating fantasy later in life (p. 181f.), by 1925 he began to express doubts as to the capacity of women to sublimate. Later he explained this in terms of the fixity of their form of gratification. "I cannot help mentioning an impression that we are constantly receiving during analytic practice. . . . A women of [about 30] . . . often frightens us by her psychical rigidity and unchangeability. Her libido has taken up final positions and seems incapable of exchanging them for others" (1933, p. 134f.).

Taken together, it is as if Freud were responding to Anna Freud's ongoing dialogue with him with a statement of recognition that the underlying conflict was indeed over masturbation as well as a recognition of the fixity of the conflict—this, counter to Anna Freud's early assertions of progression and resolution. Alongside this statement, however, Freud also seems to be taking a step back, making room for his daughter's own personal and theoretical insights and innovations— the material he has collected regarding the masochistic beating fantasy in women is, alas, not really at his "command." And Freud concludes his theoretical remarks regarding the woman's limited capacity to sublimate with an admission of his own limited knowledge in this area; he suggests, "If you want to know more about femininity, *enquire from your own experiences*" (1933, p. 135, my ital.).

Anna Freud's person influenced and shaped her theories. Her theories and the person of Anna Freud that so clearly come alive in the transmission of her ideas influenced those who heard and read her, shaping their thoughts, their feelings, and ultimately shaping their theories. "Beating Fantasies and Daydreams" contains a dialogue with Freud that draws us in as well. If we carefully read this paper, we become immersed in the questions and conflicts underlying the powerful wish to create that Anna Freud herself was so profoundly struggling with. As one enters the dilemmas regarding the value, source, and ownership of one's potential and ideas, and as one experiences the threats that these involve, a personal understanding of the role of the father in the creative process is attained. There is also made possible a more personal understanding of Anna Freud, a woman whose creative contribution to psychoanalysis has made her one of its forefathers. This is what Anna Freud wished for and feared. This can now be heard in the following lines of a poem she had written in October 1918 at the onset of her analysis with her father (in Young-Bruehl, 1988, p. 82):

> I would like to play the harp myself,
> To try the power of my own verse,
> Snatch up my soul from its despair,
> Do what cannot be done by others' words,
> . . . In my own service, I would sing my soul—
> David would I be, and King Saul as well.

## BIBLIOGRAPHY

BERNFELD, S. (1924 [1918]). *Vom dichterischen Schaffen der Jugend.* Vienna: Int. Psychoanal. Verlag.

BLASS, R. B. (1992). Did Dora have an oedipus complex? *Psychoanal. Study Child,* 47:159–187.

DYER, R. (1983). *The Work of Anna Freud.* New York: Jason Aronson.

FREUD, A. (1922). Schlagephantasie und Tagtraum. *Imago,* 8:317–332. The relation of beating-phantasies to a day-dream. *Int. J. Psychoanal.,* 4:89–102, 1923. Beating fantasies and daydreams. *Writings,* 1:137–157, 1974.

——— (1947). Sublimation as a factor in upbringing. *Hlth Educ. J.,* 6:25–29.

——— (1957). Foreword to M. Milner, *On Not Being Able to Paint. Writings,* 5:488–492.

FREUD, S. (1908). Creative writers and day-dreaming. *S.E.,* 9:141–153.

——— (1919). 'A child is being beaten.' *S.E.,* 17:177–204.

——— (1924). The economic problem of masochism. *S.E.,* 19:157–170.

——— (1925). Some psychical consequences of the anatomical distinction between the sexes. *S.E.,* 19:243–263.

——— (1933). Femininity. *S.E.,* 22:112–135.

LOEWALD, H. W. (1988). *Sublimation.* New Haven: Yale Univ. Press.

PETERS, U. H. (1985). *Anna Freud.* London: Weidenfeld & Nicolson.

YOUNG-BRUEHL, E. (1988). *Anna Freud.* New York: Summit Books.

# The Theoretical Contributions of Hans W. Loewald

## RALPH KAYWIN, D.M.H.

*An integration and dialectical reading of Hans Loewald's developmental theory is offered, demonstrating his ability to bridge theoretical dualisms. He maintains yet revises Freud's structural model and dual instinct theory in a way which embraces developmental and relational perspectives.*

IT IS NO LONGER POSSIBLE TO SPEAK OF PSYCHOANALYSIS AS A UNIFIED theoretical orientation; it is more apt to speak of various psychoanalytic psychologies. The debates which have arisen as a result of this diversity potentiate creative dissention within the field. A dialectical approach to the current debates in psychoanalysis offers a conceptual tool by which one can attempt to resolve and evaluate the otherwise dualistic polemics in the field. As I am using it, a dialectical approach is one in which seemingly contradictory viewpoints are mutually defining and dependent upon each other for meaning. There are two models for a dialectical approach. Paradox, a contradiction which one tolerates and which cannot be resolved, is one model. Synthesis, in which a third, transcendent point of view emerges out of the contradiction, is another. In contrast to these dialectical approaches, a polemical approach is one in which there is presumed superiority of one viewpoint over others.

I will use these dialectical approaches in my evaluation of Loewald's

Advanced candidate in the Psychoanalytic Institute of Northern California and Adjunct Faculty at The Wright Institute, Berkeley, CA., and The California School of Professional Psychology, Alameda, CA.

A version of this paper was read at a scientific meeting of The Northern California Society for Psychoanalytic Psychology in February 1992, and will be presented at the 1993 Spring meeting of the Division of Psychoanalysis (39) of the American Psychological Association.

ideas as they offer resolutions of conflicting points of view. To anticipate my conclusions, I will argue that Loewald is unusually successful
because he, like his counterpart in England, Winnicott, is intuitively
steeped in a paradoxical rather than dualistic approach. Loewald's
work is thus more easily translated into a dialectical perspective than
other theories. Unlike Winnicott, however, whose work is explicitly
paradoxical and dialectical, Loewald's work is implicitly and at times
inconsistently so. A Hegelian (1807) approach is not to be found in any
obvious way in his work. Thus, a dialectical reading of Loewald is
presently offered.

## LOEWALD'S THEORIES

Loewald's work was clearly influenced by the developmental perspective of Mahler. His theory manifests striking parallels with the
work of M. Klein, Fairbairn, and Winnicott and aspects of the self-
psychological perspective of Kohut. However, Loewald never aban-
dons the drive-structural model of classical ego psychology, nor the
dual instinct theory, as these other theorists have. He is unique in
bridging this theoretical discontinuity within psychoanalysis. Loewald
finds a way of applying the structural model to the study of preoedipal
psychopathology and of integrating a relational psychological perspective within a drive model. By retaining a drive theory, Loewald preserves the psyche-soma dialectic. This gets lost in theories which deny
or minimize the somatic and sexual influences in mental life. Loewald
accomplishes this through his creative capacity to redefine classical
concepts in novel ways. The interesting result of such an integrative
approach is that Loewald can be and is claimed, as it were, by adherents
to many sides of the debates which exist in psychoanalysis. However,
this is ultimately a misuse of Loewald because to do so necessitates
robbing his thinking of its paradoxical nature to bolster one side of a
debate. In fact, Loewald is a master of avoiding such pitfalls and of
finding an approach which is a synthesis of the thesis-antithesis arguments.

Loewald's writings reflect the subtlety and complexity of the workings of the mind and the analytic process. He writes eloquently, densely,
often poetically, with a gift for bringing theory to life by the use of
metaphor and creative redefinition of known concepts, rather than
clinical material per se. This makes his writings a rich challenge for the
reader, as Loewald does not lay out in any comprehensive manner the
theoretical underpinnings and developmental sequences upon which
he bases his ideas. These are only to be discovered, as in an analytic

process, by examination and synthesis of the themes which are repeated in his writings, and via the unification of the developmental
sequences which are discussed only in pieces and in random order.[1]
What follows is an integration of Loewald's developmental psychology.
I will offer an assessment of Loewald's contribution in terms of the
degree to which he succeeds in offering a dialectical approach to the
central clinical concepts of unconscious motivation, the compulsion to
repeat, and transference.

In Loewald's (1951) conception of development, the early preoedipal period is the phase when psychic structures of id, ego, and reality
are beginning to develop out of an originally unified field of primary
narcissism where "mouth and breast are still one."[2] The novel implications of this position are not immediately obvious and I shall attempt to
clarify how this one statement is both a preservation and radical reformulation of drive theory and ego psychology. We are familiar with the
concept of ego development, although we will see how Loewald's ego
psychology is unique. To this he adds the perspective that id and reality
are not simply biological and sociocultural givens; rather, they are
psychological constructions which, along with the ego, develop over
time. (Any psychological construction which is the result of development is subject to the possibility of regression, a point to which I shall
return.)

Regarding the id as a psychological construction which develops,
Loewald (1978) says, "Understood as psychic phenomena or represen-
tatives, instincts come into being in the early organizing mother-infant
interactions. They form the most primitive level of human mentation
and motivation. In their totality, and as mental life progresses toward
more complex organization of different levels of mentation and inter-

---

1. While Loewald's seminal paper about psychoanalytic process (1960) has been widely
read and recently written about (Fogel, 1991; Cooper, 1991; Schafer, 1991; Friedman,
1991), Loewald's corpus and particularly his theoretical papers have not been as extensively considered. For an excellent exception, see Fogel (1989).

2. While Stern's (1985) recent developmental observations about the remarkably related quality of infants' early functioning call into question assertions such as a phase of
autism (Mahler et al., 1975), such observations do not, in my view, call into question
concepts such as primary narcissism or Winnicott's (1956) mother-infant dual unit. These
are relational concepts, but they posit a stage of psychological functioning which precedes self-object differentiation. Infants can, in theory, manifest great interest in and
relatedness to objects which are nonetheless not experienced as psychologically separate.
Such speculations about the subjective, affective experience of infants are theoretical
constructs which have been developed to explain certain clinical data. They must be
evaluated in terms of their theoretical usefulness, rather than needing to be confirmed
or disconfirmed by observation, which, it seems likely, they could never be.

play between them, instincts constitute the id as distinguishable from the ego or superego" (p. 208). What this means is twofold. (1) The instinctual drives themselves are not simply biological-constitutional givens; rather, they are forged in early interaction with the environment. Here we see the relational perspective informing, rather than replacing, the conceptualization of that most basic aspect of psychological functioning: the definition of the instinctual drives themselves. (2) While Freud defined instinctual drives as the mental representations of biological strivings, Loewald defines them as primitive mentation which must develop and become organized in some fashion before it is appropriate to refer to the presence of a psychological structure called the *id.* In both of these ways, Loewald has preserved a drive theory while he revises the model to infuse it with a relational and developmental perspective. He has taken the Freudian concept of drive and given it full psychological status: however linked to biology they indisputably are, instinctual drives are now to be understood as psychological constructions that develop over time in interaction with the environment. They are ways of generating and containing meaning and motivation.

Loewald (1951) says that "libidinal forces arise between mother and infant. As infant (mouth) and mother (breast) are not identical, or better, not one whole, any longer, a libidinal flow between infant and mother originates, *in an urge towards re-establishing the original unity*" (p. 6, my ital.). Here Loewald is hinting at the paradox which synthesizes a central dialectic: the very forces which attempt to reunify mother and infant are those which further separate them. Or, put another way, development toward separation-individuation is driven by the yearning toward reunion. There are two crucial points in this. (1) The personality has within it both progressive and regressive motivations. (2) Development occurs not as a triumph of the progressive over the regressive aspects of the personality; rather, development requires a synthesis of these seemingly conflicting aims.

This perspective is a revitalized dual instinct theory fully exploited for its dialectical potential. Loewald believes the dual instinct model to be a conceptual advance. He maintains that when Freud shifted to his dual instinct model, it was Eros, standing in contrast to Thanatos, which represented the theoretical departure. The concept that there exists a drive for stimulation and greater degrees of complexity in intrapsychic functioning and structure building becomes central to Loewald's ideas about psychic structuralization.[3]

---

3. In his 1920 essay, Freud introduced the concept of the death instinct which opposes Eros. This dual instinct model proved controversial. This revision seemed confusing

However, Loewald (1973a) not only preserves, he advances the concept of the death instinct by equating the wish for tension reduction, which ultimately leads to a wish for psychic death, to the yearning for a return to primary narcissism. Thus, it could be said that the death instinct is not, as M. Klein (1946) saw it, the source of aggression; the death instinct is the source of regression.

It is important to sort out the various levels of abstraction which are all too often confused and mixed together in psychoanalytic theory. One level of abstraction is the clinical theory, in which it is appropriate to speak of a self contending with sexual and aggressive wishes. A second level of abstraction is the metapsychology, in which it is appropriate to speak of an ego organizing mental functioning in response to Eros and Thanatos. The life and death instincts, then, are best understood as meta-instinctual principals by which both sexual and aggressive wishes operate. From this perspective, sexual and aggressive wishes are the currency of the mind, while the life and death meta-instincts are the economic principles of the mind which determine how, why, and to what end the currency is deployed. It is in this light that Freud's last dual instinct model is a conceptual advance, in that it represents the culmination of a metatheory, as opposed to a clinical theory. Strachey's translation of "das Ich" into "the ego" rather than "the I" has been problematic for the clinical theory, but is quite appropriate for the metatheoretical level of abstraction.

Loewald characterizes the earliest phase of development as one in which the infant is immersed in a stage of primary narcissism and in which self and object are fused. The differentiated psychic structure of id, ego, and reality must subsequently develop out of this undifferentiated state. We have seen how Loewald redefines yet preserves a drive theory. What does he mean by including reality as one of the ingredients in this originally undifferentiated psychic soup? Loewald (1951) suggests that the infant's first reality is the first object, the breast. And since the breast-as-first-object exists initially in fusion with the ego, he calls this a primary reality, which is initially experienced as internal and must subsequently achieve externality. This again is a deceptively simple yet significant reformulation of Freud.

-------

since Freud's assertion that there is a second governing principle, the Death Instinct, which is beyond the libidinal pleasure principle, is in fact a restatement of the pleasure principle itself, as it was originally formulated to be a constancy principle of stimulus reduction. However, this confusion can be clarified if one views it as Freud's attempt to separate two instinctual trends, both of which had become associated with the id and the pleasure principle: seeking relaxation and seeking psychosexual stimulation. This dual instinct model also opens up dialectical potential within the conceptualization of the id itself.

For Freud, reality stands in opposition to the instinctual drives; reality frustrates immediate and total gratification. When Freud uses the term *reality,* he does not refer to a psychological construction; he refers to those forces beyond the infant's control which limit and frustrate gratification. In his view, a resolution of the inherent opposition of reality to the instinctual drives is necessary. The infant must attempt to shift from being governed by the pleasure principle to the reality principle.

In contrast to Freud's views of reality, Loewald gives full psychological status to reality. He understands reality to be a psychological construction that develops over time from early subjective forms to later more objective forms. What is the need for and significance of such a reformulation? Part of the answer to this question was hinted at earlier when I noted that any aspect of psychological functioning that develops can also regress. Loewald's reformulation is an attempt to account for certain clinical phenomena from a new perspective. The classical ego-psychological perspective would take the view that what we see in psychopathology are varying sorts and degrees of distortions in reality testing which result from the inherent opposition of reality and the drives. Patients therefore turn away from reality to fantasy wish fulfillments when reality frustrates. Loewald suggests an alternate perspective: in psychopathology reality is not turned away from; rather, reality regresses from more mature forms in which the object is experienced as external and separate from the subject, to less mature, more subjective forms where the object is experienced as internal, and therefore within the omnipotent control of the subject.

One might well wonder whether this is merely an issue of semantics were there no other ramifications of or reasons for this reformulation. However, Loewald posits this reformulation as a critique of Freud's view of the inherent opposition of reality and the drives, a view which is tied to Freud's concept of the oedipus complex. For Freud, the castration threat by the father prohibiting the incestuous wishes toward the mother is the prototype for reality. By integrating a perspective arising from clinical work with more disturbed patients, Loewald suggests that Freud's oedipal and paternal version of the psychological meaning and development of reality is not the initial version of reality. In fact, he says that such a version of the inherent antipathy of reality and the ego is emblematic not of normal development, but of obsessional neurotics' relation to reality, of which, he notes, Freud was one. What Loewald asserts is missing in Freud's obsessional neurotic view of reality, but is in evidence in more severe psychopathology, is an appreciation of the earlier, preoedipal relation to reality which has to do with separation and merger with the preoedipal mother, rather than the castration threat of the father.

The developmental yearning for a return to primary narcissism is characterized by wishes for fusion with the mother, along with the accompanying anxieties which Loewald characterizes not as castration anxiety but as dread of the womb. This early dread refers to the fear of loss of the emerging psychic structuralization in the face of wishes for a reunion with the mother. The child therefore forms an early preoedipal identification with the father, which serves to protect him or her from this anxiety. Thus, Loewald (1951) states, "The early positive identification with the father as well as the early dread of the engulfing mother, both enter into the Oedipus complex, form components of it, as much as the positive libidinal relation to the mother and the castration fear of the father" (p. 15). In this formulation, Loewald breaks down the oedipal versus preoedipal dualism. Loewald calls the preoedipal phase a transindividual phase of development, both because the preoedipal child is not yet fully psychologically separate from objects and reality, and because the child leans heavily upon the use of objects which are not fully psychologically separate in order to create psychic structure. Again, he has a relational viewpoint.

Having addressed Loewald's views on the development of id and reality, I now turn to Loewald's perspective on ego development. Here we see an example of Loewald not so much reformulating Freud as he is selecting and developing a particular threat which Freud initiated in his books *Totem and Taboo* (1913) and *Civilization and Its Discontents* (1930), and in his essay "On Narcissism" (1914), but which Freud did not fully integrate into his developmental and clinical theory. It is also Loewald's synthetic and dialectical response to the thesis-antithesis dualism between Freud's assertion as to the relative primacy of the pleasure principle, that is, the relative dependence of the ego vis-à-vis the id, to Hartmann's (1939) counterassertion of the adaptive point of view. As a jumping off point to develop this central concept which relates ego development and psychic structuralization to primary narcissism, I quote from Loewald's 1951 paper:

> The neonate does not as yet distinguish an ego from an outer world. Some sources of stimulation, in which later on he will recognize his body organs, can send him sensations at any time, while others do so at times and at other times are not available. The most important of these latter sources of stimulation is the mother's breast. It is not always available. In this way for the first time something like an "object" becomes constituted, an outside against an inside, and therewith a border between the two. . . . This state of affairs can be expressed . . . more correctly: the

ego detaches from itself an outer world. Originally the ego contains everything. Our adult ego feeling, Freud says, is only a shrunken vestige of an all-embracing feeling of intimate connection, or, we might say, unity with the environment.

In other words, the psychological constitution of ego and outer world go hand in hand. Nothing can be an object, something that stands against something else, as long as everything is contained in the unitary feeling of primary, unlimited narcissism. . . . [This repeated experience] of separateness leads to the development of an ego which has to organize, mediate, *unify*. Freud in his essay on narcissism already expresses this clearly, saying, "The development of the ego consists in a departure from primary narcissism and gives rise to a *vigorous attempt to recover that state*" [p. 5].

This position is what one could call the "big bang" theory of early development, which transcends the Freud versus Fairbairn (1941) dualism of whether drives are primary and objects secondary, or vice versa. For Loewald, ego, object, and drive—each of which are psychic structures—all emerge in one and the same developmental moment. It is not possible to say which came first or which "caused" which. Questions of linear causality are not dialectical. Each psychic structure has meaning only in light of the others: each defines, preserves, and negates the other.

Loewald's ego psychology also has untapped dialectical potential in that he implies, yet never fully asserts, that the ego has the capacity actually to achieve synthesis with respect to the basic dialectical struggle between developmental strivings for separation and individuation on the one hand, and the wish to deindividuate and return to the state of primary narcissism via a fantasy of reunion or merger with the mother on the other hand. When this synthesis is achieved, either existing psychic structure is strengthened or new psychic structure evolves.

According to Loewald (1952), the development of psychic structure takes place within a channeled environment, via psychic processes such as introjection and projection, which are utilized by the infant to create the initial boundaries between inside and outside,[4] self and object, and id, ego, and reality. He asserts that until such structural differentiations have occurred, it is not correct to conceptualize introjection and

4. The sorting out of inside from outside goes well beyond a cognitive task; it is a complex affective task which is based upon the organization of early, infantile somatic and sexual experiences and fantasies. It is essential to remember this when evaluating theoretical orientations which discount or deemphasize the roles of sexuality and the body in their developmental theories.

projection as defenses. Rather, Loewald (1951) refers to these as fantasies which are integrative processes in that they facilitate the eventual integration and differentiation of psychic structure (pp. 18, 24).

It is here that Loewald's work expands into the areas of internalization and sublimation, psychological processes which preoccupy much of his later writings. It becomes both clinically and theoretically necessary to distinguish between integrative processes which facilitate development and defensive ones which interfere. While these distinctions are essential, this is an area in which Loewald would benefit from a dialectical approach. Categorical thinking about such complex psychological processes is improved by viewing them as poles of a dialectic. For instance, in his 1973 paper "On Internalization," Loewald distinguishes repression, which he views as a defense, from internalization, which he views as a developmental process. According to this, repression does not lead to psychic structure building, but rather defends the ego's homeostasis by evacuating yet preserving conflicts in the id. By contrast, the process of internalization results in an alteration of the ego at a higher level of complexity via the destruction and reorganization of conflict. However, it is well known that repression can serve defensive or developmental processes, and one could argue the same for internalization.

Loewald's ideas on the repetition compulsion will serve to exemplify his distinction between defensive and developmental processes. Loewald (1971a) differentiates between what he calls passive repetitions, which represent psychopathology defined as developmental stasis, and active repetitions, which facilitate development. It is correct, but not sufficient, to say that Loewald is asserting that there are both nonadaptive and adaptive repetitions. Rather, the reason Loewald selected the terms active and passive has to do with the differing way the ego is operating in each case. This is where Loewald's ego psychology parts from Brenner's, who takes the position that all repetitions are forged by the ego via the identical processes of compromise formation. For Brenner (1982), the distinction is an economic one between what he calls normal and pathological compromise formations.

Drawing upon Loewald's meta-instinctual view, one could say that the ego is passive when it resolves the dual instinct conflict between the wish to dedifferentiate and the wish to differentiate, via a compromise formation. In a compromise formation the ego attempts to satisfy these conflicting unconscious motives simultaneously as they assert their aims in parallel. In contrast, the ego is active when it is able actually to synthesize the opposing aims of the dual instinct conflict

toward a third goal of a higher order rather than both aims simultaneously. That third goal is a sublimation which results in psychic structure
building. This process is not a compromise formation; it transcends
such compromises. In it the dual instincts become the catabolic and
anabolic processes which are necessary to effect structural change.

While Loewald's distinctions between such developmental and defensive processes are necessary, an approach which would orient these
distinctions in relative and dialectical relation to one another is, in my
view, more satisfactory. Loewald (1971a) is clearly striving for this approach when he says that repetition occurs "throughout life, in varying
mixtures and combinations of more or less passive reproductions
('neurotic' repetitions) and of active re-creations" (p. 90).

This approach becomes crucial in resolving the dualism about repetitions where it arises in the clinical situation, that is, in the transference. According to Freud (1916–17), transference is a repetition
which is a resistance because it is an attempt to gratify infantile, primarily sexual wishes. Similarly, according to Brenner (1982), it is a pathological compromise formation. According to M. Klein (1946), the
transference is a projection of pathological, primarily aggressive internal object relations. Alternatively, according to Weiss and Sampson
(1986), transference is not a resistance, it is an attempt to assess the
safety of the therapy situation in order to master trauma and guilt.
Similarly, according to Kohut (1971), it is an attempt to resume blocked
development. However, each of these positions is an a priori assumption about transference which derives from a theoretical orientation,
rather than arising from a clinical assessment of the quality of a specific
transference or phase of the transference. Loewald gives us a theoretical means of differentiating between those active transference repetitions which are developmental processes, no matter how much regression or aggression they entail, and passive transference repetitions
which are defensive attempts to bypass the challenges of psychic
growth. This approach does not make assumptions about the transference based upon a theoretical bias; it requires one to turn to the
analytic situation to make admittedly difficult, but necessary, clinical
distinctions. Such clinical distinctions are aided by a dialectical approach in which the assessment is never either-or. The transference is
inevitably a dialectic of developmental and defensive processes which,
on balance and at specific moments, can be said to be more or less
synthetic with respect to progressive and regressive aims.

What makes Loewald unique, then, is not just that he is an ego
psychologist who emphasizes the infant's object relatedness, attachment, and ego striving for development; it is that he understands these

ego functions to be the result of a synthesis of a complex dialectical set of developmental aims: those which strive for separation and those which strive for merger; those which strive for stimulation and those which strive for the reduction of stimulation. This is a much more sophisticated vision of unconscious motivation and development than an ego psychology which singularly asserts mastery or individuation per se to be *the* overarching unconscious motivation. It is a more sophisticated view of unconscious motivation than that which Freud ultimately offered when he "took sides" in his structural model by asserting that the gratification of instinctual wishes overrides other unconscious motivations. It is a more sophisticated, dialectical notion of the unconscious motivation than object relations theories which assert that attachment to objects is the overarching unconscious motive. Loewald synthesizes all of these motives.

Loewald (1971a) may speak about ego mastery, but he does so in an unusual way: "mastery does not mean elimination of [earlier experiences] but dissolution, and reconstruction out of the elements of destruction" (p. 90). For Loewald, developmental progress involves, along with the more familiar concepts of mastery and synthesis, regression, repetition and destruction, words not usually used by ego or developmental psychologists in the context of emotional growth. This is a theme which manifests itself not only on the theoretical level, but on the existential one in his ideas as to how superego formation results from the working through of the oedipus complex.

Integrating the clinical and metapsychological levels I have been discussing, Loewald says that the defensive process of repression would be viewed as driven primarily by the constancy principle known as the death instinct, while internalization would be viewed as driven primarily by the life instinct. This is where it seems to me that Loewald misses the dialectical implications of his own ideas. I would argue that internalization is best understood to be the result of a synthesis of the basic dialectic between life and death instincts, involving both destroying and rebuilding psychic structure.

The example par excellence of such a process of structuralization, resulting from the ego's synthesis of Eros and Thanatos, is the one which results in what Loewald calls the differentiating grade in the ego known as the superego. This then becomes a useful segue into Loewald's views of the oedipal phase of development.

Loewald (1971a) views oedipal development as "a repetition of preoedipal experiences on a new organizational level" (p. 90). It is the next phase in the process of individuation. Here again, we see that Loewald breaks down the dualism between the preoedipal and oedipal phases of development. In fact, he (1979) says, "increased understanding of pre-oedipal issues, far from devaluating oedipal ones, may in the end help to gain a deeper insight into them" (p. 386f.). According to Loewald (1985), the oedipal phase "signals the ending of transindividual psychology and the beginning of the psychology of the individual" (p. 442). He refers to individuation not only in terms of self-object differentiation, but also in terms of the altered qualities of mentation and object relatedness which derive from more differentiated psychic development.

In terms of object relatedness, Loewald (1985) views the libidinal and aggressive object cathexes of the oedipal phase, because they are incestuous, as transitional, standing midway between preoedipal self-object identifications which are narcissistic, and postoedipal true object love with objects which have achieved more complete externality. Therefore, Loewald stresses two points. (1) He emphasizes the need to make the transition out of preoedipal narcissism by entrance into the oedipal phase because "unless the oedipal level of his psychic life is available to the patient and he comes to understand it as a genuine step in his human development and not as a tragic decline from a state of grace, he remains a victim of the self-object stage and its narcissism" (1985, p. 443). (2) He emphasizes the need to achieve postoedipal object relatedness through the destruction of incestuous oedipal ties.

Perhaps Loewald's singular contribution is his 1979 paper "The Waning of the Oedipus Complex." In it, he is able to synthesize all his abstract theory into a deeply moving account of the existential aspects of working through the oedipal drama. I say working through for two reasons: (1) This is not a paper about the oedipus complex itself; it is a paper which conceptualizes the psychological work which is necessary to emerge out of oedipal level functioning into true maturity. (2) I refer to working through because the process of emerging out of the transitional phase of oedipal libidinal objects and into the capacity for whole object relating is, according to Loewald, a life task which is never completed, but is always being worked through.

Drawing upon Loewald's view, one could say that there are two ways to exit the oedipal drama: one is topographic, one structural. The topographic exit is via repression. With repression, nothing changes except the location, as it were, from conscious to unconscious. It is a homeostatic solution which maintains all the libidinal and aggressive incestuous object ties intact, only now they are unconscious and become the wellspring for continued passive repetitions which the ego deals with by forging symptoms that are compromise formations. One could say on a metatheoretical level that a compromise has been achieved by the ego vis-à-vis the dual instincts. The conflicting motives of stimulus reduction and stimulus seeking have each been gratified in parallel. The conflict tension arising from the oedipal drama has been immediately reduced through repression, yet the libidinal gratifications are maintained by being preserved in unconscious fantasy. For this reason, repression results in a pseudoexit from the oedipus complex.

The second way to exit the oedipal drama is much more complex and is best described as psychic structure formation, not compromise formation. It results from internalization, as opposed to repression. Internalization involves tolerating the conflict tensions of the oedipus complex so that the entire drama can be deconstructed and reconstructed on a higher level. This involves a shift from the patricidal and matricidal aspects of the oedipus complex, which are object-related aggressive impulses arising from incestuous ties to the parents, to the higher order, existential preoccupation of parricide. In parricide, it is the oedipal tie to the parents itself which is being killed off. Cathecting nonincestuous objects represents breaking the incestuous tie to the parents. Thus this is one aspect of parricide: the killing of the libidinal and aggressive oedipal tie to the parents by making novel forms of object choice. Parricide is also about the taking upon oneself, actually within oneself, the authority once held by the parents. One becomes one's own authority by killing off the tie to one's parents. Both of these aspects of parricide are simultaneously accomplished by, and result in, superego development.

What is internalized into the part of the ego which becomes the superego is not the parent-as-object, but is parental authority which has been taken away from the parents. This is essential to grasp, for this is where Loewald departs from those theorists who speak about the superego as an internal object. According to Loewald's ideas, an internal object or a parental introject, is not the same as the superego. Loewald is describing a process in the latest stage of individuation which is parallel to Winnicott's notion of the earliest phases of separation from the mother. For Winnicott (1958), what must be internalized by the infant is not the mother-as-object but maternal functions. In what Winnicott and Loewald are describing, if the object is introjected rather than the functions of the object internalized, it is a defensive, not a developmental process. Loewald is describing a process which is sublimatory, depersonified, deobjectified. It is a process of metamorphosis which transmutes the object cathexis of parent-child relations into internal, intrapsychic, structural relations. In this way, it involves a narcissistic regression, in that it is a movement away from the interpersonal world and into the intrapsychic world, but one which results in psychic structure building and one which paradoxically frees the individual up to have novel, nonincestuous object ties in the interpersonal world.

Loewald writes poignantly about parricide as an existential drama. In order for a person to complete the process of individuation by not only entering but exiting the oedipal phase, he or she must bear the pain and guilt of parricide. One solution is to avoid this pain, to repress and thereby to maintain the oedipal ties to one's parents in the timelessness of the unconscious. The other possibility, which is never achieved permanently but is continually worked through, is to bear the pain of parricide via the atonement reflected in superego development. By taking upon oneself the parental authority, one has internalized not just any values, but their values. Being one's own authority is both a destruction of, and a memorial to, one's parents.

## CONCLUSION

Loewald (1951) states, "The ego mediates, unifies, integrates because it is of its essence to maintain, on more and more complex levels of differentiation and objectivation of reality, the original unity" (p. 11). In saying this, he condenses many of the ideas I have been discussing: ego and reality as originally a unity (unity being primary narcissism); the synthetic functioning of the ego as heir to the wish to maintain the original unity; defensive attempts to maintain the ego's homeostasis driven by the death instinct which depletes the ego (i.e., repression), as well as structuralizing responses to conflict synthesized by the ego from the dialectic of life and death instincts, which enrich the ego (i.e., internalizations).

Loewald's developmental perspective is dialectical in that it is both synchronic and diachronic. He sees development proceeding in unfolding stages in which each subsequent stage is constructed out of the previous stage and yet can also be deconstructed and reconstructed in novel ways, depending upon whether a defensive or developmental solution has been implemented by the ego. Loewald (1951) does not view more objective ego-reality organizational levels as replacing earlier stages. They are, rather, complimentary aspects of experience: "In fact, it would seem that the more people are alive (though not necessarily more stable), the broader their range of ego-reality levels is. Perhaps the so-called fully developed mature ego is not the one that has become fixated at the presumably highest or latest stage of development, having left the others behind it, but is an ego that integrates its reality in such a way that the earlier and deeper levels of ego-reality integration remain alive as dynamic sources of higher organization" (p. 20).

For Loewald, maturity, like creativity, requires access to primitivity, not the suppression of it. Similarly, the analytic process requires regression within the transference in order for progression to occur, particularly but not exclusively with more disturbed patients. Here we have the developmental paradox: regression is necessary for progression to occur or, stated otherwise, the regressive aspects of the personality (governed by the death instinct) must participate in the developmental process, not be banned from it. Within the benign regression known as the transference neurosis, introjective and projective processes are rekindled, not solely as resistances or defenses, but as those processes which permit and accomplish psychic change in the analytic process just as in the developmental one.

Loewald distinguishes himself as someone who manages to give fresh meaning to classical psychoanalytic ideas by integrating them with object relations and developmental perspectives, thereby transforming a polemic into a higher level of synthesis. His contribution to psychoanalysis, itself a beautiful example of internalization and sublimation, mirrors his ideas about individual potential and the analytic process.

## BIBLIOGRAPHY

BRENNER, C. (1982). *The Mind in Conflict*. New York: Int. Univ. Press.

COOPER, A. (1991). Our changing views of the therapeutic action of psychoanalysis. In Fogel (1991c), pp. 61–77.

FAIRBAIRN, W. R. (1941). A revised psychopathology of psychoses and psychoneuroses. In *Psycho-Analytic Studies of the Personality*. London & Boston: Routledge & Kegan Paul, 1952, pp. 28–58.

FREUD, S. (1913). Totem and taboo. *S.E.*, 13:1–162.

——— (1914). On narcissism. *S.E.*, 14:73–102.

——— (1916–17). Introductory lectures on psycho-analysis. *S.E.*, 15 and 16.

——— (1920). Beyond the pleasure principle. *S.E.*, 18:7–64.

——— (1930). Civilization and its discontents. *S.E.*, 21:64–145.

FRIEDMAN, L. (1991). On the therapeutic action of Loewald's theory. In Fogel (1991c), pp. 91–104.

FOGEL, G. (1989). The authentic function of psychoanalytic theory. *Psychoanal. Q.*, 58:419–451.

——— (1991a). Loewald's integrated and intergrative approach. In Fogel (1991c), pp. 1–12.

——— (1991b). Transcending the limits of revisionism and classicism. In Fogel (1991c), pp. 153–190.

——— ed. (1991c). *The Work of Hans Loewald*. New York: Jason Aronson.

HARTMANN, H. (1964). *Essays on Ego Psychology.* New York: Int. Univ. Press.

HEGEL, G. W. F. (1807). *Phenomenology of the Spirit.* London: Oxford Univ. Press, 1977.

KLEIN, M. (1946). Notes on some schizoid mechanisms. In *Envy and Gratitude and Other Works.* New York: Delacorte, 1963, pp. 1–24.

KOHUT, H. (1971). *The Analysis of the Self.* New York: Int. Univ. Press.

———— (1977). *The Restoration of the Self.* New York: Int. Univ. Press.

LOEWALD, H. W. (1951). Ego and reality. In Loewald (1980), pp. 3–20.

———— (1952). The problem of defense and the neurotic interpretation of reality. In Loewald (1980), pp. 21–32.

———— (1960). On the therapeutic action of psychoanalysis. In Loewald (1980), pp. 221–256.

———— (1962). Internalization, separation, mourning, and the superego. In Loewald (1980), pp. 257–276.

———— (1971a). Some considerations on repetition and repetition compulsion. In Loewald (1980), pp. 87–101.

———— (1971b). On motivation and instinct theory. In Loewald (1980), pp. 102–137.

———— (1973a). On internalization. In Loewald (1980), pp. 69–86.

———— (1973b). Ego-organization and defense. In Loewald (1980), pp. 174–177.

———— (1978). Instinct theory, object relations, and psychic structure formation. In Loewald (1980), pp. 207–218.

———— (1979). The waning of the oedipus complex. In Loewald (1980), pp. 384–404.

———— (1980). *Papers on Psychoanalysis.* New Haven & London: Yale Univ. Press.

———— (1985). Reflections on the oedipus complex. *Psychoanal. Q.,* 54:435–443.

MAHLER, M. S., & FURER, M. (1968). *On Human Symbiosis and the Vicissitudes of Individuation.* New York: Int. Univ. Press.

———— PINE, F., & BERGMAN, A. (1975). *The Psychological Birth of the Human Infant.* New York: Basic Books.

SCHAFER, R. (1991). Internalizing Loewald. In Fogel (1991c), pp. 77–90.

STERN, D. N. (1985). *The Interpersonal World of the Infant.* New York: Basic Books.

WEISS, J. & SAMPSON, H. (1986). *The Psychoanalytic Process.* New York: Guilford Press.

WINNICOTT, D. W. (1956). Primary Maternal Preoccupation. In *Through Paediatrics to Psycho-Analysis.* New York: Basic Books, pp. 300–305.

———— (1958). The capacity to be alone. In *The Maturational Processes and the Facilitating Environment.* New York: Int. Univ. Press, pp. 29–36.

———— (1960). The theory of the parent-infant relationship. In *The Maturational Processes and the Facilitating Environment.* New York: Int. Univ. Press, pp. 37–55.

# The Temporal Framework and Lacan's Concept of the Unfixed Psychoanalytic Hour

## MOSHE HALEVI SPERO, M.S.S.W., Ph.D.

*Lacan's controversial clinical innovation of the unfixed analytic hour is evaluated within the context of Lacan's own theoretical and metaclinical views and against the classic, developmentally oriented concept of the fixed temporal analytic framework. Two clinical illustrations featuring disturbed reactions to the temporal framework of the analytic hour elucidate Lacan's proposed master/slave analogy for the treatment relationship, bringing to the fore, ironically, the basic contradictoriness of Lacan's clinical recommendation.*

THE PERTURBING RADICAL PSYCHOANALYTIC EXPOSITIONS OF JACQUES Marie Emile Lacan evoke sharply polarized attitudes. A significant proportion of this rather dramatic state of affairs is accounted for by problems of taxing style and discouraging methodology, which have been amply discussed elsewhere (Gunn, 1988; Muller and Richardson, 1982; Ragland-Sullivan, 1986; Smith, 1991; Smith and Kerrigan, 1983; Smith, 1991; Turkle, 1982). Yet even if one grants that style or *linguisterie* (the realm of verbal utterance, pun, and tonal resonance) is integral to Lacan's message (Macey, 1988, p. 175; Edelson, 1975, pp. 5–13), and agrees to put this aside temporarily in order to assess *content*, one continues to find Lacan's texts simultaneously luminescent, even prescient (such as certain elements of his critique of ego

Associate Professor, School of Social Work and Postgraduate Institute of Psychotherapy, Bar-Ilan University; Senior Clinical Psychologist and Research Scholar in Psychoanalysis and Religion, Department of Psychiatry (II), Sarah Herzog Memorial Hospital, Jerusalem, Israel. This research is supported by the continued generosity of the American Friends of Sarah Herzog Hospital.

psychology), but also anachronistic, overstated, underdocumented clinically (Green, 1986, p. 4; Schneiderman, 1980), and, perhaps most troubling from the heuristic point of view, occasionally contradictory.

However, after reviewing most of the expositions and glossifications of Lacan, I believe it is evident that contemporary psychoanalysis emerges richer for allowing itself to be informed by select Lacanian emphases that have been properly weighted, aligned with appropriate developmental perspectives, and reintegrated into classical theory (Eigen, 1981; Fayek, 1981; Friedlander, 1991; Green, 1975; Hamburg, 1991; Leavy, 1983; Modell, 1984, pp. 236–239; Muller, 1989; Smith, 1990; Spero, 1990, 1992). Lacan's tantalizing, uncannily bewildering theoretical conceptualizations—such as the "original sin" of psychoanalysis (1964, p. 12), the "castration of the letter" (1956b, p. 269; 1977, p. 65), the "alterity of the self covered in the Other" (1970; 1977, p. 49; Wilden, 1981, p. 106), and, to be considered here, the "murder and death of the analyst's time"—are nonetheless steeped within the deep perplexities of analytic theory and practice. Accordingly, it remains of great heuristic and even clinical value to winnow Lacan's *oeuvre* and glean its numerous lapidary insights, including those that serve primarily to dramatize some of the inherent paradoxes of analytic work which, as Winnicott (1971) repeatedly emphasized, must be accepted, not resolved, and respected.

A prime example of the quandary is Lacan's conflagratory technical institution of analytic sessions of unfixed, unpredictable duration. Lacan sought to dramatize eloquently one of the basic and inherently paradoxical characteristics of the analytic hour—its fostering of timelessness in a timed cell. Yet his appreciation eventually took concrete form as a destabilizing manipulation of the analytic framework; a potentially despotic, oftentimes arbitrary expedient rather than a *bona fide* parameter. To be sure, the fixed hour has certainly *not* been preserved simply because "changing the length of the session would make it difficult for the doctor to organize his day" (Wilden, 1981, p. xxv). Rather, for Lacan, the main problem of the fixed, predictable time of the hour is the very conceivability of its measured fixity, and the significance of the temporal framework in and of itself as a symbolic punctuation mark, and these issues merit perennial consideration (Gabbard, 1982; Greenson, 1974; Morris, 1989). Nevertheless, an egregious internal contradiction inheres in Lacan's unfixed hour, and I will dramatize this contradiction from the developmental perspective and (unlike Lacan) with two clinical illustrations.

## LACAN'S CONCEPT OF TIME AND THE UNFIXED HOUR

Lacan's concept of time is a quarter of his work saturated playfully, but no less thoughtfully, with stylistic and theoretical paradox (I do not yet mean "contradiction"). This emerges particularly in his two seminars on "The Purloined Letter" (1953–55; 1956a; Muller and Richardson, 1988). For Lacan, time is the measure of movements which repeat symbolically the loss of a loved object (Freud, 1895, pp. 318, 331). Although this view quite naturally begs for integration within a developmental perspective, it is not as such that time strikes Lacan. Lacan is primarily interested in the epistemic categorization of pre- and post-linguistic structures. In Lacanian terms, time is an element of the Symbolic order into which the human being is thrown insofar as time is one of the "awaiting" modes (my term) by which the presence of absence is registered and human perception constituted. Yet in these seminars, and in an even earlier paper (1945), Lacan differentiates between Imaginary time (i.e., the time frame imposed by repression and neurotic fantasy), which creates repetitiousness and endless, apparently fated recurrences, and Symbolic time, which contains the abstract structures requisite, ultimately, for limiting the automatic and ahistoric quality of compulsive repetition.

Turning to technique, Lacan became preoccupied with the degree to which the therapeutic framework—specifically, its temporally metered and fixed duration—is a given, immutable, symbolic structure, as opposed to an incidental, autochthonous creation of the analyst and patient within the realities of any given moment, subject to unpredictable alteration by the analyst in order to reveal the patient's meanings. In the "Discourse in Rome" (1977, pp. 30–113), Lacan explicitly advocated the unfixed analytic hour and short sessions where indicated. Let me emphasize, in fairness to Lacan, a useful caveat regarding the terms "unpredictable" and "unfixed" as applied to the duration of the hour. Lacan certainly did not intend for the analyst to terminate sessions in an *arbitrary* manner, but rather in a manner similar, though on a different scale, to the way in which an interpretation or a moment of insight often seems to the resistant patient to have been presented or appear unpredictably (although I believe most analysts would consider this not an ideal state of affairs). Thus, it was entirely known or "predictable" to Lacan's patients that their hours were to be of unfixed duration, although they could not predict when or where the unfixity would become manifest! Lacan's argument is that this very punctuation of the hour, this imposition of an unexpected silence or gap, is itself an analytic intervention or interpretation.

Lacan aims at preserving in brute or natural (Real), not yet Symbolized form the paradoxical fact that although the unconscious is timeless, it needs time to reveal itself; although its contents are processes in time, they are timeless. Hence, the time of the subject, as Lacan puts it, *insofar as it only reveals itself in irregularities and slips* (1953–55, Book I, p. 285ff.), must be the sole arbiter of the duration of the treatment and of each session within the treatment. The fixed, predictable adjournment of sessions is "simply a chronometric break, as such, a matter of indifference to the thread of discourse" (1977, p. 44); a category of Symbolic units of measurement, clocks, and intervals that defeat the rhythm of the patient's own natural time frames. The subject, who provides the true structure of the analysis (1977, p. 292), himself is structured as a *dis*continuity in the Real, whose holes, gaps, and slips in meaning must be enabled to determine the schedule of the psychoanalytic discourse and become its new determinants (p. 299). When the subject's speech slips, stumbles, or interrupts—which it *must* since the Imaginary, Symbolic, or Symptomatic components of discourse perpetually frustrate the primordial desires of the Real[1]—a liberating wedge is inserted between the true self and the ego that has been formed around the linguistic (and largely intransient) demands of others impinging upon the subject.[2]

Lacan thus seeks to establish an isomorphic relation between the variability of the patient's Imaginary sense of time and the substitutiveness of the patient's Symbolic perceptions of time, on the one hand, and the temporal perimeters of the hour, on the other. In this, he allegedly surrenders the structuring of the analytic hour to the patient himself, whose irregularity Lacan considers cardinal. But, in fact, Lacan also arrogates for the analyst to join in the creation of additional

1. The Real in this instance indicates the world of instinctual pleasure and the now barred or absent Other who has been surrendered as a concrete relation and replaced by abstract symbols and internalizations. The Real in Lacan's lexicon is not to be confused with "reality," for the latter is perfectly knowable whereas the Real is "impossible." The Real is best conceptualized as the brute experience of objects incompletely revealed during the initial moment of contact, prior even to the picture-thinking of the Imaginary and the linguistic abstractions of the Symbolic which, in turn, help create "reality" (Jameson, 1977, pp. 383–387).

2. How is the so-called true self to communicate if not, inevitably, through language? Others have taken up this dilemma (Hamburg, 1991; Ragland-Sullivan, 1986). Lacan may be assisted by contemporary object relations research into primitive modes of communication (e.g., projective identification) that traverse largely paraverbal channels and seem capable of transmitting even prerepresentational states (Bollas, 1987, 1989; Ogden, 1982).

irregularity by extending or terminating the hour on an unfixed basis, thereby effectively subverting the patient by introducing a Real, unanticipated puncture in the patient's discourse.[3] Lacan takes this license because he views the analyst as a scribe, a witness, the "master" of the Truth of which the patient's discourse is the progress. Inasmuch as the subject eventually learns to hide behind or usurp the Symbolically fixed termination point, it is the analyst's job to bring the punctuation process itself into the intersubjective field by corresponding creatively to the metric beat of the session and taking control of it (1977, p. 98). Lacan seeks a parallel between the dismemberment of the imaginary body or self-alienated "ego" formed during the mirror stage and the deconstruction of the imaginary conventions of discourse, allowing the short session to serve as "symbolically castrating punctuation" (Boothby, 1991, p. 213). A fixed termination point encourages erroneous passivity or *inaction* at a prime moment laden with intersubjective significances (Gifford, 1980; Knapp, 1974).

The third theme in Lacan's modified temporal framework is rooted in his twin motifs of analysis as "forced labor" and an "obsessive's shelter." The "forced labor" analogy refers to Hegel's dialectic of the slave and the master (Kojève, 1939, pp. 4–7, 34). This apprehension of the analyst as master of the value of the patient's discourse is reinforced by the analyst's prerogative to punctuate. In Hegel's view, the archetypical slave is able to survive his labors and renounce material pleasure and ownership only by virtue of knowing that his master is mortal and that by lying in wait, he may cravenly anticipate his master's death. This anticipation of death is ultimately liberating because it enables the slave to confront death itself, the Absolute Master, and in this moment of closeness to it, in this moment of extreme negativity, the slave experiences pure self-consciousness. Lacan believed that an odd form of secretive parasitism develops whereby the patient "calculates [the *fixed* session's] coming-to-term in order to articulate it upon his own delays, or even upon the loopholes he leaves himself, how he anticipates its end by weighing it like a weapon, by watching out for it as he would for a *place of shelter*" (1977, p. 98, my ital.).

Lacan in this fashion locates the intrinsic expression of the anxiety of death *within the very meter of the therapeutic dialogue,* by emphasizing the parallel between the role of death in the impacted slave/master dialec-

---

3. Compare Lacan's comment, "It is the analytic reconstruction that the subject must authenticate. The memory must be reexperienced with the help of empty spaces" (1953–55, Book I, p. 66) with Freud's undercited symbolic interpretation of material gaps in dream reports (1900, p. 332).

tic and the obsessive patient/analyst dialectic, paradigmatic of the ways in which patients squat during therapy, seduce, and hide duplicitously from the master/analyst behind the appearance of "good labor," an appearance the patient may even sustain throughout many apparently "good" hours of working through. When this pathological dialectic is left unperturbed, inevitably the slave ceases to perform his real duties, because he no longer *is* in his labors—he *is* already in the anticipated moment of his master's death. *Indeed, the slave comes to identify with the master, who is an illusion and an alienation, and thereby dies repeated deaths.* In terms of existential time, the patient *qua* slave replaces the lived future by an ethereal world of daydream which has no temporal roots in his psychologically relevant past or present (as in the case of Ellen West [Binswanger, 1944], who ultimately committed suicide). Thus Lacan seeks to prevent such servility by eradicating the deceptively reliable, mortifying guideposts of time, and reveal the indigenous temporal patterns of the true self.

Does the fixed time frame abet this pathological or false dialogue, as Lacan portrays, or does it, in fact, essentially bring such tendencies to the fore so that the patient's sense of time may be examined? Is there not something immediately and evidently contradictory in promulgating *acts* of unpredictable temporal punctuation as *symbols,* in a context where one otherwise is attempting to convert desire into *language?* I shall respond to this didactically in the Discussion. For now, note that Lacan's recommendation to foil the time-consuming patient with the unexpected termination of a maddeningly silent, boring, or deadening hour also suggests that he was essentially disinterested in the special kinds of intersubjective knowledge and understanding that is communicated to such patients precisely by sharing, surviving, and reflecting upon these admittedly painful sessions. This will be clarified in the following case illustrations.

In the first, the patient seeks to ignore time and create an illusion of timelessness to conquer death, only to fall inevitably into a bottomless culvert of sheer atemporality due to the inability any longer to distinguish treatment from original trauma (Arlow, 1984, 1986). In the second, the flow of time essentially is brought to a moribund standstill (Eissler, 1955, p. 278). This patient has available relatively well-internalized metaphors regarding time, representing modes of organizing and conceptualizing his experiences and fantasies regarding time at an essentially symbolic level (Arlow, 1984), although under the weight of an intensely archaic transference he regresses temporarily from that level. The first patient, on the other hand, continuously becomes dedifferentiated to the point where her metaphoric and linguistic structures are innundated by affective and psychophysiological pain and poorly repressed traumas, reflecting the impact of sexual trauma at almost every stage of postinfant linguistic and object relational development. In both cases, such metaphors as these individuals produce represent the efforts to interdigitate poorly structured, anarchistic (case 1) or congealed (case 2), Imaginary time frames within the Symbolic time frame made available for experimentation by the analyst. Time exists for these individuals, but the subjective qualities of its duration and substantivity are impaired by object relational and psychosexual conflicts. They hurl their time, so to speak, against the analyst's time, awaiting to infer from the nature of the rebounding echo if they have finally discerned a resilient structure.

## CASE 1

Important insights regarding time and "exit phenomena" (Gabbard, 1982) were demonstrated by a 41-year-old female patient toward the close of sessions, beginning with certain dramatic developments during the last third of her first year of psychoanalytic treatment.

The patient had a borderline personality structure with dissociative tendencies, featuring the classic admixture of high social skills and generally effective adaptive patterns in many areas of her life alongside a history of dramatic suicide attempts, hysterical epilepsy, massive dissociative episodes during the day, and disruptive and potentially life-threatening fugue and dissociative episodes at night (the degree of dissociation was variable). During these evening episodes, triggered by a complex symbolic method of interpreting the emergence of certain traumatic memory states that engulfed her during the day, she invariably found herself a partner in highly dangerous, sadomasochistic, sexual liaisons. She apparently maintained three stylistically distinct sexual liaisons with three different lovers, who had increasing degrees of psychopathic and sadomasochistic qualities. During the period relevant to the initial appearance of the exit phenomena to be described, these evening episodes, over which the patient was gradually developing greater conscious control, had become less frequent, but also limited to only the most dangerous and sadomasochistic liaison of the three.

The patient swathed herself behaviorally and self-descriptively in superlatives of all extremes. She was readily possessed by extreme hates, disgusts, loathings, and related feelings that she generally "dumped," projected or otherwise discharged as soon as possible. She was given to "high highs," states of very efficient but almost automatic functioning, manic flights of creative activity and obsessional organization, and great philanthropic acts that were similarly dispatched as quickly as possible. Her worlds of interpersonal relations and commerce typically were organized carefully enough so that her basic intolerance of frustration and poor impulse control went unnoticed. The patient exhibited prodigious artistic talent in making sweaters, often working for hours at a mindless pace, pursuing at great lengths atypical colors, yarns, or patterns. Nevertheless, her creative work was encumbered by numerous neurotic mechanisms and rituals. She could also lose interest in her projects suddenly and completely, become "stuck" by inexplicable errors, and remain severely inhibited for weeks.

She was considered to be a woman of impeccable taste, an exceptionally dedicated mother and confidante, yet she often regarded her children and her numerous devotees in a depersonalized way or through extremely distorting, free-floating projective states which induced paranoid sexual perceptions, widely split and often violent affective storms, and intense spitefulness or psychopathic apathy cloaked by episodes of dissociation.

Her complicated anamnesis included a history of chronic sexual abuse beginning with a bizarrely ritualized form of sexual molestation by an uncle at whose home she vacationed several times during the year throughout early childhood, repeated molestation and rape at age 6 at the hands of an adolescent male babysitter, rape in a neighborhood park at age 10, an incestuous relationship with a younger brother at age 13, and other actively solicited heterosexual and homosexual liaisons. Most of the early episodes were only ambiguously documented, save the violent sexual abuse she eventually suffered by her apparently psychotic husband. What medical assistance she recollected was depicted as worse than the attacks for which she sought treatment. Her dissociative episodes, with clearly sexualized, self- and object-destructive procedures, formalized during this stormy marriage which ultimately ended in divorce.

The common denominator of these sexual traumas was her parents' abject denial or disinterest in the patient's pain and their apparent ignorance of whatever signs she may have given, at least initially, of her distress. Paradoxically, her parents quashed—usually by deathly silence or impatient, pious outrage—all emotional or intellectual display. She veered from the family's stereotypical image of femininity and moral propriety, despite the fact that she was far and away the most intellectually capable and religiously knowledgeable member of the family. Paradoxically, she experienced herself as the narcissistically invested showcase child. She was never allowed to make noise and had few toys that she could enjoy.

The patient's earliest memory of losing time bore upon the fact that her father was very frequently ill and had to be rushed to the hospital at night. She would wake up looking for her parents in their beds and not find them there. She then waited alone, curled up in the bathroom reading books, during what seemed like an interminable span of hours. She also recalled that from a very early age, owing to her independent nature and her parents' indifference, she was allowed to come and go as she pleased with almost no accountability to the hour. People of means, her parents primarily supplanted normal discourse with massive shopping sprees: "We would just *kill* the stores! We'd continue shopping until we were exhausted or there was simply *no time left in the day*." This comment was typical of her mode of expression, interlocked dramatically with numerous latent and multiply determined traumatic connotations. She recounted that it was characteristic of her mother to promise to buy her whatever she desired, only to declare the patient's expressed desires as nonsense or not what she really wanted, and then subsequently purchase that very item for a cousin or a sibling. The patient always reacted to these episodes with violent abdominal pain and dissociative loss of hours. At some point after the period of work described below the patient was able to identify her physical sensations during shopping with the experience of rape, and conceptualized this symbolically by calling her mother the "thief of desire."

The patient had undergone three prior failed psychotherapies. The last treatment, which took place with a very sensitive and effective psychiatrist, began most favorably, yet foundered owing to the pressure of her unmanageable dissociative absences, exceptional projective pressures, and incessant extratherapeutic requests. Various unavoidable changes in the psychiatrist's availability led to an intractable countertransferential impasse. Thus, by the time she came to me for evaluation, a rich heritage existed for predicting an analysis rippled with acting out, splitting, and primitive projective mechanisms.

During analytic hours of the first year of treatment (five times a week), almost every session after the first month was witness to near-catastrophic anxiety reactions to her own emergent memories or to gaps in memories and in her own narrative. Every presentation began with a tedious chronological orientation of excruciating specificity, which inevitably elicited an irreversible regression into tangential data and new anxiety, derealization, dizziness, and tears. She developed a habit of constantly prefacing or interrupting her progress by asking me whether it was alright to talk. Was I yelling at her? Was I angry at her for not speaking freely? Would I scream at her? Was there time left? Would I allow her to complete her stories by providing a few more minutes extra time at the end of sessions?

These interminable inquiries were motivated by terrible anxiety, hypervigilance, and the desire to hide her destructiveness behind pseudohelplessness as she subtly created an atmosphere that apparently actualized the terrorizing ambience of the attic where she was repeatedly trapped and raped. Phenomenologically, no sooner had the memory of an object registered within her preconscious, the patient hurried to examine its most distant or peripheral details (usually chronology, colors, clothing, lineage), dreading to leave any single characteristic or detail unaccounted for, only to be shortly inundated by a plethora of toxic experiences and representations mulling about in her mind (Terr, 1984). It seemed that her condensed sense of time had crept into the very fabric of her linguistic framework, depriving her of what one might call syntactic-semantic temporal buffers, so that every word or word-chain became at once the remembered past and the anticipated future (Edelson, 1975, p. 140). Her narrative was heavily laden with overlapping sexual and aggressive allusions and metaphors which she "lived" virtually concretely (for example, she more than once described herself as speaking or acting rapaciously, but for a long time could not associate or make much deeper sense of what her choice of adjective might mean), although the observer developed the impression that he was allowed to look straight through a perfectly hierarchically layered time-tunnel, which sorely lacked signal mechanisms to cushion the journey downward.

As I increased my attention to her constant questioning and mounting anxiety, she appeared to organize herself but also began to request extra time to complete her narrative so as not to have to take home all the bad feelings. She also began to call me at home, telling me in an inaudibly "little" voice how scared she was. Yet inevitably, as she calmed, she revived and was amiably ready to intellectualize again. Highlighting these paradoxical qualities, I attempted to steer the patient away from her intellectual interest in her material and toward considering her fears and their snowballing impact on her capacity to tolerate and communicate pain. I was not getting through. In subsequent sessions, the patient claimed to experience me as suddenly bad, frightening, or as yelling at her. But equally often, after what to all intents and purposes seemed like "good" sessions, she would call or inform me timidly in the next session that she either had become enraged, blanked out, had a dissociative episode (she often "found" herself playing with razor blades or leaving the gas on in the oven), and was frightened of my very goodness. The source of these perceptions was clearly her abusive, uncaring parents, but also her own projected, archaically punitive and shaming, split-off self-representation which was exerting increasingly more influence with each session (directed apparently toward the repressed memory of terrible things done during dissociative states). However, the severely permeable index of reality in her perceptions and reactions as well as in her underlying object representations made for a very poorly differentiated quality of transference.

Two significant kinds of paradoxical atmospheres were now being created within the very first moments of almost each session and were rapidly rendering the analysis an impossibility. In one scenario, the patient entered in what she termed an "on" mood and from the doorway began flinging about a barrage of mundane details and overloaded metaphors that very quickly pulled her into some danger zone, triggering a sense of entrapment and of being "stuck" in the attic with her abusive uncle. Sometimes she accessed to apparently irrelevant side issues, leaving behind the previous story or dream that had so intensely preoccupied her only seconds before, and to which, more provocatively, I knew she would attempt to return by hook or crook before leaving my office. As the hour ran its inexorable course, it became painfully obvious that the patient was absolutely unaware or unconcerned about the approaching adjournment. As I indicated the end of the hour, she continued her verbal onslaught. When I signaled slightly more forcefully that we could continue in the next session, or even attempted to discuss her obvious dilemma with the pain at the end of the sessions, she promptly collapsed into tears, motioning me away with her hands as if I were some noxious perpetrator, and lay stoney-still for the remainder of the hour with grit teeth and clenched fists. It was not long before she was lingering on the couch almost until the next patient was about to enter.

Alternatively, she would drag herself frightened into the sessions, drop onto the couch, bury herself in a corner, and start to gag, cough, make mouth movements as if she had something disgusting in her mouth, and lay in silence. Judging from her apparent suffering and helplessness, I believed that her silence had a more authentically tormented quality; at other times, the silence seemed angry, obstinate, and rebellious. As tears rolled down her cheeks, outlining her grimaced and clenched jaws or falling upon her fists, she gave the unsettling impression of crying *through* herself. She seemed completely indifferent to time, resisted or repelled all interpretations, and began to refuse completely to leave the office at the end of sessions.

It was paradoxical that one so sensitive to humiliation appeared unperturbed by the ever-present possibility of having to encounter the next patient by remaining completely limp on the couch. At this point I had no choice but physically to lead her from the room while she maintained her almost completely flaccid deportment. She mumbled something about her helplessness, wondered plaintively if I was angry with her, and declared that she would not attend further sessions. Invariably she came for the next session, perhaps made an initial comment regarding her fears, and repeated the drama. I felt mounting pressure to discontinue the analysis, especially since my theoretical intuitions up to this point were of no help to either the patient or myself. Her obstinacy had the impact of aggravated assault even as she protested her helplessness and inability to bring herself out of paralysis. I was sure that under the childlike neediness and desire to be locked in "good" time with me, there hid, none too dormantly, murderous rage and mortification, the repetition of being trapped with someone insanely evil, and a literal mutilation of all temporal frameworks. I began gradually to offer *prima facie* interpretations that pointed to what I considered the evident seduction-and-fear pattern within the context of some kind of reenactment of dreadful sexual traumas, and her need to retain absolute control of her personal boundaries within the analytic framework. I underscored her projective provocation of me to curtail the treatment by actualizing within me simultaneously her fears and her sadistic vengefulness, by very simply forcing me to have to act out the role of a manhandler whom she could then realistically fear as well as justifiably defy.

The latter intervention brought some relief, yet her passive submission and fearfulness continued. Refusal to leave sessions still occurred. I then informed her that I thought we ought to discontinue the analytic contract, but that I was still prepared to see her on a session-to-session basis, with no commitment to the subsequent session until she could keep to the set time allotment. I assured her of her capability to defeat the analysis if she insisted on both accepting and not accepting the framework, but that for me the framework was a symbol to be preserved at all costs. I shared with her my impression that my own sanity was being denied me, as evidently she felt it had been denied her, by a nullification of the rudimentary time frames which are essential to any sense of hope, bountiful anticipation, and relief. She left that particular session thoughtfully and quickly, but called the next morning asking to continue treatment.

In formulating this intervention, I was informed by countertransference-derived representations and feelings that centered primarily on the compulsory passivity and timelessness she engendered. I experienced a certain degree of scorn for the exaggerated helplessness and limpness in this woman who behaved so utterly differently in her other walks of life—a reaction which I felt corresponded to an archaically hypercritical and unforgiving, split-off component of the patient's personality—sharply dichotomous from the tough, organized, self-possessed woman known outside the sessions, or from the bawdy, street-tough, and slightly malevolent mistress of the night. As is commonly seen in certain forms of borderline personalities featuring hysterical trends, the patient as a young girl, following the earliest sexual attacks, experienced a splitting of at least two incompatible self-components: one, a violently aggressive, sexually sadistic (by virtue of identification with the aggressor), apparently uncaring "survivor" self-component; the second, a weak, passive, numb, masochistic, and speechless "victim" self-component. Each operated within its own time framework and its own linguistic dictionary (for example, for the "victim," *complying* with treatment meant passive resistance and an astonishing lack of curiosity about her own copious associations and metaphors; for the "survivor," *complying* meant seducing me into sadomasochistic aggression so as to diminish her anticipated pain in the most expedient manner conceivable). The "survivor" was mercilessly critical of the "victim," especially concerning the patient's efforts to work through her early traumas, whereas the "victim" was necessary in order to trigger the "survivor" into acting out the violent feelings connected with these traumas.

The patient was immobilized in time as a result of early interference with the development of mature, effective symbolizing capacities and delay mechanisms as well as by virtue of the concrete annihilation of temporal boundaries she had learned to effect in order to deal with the repetitive, unpredictable coming and going of her uncle while remaining locked for days in an upstairs attic.[4] Thus, while the patient certainly did not lack a conception of time, she was able to recreate a sense of imaginary "dead time" (Green, 1986, pp. 275, 292), a paradoxical temporal state of quasi-*atemporality* recalling the traumatic interval between the loss or emotional unavailability of a "good" object and the return of a "bad" object, and vice versa. The patient prior to this stage seemed fated continuously to actualize her sense that no "good" object, and no restoration of time, ever awaited her at the end of lived experience. Or, following Fraser's recent analysis (1988), the patient was capable of entering a *prototemporal* dimension that was bereft of a true sense of the present, directionless and discontinuous, where the "arrow of time disintegrates into slivers of wood, scattered more or less along a line" (p. 486).[5]

4. From thence on, reinstated by self-hypnosis (Fliess, 1973).
5. Bearing in mind that the patient was always quite well aware of time at some dissociated or isolated level of operation, we eventually clarified another aspect of her

I clarified to the patient the hypothetical existence of two self-components and their impact upon her orientation in time. Referring to my own working representations of her, I gave her some inkling of how I experienced the complementary aspects of her split-off states, and came to sense somewhat more fully the overall experience she sought to recreate. The repeated destruction of the temporal framework of the analysis was at once a necessary mechanism for perpetuating this split as well as a painful consequence or characteristic of the split state. The intervention was successful, and brought about the cessation of this particular attack upon the framework, although it was necessary for several months to help the patient focus on the tendency to split at crisis points. Against the steadfast temporal framework, the patient was able to experience and then conceive just how real was her repetition of the original traumatic scenario, including the defensive-pathological time distortions that served as the negative integument of her memory states during that period.

CASE 2

The following, more mature analysis draws attention to Lacan's comment that the paradigmatic obsessive slave/patient anticipates the end of the session "by watching out for it as he would for a *place of shelter*" (1977, p. 98), a metaphor which we also encountered in the preceding illustration. The present, Hebrew-speaking patient used the term *miklat* to refer to shelter, which brought numerous culture-bound associations into the treatment, only the most relevant of which will be mentioned here.

The material emerged during the end of a specific session in the middle of the sixth year of psychoanalysis of a 50-year-old musician who suffered from homosexual conflicts rooted in a series of early childhood traumas and developmental disruptions. These began with leaving America and resettling in Israel when he was 4 years old, followed shortly thereafter by a two-month hospitalization (including repeated, unsympathetically administered lumbar punctures), and com-

---

acting out that was geared less toward annihilating the temporal framework than toward incorporating it into the specific contents of her memories. It seemed that she presented her important memories purposely at the termination point so that my inevitably catastrophic announcement of the end of the hour would overleaf with the repressed shock originally produced by an explosive paternal interdiction, a rapist's paralyzing command, a sadistic maternal censure of libidinal pleasure, or other experiences of sudden arrest and pain.

pulsory recuperation for two months in an isolated sanitorium. Aided by near-photographic recall and imagery, the patient portrayed his childhood and young adulthood as an unending period of loneliness, neglect, repeated shame, and disappointment in a rather arrogant yet foppish paternal figure (of whom great tales were told, but whose era had apparently come and gone), and a profoundly frustrating, negative oedipal identification with and fear of a strong, intelligent, but hypercritical maternal figure.

The patient recalled, endlessly, interminable hours of unsupervised, frightening time alone as a young child. He knew of numerous traumatic incidents that had occurred to neighborhood children during these "dead" hours, some of which were also screens for some of his own traumas. In particular, between the ages of 7 and 9 years, a complex homosexual relationship developed between the patient and a partly protective, partly abusive older adolescent. The adolescent was a frequent guest in the paternal home, but there were only dim clues to the possibility that the patient's mother sensed something amiss in his relationship with her son. This unresolved doubt had become the basis for the patient's deeply entrenched impression that the homosexual relationship, to a certain degree, saved him from complete loneliness and emotional sterility and was a tragic, unforgivable sacrifice tacitly sanctioned by his mother in order to provide him with some male image for identification.

The older boy typically initiated their encounters with some kind of game or interesting activity and slowly made more explicit sexual demands. In all instances, he approached the patient from behind and forbade him to turn around or look at him. The patient greatly intellectualized the "mild discomfort" he *supposed* he experienced during intercourse, and for a long time focused only on the existential support he gained from the attentions of this older boy. Slowly, however, these sexual liaisons drew complementary significance from the earlier trauma of having had to endure painful lumbar punctures passively, in isolation, and without explanation. Later in the analysis, he was able to link not only the quality of the two pains, but also the seeming nonmovement of time during these incidents.

Yet even early on, the patient was able to recall the sense of the endlessness of the interval between the beginning of each encounter, to which he actually looked forward with happy anticipation, and the point at which he experienced confusing sexual feelings (not yet localized) and anal pain. Although this first relationship broke off when the older boy entered military service, he suddenly reappeared in the patient's life fifteen years later, clearly in search of a renewed sexual liaison. The extent to which the patient could maintain dual tracks of time is exemplified by the fact that whenever the patient referred to this reunion, he mentioned in a rather plaintive way how he had wondered throughout those years what had happened to the man, and how he longed for his return. When the older fellow revealed that he had since married, the patient was greatly surprised and disappointed. He refused any further sexual advances and the older man again dropped out of the patient's life.

After university, the patient married a paranoid woman with severe sexual inhibitions, to whom he felt "inexplicably compelled" to reveal his sexual past. Their relationship was stormy and essentially sadomasochistic. The patient functioned valiantly and often creatively in his roles as harassed husband and father as well as highly lettered professional (through which he came into a great deal of contact with psychotherapeutic concepts), though these accomplishments were marred by a sense of frustration regarding the largely compensatory quality of his ambitions, his laggard perception of evident dangers, and his complicated and arduous sexual life.

He adopted analysis with great diligence, but also with built-in masochistic sacrifices, one of which bore specifically upon the sphere of time. In seeking treatment with me in Jerusalem, the patient had to involve himself in several long hours of travel three times a week, including the inevitable challenge of contending with the public transportation system. Nevertheless, he adapted himself well to this hurdle, never missed a session and never arrived more than a few minutes early (and even then knocked on my door only at the appointed hour), and always left on time.

The patient's narrative was characterized by an obsessive, plodding, though always forward-directed pace, highly descriptive and detailed memories that were not without affect but tended toward a grey patina, a marked insightfulness weighted down by entrenched intellectualizations, and a deep capacity for true pathos always brought up short due to shame-based timidity, hesitancy, and languid interpersonal responsivity. His sessions were usually rich, yet sluggish. As with every other achievement in his life, his analysis seemed destined to involve its participants in a process so agonizingly long that we both might be truly shocked to learn that it had finally been completed. Initially, his resiliency to work with interpretations and even enjoy certain "discoveries" was marred from time to time by the percipitous expression of manifestly transference-based fears that I was emotionally apathetic toward him. His emotional investment in the material he brought seemed intense, yet he strenuously avoided acknowledging transference feelings, giving the covert impression at the end of each session, which he dutifully adjourned exactly on time, that we had somehow passed each other on nonintersecting paths.

The patient had for half a year been progressively differentiating active and passive aspects of his homosexual identifications, and along these trends aligning a series of early memories having to do with supportive and occasionally sexually manipulative male figures. However, for a period of about one month prior to the specific dialogue presented here, the patient had become seriously bogged down by complex and repetitive quarrels with his wife and children. Whatever his wife's psychological difficulties, the patient was aware that he played masochistically into her constant ensnarements. Themes of divorce, public embarrassment, and financial loss were always in the wings. He struggled against them with an admixture of hopelessness and admirable but occasionally quixotic determination.

As domestic conflict escalated, the patient tended to itemize these crises during his hours in an increasingly monotonous and exhausting way, apparently unable to continue the analysis without clinging to mundane self-recriminations and seeking my support. He fought hard to rivet my focus on his scrupulous reportage. The pathetic, long-suffering image he cast during this period had strong roots in the lonely, sexually confused early childhood years, as did the female imagoes against which he passively attempted to defend himself. Any attempt to hold forth the analytic perspective toward the patient's thoughts and feelings was met with intense woundedness and biting perorations regarding my insensitively abandoning him in the middle of his very real life struggles and agonies. On the other hand, I did not have the impression that the analysis had become totally derailed since relevant thematic material was plainly visible even during these ruminations.

In one session, the patient presented a litigious episode having to do with the disciplining of one of his children. The assertive tendencies that had been germinating rather constructively in our work had apparently taken a major, unplanned surge toward plain aggressiveness. After a while, the opportunity presented itself to point out that major developments were taking place at home simultaneously with his continued upkeep of a logjam in the analysis. Reviewing a wide spectrum of his recent associations, I suggested that the logjam served somehow to insulate him against exposing intense anger so as to spare himself from feeling "analyzed" and dependent during a period when he needed most to feel large and powerful. Indeed, I had the impression that in some way I was being distracted by this domestic sideshow, even anesthesized, only to be apperceived by the patient (via the hostile maternal transference) as insufficiently attentive to his here-and-now dilemmas.

This interpretation was met with an immediate narcissistic collapse. The patient charged that evidently I had "all along" bought his family's perception of him as a violently abusive man, that I was at one with his mother's constant efforts to humiliate him and depress every ounce of masculinity in him. He rejected my implication that a "primitive" mechanism on the order of projective identification was involved in the recent paralysis of his analytic focus. In his ensuing rebuttal, however, his associations and demeanor confirmed this very possibility; moreover, he seemed peripherally aware of this. Characteristically, even this angry reaction was delivered deferentially, with recognizably less personal devastation compared to a similar earlier episode, and with greater aptitude for acknowledging his role in the flow of events. Nevertheless, he left that particular hour declaring that he would in all certainty not wish to attend—and he specified—the *forthcoming* session.

The patient indeed missed the next session. He called during the morning of the subsequent scheduled hour, saying amiably that he would like to come for the day's session. This hour was difficult but productive. He explained his previous absence by saying that he wished to assert himself autonomously if only "symbolically." In fact, he felt rather guiltless about it, although it was painful for him; and he wondered if this act represented the more or less constructive form of assertiveness. He had reassessed my "offending" interpretation and felt that it was accurate after all. After these comments, his material underwent a subtle change. He understood that he had allowed his wife's brand of venom to permeate the analytic container insofar as he felt forced to talk about their failing marriage. On the other hand, he was not sure about the "whole projective identification thing." In fact, he added, he considered the evidentiary material I had referred to in support of my interpretation uncompelling. He then sought to illustrate his wife's toxicity by reporting in his most lugubrious way another round of recent domestic imbroglios.

The sheer reiteration and oppressiveness of his delivery during the hour made me feel flattened. As the patient prepared to begin his next sentence, I immediately had the experience of "recalling" that I had just glanced at my watch and noticed that our time was up, and was silently preparing to announce the end of the hour. As I completed that thought, I became aware, with a disconcerting sense of fading derealization, that there in fact remained five minutes to the session and that I had *not* at any point glanced at my watch. I felt momentarily disoriented by what was obviously a *déjà pensé* experience.

Reflecting on the quality of the vast majority of his hours to date, I believed that the "signal experience" (Langs, 1976, p. 560) I had just undergone was an authentic countertransference response to the patient's developmental and neurotic difficulties with time. I shared with the patient that I had just experienced a distortion in my sense of time and that I was wondering how *he* had experienced the hour. He replied gamely and insightfully, "Perhaps you're dabbling too much in the innovations of Lacan!" I acknowledged the strength of his intuition and stated that I, indeed, had experienced a premature impression that the hour had come to its end. The patient supposed either that I wished to "close the session on him," *possibly* because he had begun to drone on again, or that perhaps I sought to end the session "while the going was good" so as to forestall his slipping back into ruminating about his family troubles. He thereby revealed his own awareness that he had, indeed, veered away from his ongoing psychoanalytic work. He was apologetic for taking up so much time, but he sorely needed a shelter (*miklat* in Hebrew) where he could unburden himself of precisely those crises which everyone, including his analyst, presumed he could handle by himself.

In the following hour, the patient expressed more thoughts about needing a *miklat* in the sense of a refuge place or sanctuary against his wife's onslaughts as well as in the sense of a hermetic vault to deposit the murderous feelings she directed at him and maybe even his own murderous feelings.[6] His impression from the previous session was that he had indeed felt pressured to *insert* forcefully a few more episodes from home before the hour ended, and he acknowledged a strangely good feeling about having had such an impact upon me as to influence my sense of time. The capacity to induce such a change in another person and the range of figurative and symbolic sexual meanings frightened him, but they also filled him with a newfound sense of presence and impressiveness.

In the immediately following session, the patient entered the consulting room 30 minutes late. Although he had been seriously late only

6. The concealment of the manslayer in the biblical *miklat* (Deut. 19:1–13: Num. 35:9–34) was not intended as an interminable incarceration. The manslayer gained release from the *miklat* with the death of the High Priest. In viewing my office as a *miklat*, the patient was expressing in a roundabout way that his freedom was in some way contingent upon my "death." Nevertheless, unlike the manslayer, the analysand enjoys the license to "sketch out several times the Imaginary exits from the master's prison" (Lacan, 1953–55, Book I, p. 287), testing or actualizing these exits repeatedly with little risk of ambush.

once before during the six years of treatment, he had been very disturbed by his lateness and apologized profusely, whereas this time he
entered nonchalantly and commenced speaking. This was surprising,
and I wondered whether he was at all aware that he was atypically late. I
said nothing. The session was rather productive, in fact, and included
the first dream in half a year. The dream seemed reparative. However,
as I shifted in my seat around the time of the close of the session, the
patient became greatly dismayed as he obviously came suddenly to the
realization that he had completely confused the scheduled time of
the session for that day. He believed he had come in promptly as usual
when in fact he was obviously a full half-hour late. He was perplexed
for a moment. He recalled that he had actually had many things on his
mind that day, and for this reason had taken several extraordinary
precautions to come on time. He related that as he stood in the lobby
waiting, he actually did have the thought that it was odd to have so
much extra time prior to the session, but he began to read the paper. It
was now clear why he had not commented on his lateness upon entering my office.

   In the subsequent hour, the patient dismissed outright his own fleeting insight that his lapse might be some form of "revenge" for my own
time distortion in the prior session—that seemed patently childish to
him. On the other hand, it was abundantly clear that his extraordinary
vigilance about time throughout the day of *his* lateness was evidence
that some kind of ambivalence was gradually deautomatizing a domain
that was otherwise routine. He then recalled the earlier episode of
lateness from about one year prior as well as an additional crisis that
had occurred when he had accidentally traveled to Jerusalem for a
session during a holiday. We had agreed not to hold sessions during the
holiday, which he acknowledged, yet he called upon arrival to inform
me that he was in Jerusalem, testing in a sense whether I would see him
anyway. Although I did spend a few moments with him on the phone, I
was not able to see him. Efforts at that time to explore the episode were
unproductive.

   He felt that in all three instances his misjudgment of time was the
result of complex processes that involved recreating the many situations of primal abandonment against which he could test whether or
not I would truly worry about him, seek him out, and care enough to
compensate him with extra time. After these comments, there
emerged some new memories in which the patient recalled a lonely
vigil as a child hospitalized in a strange place, seemingly deserted by his
parents, crying pathetically and fruitlessly in his bed for someone to

comfort him, endless nights half of whose hours were spent looking out the window, wondering in terror why no one was at all concerned about him. The patient further developed these discoveries in subsequent sessions which were marked by the resilient return of his former analytic attitude toward his material. He was able to clarify more fully the psychosexual significance of his intrusion into my time-keeping function, as it were, by projecting upon me the image of an obsessive and destructive maternal time-tending introject that had to be sadistically punctured or stretched to the breaking point.

The preoccupation in the sessions with his wife's phallic aggressiveness was to a certain degree a counterphobic defense against his anxiety regarding the male phallus and his insecurities about expressing his erotic feelings toward me. The patient had in a sense buried his own phallic counterattack within the subtle pressure of the ever-extending subjective endlessness of his hours—*within* the strictly observed temporal framework. Indeed, by mentioning the name of Lacan in his intuitive associations, the patient transformed Lacan's representation itself into a metaphor for the patient's needs and fears: though not conceived by him in this way, he had potentiated the Lacanian animus of the obsessive slave/patient and projected upon me the complementary role of despotic harvester of the patient's precious, assiduously tallied minutes. Thus, while there was certainly anger implicit in his 30-minute lateness, the patient was also able, partly as a consequence of his positive feelings regarding the impact he had had upon the analyst's sense of time, to actualize and reexperience the memory of being lost in time and the frustrated desire to be searched for.

### DISCUSSION

#### CRITIQUE OF LACAN'S APPROACH TO ANALYTIC TIME

The case illustrations make plain that the portrait of obsessive, phlegmatic, or insouciant biding of time in anticipation of the master's death is an incomplete characterization of the individual's object relational or existential attitudes toward the fixed hour, although the analogy to some kind of *preoccupation* with death at the point of termination or adjournment is a relevant notion. My first patient, for example, was not trying simply to wait out the death of the master, although this element existed superficially, such as in her sadistic fantasies. Rather, she sought to destroy the dimension of time itself and all who would be its champions (the analyst, the patient's own integrated self-image), no less ruthlessly than she experienced time as murdering her.[7]

Internal inconsistency, however, is the singular unacceptable aspect of Lacan's arguments. Lacan maintained that the "term" of the analytic hour must be unfixed because as a *substitution* for the Real, the Symbolic hour has no valid claim to fixity. The goal of the analyst was to "suspend the subject's certainties until their last mirages have been consumed. And it is in the *discourse* that the progress of their resolution must be marked" (1977, p. 43); the mediator of the Imaginary drama of treatment must be speech or a symbol, "called in another language, an act of faith" (1953, p. 425). Now we cannot simply ignore Lacan, for he is correct in saying that no symbol or linguistic form is inherently fixed, and that the true objects of discourse tend to slide under the displacements of language. However, as Lacan himself stated, psychoanalysis essentially is the *conjunction* of the Real and the Symbol, or the nullification of the Imaginary via the Symbolic. Only in their mutual interplay *within a discourse framed by dependable temporal pinions and consensual dialect* do the Real, the Imaginary, and the Symbolic eventually become approximated. The Imaginary seeks illusory comprehension by fusing the Real and the "self" into a state of timeless mirroring, while the Symbol tries *to prevent* such fusion via the rules of language and temporality, ensuring sufficient framework so that the journey in and out of the Imaginary or Real is negotiable.

By seeking to force exposure of the patient's experience of the Real through the impertinence of the unpredictable termination, Lacan abrogates his well-known axiom that the Real by definition *cannot* be sought as an absolute, and he risks disallowing the patient the struggle to fill in the space between the fixed symbol (the predictable termination point) and symbolized death with a sense of subjective time. Ironically, Hegel's vaunted dialectic deals only with Imagined death, not Real death, nor even the actualization of death—for it is only as an imagined event that death appears as central in the preoedipal and oedipal drama and in the formation of neurosis. To be sure, the path to the Symbolic is *in* the Imaginary, which the analyst must allow himself

---

7. Loewald (1980, p. 142ff.) would view this experience as *fragmented* time, where connectedness to time and the interval connections within time are annihilated, so that each instant is only its empty self, a nothing, a meaningless atemporal "now." This experience contrasts with the experience of *eternity*, where meaning is condensed in the undifferentiated unity of an extenuated, abiding instant (*nunc stans*), giving rise to a sense of unitary now that overflows into the larger world of time. My second patient was closer to the latter.

and the patient to travel through the illusions of transference—but only by *knowingly being in* the Imaginary.

The developmental focus sharpens the critique. Peraldi (1988), for example, formulated three spheres of time appropriate to Lacan's three orders of reality: mythical time (the eternal then/now quality of the structure of myth not yet actualized in the form of a tale), corresponding to the Real; fictional time (the time proper to the myth as related in the tale), corresponding to the Imaginary; and historical time (our here-and-now time to which we apply the structure of the myth), corresponding to the Symbolic. Lacan seems to have jumbled the natural hierarchical relationship between these dimensions. The fact is that successively mature, complex, abstract, and well-internalized senses of time only emerge against some previous, minimal, yet constant ordering of these realities—what Fraser (1988, 1989) views as the nested, concentric hierarchy of time. The higher the organizational level, the larger the number of stable structures that can be identified. Applied to psychoanalysis, the mythical and fictional time frames, their deeper cognitive and affective components, and the existential self-experiences to which these are linked, cannot emerge save as nested within the overall Symbolic cogwheeling of historical time, or the stable time proper to the idiosyncratic narrative of the analysis. The short-lived time of the Real, which is alien to the patient's memory traces and predatory upon chronological, emotionally viable time, and the pictorial time of the Imaginary (as encountered generally among introject-level object representations), which imposes its fantasied dimensions upon present time and tends to overwhelm it, irrupt into the treatment quite naturally, without artificial assistance from the analyst. Within a temporal framework, these two problematic senses of time become reined to the history of their own new trajectory as they unfold and gain expression during the course of treatment.

The fixed hour, then, is in truth only relatively fixed, relative to an agreed-upon, meaning-imposing chain of signifiers known as the analytic framework. No less than discourse itself, whose presence implies the absence of the loved one whose separation or insufficiency required the evocation of speech and the internalization of the processes necessary for language, the analytic framework as well is a symbol of the relinquishment of symbiotic timelessness and the internalization of a stable self that has become the permanent baseline for marking time (Arlow, 1989; Colarusso, 1979). As viewed by Bleger (1967), Green (1975, 1986), and others, the fixed time frame of the analytic hour is a nonprocess element or a *constant* of the treatment, closely linked to irreducible symbiotic "ultra-phenomena" that once preserved the rudimentary integrity of the human psychosomatic system early in life. The time frame speaks not only to the fact that human beings possess historical (i.e., dated) psychological memories, but to the very essence of the historicity and continuity of the self as it struggles constantly to balance subjective-personal and objective time. As such, the fixed time frame contains silent protective elements or values to which the primitive personality may, indeed, become pathologically attached or addicted, or attempt to supplant it with his or her own idiosyncratic internal frame. Given that these pathological fixations tend to be most resistant to interpretation, analysis depends upon the patient's inadvertent creation of "crevices" discernible against the field of an *unchanging* framework (cf. Kurtz, 1988). By surrealistically dismembering or "castrating" time itself, Lacan inadvertently renders it nonconceptual and beyond the pale of the internalizable aspects of the gradually developing analytic object.

CONCLUSION: THE "DEATH" OF THE ANALYST'S TIME

Lacan has enriched our understanding by highlighting the "deaths" of the analyst's supposed presumptions about the patient (1964, p. 232), of the analyst's own resistance to the patient's emergent self (1953–55, Book II, pp. 228, 324), of the patient's alien pseudoselves, of the patient's projected impressions of the analyst's identity, and of the Imaginary rigidity or irrelevance of time the patient seeks to impose upon the Symbolic fixed hour.

Rich clinical evidence encourages one to adopt Lacan's perspective as a guiding metaphor. Searles (1965) and others (Gifford, 1980; Hartocollis, 1983; Pollock, 1971; Segal, 1986) have documented the ways in which the patient's sense or utilization of time within the analytic hour becomes constricted or fragmented due to the advent of separation from the analyst or under pressure of unconscious fantasies of the analyst's fantasied death by "killing" the time they share. In neo-Lacanian terms, Winnicott spoke of the need for the analysand in his own time to be able to destroy or kill the analyst (and *his* own time) and to recreate the analyst (1949, 1965, 1971). Green views such destruction of the analyst as a curative component of the analytic setting, "a condition of [the analyst's] periodic resurrection, so that the analysand may be able to *use* the analyst" (1986, p. 284; Bollas, 1989, p. 36). Fayek (1981) portrays the requisite death of the patient's mirroring and narcissistic projections upon the analyst that maintain cul-du-sac communication. The case illustrations presented here amply describe the ways in which the patient may be said to murder or mutilate the analyst's capacity to create efficacious representations of the patient, to create deathly, morbid, or inert feeling states within the analyst by way of mechanisms such as projective identification and sadistic or parasitic attacks on the therapist's linking mechanisms. In both instances, such mutilation of time, and of representations in time, could perhaps be satisfactorily *imagined* merely by attending to the patients' linguistic metaphors regarding time, yet these patients further needed to induce the states of mutilated or frozen time by effecting pathological alterations in the analyst's perception of time by directly attacking the temporal framework of the session.

In conclusion, the patient's effort to return to the illusions of reality experienced prior to repression, to reexperience historically a childhood full of sexual trauma, or to attempt to articulate the prerepresentational "death" or alienation of the true self following the mirror stage, is only viable against the *a priori* backdrop of some basic analytic structure. This backdrop needs to be comprised not only of the deep syntactical structures of the language or words of the hour, but also by the temporal pattern of the hour as an integral ego function implicit in the analytic envelope. As such, the framework not only facilitates anticipation, waiting, reflection, and intentionality, but also enables the patient and analyst to mirror the intervals within the self and among its cadences of discourse. For it is not simply radical or absolute intra- or intersubjectivity that interests us clinically, but intra- or intersubjectivity that points to a well-internalized sense of individuality and separateness from and interest in the subject that has developed within a symbolic network. Thus, the termination of the hour is never only an Imaginary or Real event, nor is the patient's attitude toward it only Imaginary or Real. Since the slave/master paradigm is itself of the Symbolic, then the "death" it anticipates, including its fantasy or imaginary variations, and any countermovement to that death that may be proposed, must be symbolized as well.

BIBLIOGRAPHY

Arlow, J. A. (1984). Disturbances of the sense of time. *Psychoanal. Q.*, 53:13–37.
——— (1986). Psychoanalysis and time. *J. Amer. Psychoanal. Assn.*, 34:507–528.
——— (1989). Time as emotion. In *Time and Mind*, ed. J. T. Fraser. Madison, Ct.: Int. Univ. Press, pp. 85–97.
Binswanger, L. (1944). The case of Ellen West. In *Existence*, ed. W. M. Mendel

& J. R. May, E. Angel, & H. Ellenberger. New York: Simon & Schuster, 1958, pp. 237–364.

BLEGER, J. (1967). Psycho-analysis of the psycho-analytic frame. *Int. J. Psychoanal.*, 48:511–519.

BOLLAS, C. (1987). *The Shadow of the Object.* London: Free Association Books.

—— (1989). *Forces of Destiny.* London: Free Association Books.

BOOTHBY, R. (1991). *Death and Desire.* London: Routledge.

COLARUSSO, C. A. (1979). The development of time sense. *Int. J. Psychoanal.*, 60:243–251.

EDELSON, M. (1975). *Language and Interpretation in Psychoanalysis.* Chicago: Univ. Chicago Press.

EIGEN, M. (1981). The area of faith in Winnicott, Lacan, and Bion. *Int. J. Psychoanal.*, 62:413–433.

EISSLER, K. R. (1955). *The Psychiatrist and the Dying Patient.* New York: Int. Univ. Press.

FAYEK, A. (1981). Narcissism and the death instinct. *Int. J. Psychoanal.*, 62:309–322.

FLIESS, R. (1973). *Symbol, Dream, and Psychosis.* New York: Int. Univ. Press.

FRASER, J. T. (1975). *Of Time, Passion, and Knowledge.* New York: George Braziller.

—— (1988). Time: removing its degeneracies. In *Fantasy, Myth, and Reality,* ed. H. P. Blum, Y. Kramer, A. K. Richards, & A. D. Richards. Madison, Ct.: Int. Univ. Press, pp. 481–500.

—— (1989). The many dimensions of time and mind. In *Time and Mind,* ed. J. T. Fraser. Madison, Ct.: Int. Univ. Press, pp. 9–14.

FREUD, S. (1989). Project for a scientific psychology. *S.E.,* 1:283–397.

—— (1900). The interpretation of dreams. *S.E.,* 4 & 5.

FRIEDLANDER, S. R. (1991). "Why do (don't) you ask?" *Amer. J. Psychoanal.* 51:117–135.

GABBARD, G. O. (1982). The exit line. *J. Amer. Psychoanal. Assn.,* 30:579–598.

GIFFORD, S. (1980). The prisoner of time. *Annu. Psychoanal.,* 8:131–154.

GREEN, A. (1975). The analyst, symbolization, and absence in the analytic setting. *Int. J. Psychoanal.,* 56:1–22.

—— (1986). *On Private Madness.* Madison, Ct.: Int. Univ. Press.

GREENSON, R. R. (1974). The decline and fall of the 50-minute hour. *J. Amer. Psychoanal. Assn.,* 22:785–791.

GUNN, D. (1988). *Psychoanalysis and Fiction.* Cambridge: Cambridge Univ. Press.

HAMBURG, P. (1991). Interpretation and empathy. *Int. J. Psychoanal.,* 72:347–361.

HARTOCOLLIS, P. (1983). *Time and Timelessness.* Madison, Ct.: Int. Univ. Press.

JAMESON, F. (1977). Imaginary and symbolic in Lacan. *Yale French Studies,* 55/56:338–395.

KNAPP, P. H. (1974). Segmentation and structure in psychoanalysis. *J. Amer. Psychoanal. Assn.,* 22:14–36.

Kojève, A. (1939). *Introduction to the Reading of Hegel.* New York: Basic Books, 1969.

Kurtz, S. A. (1988). The psychoanalysis of time. *J. Amer. Psychoanal. Assn.,* 36:985–1004.

Lacan, J. (1945). Logical time and the assertion of anticipated certainty. In *Écrits.* Paris: Seuil, 1966, pp. 197–213.

—— (1953). The neurotic's individual myth. *Psychoanal. Q.,* 48:405–425, 1979.

—— (1953–55). *The Seminar of Jacques Lacan: Books I & II,* ed. J.-A. Miller. Cambridge: Cambridge Univ. Press, 1988.

—— (1956a). Seminar on "The Purloined Letter." In *French Freud. Yale French Studies,* 48:38–72, 1972.

—— (1956b). Fetishism. In *Perversions,* ed. S. Lorand & M. Balint. New York: Gramercy Books, pp. 265–276.

—— (1964). *The Four Fundamental Concepts of Psycho-Analysis.* London: Penguin, 1977.

—— (1970). Of structure as an inmixing of an otherness prerequisite to any subject whatsoever. In *The Structuralist Controversy,* ed. R. Macksey & E. Donato. Baltimore: Johns Hopkins Univ. Press, pp. 186–200.

—— (1977). *Écrits: A Selection.* London: Routledge.

Langs, R. (1976). *The Therapeutic Interaction,* vol. 2. New York: Aronson.

Leavy, S. (1983). Speaking in tongues. *Psychoanal. Q.,* 52:34–55.

Loewald, H. W. (1980). The experience of time. In *Papers on Psychoanalysis.* New Haven: Yale Univ. Press, pp. 138–147.

Macey, D. (1988). *Lacan in Contexts.* New York & London: Verso.

Modell, A. H. (1984). *Psychoanalysis in a New Context.* Madison, Ct.: Int. Univ. Press.

Morris, J. (1989). Time experience and transference. *J. Amer. Psychoanal. Assn.,* 31:651–676.

Muller, J. P. (1988). Negation in "The Purloined Letter." In *The Purloined Poe,* ed. J. P. Muller & W. J. Richardson. Baltimore: Johns Hopkins Univ. Press, pp. 343–368.

—— (1989). Lacan and Kohut. In *Self Psychology,* ed. D. Detrick & S. Detrick. Hillsdale, N.J.: Analytic Press, pp. 363–394.

—— & Richardson, W. J. (1982). *Lacan and Language.* Madison, Ct.: Int. Univ. Press.

—— & —— (1988). *The Purloined Poe.* Baltimore: Johns Hopkins Univ. Press.

Ogden, T. (1982). *Projective Identification and Psychotherapeutic Experience.* Northvale, N.J.: Aronson.

Peraldi, F. (1988). A note on time in "The Purloined Letter." In *The Purloined Poe,* ed. J. P. Muller & W. J. Richardson. Baltimore: Johns Hopkins Univ. Press, pp. 335–342.

Pollock, G. H. (1971). One time, death, and immortality. *Psychoanal. Q.,* 40:435–446.

RAGLAND-SULLIVAN, E. (1986). *Jacques Lacan and the Philosophy of Psychoanalysis.* Urbana, Ill.: Univ. Illinois Press.

SCHNEIDERMAN, S., ed. & tr. (1980). *Returning to Freud.* New Haven: Yale Univ. Press.

SEARLES, H. F. (1965). *Collected Papers on Schizophrenia and Related Subjects.* New York: Int. Univ. Press.

SEGAL, H. (1986). Fear of death. In *The Works of Hanna Segal.* London: Free Association Books, pp. 173–182.

SMITH, J. H. (1990). Ego psychology and the language of Lacan. *Psychoanal. & Contemp. Thought,* 15:143–159.

––––– (1991). *Arguing with Lacan.* New Haven: Yale Univ. Press.

––––– & KERRIGAN, W., eds. (1983). *Interpreting Lacan.* New Haven: Yale Univ. Press.

SPERO, M. H. (1990). Psychoanalytic reflections on a particular form of language distortion. *Psychoanal. Q.,* 59:54–74.

––––– (1992). Psychoanalytic reflections on language distortion and empathic listening. *Amer. J. Psychoanal.,* 52:227–245.

TERR, L. C. (1984). Time and trauma. *Psychoanal. Study Child,* 39:633–665.

TURKLE, S. (1982). Lacan and America. In *Introducing Psychoanalytic Theory,* ed. S. Gilman. New York: Brunner/Mazel, pp. 240–254.

WILDEN, A. (1981). *Speech and Language in Psychoanalysis.* Baltimore: Johns Hopkins Univ. Press.

WINNICOTT, D. W. (1949). Hate in the counter-transference. *Int. J. Psychoanal.,* 30:69–74.

––––– (1965). *The Maturational Processes and the Facilitating Environment.* New York: Int. Univ. Press, 1965.

––––– (1971). *Playing and Reality.* New York: Tavistock.

# DEVELOPMENTAL AND CLINICAL PROBLEMS

# The Social Matrix of Aggression

## Enactments and Representations of Loving and Hating in the First Years of Life

LINDA C. MAYES, M.D., and
DONALD J. COHEN, M.D.

> There is nothing we value and
> hunt and cultivate and strive
> to draw to us but in some hour
> we turn and rend it.
>
> EMERSON, 1836

*In this paper, we build on a developing body of work that addresses the various contributions to the child's emerging definition of self in the first five years of life. Described is the role of aggression in the shaping of the child's predominant modes of viewing and experiencing the world. How aggression toward another mixes with desire for another in the formation of early capacities for object relatedness is a central question for any developmental theory of aggression, for aggression is first experienced, shaped, refined, and remodeled in the context of loving relations. Studies from related disciplines provide observational data about how aggression is modified in the first five to six years of life and how the capacity to interpret the intentions of others is crucial to those modifications. Under-*

Dr. Mayes is the Arnold Gesell Associate Professor of Child Development, Pediatrics and Psychology in the Yale Child Study Center and is a candidate in the Western New England Institute for Psychoanalysis. Dr. Cohen, director of the Child Study Center, is the Irving B. Harris Professor of Child Psychiatry, Psychology and Pediatrics and is a training and supervising analyst in the Western New England Institute for Psychoanalysis. The authors gratefully acknowledge their discussions on this topic with their colleagues Steven Marans and Albert J. Solnit. Finally, this paper is dedicated to Dr. Sally Provence whose work exemplifies how careful observation of infants and their parents enriches our understanding of inner lives.

145

*standing the intentions of others relates also to the capacity to attribute affects, beliefs, and other mental states to others, a capacity referred to elsewhere as a theory of mind. The ability to reflect upon thoughts and feelings in oneself and others provides children with a fuller range of responses to their own and others' perceived aggression. Finally, external experiences of violence, abuse, and deprivation influence the child's experience of his own and others' aggression and prevent the normal modulation of aggression in the social matrix.*

CONSIDERATIONS OF AGGRESSION READILY LEAD TO POLARITIES—LOVE and hate, war and peace, creativity and destruction, synthesis and fragmentation, affection and hostility. Dichotomies such as these common in the popular world view of aggressivity parallel the prevailing classic psychoanalytic premise that aggression is an instinctual drive directed toward destruction and ultimately death. Posed as the counterforce to life-sustaining libidinal instincts, aggression and its apparent drive derivatives are a ubiquitous presence in day-to-day life; and the manifestations of aggression occasion respect and admiration as well as dread and caution in the observer and often the aggressor. Fictional and historical accounts as well as stories from the consulting room are replete with tragic individuals apparently driven by a dark, aggressive force impelling them to destroy much that is good and restorative in their own lives and those of close and distant others. As Proust's Marcel observed, pondering once again the tortuous interminglings of love and hate, "At the heart of our friendly or purely social relations, there lurks a hostility momentarily cured but recurring by fits and starts."

However, despite its ubiquity, psychoanalytic considerations of aggression have regularly led to theoretical quandaries.[1] The recurrent

---

1. As in other areas of psychoanalytic concern, terminological issues often have clouded the discussion of aggression. We shall try to distinguish the three major domains of psychoanalytic thinking in relation to aggression as (a) what can be *observed;* (b) what the individual is *experiencing,* not always consciously; and (c) what can be *inferred* and theoretically explained about the child's mental functioning.

Thus, we will refer to (a) *aggressivity* (or aggressive acts and behavior) in relation to what is observable as assertive, destructive, hurtful, etc., in a child's ongoing behavior; (b) to *aggressive feelings and mental states* (including fantasies, affects, wishes, thoughts, motives, and intents) in relation to what the child clearly or apparently is experiencing; and (c) to *aggression* (including aggressive drives, instincts, forces, impulses, striving, derivatives and the like) in relation to the psychoanalytic theory of mental organization and functioning.

We hope that the context, as well, will make the domain of discussion clear. There is obviously, and for good reasons, a slippery slope connecting these three domains of discourse; behavior, feelings, and inferred processes are intimately related, and it is easy dilemmas involve a number of issues each of which reflect in part the problematic legacy of Freud's dual instinct model as put forth in *Beyond the Pleasure Principle* (1920). Many analytic theorists have highlighted the inherent problems in considering aggression as an instinctual force on equal theoretical as well as functional footing with libidinal drives (e.g., Gillespie, 1971) or in directly equating aggression either with destruction (e.g., Stepansky, 1977) or with a death instinct (e.g., Stone, 1971). In addition, others have emphasized the apparent paradox that aggression is essential for individual and species survival despite its inherently hostile, destructive, perhaps fatal implications (e.g., Spitz, 1965; Stechler and Halton, 1987). Several have proposed different categories of aggression which allow for constructive derivations such as mastery as well as the more traditionally implied hostile aspects (e.g., Marcovitz, 1982; Parens, 1979). Those struggling to provide a biological grounding for the aggressive instinct that parallels the biology of libidinal drives have linked aggression with physical states of frustration and tension (Dollard et al., 1939) and in so doing, have vested it with a less negative cast.

Perhaps what has been most troubling theoretically for psychoanalysis is the different nature of aggression in the developing young child compared, for example, to the rageful, melancholic, suicidal or masochistic adult. In very young children, aggressivity is more frequently and directly expressed, less apparently destructive or hostile, and more apparently pleasurable or constructive at least in the first four or five years of life. Indeed, from the perspective of the child analyst, "aggression looms larger than sex in child analysis, dominates the child patient's acting out and transference behaviour" (A. Freud, 1972, p. 168). Yet a developmentally framed theory of aggression exists only in bits and pieces in various approaches to early development.

In this paper, we address one specific aspect of aggression in early development—the role of aggression in the child's moves toward individuation (e.g., Mahler et al., 1975; Winnicott, 1950) and in the shaping of the child's sense of self. How aggression toward another mixes with desire for another in the formation of early capacities for object relatedness is a central question for any developmental theory of aggression, for, at its core, aggression is directed toward others whether they be in the individual's internal or external world. The child's instinctual strivings for both loving and hating are given form and mean-

---

to switch from one level of discourse to another. Yet, we are especially interested in describing apparent paradoxes and discontinuities in the relations among these domains during the course of development and at particular moments for individual children.

ing in the child's earliest relationships with important others (Loewald, 1978); and early aggressive strivings are modified and transformed in the context of those relationships (e.g., Solnit, 1972). Conversely, the very presence of aggressive strivings in the child's relationship with others makes possible deepening libidinal ties, that is, aggression is a necessary component of the child's capacity to love others and to hold others in mind in their absence. As Downey (1984) and Loewald (1960) have also indicated, aggression makes it possible for the child to be a separate individual who is then capable of the identifications, introjections, and partial mergings so characteristic of love relationships. The very separateness fostered and facilitated by the child's early aggressivity allows the child the capacity to be close without losing his hard-won, separate sense of self. Thus, the early developmental transformations in both the frequency and character of the child's aggressivity reflect, at least in part, the child's individuation and emerging self-definition.

Most importantly, we outline how the child's maturing neurocognitive capacities for attributing affects, beliefs, and other mental states to others not only is a part of self-object differentiation (e.g., Mayes and Cohen, 1992, 1993; Mayes et al., 1993) but also contributes to the transformation of aggressive as well as libidinal strivings into the balanced form essential for mature object relations. The capacity to reflect upon thoughts and feelings in oneself and others provides children with a fuller range of responses to their own and others' perceived aggression. The mental capacities for remembering, for fantasy, and for trial action allow the child to contain the aggressive act or wish in thought and attribute aggressive motives and affects to others while at the same time maintaining both his libidinal ties to the other as well as his separateness. With an emerging appreciation of the distinction between the external world of action and perception and the inner, subjective world of thoughts and fantasies, aggressive and loving feelings are potentially more peaceably intermingled since hate contained in fantasy, thoughts, and feelings allows at least the possibility that important others remain intact.

## PSYCHOANALYTIC VIEW OF AGGRESSION

At the conclusion of the 27th International Congress, Anna Freud (1972) observed that frequent debates and discussions to that point had failed to remove "uncertainties concerning the status of aggression in the theory of drives, or the clarification of some urgent problems, such as the part played by aggression in normal infantile development; its involvement with the various agencies in the psychic structure; its role for character formation" (1972, p. 163). She went on to outline the reasons that aggression appeared so problematic to analysts despite its centrality in everyday life and its inescapable presence in the lives of young children. Aggression explicitly entered analytic theory late. Long after the erotic, relationship-building, libidinal drive had been securely placed in the context of mental functioning, Freud (1920) introduced the dualism of life and death to instinctual life.

Like a younger sibling being compared to all the achievements and characteristics of the older sibling, the aggressive drive was inevitably shaped to match the libidinal component. As a separate drive standing in parallel with the well-defined libidinal instinct, aggression needed to meet the criteria of stage development with specific body zones and to have a source, aim, and object—criteria which have been difficult to fulfill. The reasoning was essentially backward. Seeking to fit clinical observations of aggression into the framework of libidinal instinct theory did not validate aggression as a parallel, but independent drive (A. Freud, 1972; Solnit, 1972). The presumed symmetry was misleading and inaccurate and led to the conceptually troubling legacy of a parallel, separate instinct that was nevertheless not quite parallel inasmuch as the aim was manifestly not pleasure or tension reduction but fragmentation and ultimately destruction.

Such was the dilemma for understanding aggression in children where destruction and hostile intent, although present, were not apparently primary. Possibly constructive, positive functions for aggression in early psychic life were obscured by the negative valence. Understanding how such a dichotomy evolved in psychoanalytic theory is not within the scope of this paper (see, for example, Stepansky, 1977), but it is useful to explore briefly the role of aggression in psychoanalysis before it was given explicit, elevated status as a separate instinct.

Aggression was a vital, albeit implicit, presence in early psychoanalytic theory as one of the large number of functions dedicated to preserving and protecting the intactness of the self, a role that more closely approximates clinical observations of aggressivity in early childhood. Before the structural theory, aggressive impulses were subsumed under derivatives of a drive for sexual mastery (Freud, 1905). By 1915, aggressive strivings were singled out more conspicuously as primary components of a drive for mastery or self-preservation and self-nonself differentiation. However, this singular constructive place for aggression was short-lived for within the decade, with the introduction of the structural theory, the ego was no longer equipped with drives of its own (Bibring, 1941; Hartmann, 1948). With *Beyond the*

*Pleasure Principle* (1920), Freud attempted to deal with a dilemma increasingly evident in the consulting room as well as the world at large— manifestly hostile acts were not self-preservative and patients were often caught in self-destructive and self-punitive trends and cycles of self-blaming, unrelenting depression (Brenner, 1971). These repeatedly occurring manifestations of aggression in the unconscious minds of individuals in analysis in the decade of 1910–20 seemed beyond any theories of a self-protective function. Many have speculated too upon how much to emphasize the impact of either the carnage of the World War or of his daughter's death on Freud's changing view of aggression (Gay, 1988). However, in ultimately and despairingly insisting that there was an eternal antagonism between the demands of human instinctual nature and those of civilization, Freud remained true to his nineteenth-century Enlightenment views and to his profound Darwinian influence (Rochlin, 1982). In 1930, physically ill and psychologically resigned, he wrote, "I adopt the standpoint . . . that the inclination to aggression is an original, self-subsisting instinctual disposition in man, and I return to my view that it constitutes the greatest impediment to civilization" (p. 122).

In this crucial transition, Freud chose not to accept aggression in and of itself as constructively essential for normal psychic development. He placed it outside not only the pleasure principle but, perhaps more importantly, outside the shaping influences of early experience and outside any developmental framework. But, paradoxically, as Freud marked aggression the darkly primitive, ever-present destructive force always threatening to disrupt or destroy more constructive, progressive developmental gains, his students and contemporaries continued to place great weight on the role of aggression in fantasy and action as a central shaping factor in early character formation, as Freud himself had done in an earlier period (1909). For example, Abraham (1923, 1925), Reich (1933), and others grounded the analytic theory of character formation in the earliest body-based aspects of infantile experience related to aggressive, not libidinal, derivatives (e.g., the paradigmatic relations between biting or oral sadism in the infant or anal sadism in the toddler and later character structure).

Others too struggled to preserve the dual instinct model while at the same time maintaining a more constructive role for aggression in the analytic theory of early character formation (e.g., Bibring, 1941; Fenichel, 1945; Waelder, 1956). Like Freud in the earlier theories (1905), Hartmann et al. (1949) argued for the role of aggression in object-preserving needs and for the importance of the modification of aggression through fusion with libidinal instincts. In addition, they suggested there were at least three other routes for the modulation of aggression (sublimation, displacement to other objects, and restriction of the aim) so that aggressive impulses were available for psychic structure formation (e.g., superego). With the albeit somewhat difficult concept of neutralization, aggressive strivings became available again for the service of adaptive development, and a measure of ego integrity and strength was the ability to "neutralize large quantities of aggression" (p. 24).

For those analysts steeped in the tradition of infant observation and direct work with very young children, aggression is an evident and early presence in the lives of very young infants and has been considered central, if not paramount, to the infant's differentiating sense of self (Klein, 1957). Aggressivity and aggressive feelings are rooted in the earliest and most basic biologically determined patterns of behavior designed to protect the child and bring others to him in times of need. For example, the infant's cry is almost always perceived by adults as unpleasant and aversive yet indicative of need, and it generally arouses in the parent a sense of urgency to respond (Lester and Boukydis, 1984). Similarly, when infants look away during stressful interactions, they actively block out the situation which is distressing or overwhelming (e.g., Mayes and Carter, 1990). Or early motor activity and motility are manifestations of the nondestructive aspects of aggression that are a part of the process of experiencing self as effective and autonomous (Greenacre, 1971; Parens, 1979; Spitz, 1969)—the toddler's vigorous struggling or running away while being dressed or his gleefully and persistently pushing a toy off a table. Motoric activity also contributes to self-definition and the individuation process for when the infant's and young child's vigorous muscular activity is met by normal opposition during moment-to-moment physical care routines, the child gains a sense of body and of what is real (Winnicott, 1950).

These and other body-based modes of protecting self and expressing one's own effectiveness become the persistent, readily available schemas for how the child (and adult) experiences and responds to internal or external senses of danger, real or imagined. If the psychoanalytic theory of object relatedness has its biological rootedness in the infant's adaptiveness to perceive, react to, and process socially based information (Mayes and Cohen, 1993), the psychoanalytic theory of character formation is firmly grounded in these early modes of expression of aggression (Cohen, 1990). Furthermore, when the parent in Winnicott's (1950, 1969) terms "survives" the infant's earliest aggressive (e.g., motoric) strivings, he or she becomes more differentiated as an external object with whom the infant has a shared reality. In this sense, aggression precedes a capacity for loving (Downey, 1984). Aggression more than the internalization of consistent nurturing fosters individuation, self-object differentiation, and the young child's recognition of object permanence and an external reality shared with the parent (Winnicott, 1945, 1969, 1971). With such recognition, a sense of trust in the object develops and a feeling that it is safer to hate and rebel against a mother whom the child also loves.

How the child's experiences with others further shape the process of the transformation of aggressive motives and fantasies into more complex and adaptive ways of relating to the world represents a later contribution to the analytic theory of aggression and character formation—and a central paradigm shift in the theory of instincts. Loewald (1978) places the origin of instinctual life—both aggressive and libidinal—in the social context of interactions between mother and infant. The infant experiences himself as more or less aggressive in relation to the mother's experience of those and other behaviors just cited. When the 4-month-old infant vigorously sucking at the breast abruptly bites, how much the mother reacts to her unexpected pain as an aggressive attack versus a surprising but notable measure of her child's assertiveness and mastery will influence how the infant experiences such moments later on. Or when the 18-month-old about to run off to explore a new place or person looks back for his mother's reaction (e.g., social referencing; Sorce et al., 1985), his excitement and pleasure will be reinforced by his mother's encouragement or dampened by her look of fear or anger. Stated another way, how much separation and moves toward autonomy or mastery come to be experienced intrapsychically by the child as pleasurable or aggressive and hurtful depends in large part on the parent's experience and reaction.[2]

Thus, from the beginning of infancy, any aggressive act or fantasy is embedded in a social matrix. What an individual child comes to interpret and experience as aggressive and later patterns of assertiveness, self-protectiveness, and the modulation of anger and hostility toward others are rooted in these earliest interactions with others. Likewise, how much aggressivity is experienced by the individual as essential, positive, and adaptive and how much aggressive feelings and wishes in oneself and others are feared and dreaded is given initial form early in

2. Note the critical difference in this position and that, for example, of Klein (1957) who placed aggression at the center of character formation but gave almost singular responsibility to the infant with his individual level of hunger and greed (real and fantasied) and his recognition of the consequences of his insatiable needs on the mother. In this view, the mother's reaction plays little role in shaping and channeling the infant's experience in fantasy of his aggressive, assertive desires (Cohen, 1990).

the first 12 to 18 months. To be sure, aggression and aggressivity are closely tied to biological processes. There are basic neurobiological contributions to individual variations in the degree of hostile, destructive impulses, and at some point in situations of danger and mortal threat, protective biological response processes (e.g., fight or flight, rageful attack) take over both for children and for adults (Alpert et al., 1981). Indeed, driving away predators and protective destructiveness are fundamental biological processes present in all species. But what comes to be symbolized and represented in the human mind as predatory or dangerous, what kinds of events are perceived as threatening and hostile, and how aggressivity assumes adaptive and nonadaptive forms is defined and refined in the context of the child's earliest experiences. The basic biology of assertiveness and protective destructiveness is channeled by object relations, and these early patterns of experiencing the aggressivity of self and others as constructive or destructive remain available as mental representations throughout life (Loewald, 1978).

On the other hand, because much of the psychoanalytic view of aggression in early childhood implicitly focuses on the child's internal experiences of aggression—his own and others', what has been less often addressed has been (1) the specific nature of the transformations of aggressive behaviors in the first five years (e.g., are there observable differences in the types of aggressive behaviors in young children that permit a more differentiated developmental theory of how aggressive patterns are established early in life?); and (2) how maturing cognitive capacities for abstraction, symbolization, and fantasy underlie the child's ability to understand and differentiate his own and others' aggressive intentions and states. Such capacities are the neurocognitive underpinnings that make possible the transformation of early aggressive strivings contextualized by the child's experiences with important others. Studies of aggression from disciplines outside psychoanalysis provide some insight into these issues.

### OBSERVATIONAL STUDIES OF AGGRESSION IN CHILDREN

From the late 1920s on (e.g., Goodenough, 1931; Green, 1933), aggressivity in early childhood was a topic of empirical interest. In contrast to the psychoanalytic views of aggression in unconscious fantasy life, particularly from the views of the British school (e.g., Klein, 1957; Winnicott, 1945, 1950), empirical studies of aggressivity examined the external conditions and manifestations of aggression in the child's early behaviors. Taking their cue not only from drive theory and models of

frustration/tension release (Dollard et al., 1939) but also from etholog-
ical studies of animal behavior (Lorenz, 1966), many investigators
sought to understand what role aggressive behavior played in the
child's earliest socially adaptive development and how the child's environment shaped and modified aggressive behaviors (for a review, see
Parke and Slaby, 1983). For example, was rough-and-tumble play, seen
in the young of many species, an anlage of the older child's and adult's
capacities to deal with aggressive interactions with their peers (Harlow
and Harlow, 1965)? Similarly, the tantrums of early childhood were
proposed as a template for children's learning the efficacy both of
aggressive action and inhibition (Etzel and Gewirtz, 1967).

Investigators attempting to understand the roots of aggressive behavior in early childhood found that aggressivity was less often regarded as the result of a primary drive or instinct and more often, at
least in its earliest manifestations, as a more or less differentiated response to frustration of wishes and needs or to the demands of the social world on the child. For infants, these frustrations arose out of physical needs, while for older children disappointing interactions with
others were sufficient sources of frustrating experiences. Stimulus-
response models guided much of the early work on childhood aggressive behavior, and the transformations of aggressivity with maturation
were viewed through the frame of behavior modification and learning
theory (Bandura, 1973). Whether or not aggressive behaviors led a
child to his or her goal and how children responded to the evidence of
their own destructiveness or the overt pain of the injured person were
viewed as paramount events in the shaping of aggressivity. Later
studies placed childhood aggression in the context of social cognition
and in parallel with the emergence of capacities for empathy in the first
three to five years of life (Cummings et al., 1986; Dodge, 1986; Quiggle
et al., 1992). The child's ability to understand, respond to, or identify
with the person injured by an overtly aggressive act modifies acceptable
patterns of aggressivity. The social cognition model in particular permits study of how the child's social information-processing capacities
across development alters his or her own aggressive behaviors as well as
his responses to those of others.

Regardless of the theoretical frame of reference, a central contribution of empirical studies of aggressive behavior has been the various
attempts to clarify what does and does not constitute aggression in
young children. At the very least, from the standpoint of observational
studies, aggressive behavior is usually assumed to involve injury (real,
anticipated, or imagined) to a person or inanimate object (Buss, 1961;
Fesbach, 1964), but any definition of the phenomenology of aggression

in early childhood needs to consider at least five definitional issues: (1) What are the behavioral manifestations of aggression in early childhood and do these manifestations change with maturation and with the responses of the environment? (2) Are aggressive acts directed toward persons different from acts involving inanimate objects? (3) What are the instigating events leading to aggressive acts, e.g., deprivation, personal injury or attack, humiliation, or fright? (4) Are aggressive acts that are apparently responsive to the aggression of another different from aggressive behavior instigated by the child? (5) What are the goals of an aggressive act in children? How can aggressive behavior motivated by the intention to harm and destroy be distinguished from aggressive acts in which the goal is not injury but the achievement of a manifestly nonaggressive intent (e.g., to gain another's attention, to reclaim a favorite toy, to win in a game).

A number of observational studies address different aspects of these questions and have documented changes in the overt behavioral manifestations of aggression in the first five to six years of life. However, it must be noted that despite decades of study, there is still a relative paucity of data to address the issues of both developmental transformations and individual differences in aggressive behavior in preschool children (see Parke and Slaby, 1983). Aggressivity in very young children is most often manifested physically by hitting, biting, shoving, or kicking, but physical aggressivity decreases markedly after the third year of life, while verbal aggressivity (e.g., shouting, name-calling) increases between ages 2 and 4 (Goodenough, 1931). Generally, all types of aggressive acts decrease as children approach 4 to 5 years of age (Cummings et al., 1986, 1989). In comparing 4- to 6- and 6- to 7-year-olds, Hartup (1974) found that younger children were more aggressive than older children and that the difference was due to more frequent incidences in younger children of aggressivity focused on acquiring or reclaiming desired objects, that is, in asserting needs and wants.

Similarly, within the 2- to 4-year-old age group, struggles over acquiring objects decrease as the child matures (see review in Hay, 1984). Perhaps, most importantly, when aggressive acts are divided into initiated and responsive, the incidence of child-initiated aggressivity decreases as children become older, a finding interpreted as consistent with the social learning theory of aggression (Dodge, 1980; Dodge and Coie, 1987). With age, children learn what types of aggressivity are permissible in what type of situations (Cummings et al., 1989). By school age, aggressivity is more often personally directed, is instigated by threats to the child's self-esteem, and is more often overtly intended to harm the offending other. Aggressive acts intended to gain or preserve possession in which injury to another is only secondary are far less common for school-aged children (Hartup, 1974). Thus, paradoxically, as the child matures, aggressivity becomes less frequent but more often socially directed and apparently motivated by an intent to harm or injure. The instigating actions are also less often overt attacks by another, such as a toy being stolen, and more often involve perceived violations in the rules and expectations of social interactions (e.g., insults, criticism, ridicule).

Throughout these observations, however, the issue of intent or some other motivational construct remains problematic. As suggested above, the goal of an aggressive act may be as much to gain a wished-for person or achievement or fulfill an ambition as it is to harm and injure. For example, when the toddler hurls a toy across the room breaking both the toy and damaging the wall, the act is overtly aggressive but may or may not be aggressive in its intent to do damage or harm. On the other hand, if intent is excluded from the definition, certain acts that are manifestly but nonintentionally aggressive will nevertheless be considered aggressive and hostile. When a mother quickly grabs and holds her child tightly to prevent him or her from dashing out into a busy intersection, the act is manifestly aggressive though intentionally protective.

In answer to this dilemma, a number of observational schemas have attempted to distinguish various states of intentionality in aggressive acts and have divided aggressive behavior into "hostile" and "instrumental" aggressivity (Buss, 1966; Fesbach, 1964). The former is usually person-directed and requires inference by the child that the other person has behaved with the intention to hurt or harm. In acts of instrumental aggressivity, the intent is to achieve a nonaggressive goal. In the course of the act, harm to another may occur, but this is not the original intent of the act. Thus, manifestly aggressive behaviors may serve the purposes of assertiveness and protection of self and others as well as the expression of hostility and the intent to do harm—again the dilemma of constructive versus destructive goals of aggression. For young children, it is instrumental aggressivity that diminishes as the child approaches school age while acts of hostile aggressivity become more prominent (Hartup, 1974). However, the distinctions between instrumental and hostile aggressive actions are easily blurred. Both may occur in the same interchange—the mother's vigorous hold on her struggling toddler is person-directed but is not with intent to do harm. Moreover, hostile aggressive acts are not without instrumental value. Attacking a teasing, taunting child restores the self-esteem of the initially injured other, a goal as constructive and worthy as the young child's vigorously seeking to regain his lost toy.

The deeper issue in distinguishing the goals involved in an aggressive act is understanding how children come to be able to judge the intent of their peers and of adults when they feel aggressed upon and what are the given conditions for any individual child that lead to his experiencing his own or another's actions as aggressive. The judgment of hostile or injurious intent is not confined to observational paradigms dedicated to the categorization of aggressive acts but is also a fundamental aspect of the child's knowing how to respond to the perceived aggressive act of another. Children and adults commonly make errors in judgment regarding the level of intention to do injury and harm that is contained in another's actions. Distraught mothers interpret their child's lusty "no" as a call to battle just as many lovers count the hours between telephone calls as irrefutable evidence of intended, wounding rejection. Some children and adults hear only the aggressive intent in an ironic or sarcastic statement and respond in kind, while for others only a direct and sudden physical attack is perceived as threatening and dangerous.

Developmental shifts in the attribution of aggressive intent have been described for school-aged children. Boys 7, 9, and 12 years of age were presented with a variety of aggressive incidents, some involving a child accidentally attacking another, while others were more evidently intentional (Shantz and Vogdanoff, 1973). The younger the child, the less able he was to distinguish between levels of intention and accident and the more likely he was to react similarly to accidental or intentional provocation. When children are presented with unambiguous information about the intentions behind the aggressive act, even preschool children are able to alter their response based on the aggressor's intentions (Rule et al., 1974). But in naturalistic situations where cues are often subtle and ambiguous, the younger the child, the more difficulty he or she has in inferring intentionality and using such inference to guide his or her behavior (Rotenberg, 1980).

Understanding another's intentionality in any action reflects a complex series of neurocognitive operations that mature between 3 and 5 years of age and involve the child's emerging understanding that the actions of others are a reflection of the feelings, beliefs, and thoughts of others, that is, that mind or mental states guide actions and behaviors. Appreciating and interpreting the intentionality of another is a part of children's acquiring an understanding of their own and others' mental processes. Elsewhere, we have described how the capacity to

understand the notion of a subjective mental world and the link between that world and the world of directly perceivable action also
makes possible both the increasing differentiation of self and other
and the use of the mental process of imagination in the service of
deepening capacities for relatedness (Mayes and Cohen, 1992, 1993;
Mayes et al., 1993). Being able not only to attribute aggressive intentional states to another but also to attribute aggressive intentions different from one's own reflects another aspect of what is now frequently
labeled the child's emerging theory of mind (reviewed in Astington et
al., 1988; Astington and Gopnik, 1991; Wellman, 1990; and Baron-
Cohen et al., 1992).

## THEORIES OF MIND AND THE MODULATION OF AGGRESSION

In the first three to five years of life, the child's orientation to the world
of others dramatically shifts. He gradually acquires some understanding that being separate from another is fundamentally related, in part,
to having a private, subjective world defined by acts of mind. He is
aware not only of other minds but more importantly that the mind of
others (e.g., their beliefs and feeling states) may be different from his
own. With such an appreciation, the child understands that he and
others act in ways that are interpretable on the basis of these thoughts,
beliefs, desires, and feelings, that is, we do something because we love
(or hate) someone or believe that another person feels toward us in a
certain way. Achieving such understanding reflects a major shift in the
child's capacity for metarepresentation for now he is able to allow one
thing to stand for another in his private, subjective world and to attribute states he cannot directly perceive to others in his world.

Before the achievement of an appreciation of the mind of other
persons, the child's understandings of the motives of others toward
him is not differentiated. He believes that they act because he needs or
wants, and failures on the parts of others are experienced as depriving,
frustrating and threatening. As the child begins to understand the
notion of mind, he is able to explain the other's emotions and attitudes
and to act or feel accordingly. The 5-year-old oedipal-aged child's move
from dyadic to triadic relationships is facilitated by his newly emerging
capacity to attribute complex feelings, beliefs, and intentions to multiple others, which in turn makes it possible for him to be concerned
about the differing, often conflicting, beliefs and feelings of more than
one other person in his world. In the act of trying to understand or
image the mental world of other persons, the child not only demarcates
an inner world of subjectivity that is understood to be different from

the objective, veridical world, but he also creates an inner world in which people behave toward him because of certain feelings which he imagines them to have (Mayes and Cohen, 1992). Similarly, an understanding of the other's mind allows the child to imagine the other's feelings toward him and to envision how things might be were such feelings and beliefs different.

As he begins to appreciate the subjective nature of the mental world, the 4- to 5-year-old child acquires an understanding that, stated most simply, things are not always as they seem (Mayes and Cohen, 1993). In that context, he recognizes the notion of false belief—that someone may act on the basis of a belief that is presently incorrect or false because external conditions have changed (e.g., looking for something where we saw it even though the object has been moved in the interim) (Moses and Flavell, 1990; Wellman and Bartsch, 1988; Wimmer and Perner, 1983). Exactly because he is acquiring an understanding that individuals may hold to different beliefs even if the external, directly perceivable conditions appear the same, he is capable of jokes and of deception (Chandler et al., 1989). Children between 4 and 5 years of age also become able to understand that others (as well as themselves) may hold to two or more beliefs that are manifestly contradictory. They understand that someone may want or desire something very much but believe incorrectly that he knows the exact location or way to satisfy his desire (Mayes et al., 1992). Similarly, they gradually acquire the understanding that persons may feel differently about the same person at different times, or that it is possible to both like someone and be angry at them, to love and to hurt the same person.

Knowing that beliefs and feelings do not always correspond to externally perceivable conditions is crucial in being able to appreciate varying levels of intentionality in an aggressive act. For example, in a group of preschool children, there often are vigorous, competitive efforts to be close to a favorite teacher during story time. When one child pushes another out of special place, the 5-year-old child is better able to appreciate the teacher's explanations that his friend did not mean to hurt him but only wanted the special place for himself. His 3-year-old counterpart would have far greater difficulty understanding or acting on such an explanation and would be far more likely to respond to the aggressive act in kind. Similarly, allowing for the possibility that manifestly contradictory beliefs, affects, or thoughts may be held by and about the same person is a fundamental step toward the capacity for modulating one's own aggressivity and understanding another's aggressive intents. Appreciating that another may at one moment behave with the apparent intent to hurt and at the next moment be apologetic and loving allows the child to hold in closer proximity aggressive and loving feel-ings. That these capacities emerge around the same time observational studies report marked changes in the nature of children's aggressive behavior may be viewed as converging evidence for the necessary role of a capacity for attributing intentions to others in the transformation of early aggressive strivings.

In addition, the appreciation of a mental subjective world in others as well as in oneself allows the child the space of fantasy in which to play with the transformations of aggressive strivings. Feelings of neglect or disappointment that for the toddler may have contributed directly to the physical enactments of aggression may now be tempered in the child's fantasy life. Hostile, angry, destructive feelings experienced first with important others may be placed at least temporarily in the security of imaginary play and various solutions to such feelings tried on while the child is safely protected by his loving ties to the same person with whom he is angry. Parenthetically, it is particularly in this way that libidinal ties help transform and modulate aggressive strivings by providing safety as it were during the storm (Solnit, 1972). Within psychoanalysis, a fundamental premise of unconscious fantasy life is that the attribution of hostile, destructive intents first occurs with one's primary objects (e.g., Klein, 1957; Winnicott, 1945, 1950). The under-standing of a notion of mind that allows for contradictory mental states allows the child at least the mental capacity to hold both hate and love side by side in his representations of important others. With the capac-ity to allow for differing beliefs and feelings in one's own and others' minds, there is the possibility that what could previously be contained only in bad and good part objects can now be more readily mingled.

## CLINICAL ILLUSTRATION

Sophie, aged 38 months, entered analysis four times a week because of stool withholding, a symptom that her parents felt had worsened as Sophie had had increasing difficulties with separation from either of them for almost any occasion (Mayes and Cohen, 1993). A bright, verbally gifted child, Sophie seemed increasingly thwarted and con-fused by the many levels of separation demands being maturationally thrust upon her. During her first year of analysis, Sophie frequently and abruptly interrupted her play with angry outbursts of yelling and vigorous hitting. These incidents sometimes appeared connected to times when the analyst had been unable to fulfill quickly enough some-thing Sophie wanted immediately, but more often it seemed as if Sophie had been swept over by powerful feelings that she both anxiously and aggressively warded off in her physical attacks. Immediately after her outbursts, she would retreat to a far corner of the room, curl up with her blanket, and demand that the analyst not look at her. The warning about looking seemed to contain the fear that she was so aggressive that she would be left alone with no one looking at her, as well as a fear of the aggressive intent of looking as if the very act of visual contact would hold her and the analyst too dangerously close.

Interpreting Sophie's fear of her own angry feelings and her worry that she or her analyst might not survive her attacks unscathed seemed to help her return from her hiding place and resume the play she had so abruptly interrupted. Gradually, her outbursts diminished; her play became more sustained and the themes more aggressive. She often pretended to be a demanding, imperious baby whose every wish was fulfilled immediately by the "slaves" she kept close by. When her "slaves" did not respond quickly enough, she feigned indignant anger and pronounced destructive, vile threats to their bodies and very lives. Not infrequently, Sophie would interrupt stories such as these to seek out once again a safe corner in the playroom for fear that, as she clearly expressed, the bad "pirates" feelings would cut a swath of indiscriminate destruction across the playroom toward her and the analyst. During these moments, though contained within her fantasy play, she earnestly insisted that the analyst too must seek cover for there was no predicting either the appearance or the wanton destructiveness of these "pirates" once released.

Through the characters and stories Sophie created in her play, it became clearer that her struggles with her aggressivity related to both her wish, need, and demand for an evenly attentive, always available care of others and her concerns about how her aggressive feelings damaged others or drove them away. In one of her stories, a 4-year-old dragon character eagerly invited close friends to his birthday party only abruptly to hit and bite them. Puzzled and hurt, he asked his mother why his friends left the party. The mother explained how his friends did not understand why he was hitting and biting them when they were friends—they interpreted his intentions as hostile. In another story, a mother, on finding out that her baby had been quite demanding and bad during his visit to another family, says summarily, "Just throw him in the garbage." And in a third story, an indiscriminately evil character who stole from families was abruptly left alone and poignantly searched for friends. Even the revenge heaped upon him by the family he had previously injured paled as Sophie embellished the story of his lonely search for others like him. Suddenly he was lovingly taken in by the very family he had so grievously injured.

As she explained soberly to some of her dolls, it was possible to be angry with someone they also loved; and even when they were angry, they could also be close.

Each of these examples illustrate Sophie's profound, deeply felt struggles to understand how it was possible to have aggressive feelings toward those she loved and depended upon. As she gradually acquired the ability to appreciate and represent the differing thoughts and feelings of others and their different states of aggressive intention, she began to wonder and worry about the responses of others to both her fantasied and enacted aggression. Her play acquired a new depth and her characters, assuming more complex, multidimensional mental lives, became simultaneously emancipated and tragic. Through their aggression, they established for themselves a world in which they were feared, dreaded, and able to do whatever they wished but where they were left alone and denied the closeness they had so deeply desired. With a maturing capacity for attributing meanings, feelings, and different states of intention to others, Sophie was able to experiment with a multicausal view of aggressivity. Not only was it essential for her ongoing shaping of her own sense of self, but now she could see aggressive thoughts and wishes, as well as behavior, through the eyes of others and explore how love and hate exist side by side.

Children such as Sophie or Winnicott's *Piggle* (1977) illustrate not only how aggression fuels individuation and a sense of separateness but also how it contributes to the shaping of psychic structure. With a deepening understanding of one's own aggressive wishes and fantasies and an appreciation of the same in others, there comes also the fuller recognition of the potential impact of aggressive acts on others. Accepting a growing sense of personal responsibility for one's intentions, wishes, and fantasies is a part of the ongoing definition of self (Loewald, 1978) and a part of the building up of the superego and the experiencing of guilt for one's own potential destructiveness toward others, especially those we care the most about. Concern for and about the other modifies and shapes the child's experience of his own aggressiveness. Libidinal and aggressive wishes are intermingled as the child struggles to repair what he perceives and accepts as the results of his aggressivity. In this sense, the building up of superego functions, like the capacity for loving, is deeply rooted in the child's sense of his own aggressivity and the effect on others. Once again, individual variations in the child's internal representations of the values and rights of others have their roots not only in libidinal ties to parents and in the working through of oedipal love (Hartmann and Loewenstein, 1962), but also in how much aggression has been experienced as constructive or destructive in the context of relationships with others.

## SUMMARY AND RESEARCH IMPLICATIONS

The capacity to attribute aggressive intentions and motives to oneself and to others represents a synthetic ego function that plays a significant role in the transformation of aggressive strivings in the preschool child and in the more differentiated use of aggression in the service of both self-definition and relations with others. Aggression is experienced, shaped, refined, and remodeled in the context of loving relations, and it is a central psychoanalytic observation that young children first experience their own aggressive feelings in response to and in the presence of those whom they love the most. With the maturing ability to understand and reflect upon one's own and others' mental states, the experience of being or feeling aggressive toward another gains new meaning.

Observational studies indicate that aggressive behaviors change markedly in the preschool years, or in the terminology of psychoanalytic observation, direct discharge of aggressive drive derivatives is muted and shaped by the child's relations with his parents or with those who most actively care for him. Children become less physically aggressive and aggressive responses to frustration of physical needs or desires are less often the eliciting events. However, paradoxically, by 4 to 6 years of age, while generally less aggressive, children more often direct their aggressivity to others and are more often aggressive in response to perceived threats to their sense of self. At the same time, because of maturing capacities for symbolization and abstraction, children are able to use pretense and fantasy to work out their experiences of their own and others' aggression. For the oedipal-aged child, the transformation of aggression and the blending of aggressive and libidinal wishes toward the same person are made possible by the ability to understand the nature of one's own and others' mental states and of the relation between mind and action. In a very real sense, understanding aggressive states of mind and intentions is a more difficult, or at least equally essential, task in the child's developing and expanding relationships with multiple others. Appreciating the neurocognitive contributions to the transformations of aggression makes possible more detailed studies of how children may fail to use aggression constructively for self-other differentiation, of the environmental contributions to the early transformations of aggressive strivings, and the individual differences in how much children or adults attribute hostile intentions to the actions of others.

The latter point brings us back to the psychoanalytic theory of the role of experience in mediating the child's sense of his own aggressiveness and raises several areas for investigation. The theory presented thus far for the modulation and transformation of aggressivity in the preschool-aged child permits us a conceptual frame for thinking about the circumstances in which the child's external world is chronically violent and/or depriving and physically hurtful. Young children who are chronically ill or physically restrained in the first months of life because of illness have both the experience of being hurt by others and of having fewer and different opportunities to use their bodies to assert their needs or protect themselves. Or when the child's normally occurring assertive or aggressive acts (e.g., the toddler's tantrum) or even fantasies of aggression are met by real, often life-threatening aggressive responses, the child's experience of himself as aggressive is shaped in ways that are dramatically different from those which contain and accept his aggressive assertiveness. Similarly, children who are the habitual witnesses of physical violence both to those they love and to those who randomly pass through their world will likely experience a greater and earlier sense of danger when confronted with their own aggressive feelings and wishes. Or they may experience their own aggressivity and fantasies as compatible with that which commonly occurs around them and permissible by those whom they have experienced as equally violent and destructive.

How each of these situations influences the transformation of aggression as the child gradually acquires more sophisticated capacities to reflect upon his and other's aggressive intentions is a question most relevant to psychoanalytically informed investigations. For example, relationships with important others that are marred by explicit violence and abuse may bring the child face to face with the mind of another that is too frightening and dangerous to try to understand. In such cases, despite maturational readiness, the capacity to understand others' minds and different states of aggressive intention may be seriously impaired. In addition, when the child's mode of experiencing the world early on has been predominantly colored by aggression, danger, and hurtfulness, it is not clear how, or if, the capacity to attribute beliefs and intentions to others allows the child to imbue those others or himself in fantasy with less aggressive, hurtful minds. In other words, in these instances, how much is the child able to work out his real experiences of destructiveness and rage through his play and in the privacy of his inner subjective world? And even with the capacity to reflect upon the aggressive wishes and fantasies of self and other, children exposed to chronic, intense violence will likely have a different sense of their own intentionality and responsibility.

Questions such as these are deeply germane to child psychoanalysts who are increasingly called upon to care for the children from substance-abusing homes and neighborhoods and children of the inner city whose external worlds are so unsafe that their inner fantasies are daily given voice and reality in their immediate and observed experiences (Marans and Cohen, 1993; Mayes et al., 1992). Such questions also provide us with the broadest outlines of a theory that distinguishes between the conduct or disruptive behavior problems of young children bounded by anxiety and fear as with Sophie and those who seem unmoved by their effects on others. Finally, from its earliest beginnings, psychoanalysis has been profoundly concerned with the experience and nature of early trauma and how that experience is mediated and modified by the child's inner fantasy and shapes the child's ongoing modes of apprehending the world. When children are still evolving a sense of what is inner and outer, pretend and real, and what it means to hold aggressive wishes and feelings toward those they love and depend upon, early exposure to violence and deprivation shapes their view of themselves in relation to their own and others' aggressivity and their view of the world as hostile or protective, constructive or destructive, forgiving or punishing, loving or hating. In these ways, aggression remains central to the psychoanalytic theory of character formation and to the child's developing ability to integrate and synthesize loving and aggressive feelings in the service of deepening relations with others.

## BIBLIOGRAPHY

ABRAHAM, K. (1923). Contributions to the theory of the anal character. *Int. J. Psychoanal.*, 4:400–418.

—— (1925). Influence of oral erotism on character formation. *Int. J. Psychoanal.*, 6:247–258.

ALPERT, J., COHEN, D. J., SHAYWITZ, B. A., & PICCIRILLO, M. (1981). Neurochemical and behavior organization in disorders of attention, activity and aggression. In *Vulnerabilities to Delinquency*, ed. D. O. Lewis. New York: S. P. Medical and Scientific Books, pp. 109–171.

ASTINGTON, J. W. & GOPNIK, A. (1991). Theoretical explanations of children's understanding of mind. *Brit. J. Develpm. Psychol.*, 9:7–31.

—— HARRIS, P. L., & OLSON, D. R. (1988). *Developing Theories of Mind.* Cambridge: Cambridge Univ. Press.

BANDURA, A. (1973). *Aggression.* New York: Holt.

BARON-COHEN, S., TAGER-FLUSBERG, H., & COHEN, D. J. (1992). *Understanding Other Minds.* Oxford: Oxford Univ. Press.

BIBRING, E. (1941). The development and problems of the theory of instincts. *Int. J. Psychoanal.,* 21:102–131.

BRENNER, C. (1971). The psychoanalytic concept of aggression. *Int. J. Psychoanal.,* 52:137–144.

BUSS, A. H. (1961). *The Psychology of Aggression.* New York: Wiley.

———— (1966). Instrumentality of aggression, feedback, and frustration as determinants of physical aggression. *J. Pers. Soc. Psychol.,* 3:153–162.

CHANDLER, M. J., FRITZ, A. S., & HALA, S. M. (1989). Small scale deceit. *Child Develpm.,* 60:1263–1277.

COHEN, D. J. (1990). Enduring sadness. *Psychoanal. Study Child,* 45:157–178.

CUMMINGS, E. M., HOLLENBECK, B., IANNOTII, R. J. RADKE-YARROW, M., & ZAHN-WAXLER, C. (1986). Early organization of altruism and aggression. In *Altruism and Aggression,* ed. C. Zahn-Waxler, E. M. Cummings, & R. J. Iannotti. New York: Cambridge Univ. Press, pp. 165–188.

———— IANNOTTI, R. J., & ZAHN-WAXLER, C. (1989). Aggression between peers in early childhood. *Child Develpm.,* 60:887–895.

DODGE, K. A. (1980). Social cognition and children's aggressive behaviors. *Child Develpm.,* 51:162–170.

———— (1986). Social-information processing variables in the development of aggression and altruism in children. In *Altruism and Aggression,* ed. C. Zahn-Waxler, E. M. Cummings, & R. J. Iannotti. New York: Cambridge Univ. Press, pp. 280–302.

———— & COIE, J. D. (1987). Social-information processing factors in reactive and proactive aggression in children's peer groups. *J. Pers. Soc. Psychol.,* 53:1146–1158.

DOLLARD, J., DOOB, L. W., MILLER, N. E., MOWRER, O. H. & SEARS, R. R. (1939). *Frustration and Aggression.* New Haven: Yale Univ. Press.

DOWNEY, W. (1984). Within the pleasure principle. *Psychoanal. Study Child,* 39:101–136.

ETZEL, B. C. & GEWIRTZ, J. L. (1967). Experimental modification of a caretaker-maintained high-rate operant crying in a 6- and a 20-week-old infant (Infans tyrannotearus). *J. Exp. Child Psychol.,* 5:303–317.

FENICHEL, O. (1945). *The Psychoanalytic Theory of Neurosis.* New York: Norton.

FESBACH, S. (1964). The function of aggression and the regulation of aggressive drive. *Psychol. Rev.,* 71:257–272.

FREUD, A. (1972). Comments on aggression. *Int. J. Psychoanal.,* 53:163–171.

FREUD, S. (1905). Three essays on the theory of sexuality, *S.E.,* 7:125–243.

———— (1909). Character and anal erotism. *S.E.,* 9:169–175.

———— (1915). Instincts and their vicissitudes. *S.E.,* 14:111–140.

———— (1920). Beyond the pleasure principle. *S.E.,* 18:3–64.

———— (1930). Civilization and its discontents. *S.E.,* 21:59–145.

GAY, P. (1988). *Freud.* New York: Norton.

GILLESPIE, W. (1971). Aggression and instinct theory. *Int. J. Psychoanal.*, 52:155–160.

GOODENOUGH, F. L. (1931). *Anger in Young Children*. Minneapolis: Univ. Minnesota Press.

GREEN, E. H. (1933). Friendships and quarrels among preschool children. *Child Develpm.*, 4:236–252.

GREENACRE, P. (1971). Notes on the influence and contribution of ego psychology to the practice of psychoanalysis. In *Separation-Individuation*, ed. J. B. McDevitt & C. F. Settlage. New York: Int. Univ. Press, pp. 171–200.

HARLOW, H. F. & HARLOW, M. K. (1965). The affectional systems. In *Behavior of Nonhuman Primates*, ed. A. M. Schrier, H. F. Harlow, & F. Stollnitz. New York: Academic Press, vol. 2, pp. 287–334.

HARTMANN, H. (1948). Comments on the psychoanalytic theory of instinctual drives. *Psychoanal. Q.*, 17:368–388.

———— KRIS, E., & LOEWENSTEIN, R. M. (1949). Notes on the theory of aggression. *Psychoanal. Study Child*, 3/4:9–36.

———— & LOEWENSTEIN, R. M. (1962). Notes on the superego. *Psychoanal. Study Child*, 17:42–81.

HARTUP, W. W. (1974). Aggression in childhood. *Amer. Psychologist*, 29:336–341.

HAY, D. F. (1984). Social conflict in early childhood. In *Annals of Child Development*, ed. G. Whitehurst. London: JAI, vol. 1, pp. 1–44.

KLEIN, M. (1957). Envy and gratitude. In *Envy and Gratitude and Other Works*. London: Hogarth Press, 1975, pp. 176–235.

LESTER, B. M. & BOUKYDIS, C. F. Z. (1984). *Infant Crying*. New York: Plenum Press.

LOEWALD, H. W. (1960). Internalization, separation, mourning, and the superego. In *Collected Papers*. New Haven: Yale Univ. Press, 1980, pp. 257–276.

———— (1971). On motivation and instinct theory. *Ibid.*, pp. 102–137.

———— (1978). *Psychoanalysis and the History of the Individual*. New Haven: Yale Univ. Press.

LORENZ, K. (1966). *On Aggression*. New York: Harcourt, Brace & World.

MAHLER, M. S., PINE, F. & BERGMAN, A. (1975). *The Psychological Birth of the Human Infant*. New York: Basic Books.

MARANS, S. & COHEN. D. J. (1993). Children and inner city violence. In *Psychological Effects of War and Violence on Children*. ed. L. Leavitt & N. Fox (in press).

———— DAHL, K., MARANS, W. & COHEN, D. J. (1993). Aggressivity in play. In *The Many Meanings of Play*, ed. A. J. Solnit, P. B. Neubauer, & D. J. Cohen. New Haven: Yale University Press, pp. 275–296.

MARCOVITZ, E. (1982). Aggression. *Psychoanal. Inq.*, 2:11–20.

MAYES, L. C. (1992a). Experiencing self and others. *J. Amer. Psychoanal. Assn.* (in press).

———— (1992b). Playing and therapeutic action in child analysis. Submitted manuscript.

———— (1993). The child's emerging understanding of other minds. *J. Amer. Psychoanal. Assn.* (in press).

———— & CARTER, A. S. (1990). Emerging social-regulatory capacities as seen in the still face situation. *Child Develpm.*, 61:754–763.

———— & COHEN, D. J. (1992). The development of an imaginative capacity in young children. *Psychoanal. Study Child*, 47:23–47.

———— ———— (1993). The role of constitution in psychoanalysis. In *Concepts in Psychoanalysis*, ed. B. E. Moore. New Haven: Yale Univ. Press (in press).

———— GRANGER, R. H., BORNSTEIN, M. H., & ZUCKERMAN, B. (1992). The problem of intrauterine cocaine exposure. *J. Amer. Med. Assn.*, 267:406–408.

———— & KLIN, A. (1993). Desire and fantasy. In *Understanding Other Minds*, ed. S. Baron-Cohen, H. Tager-Flusberg, D. J. Cohen. Oxford: Oxford Univ. Press (in press).

———— ———— & COHEN, D. J. (1993). The effect of social context on children's developing theory of mind. Submitted manuscript.

MOSES, L. J. & FLAVELL, J. H. (1990). Inferring false beliefs from actions and reactions. *Child Develpm.*, 61:929–945.

PARENS, H. (1979). *The Development of Aggression in Early Childhood*. New York: Jason Aronson.

PARKE, R. D. & SLABY, R. G. (1983). The development of aggression. In *Handbook of Child Psychology*, ed. E. M. Hetherington. New York: Wiley, 4th ed., vol. 4, pp. 547–641.

QUIGGLE, N. L., GARBER, J., FRANK, W. F., & DODGE, K. A. (1992). Social information processing in aggressive and depressed children. *Child Develpm.*, 63:1305–1320.

REICH, W. (1933). *Character Analysis*. New York: Simon & Schuster, 1945.

ROCHLIN, G. (1982). Aggression reconsidered. *Psychoanal. Inq.*, 2:121–132.

ROTENBERG, K. J. (1980). Children's use of intentionality in judgements of character and disposition. *Child Develpm.*, 51:282–284.

RULE, B. G., NESDALE, A. R. & MCARA, M. J. (1974). Children's reactions to information about the intentions underlying an aggressive act. *Child Develpm.*, 45:794–798.

SHANTZ, D. W. & VOGDANOFF, D. A. (1973). Situational effects on retaliatory aggression at three age levels. *Child Develpm.*, 44:149–153.

SOLNIT, A. J. (1972). Aggression. *J. Amer. Psychoanal. Assn.*, 20:435–450.

SORCE, J., EMDRE, R. N., CAMPOS, J., & KLINNERT, M. (1985). Maternal emotional signaling. *Develpm. Psychology*, 21:195–200.

SPITZ, R. A. (1965). *The First Year of Life*. New York: Int. Univ. Press.

———— (1969). Aggression and adaptation. *J. Nerv. Ment. Dis.*, 149:81–90.

STECHLER, G. & HALTON, A. (1987). Assertion and aggression. *J. Amer. Psychoanal. Assn.*, 35:821–838.

STEPANSKY, P. E. (1977). *A History of Aggression in Freud*. Psychol. Issues, monogr. 39. New York: Int. Univ. Press.

STONE, L. (1971). Reflections on the psychoanalytic concept of aggression. *Psychoanal. Q.*, 40:195–244.

WAELDER, R. (1956). Critical discussion of the concept of an instinct of destruction. *Bull. Phila. Assn. Psychoanal.*, 6:97–109.

WELLMAN, H. M. (1990). *The Child's Theory of Mind.* Cambridge, Mass.: MIT Press.

———— & BARTSCH, K. (1988). Young children's reasoning about beliefs. *Cognition*, 30:239–277.

WIMMER, H. & PERNER, J. (1983). Beliefs about beliefs. *Cognition*, 13:103–128.

WINNICOTT, D. W. (1945). Primitive emotion and development. *Int. J. Psychoanal.*, 26:137–143.

———— (1950). Aggression in relation to emotional development. *Collected Papers.* New York: Basic Books, 1975, pp. 204–218.

———— (1969). The use of an object. *Int. J. Psychoanal.*, 50:711–716.

———— (1971). *Playing and Reality.* London: Tavistock Publications.

———— (1977). *The Piggle.* Madison, Conn.: Int. Univ. Press.

# Problems in Female Development

## Comments on the Analysis of an Early Latency-age Girl

### RHODA S. FRENKEL, M.D.

*A 6¹/2-year-old girl's clinical material relevant to the emergence of clitoral and vaginal masturbation and masturbation fantasies during analytic sessions is presented. The intense genital excitation, which she called "jeebies," often overwhelmed her ego functioning. She assumed the jeebies and the fantasies that precipitated and accompanied them would cause bad things to happen to her. External events and the nature of her object relations reinforced and confirmed her belief that being only female was unacceptable. Her penis envy, a wish to be a boy-girl, had multiple determinants. A detailed description of her evaluation and subsequent treatment reveals how her unconscious conflicts were resolved in analysis through the evolution and resolution of her transference neurosis, validating the psychoanalytic approach.*

SINCE THE EARLY YEARS OF PSYCHOANALYSIS FREUD'S VIEW OF FEMALE development has been a source of dispute (Horney, 1926; Jones, 1935). Only sparce data from the psychoanalysis of children have refuted Freud's (1925) phallocentric theory that little girls, unaware of their vaginas, feel castrated and inferior because the clitoris is not only smaller than the penis, but provides less pleasure. During the past two decades a variety of disciplines have contributed to our modifying and expanding our concepts about female development (Masters and Johnson, 1966; Kleeman, 1971; Money and Ehrhardt, 1972; Stoller, 1973; Blum, 1976a; Chehrazi, 1986). Although the contemporary view

---

Training and Supervising Analyst, Dallas Psychoanalytic Institute; Clinical Professor of Psychiatry, University of Texas Southwestern Medical Center at Dallas, Texas.

is that penis envy is a secondary phenomenon, a pathological defense and/or an understandable response to interpersonal and sociocultural influences (Horney, 1926; Jones, 1935; Applegarth, 1976, 1988; Blum, 1976b; Grossman and Stewart, 1976; Karme, 1981; Chehrazi, 1986, Lax, 1990; Frenkel, 1991a), most of the clinical data have come from reconstructions of adult analysis. Since formation of a fairly rigid superego is the hallmark of latency, data about masturbation are difficult to elicit even in analysis.

The present case offers some unique opportunities to view in statu nascendi many of the vicissitudes of the instinctual drives in a 6½-year-old girl who was unable psychologically to enter latency until she was 9. The analysis took 2 years and 8 months, during which the patient was seen four times a week. In addition, during the first few months at least one parent was seen weekly. Thereafter, the mother was seen only once every month or so. Extensive details of the evaluation, developmental history, opening and first half of the midphase of the analysis will be presented in order to demonstrate the meaning and evolution of the transference neurosis which allowed the patient's masturbatory activities and fantasies to emerge. Relevant aspects of the resolution of the transference and termination will be summarized.

The data from the analytic sessions demonstrate a young girl's capacity for intense genital pleasure and orgasm, achieved by self-stimulation of the clitoris and vaginal introitus. This adds to the growing evidence refuting the notion that women are biologically inferior. In addition, the findings support current views of female development in which penis envy is viewed as a secondary phenomenon, and intense and persistent penis envy is considered defensive and aberrant.

## OVERVIEW OF THE LITERATURE

Bornstein (1953), referring to her analytic experience with latency children, wrote that some masturbation with limited orgastic gratification is normal in latency, especially in boys. Nevertheless, she described three girls who experienced intense orgastic sensations from thigh pressure alone. From this she assumed vaginal sensations were involved. She wrote that girls experience orgasms with sensations of dizziness, confusion, fears of sickness, death, and the world perishing. She did not describe in what context within the analytic process she learned about her patients' masturbation. Fraiberg (1972) gave detailed analytic vignettes of two latency-age girls who reported transient genital anesthesia. In each, the core conflicts centered around masturbatory activities and fantasies. Both girls reported vaginal exploration and experiencing pleasurable excitation from the clitoris, labia, introitus, and probably the vagina. Fraiberg proposed that for some girls an unsuspected capacity for explosive discharge, similar to if not identical with adult orgasm, might transiently threaten their ego boundaries and result in genital anesthesia. Linking this to frigidity in adult women, she wrote, "The analysis of childhood masturbation might then include the original flight from the genitals as the results of insupportable, overwhelming excitement and an anesthesia in childhood which was the prototype for frigidity in later years" (p. 474).

With regard to Fraiberg's hypothesis, my reports of the analysis of an adolescent girl (Frenkel, 1991a, 1991b) are of interest. Early in her analysis my patient complained of vaginal anesthesia with coitus. Later she shamefully recalled that, at the age of 4 or 5, her older sister had caught her manually masturbating in bed and had slapped her hands. During her termination she became conscious that since latency, while showering, she achieved orgasm by directing a stream of water over her clitoris. Until then she had totally repressed the sexual nature of this activity. She did not seem to be concerned, at least in the present, about loss of ego boundaries, but did express fear of the consequences for the contents of her masturbatory fantasies. Kramer (1954) wrote about three women in analysis who reported early childhood masturbation to orgasm. Believing little boys might be incapable of orgasm, he thought lack of relief in either sex led to behavioral disturbances. Barnett (1968) reported that girls are aware of their vaginas and physiologically, unlike boys, are capable of orgastic release. Barnett (1966) and Kestenberg (1968) also presented several less detailed analytic vignettes of young girls in whom internal vaginal arousal caused anxiety.

## CASE MATERIAL

Erica, age 6½, was brought for psychiatric evaluation because she was constantly fighting with her younger sisters, with her peers, and especially with her mother, Mrs. G. Nearing the end of a bitter divorce proceeding, Mrs. G. was distraught and felt unable to tolerate the escalating battles with Erica. Mrs. G. feared she was about to repeat the physical abuse of her childhood. Although the increase in Erica's belligerent behavior paralleled the increasing friction and physical fights between the parents during the previous year, Mrs. G. complained that she could do nothing to stop Erica's constant opposition, bickering, and demands for attention.

### DEVELOPMENTAL HISTORY

Two months after Erica's birth, Mrs. G. sought treatment with me for depression and incapacitating phobic symptoms. She had an underlying hysterical character and was seen twice a week in psychoanalytically oriented psychotherapy. Before her pregnancy, she consciously believed that her marriage was idyllic. She viewed her husband, a doctor who later became a medical missionary, as a messiah who, as part of his grand plan to save the world, first had rescued Mrs. G. from her family. Mesmerized by his good looks, brilliance, and verbal skills, she did not recognize the pathology of his grandiosity. Although the pregnancy was planned, Mrs. G. felt guilty. Unaware of her own ambivalence, she blamed others for her guilt: her parents' anger at her interrupting her academic career and her in-laws' complaints that she and Dr. G. could not financially support a family. As she gained weight during the pregnancy, Dr. G., suffering from a fat phobia, found her physically revolting and could not tolerate her touching him. In the fifth and seventh months of her pregnancy, Mrs. G.'s reckless driving caused two minor car collisions. However, Erica was a healthy neonate, the product of a full-term pregnancy and normal delivery. Dr. G., the scion of two generations of proud male chauvinists, angry at not having a son, refused to visit his wife and daughter in the hospital. For six months, using his job as an excuse, he was rarely at home. Mrs. G., frightened of being alone at night, would barricade herself in the bedroom, unable to leave even if she heard Erica crying. After the delivery Mrs. G. felt exhausted and upset by the ugliness of her child. She gave up breast-feeding after several days due to insufficient milk. Although she expressed both resentment and fear of the responsibilities of motherhood, she must have been more nurturing than she described. Despite the above-mentioned turmoil, Erica was an easygoing baby, who slept through most nights by 4 weeks, and had no feeding problems or colic. Erica was smiling and cooing by 10 weeks and was above normal in growth and weight. During her therapy Mrs. G. decided not to wean Erica abruptly at 3 months, so Erica easily gave up her bottle at 9 months.

Mrs. G.'s treatment revealed her intense guilt over her sexuality, femininity, and passive longings, which caused her to deny the pleasure she experienced with Erica. Repeating her own family history, she saw her firstborn as herself, the bad child. Thus Mrs. G. always felt the need prematurely to separate from Erica, whose natural endowments allowed a precocious pseudoindependence. When Erica was 6 months old, Mrs. G.'s parents came for a long visit and were very critical of Mrs. G.'s homemaking and mothering skills. In response, Mrs. G., unconsciously identifying with her mother's hostility, became quite careless, leaving dangerous items, like open diaper pins, within Erica's grasp. Once after diapering, she left Erica unattended on a high counter. Erica fell, broke her leg, and had to be in a body cast for several months.

Nevertheless, Erica managed to pull herself to a standing position by 8 months and was walking and talking before she was a year old. At this time Mrs. G. "accidentally" became pregnant with her second daughter, who was born when Erica was 20 months old. Several months later she decided to stop treatment, stating she was no longer phobic or depressed. Mrs. G. had made excellent progress, but was fearful of facing core oedipal conflicts. I sensed that unconsciously she knew that her further growth would lead to a divorce. Unable to accept the fact that her husband had severe psychiatric problems, she preserved her fantasy of his greatness.

Inconsistent toilet training began at 18 months, but Erica was not fully trained until she was 3 years old. Besides the marital discord, other significant developmental traumas were two years of intermittent, severe ear infections resulting in bilateral myringotomies with tubal implants at age 4. They were removed after 18 months without further sequelae. When she was 4½, her youngest sister was born. At age 5, when she was alone in the car with her mother, Mrs. G. ran a traffic light causing a major accident. Their car was totally destroyed, but fortunately physical injuries were not major. Nevertheless, Erica "went flying," badly bruising her head on the car window. Although she suffered no other physical injury, for a year she remained terrified by being in cars. Erica began preschool at age 4, crying for a month, before settling down and enjoying it. She repeated kindergarten due to emotional immaturity and lack of reading readiness. Mrs. G. blamed her teacher for being too strict.

In the 4½ years between Mrs. G.'s treatment and Erica's evaluation, Mrs. G. had been reasonably content. While taking a few postgraduate courses, generally she maintained good rapport with her children. Viewing Erica's independence and drive as masculine, Dr. G. clearly preferred her to his wife and other children. He took pride in and encouraged Erica's aggressiveness and often roughhoused with her as if she were a son. Mrs. G. was jealous of the attention that her husband gave to Erica. As Dr. G.'s career progressed, they were able to move to a larger house which temporarily placated Mrs. G. After the birth of a third daughter, however, Dr. G. became increasingly hostile both at home and work. He had to change the location of his practice and his fights with Mrs. G. escalated. No longer able to maintain her illusions about her marriage, divorce became inevitable. Once again, Dr. G. rarely came home. Mrs. G. became irritable, unreasonable, and intolerant of her children, but especially Erica. She could not tolerate Erica's presence for more than an hour or two and was unaware that her anger, impatience, and outright rejection of Erica provoked much of

Erica's combativeness, which Mrs. G. claimed she was unable to stop. Thus Mrs. G. said, "Erica's following the script I followed, a bully with few friends. Although I don't hit her as much as I was hit [by both parents], she's aware I'm the authority figure."

In contrast, Dr. G. disclaimed any problems with Erica. Pleased with her assertiveness, he said, "I just negotiate with her as if she were a small adult." When his children visited, he seemed proud that Erica enjoyed playfully wrestling with him and sleeping in his bed, while his other daughters slept in the living room. He was scornful of his wife and parents who disapproved of Erica sharing his bed. I told him I shared their concern. Nevertheless, he continued for some time to sleep with Erica. Once, when the paternal grandparents were on a brief visit, they requested to see me. They wanted me to know that both the parents ignored all the children until their behavior became unbearable. They felt the children were wild, lacking in discipline, and that their son encouraged Erica to pit his approval against her mother's disapproval. They also wanted to be sure I knew that when the children had their weekly visit with their father, Erica shared his bed.

### INITIAL ASSESSMENT

When I met Erica in the waiting room, her demeanor was awkward, unhappy, and unappealing. Tall for her age with a comely face, she was well developed with good coordination when she chose. With dirty and torn clothes, she appeared as a waif. Thus, in spite of her real assets, she projected what she later described to me as her image of herself, that of a deprived and unlovable child. Separating easily from her mother, she went directly to the playroom, where she spent some time arranging and rearranging the furniture in the dollhouse. She complained that none of the arrangements would do, that they were all bad, and that the furniture was ugly. She wanted a larger house with a large chimney and a real fireplace. When encouraged to tell a story about the house, she added a mother and father doll, placing them in adjacent cribs and said that they were asleep. She then added three child dolls: a boy and girl who were 7-year-old twins and an infant girl. After she made lunch for them, the 7-year-old girl put the baby in the sand box and went off with the twin brother to a swing set, where they rapidly swung back and forth, hugging and kissing on the same seat. During this time Erica referred to the infant as the twins' child and also had the infant call the older sister Mommy. The play ended in tragedy: while the twins were kissing, the baby got out of the sand box, screamed as she fell down a slide, and then appeared to be dead. The twins ran over, realized the baby had only broken her leg, and took her to a hospital.

The sequence of her play seemed to illustrate some of her nuclear problems. First her dissatisfaction with being female; no matter how the house and furniture were rearranged, they were ugly and bad. That is, the house served as a metaphor for her body, psychologically the place where she lived. Her wish for a larger house with a big chimney and a real fireplace seemed to compensate for this feeling, which became a persistent theme of wanting to be both a girl and a boy. The subsequent play with the dolls appeared to express her concern that her parents would abandon her; they were asleep in cribs, perhaps a perceptive comment that they were behaving like infants. Subsequently, her play seemed to dramatize oedipal wishes and fears of the destructive consequences, to herself and others, of her libidinal and aggressive drives. After the twins "love-play," the baby was hurt, maybe even dead. The baby might represent either of her hated sisters, her mother, already represented as an infant, or herself as she had suffered a leg injury. Some evidence of guilt may be seen in the oversolicitousness of the twin (herself) to the infant (sister/mother) or punishment to the infant (herself) for jealous feelings toward the parents, concerns that she caused her parents' divorce and her abandonment, or the dangers of autonomous functions. The subsequent evaluation sessions as well as the course of her analysis reinforced and elaborated on these initial impressions.

During psychological testing, Erica was uncooperative, responding to queries with the first thing that came to her mind. Her precocious seductiveness made the male psychologist uncomfortable. He concluded that her motivation and concentration were quite poor. (Notably, while resisting testing, she was highly motivated and concentrated in her seductive efforts.) Her IQ was average. However, given her behavior and the scatter in the scoring, high in vocabulary and verbal comprehension, she probably was more intelligent. Erica's coquettish behavior and frequent nonsensical responses in part seemed motivated by a fear she would be seen as inadequate; e.g., her story about a girl with a broken leg, who is thrown out of the window by her "dumb mother." Mothering figures were depicted as so preoccupied with their own problems that they were incapable of responding to their children's needs. She equated femininity with inadequacy and rejection as seen in her story of a child who kills a baby because it is a girl and not a boy. In addition, the projective tests showed a wish for independence from which she recoiled because she feared danger from a hostile environment. She expected that such autonomous moves would be too willingly granted and she would be cut off from her sources of nurturance. She was seen to be extremely competitive with her youngest sister, stating if she could change anything about herself, it would be to be a baby again because then you were given all kinds of candies. The examiner felt that despite some evidence of an attention deficit disorder, Erica was in the process of forming a hysterical character structure and would benefit most from insight-oriented psychotherapy.

OPENING PHASE

The establishment and maintenance of the analytic process was prolonged and difficult due to multiple resistances of both Erica and her mother. Unable to resume her therapy with me, Mrs. G. did agree to supportive therapy with a colleague. Initially Erica portrayed not only her anxiety about beginning analysis, but also an almost sequential reenactment in her play of her developmental conflicts and defenses. Throughout this progression from oral to phallic-oedipal concerns, I mainly observed and then described Erica's activity to her, remarking occasionally on what seemed to be her predominant affect, i.e., you look like you feel angry, excited, sad, or happy, etc. Although told it would be helpful for Erica to eat either before or after her sessions, Mrs. G. made no effort to prevent Erica entering each session with her hands full of candy and soft drinks. Erica rapidly consumed her snacks. In the remaining time, presenting herself as an insatiable infant, she would lie on the analytic couch sucking water from a baby doll bottle, repeatedly requesting that I refill the bottle. Noting her hunger, I added that often children who were afraid of grownups and new situations would eat and drink to help them forget scary feelings. As her anxiety decreased, she stopped bringing food to her sessions. For a time she gave the bottle to a baby doll, often forgot to diaper the doll, and left small puddles in the play area. As she spanked the doll calling it a bad girl, I would say that the baby was not bad, that her mother had just forgotten to diaper her.

There was a brief period of simply making a mess in the playroom by pulling out toys and games and dumping them in the middle of the floor. She agreed that she was angry at me, but insisted that the mess was my fault. She would not say what I had done and made no reply when I asked if maybe she felt I did not spend enough time with her or was angry that I spent time with other children. (I thought she was reenacting her anger at her second sister's birth.) She gave me an exasperated look and in the following weeks she repeatedly acted out with dolls and puppets, play-acting her earlier traumas and listing her multiple reasons to be angry at her parents. There were many scenes of broken legs, hospitalizations, automobile accidents, parental arguments followed by her attempts to deal with them by denial, reversals, reaction formations, and regressions. When a doll or puppet was injured, I commented that it was frightening to get hurt. There were also recurring scenes of children being lonely, confused, and disappointed when an adult they had counted on disappeared at the moment he or she was most needed. She then returned to making a mess with all the toys thrown about the playroom. Her mother told me that during this time the divorce had been finalized. Thus, the next "messy" session, I was able to comment that maybe Erica was blaming me for her parents' divorce. She nodded her head in silent agreement. Exploring this, she realized that she only hoped I would stop it and had blamed herself, noting with surprising insight that it was easier to blame me. None of my comments or interpretations altered her conviction that her "badness had caused the mess."

Because of Mrs. G.'s inconsistency and hostility, Erica feared that I would behave similarly; so a long period was needed to establish a therapeutic alliance in which Erica could trust me to be a noncritical, consistent, empathic adult. This allowed a more affective portrayal of her highly charged oedipal conflicts. In the sixth month of her analysis, Erica began her Monday session describing plans for her father's birthday, which she seemed to confuse with her own earlier birthday. When I questioned her, she gave me an exasperated look, which meant I did not understand; so I asked her to explain it to me. As she talked of her spending the weekend with her father to celebrate "our birthday," she became excited. Wiggling in her chair, she started to giggle and then fell to the floor; rolling back and forth, saying she was a monkey, but would not do her monkey dances for me. For several days her play was disorganized and she seemed out of control. Over the weekend on her father's birthday, he took her to a fair and she spent the night with him. She began her next session on the floor in the waiting room, tearing up pictures from a coloring book. Once in the office she made a face with playdough, said it was me, then made a knife and slashed the face. Next, she fashioned a long tube from paper towels, and put some small wads of paper into her mouth and spit them through the tube onto the floor. She started rolling on the floor, first saying she was angry with me, then laughing and wiggling her whole body in a clearly erotic fashion. She said she had gone to the fair with her daddy and did the monkey dance. When I asked if she was doing the monkey dance now, she said she would show me. Taking a cylindrical building block, she affixed a sphere of playdough to one end of it, labeling it "a thing" (a clearly phallic object). She began the monkey dances standing on a chair, sensually gyrating her body while caressing the "thing" against her chest. Moving to the floor, she continued to move her body seductively. She seemed unaware of my presence as the tempo escalated, and breathing heavily she began to masturbate, rubbing the "thing" around her clitoris. Throwing it aside she used her hand to stimulate both her clitoral and vaginal areas. As she seemed to be reaching a climax, she stopped abruptly. Appearing fearful, but unable to verbalize her feelings, she insisted on going to the bathroom to avoid having an accident. On returning she crawled on the floor and wiggled her bottom at me, saying, "I'm a dog and this is the story of stinker-butt." She nodded no when asked if this was part of the monkey dance. Then she gave me a piece of paper on which she had written, "I luv you." Next she crawled and hid under a small covered table making sounds of urinating and defecating. After agreeing not to end her session early, she said, "I am you and you are me. If I were me, I be stinker-butt. But, if I am you, I am not stinker-butt. Now you see!" She agreed when I said she wanted to leave early because feeling like a stinker-butt made her unhappy.

In the next two months Erica intermittently masturbated during her sessions, usually following visits with her father, which were now restricted to daytime and only with her sisters. Most often she would interrupt her excitement and go to the bathroom, but several times she seemed to reach a climax in the session. Using her hand she would begin in the clitoral area and, with increasing frenzy, she then reached into her vagina. Sometimes using one hand on top of the other, she tightly squeezed her perineal area, both intra- and extravaginally, held her breath for a few seconds, and then made a pleasurable sigh. Releasing her hands, she remained on the floor for a few moments with a dreamy look in her eyes. During these episodes, she seemed totally unaware of my presence. After regaining awareness of her surroundings, she would say only, "Another monkey dance . . . I'm just a stinker-butt." When asked, she related that sometimes she did it at home, but never around her mother, because her mother would hit her if she started. She agreed when I asked if she expected me to hit her. She thought that she was bad and deserved to be hit. I told her she did not deserve to be hit and that I would not hit her, but we needed to understand what she meant by being bad, what she was thinking about during the monkey dances and why she did them.

These sessions troubled me. Other little girls had masturbated briefly during a session or described to me more extensively what they did at home in private. However, Erica was the youngest to so explicitly masturbate during a session, clearly spreading her legs so I could see exactly what she was doing. Undoubtedly she wanted to provoke me; but more importantly, lacking the words, she wanted to show me exactly where and what her problem was. I wondered if analysis was too regressive for her, if her ego was too weak. My decision to continue was based on my reasoning that although Erica was of latency age, she had failed to achieve certain latency capacities. If her oedipal and preoedipal conflicts had precluded her developing a tolerable superego, then analysis was the only treatment to help her.

An environmental change helped. Dr. G. developed a relationship with a woman from his church. When his children visited, his girlfriend was always present. With the appearance of the girlfriend, Erica's open masturbation decreased. Several weeks later Dr. G. and his girlfriend went to another city, where Dr. G. planned to finish his training to be a missionary. After this, Erica virtually ceased masturbating during her sessions. She began playing out stories of dogs having babies. In one session I asked if the story had something to do with her calling herself a dog after the monkey dance, she said, "Shut your mouth." She then played out a series of stories. In one a young girl went to live with her mother after her father died in an accident; in another a family of five dolls tried to live together, but a disaster caused the dolls to be thrown all over the playroom. I commented how nice feelings in your body could often be very scary. Of course it took us more than a year to get an explanation of just what her feelings were. She did not consider them nice, but agreed they gave her pleasure.

Reassured that I understood her feelings without being threatened by them, Erica needed to know if I would hurt her, as her mother did, if she tried to destroy major property in the office, or hurt me or herself. Sometimes physical restraint, firmly holding her without hurting her, was needed. I commented that Erica wanted to be held, but there were more pleasant ways to get this need met. Understanding that the limits were real, consistent, and safe seemed firmly to establish a therapeutic alliance.

More comfortable in the analysis, Erica allowed her positive transference feelings to emerge. Thus, she had an intense mourning and rage reaction anticipating a one-day absence. This was followed by a jubilant, but somewhat shamefaced reunion the next session. Erica's play then shifted to her concerns over feminine identification. She drew pictures of girls and flowers which combined both male and female features, an early expression of her wish to be both sexes. Now eager to come to her sessions, she was more tolerant of and interested in my comments.

MIDPHASE

Erica entered this phase with a remarkably strengthened ego. Her acting out diminished, and her use of verbalization and organized symbolic play increased. Positive transference appeared in a series of pictures entitled "I love you." These drawings were more organized, complex, and affectively charged, with age-appropriate printing and correct spelling. They depicted her sitting on my lap while holding on her lap a pot with a flower displaying clearly both masculine and feminine components. As we neared a summer break, she became furious at my refusal to let her take an office pencil home with her, but she was able to tolerate the frustration. Acknowledging she had many pencils at home, she agreed she wanted something special from me. In addition to the phallic significance of the pencil which will be detailed later, she wanted something, like a transitional object, to remind her of me during the summer. As the break approached, our work shifted to her fears about separation and abandonment.

As Erica's life centered more around her analysis, her transference feelings were expressed directly and were integrated into the content of her play. For example, after the break, she cried inconsolably throughout her first session, refusing to play, only saying she no longer wanted to come to see me. I commented that as Erica often expressed her feelings backward, perhaps she had missed me and our time together. The next session, she continued to cry. Repeating my previous comment, I added that perhaps Erica felt I had forgotten her or did not want to see her, so that she might want to pay me back by saying she did not want to see me. Her crying subsided, then stopped quite suddenly as she said, "Oh well, that was really yesterday."

The following months Erica portrayed primarily with dolls and the dollhouse her previously described conflicts over feminine identity, her unresolved oedipal wishes, her fears of retaliation, and her subsequent regression to oral and anal concerns. The following vignettes sequentially illustrate our progress. One session began by her undressing a doll she identified as me. Simultaneously she tried to look up my skirt and then pick up her own skirt to show me her bottom. Noting that her curiosity was helpful in our work, I asked, "Do you want to know what my bottom looks like?" She replied, "Shut your mouth." Then repeatedly she asked me, "What time is it?" I commented that when I started talking about thoughts or feelings that were upsetting, she often asked about the time. Knowing that her mother often did this, I continued, "Maybe you are acting like someone else who is concerned about time." Eventually she agreed that her mother often was agitated about the time. I then explained that Erica's demands to know the time might be one way she handled scary or angry feelings, by imitating her mother. This led to frequent requests to take home office pencils, rulers, and crayons, and her subsequent anger at me when her wishes were not gratified but analyzed. During one such session, she drew a picture of a girl's bottom with a penis. I told her girls did not have penises. She called me a liar and said they had them up inside. With exasperation, she said, "I have to have a pencil to put up inside me. I'll die if I don't get one." Now shouting at me, she said, "I have to have a penis or have a baby, because you know, you know being a girl is bad." She explained bad meant that, "Only boys get the best love." Then she whispered, "Boys don't have jeebies." Refusing to explain "jeebies" (McKechnie, 1979), she started to cry, complaining, "I don't know why, but only boys are loved and girls aren't." She was expressing a concept reinforced by the thinking and behavior of her family in which throughout three maternal and paternal generations, women were both feared and degraded. I acknowledged that this was true in her family, but it was not true in all families. Again she called me a liar, but gradually she was able to explore the possibility that being a girl was not bad. She became less bossy in her sessions and dressed with more care. Occasionally she twirled around with pleasure, showing off a new dress and "my bottom." Mrs. G. reported Erica was making friends her own age and had refused to wear the boys' clothes sent to her by a relative.

After a brief period of pleasure with her increased acceptance of being female, Erica once again became anxious. Her doll play displayed multiple variations of a story in which a girl and an older boy or adult male end up hugging and kissing, then go to bed tightly holding one another, after which the girl is injured. Most of my comments were met with, "Shut your mouth." Once she explained that the couple in bed were trying to make a baby. One day when I again inquired if the little girl was being punished for her feelings, Erica resumed her monkey dances. This time, interrupting the dance, she fell from the chair, exaggerating her pain to show me invisible bruises. At the same time after a bike accident or fight at school, she came to the sessions with obvious cuts or bruises, which she casually discounted. In time she understood that she was punishing herself, as she had the doll, for genital sexual feelings, which she called "jeebies." She blamed "the jeebies up inside me" for making her do the monkey dances. Before telling me more about the jeebies, she wanted to make sure I had seen her injuries, both visible and hidden. She needed me to acknowledge that she had already been hurt, as she was still fearful that I would punish her for her competitive sexuality. Less fearful, she became furious at me for canceling a session and revealed her fantasy that I was going away for a weekend with my husband. I asked if she felt the same way when her mother left to spend a weekend with her new boyfriend. She agreed. I commented that feeling left out or abandoned was like the invisible injuries she had tried to show me. In another session she interrupted her monkey dance to tell me that when she danced for her daddy, he had laughingly called her his little monkey and then hugged and kissed her. She said that made the jeebies worse. When I asked her to explain, she pointed to her clitoral area and said, "They start here and then go up inside me. They go all over me and I can't stop them; then where they go nobody knows." With much consternation she whispered it was her jeebies that made her mother so mad at her and that they had caused her parents' divorce. In the following sessions Erica portrayed triangular relationships in which primarily a girl doll tried to win one parent away from the other. In one scene after the father went to work, the girl hugged and kissed her mother, who then picked up the girl and threw her out a window, breaking her arm. Alternately, scenes of the father and girl hugging and kissing would be followed by car accidents in which the little girl was either killed or seriously injured. I commented that Erica had earlier injuries that no longer showed, but still upset her. She agreed, adding the jeebies had caused it all. She thought that she had always had bad jeebies for which her mother punished her, explaining to me that was why her mother often talked of Erica's broken leg and the car accidents. After a period of disbelief, Erica experienced considerable relief that she could play and talk about the jeebies without upsetting or angering me. She agreed when I suggested that her frequent accidents might be her way of trying to control her thoughts and feelings. She added that if she hurt herself a little, she could stop a worse punishment and still keep her jeebies. She knew jeebies were bad, and that she was bad for liking them. But as she did not want to give them up, that explained her mother's anger and withdrawal. She knew all girls had jeebies, but was surprised that other little girls had similar wishes. Not understanding the difference between thoughts and actions, Erica was sure her fantasies and jeebies were worse than those of other girls, as they had caused her to lose both her parents.

Approaching a long summer break, Erica started shaking her head at me, calling me a liar. Accusing me of leaving because of her jeebies, she said, "Whenever I love someone, my jeebies make them go away." In her sessions she appeared forlorn and disheveled, refused to play or speak to me, and often spent the hour on my couch pretending to be asleep. She ignored my comments that she was leaving me before I left her. After a time she found a life-sized baby infant girl doll which she put under her dress pretending to be pregnant. Continuing to ignore me, she lay on my couch; using the doll, she repeatedly acted out, rather realistically, a fantasied pregnancy and vaginal delivery. She lavished the baby with love and promised never to leave her. Continuing to avoid any interaction with me as she fed the baby a bottle, she appeared to be in a state of blissful symbiotic fusion with "her baby." I commented on her activity and affect and reminded her that I had not yet left. One day she replied that I had left, but that I could be the male doctor who would take care of her in the hospital and help with the delivery. Later I became the father who was too busy to care for either mother or child. Although she wished it were not true, she said she felt girls were not lovable and that was why her father had left. She thought I was going to leave her permanently like her father, or just not want to be around her like her mother. I acknowledged that when you missed someone, time seemed endless, and I asked Erica what she thought might help. With a smile, she suggested we make a "program," knowingly making a pun with her name. The double entendre implied our making a baby. This was the first humor she had shown and was also an age-appropriate defense. In the last few sessions we constructed and decorated the "program"; we marked the days when the vacation would begin and end, adding her activities during this time. Contrary to my usual policy, I allowed her to take the "program" home with her at the end of the session before the break.

After the vacation, having the "program" seemed less important to Erica than my willingness to acknowledge her pain and fear, and to help her deal with her feelings. On one level it was a sublimation of her wish for me to give her something, a penis or a baby. On another level, the analysis gave her a safe milieu and her first stable object relationship. In this sense the "program" was an age-appropriate version of a transitional object. Most importantly, I believe what was given was a way of coping. By identifying with me, using her mind and her imagination, she was able to tolerate the frustration of the summer break, a significant growth in her ego functioning.

### SUMMARY OF REMAINING MIDPHASE AND TERMINATION

When treatment resumed, Erica's emotional maturation was striking. Physically her growth was unremarkable, yet now she appeared and acted her age, as if in a month she had aged two to three years. Despite several stressful external events, she was able to maintain her gains as seen in her increased understanding and ability to use the analytic process and symbolic play to communicate and understand her feelings. The first stress, related by Mrs. G., was that Erica's father had remarried and moved out of the country. Shortly before leaving, he said good-bye to Erica by phone, but had not yet fulfilled his promise to write her. According to Mrs. G., none of the children seemed to care.

As Mrs. G.'s boyfriend J. moved in with her several weeks later, the second event, it seems likely she was too preoccupied to be aware of Erica's feelings. The third event, several weeks after resuming the analysis, I had to cancel several sessions to have a lesion excised from my foot. Working primarily with drawings, Erica expressed some disappointment about my vacation, but worried most about the consequences of her angry and jealous feelings toward her mother. Erica showed no feelings about the impending break.

When I returned, Erica outwardly ignored my limping with a swollen bandaged foot. However, she began to paint a series of brightly colored stylized pictures of little girls carrying baskets of flowers. In all the pictures, each girl was missing one arm, had fake smiles, and worried eyes. Some pictures had poems such as "It's spring, I love the flowers, I love the tree, I love the sun and I love me." Thus, fears of bodily injury, castration, masturbation, and femininity were brought directly into focus. However, Erica maintained a cheerful façade, insisting her pictures were as sunny as she was. Two weeks later I was walking normally in regular shoes without a bandage. Then Erica began to tell me that she thought her angry feelings had hurt me. She believed my foot had been cut off and she feared retaliation. Recalling that previously her concerns about jeebies had led her actually to hurt herself, I asked if now she was drawing these fears rather than acting them out. She agreed and I said that drawing and talking were much better ways to solve problems, because no one got hurt. She then related her current fears that her jeebies, anger, and jealousy would drive away J., yet sometimes she even wished that would happen so she could have more time with her mother. Worried about her mother's limitations, she was annoyed that her mother needed J. and feared J. would take her mother away. Behind this fear she was able to find her wish that J. would take her away. Nevertheless, she did realize that her mother was much happier and spent more time with all the children.

Transference issues reemerged when Erica asked if the "slit" on my foot could reopen. I asked if she was not concerned about another "slit" on my body. Alarmed, she responded, "They didn't cut something else off you, did they?" Asked what she meant, Erica became tight lipped and determinedly drew a series of phallic flowers. Identifying what appeared to be a vagina with a penis, I asked if Erica wished I had both. Refusing to answer, Erica took a boy and girl doll, winding their arms around one another; she tied them together, naming them Leslie. I said that the name could be used for both a boy and a girl. She missed her next two sessions, complaining of a flulike illness. On returning, she resumed her play with Leslie, adding a mother and father doll who were constantly hugging and kissing each other and Leslie. I wondered why they needed to hug and kiss so much. Erica laughed and said, "That's love." I asked if it was not pretending to love. Several sessions later Erica stopped this theme, commenting sadly, "They're not real, you know." I noted how unhappy she looked. She said that she was upset that she could not make a real boy-girl doll. This led to her admitting her profound disappointment that I was "just a girl" and could never give her a penis. I asked if she still felt she would die without one. Looking at me with disgust, she said, "You know they stop the jeebies."

During the following weeks, in a pleasant but serious mood, Erica worked steadily. While talking about the jeebies and the differences between male and female feelings and fantasies, we drew pictures showing male and female anatomical differences in children and adults. She always tore the pictures and threw them out. Then she untied Leslie and announced they were twins, Leslie and Laura, who would marry and have babies when they were older. Later she said brothers and sisters could not marry and that Leslie had to go away to live with his real father. When she said Laura felt sad without Leslie, I noted that she rarely spoke about her own father. Nodding her head in agreement, she said that sometimes she really missed him. She sat silently for a while and then returned to Laura who was preoccupied with a role in a school play. Laura soon forgot Leslie, and Laura's name was changed to Diane. Shortly after Diane's appearance, Erica said she was bored with the dolls and was thinking of stopping analysis to be in a school play. Splitting the transference, she talked glowingly about her music teacher, who had told her she was very talented. I agreed that Erica might be close to stopping, but thought she was still avoiding some feelings about me. Denying this she continued to complain of nothing to do and some anger about missing the school play. I suggested she was still angry at me for being female and not helping her to be a Leslie, a boy-girl. She acknowledged with some surprise that she had almost forgotten about Leslie and agreed she was angry and disappointed, but she knew there were no boy-girls, that was just make-believe.

With her increased ego strengths Erica reluctantly worked through fears of her genital strivings and her frustrated transference wish that I, as a phallic woman, would give her a penis. The increased acceptance by peers, decreased rejections by her mother, and J.'s genuine affection, the most she had ever known, helped affirm her positive identification with me and her mother. Less threatened by her genital strivings and fantasies, she no longer needed to be a boy-girl. She was ready for termination.

With her improved self-image, Erica had less need for make-believe, and spent her sessions talking about her activities at school, at home, and with friends. As her sessions seemed too staid, I inquired if something was bothering her. She said that she knew it was time to stop, but the idea scared her. I assured her that she could spend several months or more just talking about stopping, that we did not have to set a date until she was ready, and that, if she needed to, she could return. She then told me her mother was planning to marry J. in a few months and that she wanted to stay in treatment until after marriage. It bothered her that she could love J. more than her father, but everything about J. was nicer. She was relieved that I might be right, because she still had jeebies, but they did not make her mother mad and J. had not left or taken her mother away.

We set a date for termination and in the last months worked through her oedipal wishes and fears. Moving back and forth between the playroom and the adult area, she played out fears of being abandoned if she moved into latency and worried how she could manage without me. Around Thanksgiving she began drawing pictures of a Puritan girl in a number of threatening situations. In the last picture, the girl was saved from falling off a cliff by a founding father, and then she became an industrious helper preparing for the Thanksgiving feast. The last session, she brought some daisies she said were from her garden. As she tried to arrange them, she realized many of them had wilted. As she threw them out, she expressed her sorrow at leaving treatment, but said, "There's not much more to do here." She said it helped to know she could write, call or come to see me, but she thought she might be too busy. After we said our good-byes and the session ended, I noticed she had left one fresh daisy that was just beginning to bloom.

### DISCUSSION

Erica's analysis presents some unique clinical data that provide additional evidence refuting Freud's hypothesis (1925) that penis envy is the immediate result of a little girl's discovery of the inferiority of her clitoris. The clinical material is significant because Erica's masturbation fantasies and masturbatory activity led on several occasions to orgasm during her analytic sessions. Although in part it was a reenactment from recent memory and a report of activity outside the analysis, its primary importance was that it occurred as part of the analytic process so that the exact nature of the activity not only was observed, but its meaning was analyzed and understood. Erica dramatically demonstrated that her clitoris was not physically inferior, but rather was the locus of the beginning of intense, pleasurable genital arousal, which she called the "jeebies." Moreover, the psychological significance of Erica's genitalia and jeebies was almost the opposite of what Freud proposed. Erica imbued her erotic capacity and fantasies with a magical potency so dangerous that she believed it caused her parents' divorce and her abandonment and rejection by them. Since she accurately observed that in her family boys were loved and girls were not, she was convinced that boys did not have jeebies. She wanted a penis to get rid of her jeebies or at least to diminish their power and destructiveness, so that she could be loved and valued. She never expressed a wish to be a boy, but rather a boy-girl. Clearly aware of her vagina and its erotic connection to her clitoris, she enjoyed her jeebies and did not want to lose them or her genitalia. Her solution was to have a penis inside her vagina. Aware that some girls and women got affection, she imagined they must have hidden penises in their vaginas which somehow made their jeebies acceptable. Thus, her persistent intense penis envy was pathological and occurred as a secondary phenomenon in response to her perception that being only a girl was unacceptable.

While it is true that Erica's development was not normal, biologically she appeared to be a normal girl. One can argue that her genetic endowment gave her stronger than normal genital strivings. This cannot be proved or disproved. However, Erica did respond to psychoanalytic treatment. So, without biologic (psychopharmacologic) intervention, when the analysis ended, Erica's behavior and attitudes about herself and others were consistent with what we know about 9-year-old girls. Alternately, it seems likely that as Mrs. G. was not a gentle or controlled woman, when she cleaned and diapered Erica, she may have overstimulated the perineal and anal areas. We do know that Mrs. G. prematurely separated from Erica, pushing her to form an early close relationship with her father. Undoubtedly Dr. G.'s roughhousing, wrestling, and sleeping with Erica were other sources of overstimulation, both physically and psychologically.

We have not yet developed a cohesive theory of normal female development. But the knowledge that many little girls are aware of their vaginas and have the capacity to experience pleasurable clitoral and vaginal sensations that can result in intense orgastic experiences increases our understanding of women and needs to be integrated into our developmental formulations. In contrast to current psychoanalytic theories of femininity which place primary importance on introjects and identifications that result from child-parent interaction (Lax, 1990), Erica's primary problem arose from her unacceptable genital drives. Sociocultural, environmental, and interpersonal influences were critical in Erica's conflicts, as they secondarily reinforced, amplified, and validated her belief that her instinctual drives not only were bad but dangerous. Further studies are needed to clarify this issue. Perhaps both factors are equally important. What is most germane may be the consequences of their particular interaction in each individual.

Initially Erica met most of the criteria of the attention-deficit hyperactivity disorder. That is, before she was 7, she had a disturbance lasting at least 6 months during which she was excessively fidgety, had difficulty remaining seated when required to do so, appeared to be easily distracted by external stimuli, often blurted out answers to questions before they were completed, had difficulties with sustained attention to tasks and playing quietly, often did not listen to what was said to her, and frequently engaged in physically dangerous activities without considering consequences. This disturbance is generally attributed to a biochemical imbalance that can be corrected with pharmacologic agents. In recent years it has become one of the most commonly diagnosed ailments of childhood. One of the purposes of the length and detail of this presentation was to provide evidence that at least in one child, this behavior resulted from psychological problems. The evaluation indicated that Erica was suffering from an inability to resolve unconscious conflicts from the oedipal and preoedipal phases which had prevented her stable entry into latency. This was the indication for psychoanalytic treatment. It took some time to establish a therapeutic alliance and analyze Erica's transference resistances and negative transference feelings. Thus, a transference neurosis emerged which allowed Erica to show me her jeebies. Her intense genital strivings and associated fantasies evoked much fear, guilt, and regressive behavior. In time I dealt with her anger and disappointment at the frustration of her transference wish that I, as a phallic woman, would solve her problems by giving her a penis so that she could be a boy-girl. Analyzing her positive transference feelings, she was able to identify with my analyzing functions and with my acceptance of her as a female. This enabled her sufficiently to resolve her oedipal and preoedipal conflicts. The ensuing stable structural changes reflected increased ego functions and an operative and less punitive superego. She progressed into latency where her drives were sublimated effectively in phase-appropriate defenses, allowing for realistic scholastic achievement, creative work, and improved peer and family relationships. There were no longer any manifestations of an attention deficit disorder, with or without hyperactivity.

It is difficult to see how psychoanalysis could have corrected a biochemical imbalance. Admittedly, drugs might have improved some of her behavior. Being given something that she could orally incorporate might have had magical significance for her. It might have calmed her and elevated her mood, but such an approach would have masked the underlying real pathology. It would also have made her dependent on an external agent rather than on her own mind and body to achieve comfort, security, and growth in her life. These clinical data provide the rationale for psychoanalytic treatment.

## BIBLIOGRAPHY

APPLEGARTH, A. (1976). Some observations of work inhibition in women. *J. Amer. Psychoanal. Assn.*, 24(suppl.):251–268.

——— (1988). Origins of femininity and the wish for a child. *Psychoanal. Inq.*, 8:169–176.

BARNETT, M. C. (1966). Vaginal awareness in the infancy and childhood of girls. *J. Amer. Psychoanal. Assn.*, 14:129–141.

——— (1968). "I can't" versus "He won't." *J. Amer. Psychoanal. Assn.*, 16:588–600.

BLUM, H. P., ed. (1976a). Female psychology. *J. Amer. Psychoanal. Assn.*, 24(suppl.), no. 5.

——— (1976b). Masochism, the ego ideal, and the psychology of women. *J. Amer. Psychoanal. Assn.*, 24(suppl.):157–192.

BORNSTEIN, B. (1953). Masturbation in the latency period. *Psychoanal. Study Child*, 8:65–78.

CHEHRAZI, S. (1986). Female psychology *J. Amer. Psychoanal. Assn.*, 34:141–162.

FRAIBERG, S. (1972). Genital arousal in latency girls. *Psychoanal. Study Child*, 27:439–475.

FRENKEL, R. S. (1991a). The early abortion of a pseudocyesis. *Psychoanal. Study Child*, 46:237–254.

——— (1991b). Termination in the analysis of an adolescent girl. In *Saying Goodbye*, ed. A. Schmukler. Hillsdale, N.J.: Analytic Press, pp. 211–229.

FREUD, S. (1925). Some psychical consequences of the anatomical distinction between the sexes. *S.E.*, 19:243–258.

GROSSMAN, W. I. & STEWART, W. A. (1976). Penis envy. *J. Amer. Psychoanal. Assn.*, 24(suppl.):193–212.

HORNEY, K. (1926). Flight from womanhood. *Int. J. Psychoanal.*, 7:324–339.

JONES, E. (1935). Early female sexuality. *Int. J. Psychoanal.*, 16:262–273.

KARME, L. (1981). A clinical report of penis envy. *J. Amer. Psychoanal. Assn.*, 29:427–446.

KESTENBERG, J. S. (1968). Outside and inside, male and female. *J. Amer. Psychoanal. Assn.*, 16:457–520.

KLEEMAN, J. A. (1971). The establishment of core gender identity in normal girls. *Arch. Sex. Behav.* 1:103–129.

KRAMER, P. (1954). Early capacity of orgastic discharge and character formation. *Psychoanal. Study Child,* 9:128–141.

LAX, R. (1990). An imaginary brother. *Psychoanal. Study Child,* 45:257–272.

MASTERS, W. & JOHNSON, V. (1966). *Human Sexual Response.* Boston: Little, Brown.

MCKECHNIE, J. L., ed. (1979). Heebie-jeebies, n.pl. [coined by Billy De Beck in his comic strip, *Barney Goggle*], an attack of nervousness, jitters [slang] *Webster's New Universal Unabridged Dictionary.* New York: Simon & Schuster, p. 840.

MONEY, J. & EHRHARDT, A. (1972). *Man and Woman, Boy and Girl.* Baltimore: Johns Hopkins Univ. Press.

STOLLER, R. (1973). The impact of new advances in sex research on psychoanalytic theory. *Amer. J. Psychiat.,* 130:241–251.

# The Impact of Divorce on a Preadolescent Girl

## E. KIRSTEN DAHL, Ph.D.

*This paper presents clinical material from the psychoanalysis of a 12-year-old girl whose parents had divorced several years earlier. Material drawn from her analysis permits us to examine the question: given the intrapsychic demands of the prepubertal period, how was the experience of divorce registered, what aspects of intrapsychic functioning became distorted, and what, if any, remained uncontaminated? The impact of the parental divorce lay in an intensification and entrenchment of characteristic latency defenses which, as puberty approached, contributed to heightened internal conflict and an insistent turn to reality as both explanation for and solution of intrapsychic conflict.*

JUDITH WALLERSTEIN, USING DATA FROM HER LONGITUDINAL STUDY OF the impact of divorce on children's development (1980, 1989), concluded that the impact of divorce is mediated in part by the developmental level of the child and that with the entry into new developmental territory the impact of the divorce may be reexperienced in new ways. My paper demonstrates how the impact of divorce can be understood through the lens of the inner world. I will examine the ways in which multiple, complex, external factors were reworked intrapsychically as a preadolescent girl tried to negotiate the internal demands of the prepubertal period. In this case we can see the apparently delayed effects of divorce on a child who appeared to have coped well at a younger age, but who, facing the developmental crisis initiated by prepuberty, appeared to feel bereft and abandoned in a new way.

The case of 12-year-old Lizzie represents an atypical postdivorce

Associate Professor, Yale University Child Study center, New Haven, Conn.

An earlier version of this paper was presented at the annual meeting of the International Psychoanalytic Association in Buenos Aires, Argentina, July 30, 1991.

family constellation; although Lizzie had spent her early years in the care of both parents, by the time of the divorce her mother had assumed the role of the absent, but regularly visiting, parent. There were many other unusual features of the family situation, any one of which might be examined for its impact on Lizzie's subsequent development. Material drawn from Lizzie's psychoanalysis permits examination of the question: given the intrapsychic demands of the prepubertal period, how was the experience of divorce registered, what aspects of intrapsychic functioning became distorted and what, if any, remained uncontaminated?

## CLINICAL MATERIAL

Lizzie H. was 12 years 3 months old when she was referred for psychoanalysis. Although her complete analysis lasted two and a half years, only material from the first year will be presented as this most clearly illustrates the phenomena under study in this paper.

At the initial consultation interview, Mr. and Mrs. H. reported that over the past few weeks, Lizzie had been increasingly preoccupied by obsessive suicidal thoughts and that the previous week, Lizzie had been sent home from school following her breaking down in uncontrollable and inconsolable crying. Since then Lizzie had felt herself unable to return to school. Both parents expressed concern that their daughter might be suicidal. With some irritation, Mrs. H. said that recently her daughter had become quite clinging toward her as if Lizzie was trying to control her mother's every move. In addition, Lizzie had begun compulsively confessing all her transgressions to her father. She also had begun to have difficulty falling asleep at night.

During the initial consultation, the following history emerged. Lizzie was the second of a sibship of two; her brother, Charles, was 3 years older. There was a significant age difference between Mr. and Mrs. H. who had met when the mother was a student of the father's. When Lizzie was 6, the family moved to Connecticut and settled in a suburb close to the father's job. The mother's job was in a city some distance away; although the mother might possibly have commuted between home and job, instead she chose to live in an apartment close to her job during the week, returning to the family home each weekend. From Friday evening until Monday morning, the mother lived with her family.

Two years later, when Lizzie was 8, the parents divorced. Mr. and Mrs. H. agreed that their marriage had always been a difficult one, but the most immediate cause of the divorce was that Mrs. H. had taken a lover and wished to live with him. The parents were concerned about the impact of a divorce on their children and wished to minimize its consequences as much as possible. For this reason, they decided not to change their living arrangements in any way; Mrs. H. continued to return "home" every Friday night, leaving again on Monday morning. As the parents had had separate bedrooms for a number of years, they felt the divorce had a minimal impact, as far as they were concerned, on their living arrangements. Again, in the hopes of not hurting their children unnecessarily, the parents thought there had never been any significant discussion about the divorce and they were unsure what the children actually had known about it at the time. Retrospectively they thought the situation must have been hard on both children, although until their daughter's recent troubles they would have said the divorce had had a greater impact on Charles, who, they felt, was a somewhat isolated adolescent. Recently Mrs. H. and her companion had bought a house together several hours away. Both Mr. and Mrs. H. anticipated that the children would occasionally visit Mrs. H. at her new home, but Mrs. H. did not intend the purchase of this new home to interfere in any substantive way with her current visiting arrangements. Both parents reported that their children were aware of and apparently liked mother's companion, although they saw very little of him as visitation usually took place as described and the children rarely visited their mother at her apartment. Mother's companion did not accompany her during her visitation with her children as both Mr. and Mrs. H. felt this would make all concerned uncomfortable.

Lizzie's developmental milestones were normal. The parents described their daughter as a "perfect little girl" and "a superkid." They had always found her "easy to read" because "she wore her heart on her sleeve." They thought she had adapted well to all the changes in her life and had always been a child who did very well both academically and socially. Mr. and Mrs. H. said that Lizzie's obsessive thoughts and "Mommy clinging" had started four months prior to the consultation. In passing, Mr. and Mrs. H. mentioned that on those nights when Lizzie had trouble sleeping, she would sometimes climb into bed with her father. On weekends when Mrs. H. joined the family, Lizzie often slept with her mother. Recently Lizzie had developed some compulsive rituals, particularly around speaking to her mother on the telephone and the need to "confess" her "bad" thoughts and deeds to her father. At 12 years 3 months old, Lizzie was not yet menstruating, although her pediatrician had suggested at Lizzie's 12-year exam that she would begin sometime within the next 18 months. The pediatrician's prediction proved correct as Lizzie reached menarche at 13 years 4 months.

I found Lizzie to be attractive and feminine, her blossoming figure clearly indicating the approach of puberty. Although visibly depressed, she was dressed appropriately and stylishly in a manner typical for a girl of her age and social class. Lizzie was very tearful, but
she was nevertheless quite articulate and surprisingly "psychologically
minded." She stated several times that she wanted to "figure things
out" so that she wouldn't be so depressed. She described herself as
feeling helpless to stop her obsessive thoughts and actions and implied
that her depression was the result of feeling overwhelmed by these
thoughts. She was able to give a coherent and vivid history of herself
and her family as well as of the onset of her symptomatology; she knew
when her parents had divorced and she knew that the cause had been
longstanding difficulties between her parents as well as the presence of
her mother's lover. With some help from me she was quick to make
connections between present experiences, thoughts, fantasies, feelings, and memories; as she began to make connections, she began to
experience a lightening of her mood, revealing a good sense of humor
as well as a lively intelligence.

Lizzie said she thought she had started to feel bad around Mother's
Day; she connected these depressive feelings with discovering her
mother's birth control device and her learning that her mother and
mother's lover had bought a house together. Although Lizzie said that
she and her mother were very close, she described a number of incidents in which she depicted her mother as neglectful, unfair, and
insensitive. Lizzie said that when she first started to feel bad four
months ago, she had been aware of feeling angry with her mother but
then found herself worrying obsessively that her mother might die in a
car wreck after a visit with her. Lizzie's next obsessional thought had
been that she might kill her mother's dog (who lived with Lizzie). Lizzie
reported that these consciously hostile, obsessional thoughts had then
been replaced by obsessive "visions" of stabbing herself with a kitchen
knife. These obsessional thoughts were followed by the ritual actions of
confessing to her father and a daily telephone conversation with her
mother. The immediate precipitant for Lizzie's breakdown in school
had been that her best friend had not invited Lizzie on a weekend trip
because she felt Lizzie "ought to spend more time with her mother." As
Lizzie and I noticed together over several sessions how uncomfortable
Lizzie became when she felt angry toward her mother, she reported a
diminution of her suicidal thoughts. Lizzie then recalled two incidents
in the preceding year which she thought contributed to her present
troubles; both could be understood as representing a fantasy of being
overwhelmed by her sexual impulses. These incidents were followed by

increasing anxiety about menarche. Lizzie believed that her pediatrician had told her the exact date on which she would begin to menstruate and that this date fell 18 months from her twelfth birthday. Lizzie wanted to believe that menarche could be predicted and thereby controlled, but feared that instead she would be taken by surprise.

Strikingly absent from Lizzie's material was any mention of her father. When I tried to explore with Lizzie her parents' report of her sleeping in their respective beds and her ritual confessions to her father, she denied sleeping with her father and was quite bland in her account of her confessions to him. She said she did sometimes climb into her mother's bed "to cuddle, but it's no big deal."

Lizzie readily acknowledged that she preferred being able to figure things out in advance so that she would know what to do and not be taken by surprise. She thought that perhaps her obsessive thoughts had something to do with this preferred style of coping. She agreed enthusiastically to undertaking analysis.

Mr. and Mrs. H. were very pleased with Lizzie's decision to begin an analysis. Mrs. H. had been involved in psychoanalytically oriented psychotherapy for several years and had found it very helpful; feeling that her own psychotherapeutic work was sufficient, Mrs. H. did not wish to meet with anyone at the Child Study Center. Mr. H. readily agreed to meet on a weekly basis with a senior faculty social worker especially skilled in work with parents of adolescents. These parallel treatments continued throughout Lizzie's psychoanalysis. Through his treatment, Mr. H. became more sensitive to the developmental needs of his daughter and became more appropriate, firm, and consistent in the setting of limits for Lizzie. In spite of the failure of their marriage, both parents were very committed to their joint parenting arrangements and were well able to discuss issues raised by parenting Lizzie. Certainly both parents gave evidence of having personality difficulties that, in spite of their love and genuine concern, interfered at times with their capacity to parent Lizzie appropriately. However, the focus of this paper is not an examination of the impact of the family system on Lizzie. The material from Lizzie's psychoanalysis gives us a powerful lens through which to view the particular meanings she gave intrapsychically to her parents' divorce and the ways in which her experience of their divorce became interwoven with other aspects of her inner world. The psychoanalytic data allow us to explore what uses *Lizzie* made of her parents' divorce as an organizer within her inner world.

At the conclusion of Lizzie's analysis, she had become a popular, academically successful girl well launched into midadolescence. No longer anxious or symptomatic, she employed a variety of defenses in a flexible manner. She continued to demonstrate a gift for observing the ways in which her mind worked, but this had lost its earlier intellectual, obsessional quality. She demonstrated a particular sensitivity to the psychology of others, including her parents. Lizzie developed an understanding and acceptance of her parents' limitations as well as their strengths; her capacity to view her parents tolerantly and objectively contributed to a loving detachment from them, unusual in someone her age.

At the start of her analysis, Lizzie was very preoccupied with her anxiety generated by her obsessional thoughts; the content of these thoughts had to do with the need to confess and repetitive recitations of activities of hers about which she felt guilty. Later it emerged that she sometimes relied on obsessional thoughts (e.g., visualizing typing letters on a typewriter) to control painful affects as well. As we explored this material, her severe separation anxiety related to her mother's comings and goings emerged more clearly; her rage at her mother for what Lizzie experienced as her mother's abandonment exacerbated Lizzie's anxiety around separations. Lizzie began to understand that all of her anxious, solicitous concern for her mother (e.g., she would warn her mother to drive carefully and worry mother would have an accident) around her mother's leave-takings masked a deep fury related to the mother's original "abandonment" (perceived as being at the time of the parental divorce) and her taking a lover "instead" of her daughter. The separation anxiety was also linked to her fears about what becoming a teenager would bring which had crystallized around her anticipation of menarche; although somewhat vague, her anxious fantasies reflected her fear that to menstruate meant to lose control of her body, an anticipation of feeling ashamed and soiled, and the worry that "everyone would see." This material was expressed directly in relation to her mother and then in displacement around her current babysitter, Marty. We began to understand the intensity of her wish that her mother help her regulate her drives as Lizzie believed her mother had when Lizzie was younger. In the context of her sexually maturing body, Lizzie's longing for this early, active, preoedipal mother also made her very anxious as the longings stimulated homosexual fantasies.

Lizzie began a Monday hour early in her analysis saying that she felt "really upset" because her mother had just left. But now she could see these feelings were cyclical; she knew she would feel better by the end of the week. She felt she had a little better control over her feelings. She could see they were closely connected to her feeling that she needed her mother and how cross she felt then when her mother left. Lizzie said, "I wonder now how I ever managed before when she left me? How could I ignore her going?" Then she began to describe her new obsessional thoughts, how she imagined typing words over and over, whatever words she was thinking; she did this to stop feeling anxious. Lizzie then reported a dream she had had the night before, "I dream I am Private Benjamin and I am swimming in the pool with friends." She thought she had this dream because she recently saw *Private Benjamin* on TV and also because she really wanted to own a swimming pool. Lizzie described the movie as a really funny comedy about a girl who joins the army, a statement that conceals the complexity of the film's depiction of its heroine's aggressive and sexual conflicts. She said that she spent Friday night at her best friend Emma's house and they had fun watching a favorite movie together. But later in the evening Emma's older sister came home drunk. Lizzie said this was very disturbing and the next day the sister talked about mixing alcohol and marijuana; she hadn't done that, but she said her boyfriend had. When Lizzie looked shocked, Emma's sister laughed and said, "I thought when I was your age, I'd never do any of that stuff, but you know you always do." As Lizzie reported this to me, she looked very worried and wondered whether I thought that was true. "All my friends' parents use marijuana, but *my* parents *never* have; they *really* disapprove of that sort of thing." She said emphatically *she* would never use drugs or do wild things. Lizzie looked worried again and said, "But then I get to thinking; what if I *do* try it out once or twice? I'll feel like such a terrible failure. My mom wouldn't like it." I commented that when she thought about becoming a teenager, a lot of exciting, scary feelings got stirred up and then she felt like she really needed her mother to help her stay in control, but at the same time she felt it was sort of babyish to need her mother that much. Lizzie said maybe she wouldn't feel like she needed her mom so much if she had had more of her when she was younger. "Like I still like her to cuddle me a lot, but I wouldn't want my friends to know that." After a pause, Lizzie said that her parents were going to rehire her old baby-sitter, Marty; Lizzie felt very excited about that, "because I really LOVE Marty and we have lots of fun together."

As we analyzed this material, Lizzie began to turn to her best friend, Emma, both as a displacement from the tie to her mother and as a transition to boys. The relationship with her best friend took on all the characteristics of a great romance, with Lizzie and Emma celebrating their "second anniversary" and then the introduction of a (female) rival so that there were many "terrible misunderstandings," "lovers' quarrels," and loving reunions. In this relationship, it was possible to see the imprint of the phallic-oedipal tie to the mother in Lizzie's wish for exclusive possession of the love object and her jealous fury when she felt spurned.

Other themes that emerged during the first year of Lizzie's analysis were:

Lizzie thought that her family was "strange." Lizzie felt that the nature of her family was strange and that the individual members of her family were strange. Although on the surface, her notion of her "strange family" had to do with her embarrassment both about the divorce and her parents' custodial arrangements, at a deeper level this idea reflected a fantasy of her "strange" inner world with its "strange" eruptions of intense feelings. Lizzie wondered anxiously whether she herself was all right. This anxiety along with her preoccupation with her maturing body and her tendency to experience these bodily changes as negative suggested a deeper anxiety about bodily integrity as well.

Early in this first year of analysis, Lizzie seemed to experience her father primarily as an externalization of her superego, that is, someone to whom she could and should "confess" as well as someone who stood on the side of being a good latency girl. In the course of the year there were fleeting glimpses of a more oedipal valence to Lizzie's tie to her father; this was expressed primarily through Lizzie's anxiety about being alone with him and about leaving him alone. She presented herself as functioning as her father's wife, cooking, cleaning, and washing clothes. Initially these longings found some confirmation in reality, as Mr. H. very much relied on Lizzie to handle many household chores. One might speculate that the age difference between the parents lent plausibility to Lizzie's fantasy of "daughter as wife" as well. However, as the father began to treat his daughter more appropriately, Lizzie's longing to be her father's wife and the attendant anxiety, rather than subsiding, emerged more clearly, suggesting that it was not simply Lizzie's *experience* of her father putting her in a "wifely role" that awakened her anxiety but that her oedipal fantasies significantly shaped her feelings about the household chores.

Much of this material emerged through the vicissitudes of the transference. Treatment began with Lizzie openly wishing to have me as her "good mother"; she avoided noticing or expressing any negative feelings toward me. Lizzie was very anxious about my leaving her for the long summer vacation and although she was able to recognize the link to her mother, she nevertheless insisted that she needed to be able to correspond with me during the break.[1] During the vacation she did

---

1. This was not a usual practice for me, but the holiday interruption occurred only two months after Lizzie began her analysis. It was not possible to analyze fully the meanings of her wish for my summer address. Further, I remained concerned about her depres-

indeed write to me once: a long affect-laden letter about how she had gone to a duck pond with her best friend and somehow cut her foot, requiring stitches. The emphasis in the letter was on blood and pain and her account suggested an unconscious fantasy of menarche as castration occurring in the absence of the mother while alone with the oedipal father.

When we resumed in September, there was more evidence of her struggle with negative feelings toward me: coming late to appointments, "needing" to cancel, and dozing off during sessions. As we analyzed her resistance, she brought in a board game for us to play. We came to understand it as permitting a situation in which she could express extremely destructive "killing" feelings while she also felt close to me. As this material was analyzed, it became clear that the risk in being "too close" was not only that her anger might destroy me but, more frighteningly, her fear that her longings for me, which contained the unconscious wish for her mother's bodily care now in the context of her sexually mature body, would become homoerotic. At this point the "love affair" with her best friend became a way via displacement to express these transferential themes.

During September, Lizzie anticipated a visit from Mrs. G. who had been her baby-sitter until Lizzie moved East. Lizzie said the thought of Mrs. G.'s visit made her feel furious; she wished she wouldn't come. She thought Mrs. G. would just want to fatten her up and would want Lizzie to wear "little girl's clothing." Lizzie thought she would just be too busy with her girlfriends to spend any time with Mrs. G. However, when Mrs. G. arrived, Lizzie was surprised by how much she enjoyed Mrs. G.'s visit. She found that Mrs. G. didn't treat her like a baby. In fact, to Lizzie's delight, Mrs. G. wanted to take her shopping for some really nice clothes. Immediately following this thought, Lizzie commented ruefully that Mrs. G. *did* cook very big meals and Lizzie felt she had to spend a lot of time bike riding so that she wouldn't put on any weight. After this thought, Lizzie remembered that she had had trouble sleeping the night before. But, "thank goodness," she said, "I didn't try to sleep in my dad's bed." She recalled then being asked to write down three wishes for a class at school; her wishes were that her dog be better housebroken, that she be given an air conditioner for her bedroom, and that she had a "decent boyfriend." Lizzie laughed recalling these wishes and then said she had been really busy with Girl Scouts lately. Also at night she found she was having some confusing "sexy"

---

sion and thought that the knowledge that she could write to me might help her weather the summer holiday more successfully.

thoughts. She was reminded of how four years ago she and an older girlfriend had watched "porno" movies: "She got me into a lot of weird stuff." Lizzie said she thought that maybe at night sometimes she got worried those old sexy feelings would come back and that then she would masturbate. After a pause she said she was thinking of this girl who got her period in the *fourth grade;* "It was yucky; it ran all down her legs! Emma's periods are very messy too. And my mother's flow is very heavy. I don't like that. I want to be able to still wear white pants."

A few sessions later, Lizzie began by reporting crossly that her mother had promised to take her shopping for clothes and then had reneged on the promise. Lizzie complained about her mother buying her "only cheap clothes and not even very many of those." Apparently changing the subject, she described how she and her girlfriends had gotten to know a slightly older boy, Jimmy, who was from another school. Lizzie said that originally Jimmy was "going with" one girl, but that she and her friends had all made friends with him so Jimmy wouldn't go with just one. They had all begun to hang out every afternoon at what had earlier been Lizzie and Emma's special place, the duck pond. Lizzie said she felt especially drawn to Jimmy. She found this very mysterious. She reported gravely that she had had an uncanny thought about Jimmy: she felt convinced that one day she and Jimmy would marry. She thought that she and Jimmy had a special, but secret, bond because she knew that Jimmy's mother had died leaving Jimmy an orphan. Lizzie went on to say that she had gotten all the girls to agree to a pact that no one would see Jimmy alone. However, in spite of this pact, she, Lizzie, had immediately broken it by arranging to meet Jimmy alone. She said that the two of them had just talked and he had touched her hand. Lizzie said that then she had felt panicky and had had the thought, "Things are going too fast!" Lizzie said then "somehow" all her girlfriends had discovered that Lizzie had broken their pact and that Emma had gotten especially angry, threatening not to be Lizzie's best friend any more. Lizzie said she couldn't stand the thought of her and Emma breaking up and so she had decided to write Jimmy a note saying she would never see him again. Following this narrative about Jimmy, Lizzie fell silent for a while; she looked sad. After a bit she spoke of missing her mother. She said she had decided to see her mother "no matter what" the coming weekend, even if she had to go visit her. She thought maybe she *would* go visit her mother instead of going to school. Lizzie announced suddenly that maybe she would go to *live* with her mother. As mentioned earlier, the parents apparently had never considered having the children live with the mother following the divorce, their conscious reasoning being that this would be too disruptive for the children. Consciously, Lizzie very much held this attitude. She insisted that she did not want to live with her mother as it would mean leaving all her friends and her school, but occasionally she "played" with the idea. This fantasy had less to do with imagining "life with mother" and was utilized primarily defensively as a way of representing the wish to remove herself from current internal conflict.

Another aspect of the transference during this first year was Lizzie's inability to anticipate sad or negative feelings around separations from me, so that she would find herself in the middle of my absence "suddenly" terribly upset. We could see how this not noticing was defensive against both her rage and her longings.

As the year drew to a close, the transference appeared to be fully organized around the following themes: (1) the wish to have me all to herself; (2) the fear of the homosexual tie; (3) jealousy of my "others"; (4) and the defensive need to be the good, bright latency girl who understood "everything." The transference neurosis was represented most vividly very late in the Spring when she felt unable to come to sessions because she was so upset over her best friend who had taken "another"; Lizzie feared that if she came to her sessions, I would simply remind her of this painful "jilting" and she wouldn't be able to be a good student in school.

During this first year, Lizzie seemed to be struggling with reawakened oedipal conflicts as she approached menarche. Although these conflicts appeared to be age typical, the environmental situation seemed to contribute to Lizzie's experience of her fantasies as more dangerous, more capable of realization. Internally, her fear that, under increased pressure from both the drives and her oedipal wishes, she would be unable to regulate either her aggression or her sexuality seemed to have initiated an attempted solution via regression to a preoedipal level both in the content of her fantasies and in her defensive maneuvers. Internally, Lizzie fell back on a defensive use of magic (in thought and action), and an overvaluation of intellectual activity; when this threatened to fail, she resorted to the demand that external reality via either her mother or father reestablish internal control.

With the reinstatement of a more infantile relationship with her parents in reality, Lizzie accomplished a partial oedipal victory in fantasy, but one that was experienced as dangerously regressed. It is probably quite significant that the precipitant of the breakdown in school was when Lizzie's best friend refused to invite Lizzie on a weekend trip, instead insisting that Lizzie spend more time with her mother. The longing for the magical mother of infancy who could "make everything better" in the context of puberty brought with it homoerotic fantasies now felt as dangerously realizable. Her attempt to make her father serve as an external superego (through her daily "confessions" to him) in an effort to control the re-erotized longing for the mother also brought the "positive" oedipal fantasy too close to realization. It is in this context that the depressive withdrawal from school and friends could be understood: as a refusal to go anywhere because every step seemed too dangerous.

## DISCUSSION

In her longitudinal study of the impact of divorce on children, Wallerstein found that the most striking response of children 6 to 8 years old at the time of divorce was their "pervasive sadness." She found that their usual defenses and coping mechanisms did not function successfully under the press of such increased painful affects, and that the majority of these children were openly grief-stricken. The children's thinking was colored by fantasies of deprivation and of the loss of things essential to continued life. The children openly yearned for and inhibited the expression of aggression toward the departed parent. Fantasies of reconciliation between the parents were widespread and tenaciously held (Wallerstein and Kelly, 1980).

Perhaps we can understand Lizzie's failure to manifest these common reactions to her parents' divorce at the time it occurred as representing in part an identification with her parents' own style of coping with their divorce through the employment of massive denial. We can speculate that the divorce found registration through the intensification and heightening of certain defensive strategies which appeared to become characteristic of Lizzie during latency: intellectualization, aggression turned inward in the service of being good, an increase in obsessionality, and the return of a belief in magic.

With the approach of puberty Lizzie's cherished defensive strategies proved insufficient in the face of increasing pressure from the drives and she broke down, exhibiting many of the reactions Wallerstein describes for the early latency period: grief, a clinging to the departed parent, an insistence on parental reconciliation manifested in Lizzie's denial of her mother's lover, an inhibition of aggression toward the departed parent, and fantasies of loss and deprivation.

Should Lizzie's breakdown be understood primarily as a delayed reaction to her parents' divorce, a reaction no longer capable of being warded off because of a weakening of the defenses secondary to the prepubertal upsurge in drives? I think that Lizzie's breakdown is better understood as resulting from the particular intrapsychic demands of the prepubertal period and the specific ways in which the parental divorce resonated with and intensified the dilemmas of that internal landscape. Lizzie's fantasies about the meaning of her parents' divorce for her became a metaphor or personal myth that functioned as an organizing and explanatory construct in her inner world.

Psychoanalytic theory concerning female preadolescence (Blos, 1962; Deutsch, 1944; Laufer and Laufer, 1984; Burgner, 1988) emphasizes that the biologically based upsurge in drives and the reawakened oedipal fantasies are initially defended against by a regressive turn to the preoedipal tie to the mother and an indiscriminate cathexis of all earlier libidinal and aggressive modes of gratification.

The reawakened longing for the active mother of infancy brings with it the danger of passive surrender. The girl is caught between longing to submit to the internalized infantile mother for gratification and the fear of being forced to submit, thereby losing her hard-won activity and sense of bodily integrity. The biologically based upsurge in the drives creates an internal climate of excitement that mirrors the primitive excitement of the infantile relationship to the mother. During infancy the mother is experienced as the regulator of affects, particularly excitement; now, as the child enters adolescence, the affect-regulating aspect of the mother is both longed for and feared. Just as the young adolescent struggles to free herself from this internal mother and simultaneously to keep her as a part of the self forever, she also moves toward a further psychological differentiation of her body from her mother's.

The material from Lizzie's first year of analysis illustrates this prepubertal landscape. We can see how the approach of menarche and the increase in excitement secondary to the upsurge in the drives reawakened the oedipal conflict and stimulated her longing for the affect-regulating mother of infancy with the accompanying fear not only of engulfment but of the homosexual object choice. Although these conflicts appear age typical, the environmental situation seemed to contribute to Lizzie's experience of her fantasies as more dangerous, more capable of realization. As we have seen, Lizzie initiated an attempted solution to these internal dilemmas via regression to a preoedipal level both in the content of her fantasies and in her defensive maneuvers. When these defenses threatened to fail, Lizzie resorted to the demand that her actual parents, especially her mother, reestablish internal control.

The reawakening of infantile sadism presented yet another danger for Lizzie; she did not feel safe externalizing this sadism onto her absent mother, linked internally to the mother she felt she needed as a regulator of excitement, nor was it safe to direct it toward her father on whom she felt dependent for care. To reverse the direction of the sadism would result in an intolerable level of masochism. Lizzie's separation anxiety, obsessive thinking, and magical operations can be understood as extreme defensive maneuvers in the service of inhibiting her sadism, thereby preserving the tie to the parents-in-reality on whom she felt so desperately dependent.

Lizzie responded to her reinstatement of a more infantile relationship with her parents in reality, as if it were a partial but nevertheless dangerous oedipal victory. Lizzie created a defensive fantasy of a magical, "always present" mother who would "make everything better," but in the context of her sexually maturing body this fantasy now felt dangerous as it implied a homosexual tie to her mother. Her effort to make her father serve as an external superego in an attempt to control the re-erotized longing for the mother also brought the "positive" oedipal fantasy too close to realization. At the time of her breakdown, Lizzie found herself surrounded by danger, from within and without; no further intrapsychic maneuvers remained and her ego was threatened with being overwhelmed.

Lizzie appeared to experience her parents' divorce as the loss of her mother; in an effort to master this psychological loss, normal intrapsychic processes became deeper and more entrenched. For Lizzie this had the effect during latency of a precocious but tenaciously accelerated developmental leap ahead into a pseudomaturity. Lizzie "overidentified" with her mother's wifely function. With the entry into the prepubertal period this tenacious, brittle identification with her mother as father's wife left her dangerously vulnerable to the reawakened incestuous fantasies. Lizzie attempted to regulate her heightened anxiety and excitement by a turn back toward the internal mother of infancy, but the attendant sadistic wishes proved intolerably dangerous as well. Because Lizzie could not find a satisfactory resolution within her inner world, she turned insistently, tenaciously, and despairingly to her real parents, demanding that they unite to take care of her as she imagined they had when she was very little, before the divorce.

For Lizzie the impact of her parents' divorce lay in the ways in which it became interwoven with aspects of her inner world. Her experience of the divorce as the loss of her mother intensified a brittle identification with her mother-as-wife which increased the anxiety generated by the reawakened oedipal fantasies as she approached puberty. Lizzie also employed her parents' divorce as an "explanation" for her fantasy of maternal abandonment, a fantasy created to defend against the newly dangerous longings for the old, active, pleasure-giving and excitement-regulating mother of infancy. Lizzie tried to solve the dilemmas of her inner world by an insistent turn to external reality: if only her parents had not divorced, everything would be all right "inside." Her symptoms at the point of breakdown may be understood in part as representing an unsuccessful compromise formation reflecting an unconscious fantasy that if she brought about her parents' reunion, she would be able to move forward into adolescence without encountering internal conflict.

## BIBLIOGRAPHY

BLOS, P. (1962). *On Adolescence.* New York: Free Press.

BURGNER, M. (1988). Analytic work with adolescents terminable and interminable. *Int. J. Psychoanal.,* 69:179–187.

DEUTSCH, H. (1944). *The Psychology of Women,* vol. 1. New York: Grune & Stratton.

LAUFER, M. & LAUFER, M. E. (1984). *Adolescence and Developmental Breakdown.* New Haven: Yale Univ. Press.

WALLERSTEIN, J. S. & BLAKESLEE, S. (1989). *Second Chances.* New York: Ticknor & Fields.

——— & KELLY, J. B. (1980). *Surviving the Breakup.* New York: Basic Books.

# Reality, Fantasy, and Adolescence

## H. SHMUEL ERLICH, Ph.D.

*Psychoanalytic views of reality and fantasy are contingent upon a theory of ego/mind: A mental-apparatus-objective approach is distinguishable from an experiential-subjective approach. These two views are highly correlated with Being and Doing as underlying modalities of processing experience. Adolescent development necessitates the integration and amalgamation of these two modalities, which are reflected in relating to reality as objective and separate from, or as merged and fused with, the ego, with corresponding fantasy contents and ego states. As social reality exists as an independent variable, it poses real problems for such crucial aspects of adolescence as identity formation, psychosocial moratorium, and the generational gap.*

I WOULD LIKE TO BEGIN WITH A QUOTE FROM WINNICOTT: "growing up means taking the parent's place. *It really does.* In the unconscious fantasy, growing up is inherently an aggressive act. And the child is no longer child-size" (1971, p. 169).

In this brief quote, Winnicott (1) takes pains to point out that the growth that endangers the parental position is a reality event; (2) distinguishes what really happens from an (underlying) unconscious fantasy; (3) returns to making a reality-based observation concerning the actual present size of the child; and (4) apparently feels compelled to make all these statements in the context of describing growth in adolescence.

I submit this statement in order to demonstrate the main points of my argument: (1) The conceptualization of the relationship be-

Director, Sigmund Freud Center for Study and Research in Psychoanalysis, and Clinical Associate Professor, Department of Psychology, Hebrew University of Jerusalem; Training Analyst and Faculty, Israel Psychoanalytic Society and Institute.

Earlier versions of this paper were presented at the Conference on Fantasy and Reality in Late Adolescence, Kassel University, and at the Lindau Psychotherapie Wochen, Germany, April 1992.

tween reality and fantasy plays a crucial role in psychoanalytic theory. (2) There are essentially two opposed approaches to this issue, which may be viewed as reflecting a more fundamental and underlying duality of experiential modes. (3) While the relationship fantasy/reality is of great importance in understanding all development and functioning, it is of special significance with regard to adolescent development. This has to do with the unique transformation in the above-mentioned experiential modes that is essential to adolescence.

## PSYCHOANALYTIC VIEWS ON REALITY AND FANTASY

Starting with Freud's earliest work (1895), there is a tension inherent in psychoanalytic conceptualizations of the relationship between the individual and his reality. Freud early on set himself the task of creating a working model of the mind in the form of a mental apparatus. The major adaptive aim of this mental apparatus is the handling of external and internal stimulation in accordance with the pleasure principle. The relationship between the organism and its internal and external reality is conceived of as the mediation, by the mental apparatus, between the organism and its environment, the latter quite schematically and reductionistically consisting of stimulation.

Freud, however, suddenly also speaks of the active role of "*extraneous help,* when the attention of an experienced person is drawn to the child's state. . . . In this way this path of discharge acquires a secondary function of the highest importance, that of *communication*, and the initial helplessness of human beings is the *primal source* of all *moral motives*" (p. 318).

This unexpected inclusion of the "experienced person" in the mental apparatus scheme is actually the precursor of Hartmann's "average expectable environment," Erikson's "mutuality," and Winnicott's "good enough mother." With this one brief interjection, we are witness to the essential failure of the task Freud had set himself, of devising "a psychology for neurologists," couched in and developed entirely out of physical properties and assumptions. It is the failure of the mechanistic model of the mind which requires an equally mechanical, passive and restricted environment. Surely the "experienced person" must have gained his experience by having been raised himself by other human beings. He or she is not sophisticated "humanoid" machinery, but the repository of cumulative human experience, transmitted in social containers which are ready to meet and interact with the neonate. All the tension between mental apparatus psychology and a psychology of human experience, meaning, and symbolization is inherent in the one word "communication."

The tension between these two approaches—the mental apparatus vs. the experiential—is reflected in the polarized views of *reality* in psychoanalytic thinking. Let us address first what I would call the "traditional view" of reality, namely, the mental apparatus approach. Freud preferred to ignore reality and to treat it as "what is out there."[1] The advent of ego psychology put reality back within the scope of psychoanalysis by adding the adaptive point of view to the others. Yet the nature of this adaptation continued to be, in Wallerstein's (1973) words, "from the inner perspective looking outward." The organism is equipped with preadapted ego apparatuses, geared toward an "average expectable" environment (Hartmann, 1964). While these apparatuses change and mature with development, the environmental dimension remains fixed within such broadly defined limits. In this view, reality is always *external* to the mental apparatus; it is inherently *objective* in relation to it. There must be a *boundary* between reality and the apparatus; this is as much true for *external* reality (environment) as for *internal* reality (soma and drives). I would also include here the Kleinian view, which is essentially based on the separateness of ego and object. Recent findings on neonate development (e.g., Stern, 1985) support the availability of such early discriminatory capacities.

The existence of a boundary requires mediation across that boundary. The ego, says Freud, is such a "frontier-creature" (1923, p. 56). Borrowing from social system terminology, I would say that "the ego functions and exercises its leadership 'on the boundary'" (Erlich, 1992). There can be no question about the adaptive value of the ego's functioning at this boundary. A breakdown of what constitutes relating to reality (e.g., reality testing, sense of reality, perception, thought, fantasy, judgment, motility, defense, etc.) is actually a catalogue of ego functions (Hurvich, 1970; Sandler and Nagera, 1963; Wallerstein, 1983). It is also implicit in this conception that the ego employs secondary processes in its reality relationships.

Let me attempt at this point a partial summary of this traditional view of reality in psychoanalysis. I would say that in this approach, reality consists of the intrapsychic elaborations by the ego of what it is capable of processing at the boundary between what is internal and

---

1. The shift from the seduction theory to the wishful oedipal fantasy was, of course, a further step in the same direction, and is intrinsically relevant to the subject matter of this paper.

what is external to the mental apparatus. It is a view of reality as *outside* of, and capable of being *objectified* by, the ego.

There is another view of reality within the scope of psychoanalysis, but it appears to be regarded as a more subversive, "less scientific" point of view. This view does not proceed from the inside out, as the former one does. Instead, it is based on the *original unity and oneness of ego and reality* (Erikson, 1962, 1968; Loewald, 1951; Winnicott, 1971). Here the original relationship of ego and reality (as represented by the mother) is one of unity and oneness. The ego is "a participant in the creation of reality," better defined as "actuality" (Erikson, 1962).

The primary relatedness between infant and mother is one of unity and oneness, which Winnicott terms BEING. The discovery of reality proceeds via the *illusion* of the creation of this reality by the infant. The cooperation and participation of the environment, which leaves this illusion unchallenged, allow for the creation of potential space and the transitional object, which are the basis of the infant's subjective experience of reality. The gradual discovery of objective reality is a later achievement, contingent on the prior creation of potential space and transitional phenomena. The ego, in Loewald's terms, gradually *detaches* reality from itself, *allowing* it to become objective.

To summarize this view of reality, which I call the "experiential" view: it proceeds from the initial *psychological unity of ego and reality.* The earliest experience and notion of reality are that it is part of oneself. There is no room even for such a thing as an interaction, since self and object *are* one. Events take place within a reality subjectively experienced, yet as vivid and related as can be. The ego is certainly operative here, but in a different way than we are perhaps accustomed to think of it. Mental processes conform to the primary process type; yet it would be incorrect to assert that this is therefore necessarily a "primitive" mode of functioning.

I have thus far addressed myself to what I described as the two opposite views of the nature of the relationship of ego and reality. I can now ask whether and to what extent a similar situation prevails with regard to *fantasy.* Three major categories must be distinguished in the psychoanalytic literature with regard to fantasy. These should be thought of as different *approaches* to fantasy, rather than definitions of what constitutes fantasy:

1. A specific wish or ideation, or, in general, the *content*-aspect of a psychic process, which may be conscious, preconscious, or unconscious. This meaning of "fantasy" is prevalent in clinical usage. It also concurs with the Kleinian view, in which fantasies are *always* regarded as the ideational components of instincts. In this sense, fantasies "are"

instinctual drives or wishes, originally experienced both somatically and mentally, but gradually becoming more refined and ideational (Isaacs, 1948; Segal, 1964).

2. A mental *process* or psychic *structure*. Here the emphasis is on the capacity of fantasy to take part in mental regulation, by playing a defensive, anticipatory, or adaptive role, and in this way to bind anxiety, stabilize internal processes, and possibly govern behavior in a consistent manner (Sandler and Nagera, 1964). Used in this sense, fantasy appears to qualify as a mental structure (Rapaport, 1960). Once again, such a structure could function at various levels of consciousness. It would probably be found to be largely unconscious, however, especially if it integrates many diverse and complex bits of affect, ideation, and instinctual wishes. This corresponds primarily to the ego-psychological view of fantasy, but in part also to some of the meaning it has within the Kleinian approach.

3. An *ego state*, characterized mainly by its prevailing mode of altered consciousness. Of all the different meanings of the term, this is the one that Freud consistently seemed to prefer (Laplanche and Pontalis, 1985). Here fantasy corresponds to the phenomenology of the daydream state, which is best captured by the fact that the ego indulges itself in turning away from objective, factual reality, while it maintains a constant background awareness of its unreality. Rather than invoking the continuum conscious/unconscious, or internal/external, as in the first two dimensions, this experiential dimension partakes of the continuum subjective/objective, or "psychic reality" (Freud, 1900, p. 620).

It seems to me that these three areas—reality, fantasy, and our theory of mind—are closely linked and intertwined. It appears that fantasy falls into the same division we encountered concerning the notion of reality. In the traditional psychoanalytic approach, the relationship between fantasy and reality is essentially a *causal* one—fantasy is always caused by inner or outer reality. In turn, fantasy formation will affect or cause events in reality. In this view, fantasies (particularly in the form of daydreams) are primarily created in response to the failure of reality to meet needs and instinctual wishes: it is their frustration that leads to wish-fulfilling fantasies. Fantasies are the ego's temporary indulgence in substitute gratification, in lieu of actual fulfillment in outer reality. This causal model thus links fantasy with ego functioning and defense, as much as with the regulation of the mental apparatus.

What is the view of fantasy in the experiential approach? Here it is not the case that the ego has a fantasy *about* reality, which is then a *substitution* for reality. Rather, fantasy *is* reality, or "a reality." It is experienced as real, in the sense that it is enjoyed or abhorred as such. More importantly, however, the discrimination between what is and what is not "objectively real" is not the pertinent or the paramount question here. The central experience is one of unity of subject and object, of ego and reality. Inner and outer, subjective and objective reality are experienced and regarded as one. In the same vein, though more difficult to comprehend from a factual point of view, reality *is* fantasy. The attempt to split fantasy from reality must lead to disillusionment, and eventually to loneliness and despair.

## THE TWO EXPERIENTIAL MODES

So far I have reviewed the psychoanalytic concepts of reality and fantasy, and found them to be intrinsically related to models of the mind and in particular to the ego. I was able to differentiate two diametrically opposed views. One proceeds from the notion of a mental apparatus, regards reality from the inside outwardly, and involves objectification of reality, an emphasis on boundaries, causal relationships, and secondary process thinking. The other, which stems from an experiential-psychological view, stresses the initial unity of ego and reality, and involves subjectification of reality, the absence of causality and boundaries, and primary process thinking.

These two seemingly opposed views bear striking similarities to the two experiential modalities I have described (Erlich and Blatt, 1985; Erlich, 1988, 1989, 1990, 1991, 1992). I suggested that the experience of self and object occurs and is processed within two psychological modalities. These modalities operate continuously and in parallel, and eventually also complementally, yet only one modality will be ascendant or dominant at any given moment. The two modalities give rise to fundamentally different experiences of self and object: in the first, self and object are clearly demarcated by boundaries; the relationship between them is causal and functional, and is dominated by purpose and intentionality, directionality and chronology. Logical and critical thought is characteristic, and hence thinking strives toward objectivity, and is of the secondary process kind. This is, however, also the modality in which instinctual drives and conflicts are experienced. The central question here might be phrased as, "Who is doing what to whom?" which is why I termed this dimension as Doing.[2] In the second dimension, the fundamental quality is that of merger, identity, and fusion

2. The terminology of Doing and Being has its origins and clear parallels in Winnicott's work (1971), yet there are also some significant and fundamental differences between his conception and mine.

between self and object. Boundaries hardly exist at all, and are met only when they encompass both self and object together. Time, space, and other dimensions of physical or factual reality are secondary and unimportant, and thinking is subjective and primarily of the primary process kind. The central experience is one of Being (hence its name) in fusion and togetherness. There are no conflicts or drive wishes here, but only experiences of being vs. nonbeing, with needs, wishes, and wants along these lines (Erlich and Blatt, 1985; Erlich, 1990). These modalities have important implications for theory, but obviously also for treatment and clinical understanding (Erlich, 1991). They also have developmental implications, and especially so for adolescence; I will discuss these presently.

The issue of fantasy/reality, and the ego's participation in it, seems to resolve itself around these dimensions. The reality testing and adaptive aspects of the relationship between ego and reality take precedence and are reflective of our thoughts and fantasies in the mode of Doing. It is in this mode that the notion of a mental apparatus is conceived and takes precedence. In the mode of Being, on the other hand, we are concerned with the survival of the self—not in the adaptive sense, but in terms of its being able "to be with" the object, the environment, and also oneself, in the sense of feeling alive and thriving, and in Winnicott's sense of "the capacity to be alone" (1958).

## FANTASY AND REALITY IN ADOLESCENCE

Adolescence poses a critical developmental juncture for the two experiential modes of Being and Doing in that it calls for their integration and amalgamation (Erlich, 1990). Such an integration is a necessary prerequisite for the achievement of the developmental milestones that adolescence must secure, which are identity formation and intimacy (Erikson, 1959). The coming together of Being and Doing enables the adolescent to experience himself as fully merged with a particular role provided by society, while at the same time he can also be fully engaged in the acquisition and mastery of the functional, technical, factual, or mechanical skills it calls for. Where such an integration of the two modalities has not been accomplished, we will meet with various forms of lopsidedness: for example, an arid absorption in technical aspects (computers, electronics, motorbikes) at the expense of feeling fulfilled by and enjoying these as the expression of a facet of one's self. Or, conversely, we may see an adolescent who wanders off alone into nature to seek communion with it, but feels indifferent or unable to find his bearings, negotiate a map and compass, care for his apparel, and manage his food and water supplies. There are, of course, innumerable variations on these themes, and frequently these involve the most basic and earliest maintenance functions of body and soul. The point is always, however, a failure of the integration of the two modalities, with an ensuing emphasis of one at the expense of the other. It should be borne in mind that both Being and Doing involve *relating* to reality (environment, objects); they differ in the *experience of ego/reality*, which proceeds through merger and fusion in one mode, and through separateness and functionality in the other.

The adolescent, just like the psychoanalyst, can view and experience himself and reality in these two opposed ways, and these will then be reflected in the different contents and organization of his fantasy productions. When experiencing himself and his objects along the Doing dimension, the emphasis will be on what he does to reality, or reality to him. This is typically related either to the direct expression of drive wishes and conflicts or to the defensive maneuvers against them. The following brief vignette provides an illustration of this type of fantasy.

Mr. A. was a young man in his 20s with severe problems in the area of his sexual and work identity. The analysis was in its initial stages; there were, however, signs and symptoms of his conflicts, such as premature ejaculation and impotence, a general listlessness and dissatisfaction, and a denigration of women. His parents' marriage was seriously disruptive, the father carrying on an open affair with a "young chick," while the mother was a depressive "nothing."

In this particular session he talked about his adolescent relationship with two other boys. They were experienced by him as manly and strong, compared to his own weakness and lack of manliness. Various escapades were described, involving the adolescent boys' wishes for female closeness, in which he felt himself to be pushed out and ridiculed. He then related the following fantasy for the first time: He used to imagine himself in his adolescence as leaving home, with its incessant fights and quarrels, with his father and his "chick" and his nothing-mother, and go to a military boarding school. There he would imagine himself becoming a soldier, a fighter, a macho-hero. Then, with a few more turns to the story, he would imagine himself sent abroad and given undercover intelligence training. He would then finally learn what he most desired—to be able to control himself totally and completely, so as to be absolutely unruffled by anything that happened to him in reality.

This particular adolescent fantasy centers around Doing—the issues are his power and impact on the environment, as well as the latter on him, both of which will be discussed below. The adolescent may, however, also experience himself and his objects along the dimension of

Being. In this case, his experience of reality will be fluid and indefinite; he will tend to experience himself as part of reality, and reality or others as part of himself. The quality will be of various states and stages of merger, and the emphasis will be more on relatedness and experiencing, and not so much upon causing and functioning, doing or being done to. The following vignette illustrates this.

J. was a 17-year-old adolescent boy in analytic treatment for a year and a half. His parents were divorced, and his mother had a relationship with another man. He shared artistic talents and tendencies with his mother and was close to her, but angry and standoffish with his father. In the early phases of the analysis, the analyst found it difficult to remember and reconstruct the sessions. This particular session took place after J. missed many sessions, his mother wanted to stop treatment, and a meeting took place between J., his mother, and the analyst.

In the meeting, I felt as if I was returning my mother to me, like when I was little. [When you were her special boy.] My 6-year-old cousin, I watch her and see how she understands things better than the adults, and I understand her. [It brings you back to yourself, to the little boy that felt special for mother, belonging to her, taking up the place father did not occupy.] I only remember I didn't like it when she slept in the living room. I have no memory of when they were together. I used to think they are together, one, that it's a regular family. Perhaps I knew even then that something was amiss. But I always knew I was special for her. [Analyst interprets his anger at his father.] He can drive you crazy. I can erase him, make him nonexistent. Kill him, as you would say. Just like I can erase you too—when I escape into fantasies. Something in you took care to join between me and mother, that she and I would be together, and you would be outside [smiles]. I had this thought that you two would talk and get together, join. Some fantasy like that. I can altogether get lost in my own fantasies. [They become so real that they are too close to reality.] [He sheds some tears.] It can drive you crazy! And I try to get out of it myself, by going all the way with my fantasies, so as to come out on the other side. It also frightens me here, with you, like when I think you are going along with me, with my fantasies, and don't keep a distance. When you stop letting me feel they are fantasies. As if we are both gliding in this, and it scares me. And then I don't want to come [tearfully].

In this material the Being modality is powerfully present, as, for instance, in the numerous allusions to joining[3] and merger, and the experience of "gliding," suggesting weightlessness and suspension in

3. Some of these joining wishes also have clearly oedipal overtones, reflecting integrative tendencies at work, but also the parallel-process existence of the two experiential modalities.

time and space, which are typical of this experiential mode. It is even more striking, however, when he describes fantasy as a process as well as a specific content. He is capable, for instance, of "erasing" someone subjectively, leaving it unclear whether this takes place in subjective or objective reality. Fantasy obliteration and reality eradication are, for the moment, one and the same. His tendency toward immersion in fantasy, as an ego state akin to daydreaming, is definitely and powerfully prominent. It is clear that reality and fantasy are interspersed and merged for him at such moments. He speaks of going in and trying to arrive at the other side, as though it were a physical entity—a tunnel or a cloud. It is also obvious that despite his clear penchant for such fantasy states, it is at this point a frightening and unpleasant experience for him. It should be pointed out that this represents a therapeutic gain for him: he came to treatment with an attitude of boastful familiarity toward such states, which served a defensive function for him. This was also reflected in the analyst's initial difficulty in reconstructing sessions, because the sequence was not ordered logically (secondary process). He gradually became somewhat more capable of relatedness in the Doing modality as well, and now regarded these states ambivalently.

So far I have traced the developmental vicissitudes of the experiential modes of Being and Doing in adolescence, and their influence on the adolescent's stance vis-à-vis the reality/fantasy issue. We can now look at some *specific fantasy contents* that are met with in adolescence. Rather than provide a complete checklist of such fantasies, I would like to offer several content categories that are frequently met with as overt themes in adolescent treatment material, which may also constitute underlying or inferred unconscious categories.

The first such fantasy category has to do with *power*. The displacement of parents, as Winnicott says, is actual. It requires power, but it also bestows power. The displacement of parental authority and the actualization of one's own power serve as a catalyst that may further expand the adolescent's fantasy of his powers and omnipotence. But power also has to do with producing real change in the environment, through whatever means one commands. This is linked to the Doing dimension, and to functional relatedness with reality. Yet another aspect of the power fantasy has to do with the Being mode, and with omnipotent fantasies and cravings. The fact that the adolescent is no longer child-size calls for a particular form of denial (Erlich, 1986) in order to deal with frightening aspects of his actual power now aggressively marshaled, in fantasy, against his parents.

Hand in hand with power comes the fantasy of *submission vs. displace-*

*ment*. The implication of power is conflict, and conflict must lead to one of two outcomes: one's own or the other's defeat, submission and subjugation, or to being displaced from one's potential or rightful place. The adolescent is extremely concerned about issues of space and position. The separation and extrusion from the family of childhood lead to another dangerous outcome of his struggle for power; they sensitize him to potential dislocations and dislodgements of himself and of others. He may fight heatedly for privacy and ownership in a way he has eschewed till then.

The related fantasy of *passive surrender* is extremely attractive to many adolescents. It represents the temptation to relinquish oneself to the care, nurturing, and assimilative pull of greater powers—army, church and religion, ideology, and even university—which promise to fashion and mold the self. Another variation on this theme is the particularly regressive fantasy of *engulfment*. This fantasy and the anxiety associated with it are commonly found in severe narcissistic and borderline pathology. This is, of course, related to the primary and most severe underlying anxiety within the Being modality, which is that of *annihilation*.

The Doing modality also gives rise to the fantasy of the *penetration* of reality, or of being penetrated by it. This fantasy, which can have serious regressive implications, may be found in either male or female adolescents, with corresponding gender-related issues and complications. At the nonregressive level, however, it has to do with the phallic fantasy of causing the environment to feel one's power and presence and respond to it, and to allow reality to affect oneself, without fearing the outcome of such intercourse.

I have not spelled out sexual fantasies as such, because I believe that in adolescence proper these are usually subsumed under those fantasy categories that I have described. In late adolescence and young adulthood, however, with the increasing importance of intimacy, overt sexual themes do emerge. Laufer (1976), however, stressed the "central masturbation fantasy," which is fixed by the oedipus complex and contains regressive satisfactions of the main sexual identifications, but is important, in his view, in adolescence. Its pathological effects seem to contain some of the fantasy themes I have enumerated: for example, a feeling of deadlock and lack of choice, which involves power, submission, and passivity. The specific sexual contents are traced by Laufer to specific patterns of erotized childhood interactions. I prefer to regard such masturbation fantasies as idiosyncratic, i.e., specific to a given adolescent but not to adolescence; or as masturbatory fantasies and practices idiopathically related to individual childhood experiences.

ADOLESCENCE AND SOCIAL REALITY

In closing, I want to focus briefly on three issues that involve the adolescent's actual relatedness to reality: identity formation, the generation gap, and the psychosocial moratorium.

Ego identity refers to the ego's finding its expression within a particular social role provided by the social environment (Erikson, 1968). Identity and reality are thus intrinsically and completely interdependent. Identity, as the incarnation of an individual ego and a given social role, is the strongest bridge that spans inner and outer reality. Social role, however, is affected by events in social reality over which the developing ego has no say. I have in mind the rapid shifting of role models in Western society over the last few decades. An adolescent does not jump into a given role: he is prepared for it gradually, from birth onward. Constantly changing and diffusely defined roles make it difficult for the ego to identify decisively and vigorously. We need only reflect on such recently changed and still mutating roles as the homosexual, the craftsman, or the career woman, to understand the scope of this issue. Identity formation is perhaps enriched by a rapidly transforming social reality; but it is certainly not made any easier by it.

One area in which change has turned into erosion is that of the generational gap. The authority and respect usually accorded to the parental generation depend to a large extent on the degree to which this generation identifies itself in postadolescence and adulthood with permanence and stability, with upholding and maintaining its values and ideologies. The older generation's postadolescent conservatism thus guarantees the adolescent generation's freedom to oppose and challenge and to reach out for its fantasy of a better world and social order. Parental identification with change may therefore interfere and compete with the adolescent's needs.

Late-adolescent and youth's quest for moratorium may also be viewed as the search for a better environment, which could enhance one's chances for a successful identity formation. An "average expectable" reality is too static and restrictive for the adolescent's need for experimentation. The ego, it must be remembered, answers to considerations of safety. In terms of present conditions in many areas in the world, the adolescent's ego must be faced with considerable danger when encountering particular social roles. These reality attributes must make it at times highly explosive and prohibitive for an adolescent to complete his assumption of an identity, when it is connected with dangers too severe for the ego to handle. On the other hand, youth has always been known to throw away, at the right moment, considerations of rationality and safety, and to risk and sacrifice body and soul for a cause or ideology that becomes identified with the ego ideal. We may, perhaps, better understand this contradiction if we think in terms of the Being and Doing modalities. It is in the Being mode, in the unity of ego and reality, that life itself—the "being" of self and object—seems eternal, ego ideal and ego are fused so that ideals *are* life itself, and one is beyond "petty" considerations of safety which the ego recognizes and implements so well in the Doing mode.

Can we really then look away and not recognize it when the environment is in a dangerous state of flux, when it is too unstable, or conversely, too rigidly fixed? There is a need for "reality constancy" (Frosch, 1966) as much as for object constancy. The social implication is for a needed rate of change that is attuned and suitable to what can be experienced as safe, and be safely experienced. For psychoanalysts, it is difficult to do more than point this out. Perhaps we must think of better ways in which we may influence and shape reality in accordance with our fantasies-theories.

### Summary

I have developed the argument that psychoanalytic views of reality, and also of fantasy, are contingent upon the conceptualization of the ego/mind. I have distinguished a mental-apparatus-objective and an experiential-subjective approach to reality and fantasy, and have correlated these two views with Being and Doing as two underlying dimensions of processing experience. Adolescent development critically necessitates the integration and amalgamation of these two modalities. The adolescent's degree of success at this developmental task will be reflected in the nature and quality of his integration of Doing and Being relatedness to reality, as objective and separate, and as merged and fused with him, with corresponding fantasy contents and ego states. Finally, looking at social reality as a dimension independently capable of change and flux, I outlined some of the issues this may pose for such crucial adolescent accomplishments as identity formation. The adolescent requires an optimum of reality constancy and a modicum of social conservatism in his social environment. These will help him reach out and aspire for the fantasies that he carries, and through which he embodies the hope for a future of development and progress for all of us.

## BIBLIOGRAPHY

ERIKSON, E. H. (1959). The problem of ego identity. In *Identity and the Life Cycle, Psychol. Issues*, 1:101–164. New York: Int. Univ. Press, pp. 101–164.

———— (1962). Reality and actuality. *J. Amer. Psychoanal. Assn.*, 10:451–474.

———— (1968). *Identity, Youth and Crisis*. New York: Norton.

ERLICH, H. S. (1986). Denial in adolescence. *Psychoanal. Study Child*, 41:315–336.

———— (1988). The terminability of adolescence and psychoanalysis. *Psychoanal. Study Child*, 43:199–211.

———— (1989). On loneliness, narcissism, and intimacy. Read to Israel Association for Psychotherapy.

———— (1990). Boundaries, limitations, and the wish for fusion in the treatment of adolescents. *Psychoanal. Study Child*, 45:195–213.

———— (1991). Die Erlebnisdimensionen "Being" und "Doing" in Psychoanalyse und Psychotherapie. *J. Psychoanal. Theory & Practice*, 4:317–334.

———— (1992). Ego and self in the group. Read to Israel Association for Group Therapy.

———— & BLATT, S. J. (1985). Narcissism and object love. *Psychoanal. Study Child*, 40:57–79.

FREUD, S. (1895). Project for a scientific psychology. *S.E.*, 1:281–397.

———— (1900). The interpretation of dreams. *S.E.*, 4 & 5.

———— (1923). The ego and the id. *S.E.*, 19:1–66.

FROSCH, J. (1966). A note on reality constancy. In *Psychoanalysis—A General Psychology*, ed. R. M. Loewenstein et al. New York: Int. Univ. Press, pp. 349–376.

HARTMANN, H. (1964). *Essays on Ego Psychology*. New York: Int. Univ. Press.

HURVICH, M. (1970). On the concept of reality testing. *Int. J. Psychoanal.*, 51:299–312.

ISAACS, S. (1948). The nature and function of phantasy. In *Developments in Psycho-Analysis*. London: Hogarth Press, 1970, pp. 67–121.

LAPLANCHE, J. & PONTALIS, J.-B. (1985). *The Language of Psychoanalysis*. London: Hogarth Press.

LAUFER, M. (1976). The central masturbation fantasy, the final sexual organization, and adolescence. *Psychoanal. Study Child*, 31:297–316.

LOEWALD, H. W. (1951). Ego and reality. *Int. J. Psychoanal.*, 32:10–18.

RAPAPORT, D. (1960). *The Structure of Psychoanalytic Theory. Psychol. Issues*, 2:7–158. New York: Int. Univ. Press.

SANDLER, J. & NAGERA, H. (1963). Aspects of the metapsychology of fantasy. *Psychoanal. Study Child*, 18:159–196.

———— & ———— (1964). Symposium on fantasy. *Int. J. Psychoanal.*, 45:190.

SEGAL, H. (1968). *Introduction to the Work of Melanie Klein*. New York: Basic Books.

STERN, D. N. (1985). *The Interpersonal World of the Infant*. New York: Basic Books.

WALLERSTEIN, R. S. (1973). Psychoanalytic perspectives on the problem of reality. *J. Amer. Psychoanal. Assn.*, 21:5–33.

—— (1983). Reality and its attributes as psychoanalytic concepts. *Int. J. Psychoanal.*, 10:125–144.

WINNICOTT, D. W. (1958). The capacity to be alone. In *The Maturational Processes and the Facilitating Environment.* London: Hogarth Press, 1979, pp. 29–36.

—— (1971). *Playing and Reality.* London: Tavistock Publications.

# Play in Adulthood

## A Developmental Consideration

## CALVIN A. COLARUSSO, M.D.

*This paper is about normal development, addressing the basic charac-teristics and evolution of play throughout life, with particular emphasis on the nature of play in adulthood. Although the psychoanalytic litera-ture on play in childhood is extensive, undoubtedly because of its rele-vance to child analysis, very little has been written on the subject of adult play or on the relationship between adult play and its childhood anteced-ents.*

### DESCRIPTIONS OF PLAY

ALTHOUGH PLAY IS A COMPLEX PHENOMENON WHICH IS NOT EASILY DE-fined (Neubauer, 1987), there are many descriptions. The following few come closest to framing the issues I wish to address. Solnit (1987) described play as "a mental-physical activity that has normative, development-promoting functions" (p. 221). Central to this activity is pretending. The lack of realistic consequences allows the ego to use its symbolizing capacity in "a synthesizing exercise or practicing to adapt or to resolve conflicts in an exploratory, make-believe manner" (p. 211).

I am particularly interested in play as a mechanism for achieving what Neubauer (1987) called "a new level of competence or develop-mental organization" (p. 3). Since development is lifelong (Colarusso and Nemiroff, 1981), play may serve the same functions in adulthood as it does in childhood, promoting the engagement and mastery of phase-specific developmental tasks. As the capacities of the ego grow and life experiences multiply, play becomes "an indirect approach to

Training and Supervising Analyst in Adult and Child Psychoanalysis at the San Diego Psychoanalytic Institute; Clinical Professor and Director of the Child Psychiatry Res-idency Training Program at the University of California at San Diego.

seeking an adaptive, defensive, skill-acquiring, and creative expression. *It is a mode of coping with conflicts, developmental demands, deprivation, loss, and yearnings throughout the life cycle"* (Solnit, 1987, p. 214, my ital.).

Thus, play is engaged in by both children and adults because it relieves the stress of living in reality and the frustration of basic conscious and unconscious needs; it provides a mechanism for confronting a challenge and overcoming it in a gratifying manner. The challenge in the play resembles a challenge in the real world but is more manageable because the goal of play is victory, not defeat. For these reasons play is a mechanism facilitating recuperation and mastery (Ostow, 1987).

Although childhood and adult play serve the same developmental functions, they are qualitatively different because the mind and body of the adult are not the same as those of the child. As Plaut (1979) described it, "play activity in adulthood reveals the masterful mature function of the ego, which temporarily dominating id and superego, integrates their components into ritualized expression within a structured, articulated framework" (p. 221).

### Basic Characteristics of Play

The nature of play may be elaborated more fully by considering some of its basic characteristics rather than attempting to formulate an all-encompassing definition. By so doing I plan to set the stage for a discussion of the similarities and differences between play in childhood and adulthood.

#### THE ROLE OF MENTAL ACTIVITY AND PHYSICAL ACTION

Childhood play is usually described as consisting of two interlocking components: conscious or unconscious fantasies or wishes, and physical acts which carry these into an observable enactment (Neubauer, 1987). Fantasy play during the oedipal state ("Let's play house, I'll be the Mommy. You be the baby.") and organized games (such as kickball or hopscotch) during latency are examples.

However, motoric expression may be greatly minimized or entirely absent in both childhood and adulthood, although much more so in adulthood. The motoric component may be expressed by others who act for the person at play; for example, when an individual, child or adult, is a spectator at a sporting event or at a stage play. In these instances the person at play *identifies* with the athlete's or actor's actions, elaborating fantasies in response to what is seen and heard. This form of passive, nonmotoric participation in play activity through identification with others is a key component of all spectator activities. Extremely common and ubiquitous, particularly in adulthood, this form of play has not received much attention in the psychoanalytic literature. Although peripheral to my primary objective in this paper, I hope that the ideas presented here will focus increased analytic attention on the active and passive play activities of adult analysands.

On other occasions the motoric component may be greatly reduced because of the nature of the game being played. Board games such as checkers or Monopoly require very little physical action, as do more complicated mental games such as bridge or chess. All may be played by both children and adults, although not with the same frequency or capability.

It is important to note that although games which require strenuous physical action are less common in adulthood, particularly middle and late adulthood, motoric expression remains a component of play throughout life, as exemplified by the 80-year-old golfer or tennis player.

### PLAY AS A NONSUBLIMATED ENACTMENT

Play is an attempt through enactment to master traumatic stimulation, the natural state of the child (Waelder, 1932); and to resolve, in both children and adults, internal conflicts which are generated by the engagement of phase-specific developmental tasks. Those at play must recognize that what is being enacted is not real.

"Play stays too close to the drives to qualify as sublimation" (Neubauer, 1987, p. 4), but in its expression of the pleasure principle it serves as an experimental way to pursue the road to reality. Because adults have a more developed sense of reality testing and an increased capacity for sublimation—drives and conflicts which can be easily sublimated do not need to be addressed through play—they play less frequently. But when adults do play, they play for the same reasons as children: to attempt to organize and control the intrapsychic world of drives and conflicts, expressing themselves, alone and with others, in gratifying ways.

### PLAY AS A FORM OF PRETENDING WHICH IS FREE
### OF EXPECTABLE CONSEQUENCES

Play ceases to be play when the "observing ego loses its role and the capacity to pretend is lost, or at least sharply changed from one of primary significance to a secondary or tertiary role in the behavior and subjective experience of the individual, allowing for maturational and developmental changes in such capacities and tolerances" (Solnit, 1987, p. 210). These maturational and developmental changes in capacities and tolerance account for some of the differences between play in childhood and adulthood. Because of the relative immaturity of the observing ego, children are less likely to sustain the capacity to pretend than adults. Thus adults can play for longer, uninterrupted periods of time even when intense emotional states or physical exertion are involved; attending a Wagnerian opera or running a half-marathon are examples.

Another of the basic components of play is "freedom from expectable consequences. Play is an activity that is enjoyed for the moment; after it is over, nothing that has happened is to carry over into the real world" (Ostow, 1987, p. 194).

Although basically true, the idea that play is *entirely* free of expectable consequences is misleading. There is some carryover into the real world be it the repetition of a similar theme in later play by an oedipal-aged child because aspects of the oedipal conflict have not yet been resolved, the awarding of a Little League trophy or a number one college football ranking, or the discussion with friends of a scene from a musical or play. Although none of these results has any serious consequences (a statement which would be disputed by any rabid fan), all are aftereffects carried over into the real world.

As Ostow (1987) recognized, "the spice of play is contributed by whatever reality factors are invoked. A game becomes more exciting if there is even a small reward to the victor, or a prize for the winner of a contest. A novel or a drama becomes more engrossing if the reader or viewer recognizes himself in a character and identifies with that character in his fictional experiences. The historical novel, the roman à clef, the drama that portrays the human situation—these are all more compelling than the fantasy in which no aspect of life can be recognized. In fact one can list a number of human activities in which it is difficult to sort out the play from the serious elements, for example, social activities, sports, sexual relations, and humor" (p. 194).

In some instances when adults lose the capacity to pretend, particularly when aggressive feelings have been aroused, the real consequences may be considerable. Fights among hockey players or fans at a European soccer match are examples, as is the following adult observation (Colarusso and Nemiroff, 1981). In the midst of an "important" Little League baseball game, the two opposing coaches confronted each other and the umpire over a disputed call. Soon they were exchanging punches, while their 8-year-old players watched. In "real" life, one was a lawyer, the other a judge.

## DO ADULTS PLAY?

As surprising as it may seem, this is a question which must be addressed because of Freud's (1908) observation that adults do not play. Even though Freud modified his statement later in the same presentation, the idea has persisted, supported by Anna Freud's (1965) suggestion that childhood play is replaced by adult work.

After describing the characteristics of play in early childhood and the oedipal phase, Anna Freud begins to describe a shift from play to work during the latency years. "Direct or displaced satisfaction from the play activity itself gives way increasingly to the pleasure in the finished product of the activity, a pleasure which has been described in academic psychology as pleasure in task completion, in problem solving, etc." (p. 81).

The shift from play to work is completed in the last substage in the developmental line, covering the period of latency and adolescence, when the "ability to play changes into the ability to *work*" (p. 82) due to the increased ability of the ego to (a) control impulses and use materials constructively; (b) delay gratification and carry out preconceived plans; and (c) achieve the transition from primitive instinctual to sublimated pleasure and from the pleasure to the reality principle.

I have two criticisms of this line of thinking. First, I wonder if two developmental lines are not being truncated into each other. Later in this paper I propose a developmental line of play which encompasses the entire life cycle. Does a similar developmental line exist for work? At the very least if play and work have the same origins in early childhood, it is more plausible to hypothesize that the two activities begin to differentiate from each other in childhood, not that work replaces play.

My second criticism concerns the fact that the developmental line of play ends in childhood rather than continuing into adulthood. If this is true, how are such adult games as soccer, football, cricket, chess, and cards to be explained? How is the enormous adult involvement in spectator sports to be understood within such a framework?

Solnit (1987) recognized that adults do not stop playing: "What appears to be a renunciation is really the formation of a substitute or surrogate" (p. 207). So did Plaut (1979), who related Freud's view that play was "inappropriate to adulthood" to the European culture's "highly ambivalent attitude toward pleasure and an elevation of work to a dominant position in its value system" (p. 219). The same idea is contained in Freud's definition of health as the freedom to love and work, but not to play. Plaut would elevate play to the same level as love and work. "From a psychological point of view, *love, work, and play are the three ideal types of action*" (p. 219).

And he states categorically that play continues into adulthood. "In keeping with the Freudian dictum that nothing disappears from mental life, it is more accurate to say that both the capacity to fantasy and the capacity to play coexist in human mental life, from infancy through old age, and their functions, genetically and dynamically linked, continue throughout life" (p. 229).

I agree completely. Play exists in various forms from early childhood through late adulthood. Although there are great similarities between some forms of childhood and adult play, there are also considerable differences, a reflection of the evolution of psychic structure and developmental processes throughout the life cycle.

That the capacity to fantasize and the capacity to play coexist throughout life seems so obvious that the statement need not be defended. What has not been addressed thoroughly in the psychoanalytic literature is the *relationship* between fantasy and play throughout life, particularly in adulthood. This issue will be discussed in the section on a developmental line of play based on levels of ego functioning and motoric expression.

## WHAT MOTIVATES CHILDREN AND ADULTS TO PLAY?

Waelder (1932) suggested that children play in order to master experiences which are too overwhelming to be mastered easily. Peller (1954) related the need to play in children to the engagement and mastery of phase-specific developmental tasks.

Whereas Waelder and Peller only address the motivation for play in childhood, Ostow (1987) suggests the following reasons for play to occur in both children and adults. First, play provides a mechanism for disengaging from frustration and disappointment in the real world by providing an illusory gratification which reduces tension and distress. Second, play also provides relief from intrapsychic conflict by offering pleasurable alternatives. But most importantly of all, particularly for the adult, "Play seems to provide, not for the unrestrained pursuit of pleasure, but rather for the exposure to realistic or realisticlike challenges, the overcoming of which relaxes tension and replaces it with pleasure. . . . Play is a simulated, attenuated, and controllable reality. When the pain becomes too great, or the threat too formidable, the play can be terminated" (p. 200).

Ostow recognizes that both children and adults play for the same reasons, but he describes a qualitative difference in what they are attempting to master: "whereas children's play anticipates future, more difficult tasks, adult play attempts to master simplified versions of the external world, problems of limited complexity, and posing limited threats. Under certain circumstances, adults too may fear assuming new tasks or roles, and use play to help them to master their fears, either realistically by practicing the new roles, or unrealistically by denying them" (p. 200).

Adult developmental theory suggests that adults are not dealing with simplified versions of the external world or problems of limited complexity and threat. In the engagement of the phase-specific developmental tasks of adulthood, adults confront external realities and internal issues and conflicts which are every bit as complex and difficult to master as those encountered in childhood (Colarusso and Nemiroff, 1981). Because the psychic apparatus of the adult is more complex and has a greater repertoire of ego mechanisms available to it, play is not used as commonly by adults; but when they do play, their play is as psychologically determined as the play of children.

## A Conceptualization of Play According to Levels of Complexity

This developmental line of play according to levels of complexity is based on the capacity of the ego and superego to manage internal and external stimuli and to resolve conflicts through the use of increasingly sophisticated mechanisms, thus accounting for some of the similarities and differences between the play of children and adults. A second, interrelated formulation based on developmental phases and tasks follows.

The four levels are:

Level I. This simplest form of play which is confined to the first several years of life consists of simple motor activity and thought, reflecting the limited physical and mental abilities of the infant and toddler.

Level II. Occurring primarily during the oedipal years and latency, this is the typical fantasy play of childhood. It is made possible by the attainment of object constancy, the ability to symbolize and fantasize, and the emergence of complex motoric capabilities.

Level III. Occurring for the first time during latency and *continuing throughout the remainder of life,* this level of play has many forms of presentation and is an expression of some or all of the following physical and mental functions: highly complex motor skills; sophisticated object relatedness, sometimes in interlocking roles; the capacity for abstract thought; and the ability to channel the expression of sexual and aggressive impulses in highly regulated and ritualized ways, reflecting the influence of the mature ego and superego.

Level IV. Essentially nonmotoric, Level IV play is an expression of the highest levels of ability of the human psyche to fantasize, symbolize, and abstract. Although most common in adults, it is by no means limited to adulthood, occurring with increased frequency from the oedipal phase of development onward.

### LEVEL I PLAY

Infants and toddlers at a presymbolic level do not play (Neubauer, 1987). However, they are taught the rudiments of play by their parents through "peek-a-boo" and other playful interactions. "Thus, play becomes a source for initially trying on, practicing, and imaginatively elaborating the capacity for wit, humor, pathos, and a whole host of affective experiences (tolerating the feelings) and their expressive communication to others" (Solnit, 1987, p. 209). Level I play is also well described by Mahler et al. (1975) during the practicing and rapprochement subphases.

Winnicott (1953) emphasized the relationship between the transitional object and phenomena and early play, ascribing great importance to the connection. "On the basis of play is built the whole of man's experiential existence" (p. 94). He also proposed a developmental line of play which evolves from transitional phenomena, to fantasy and shared play, to cultural experience.

Although Level I play is rudimentary, it performs a vital function in early development. "Play facilitates emerging ego functions, such as the establishment of body boundaries; or the acquisition of sphincter control (e.g., through toys which involve filling and emptying); or motility (movable toys). . . . The information-processing activities associated with play exercise and enhance the development of cognitive schemas. . . . Play material helps the child to discharge instinctual trends in bringing things together (constructive activities) and dispersing them and breaking them apart (destructive activities)" (Moran, 1987, p. 12).

### LEVEL II PLAY

Level II play is characterized by an endless variety of oedipally based fantasies enacted through resourceful and sometimes highly original characterizations. Because the ability to pretend is more fully developed and the superego is not yet a dominant force, as Freud (1908) pointed out, Level II play is unabashedly exhibitionistic and unembarrassed.

Although play at this level is largely confined to the oedipal phase and latency, adults occasionally used modified aspects of this form of play on special occasions such as Halloween. Because of the developmental urgency involved oedipal-aged children identify more strongly with their play characters than adults do and are not as capable of maintaining a well-defined sense of pretending.

## LEVEL III PLAY

Level III play is exemplified by organized games and sports. They occur consistently for the first time during the latency phase, an expression of the physical and mental capabilities which are emerging then. For the first time in life the child is capable of a variety of complicated motor skills, the ability to read and write, independent peer relationships, and the capacity consistently to adhere to rules, tolerate frustration, and channel drive expression.

Once the capacity for Level III play emerges in latency, it continues to be utilized throughout life. Although the form remains the same, the developmental themes and conflicts which are expressed through games and sports change dramatically from developmental phase to developmental phase.

In adolescence and young adulthood when physical prowess is at its peak and peer relationships are a major form of relating, organized games are the most characteristic form of play. This is reflected in the importance placed in nearly every culture on games played by individuals in this age group, be it participation in a high school football game or the Olympics. Nor is the psychological significance of games limited to the actual participants. Be it that high school football game seen by a few or the world cup soccer match watched by millions, spectator involvement in organized games is a major form of play, by far the most common in adulthood.

## LEVEL IV PLAY

Level IV play is *mental* play. Although it reaches its most mature form of expression in the second half of life, it is also very common in childhood. Neubauer (1987) spoke of "Playing with words, the substitution of acts by words" (p. 8). Cohen (1987), speaking of the transformation and abstraction which occur in children's play, called it "nonphysically oriented play" (p. 94). When play material is involved, what it is or what it represents is not critical; "it is more important how it fits into a symbolic network" (p. 94). Eventually, play materials may become totally unnecessary. As described by Anna Freud (1965), "When toys and the activities connected with them fade into the background, the wishes formerly put into action with the help of material objects, i.e., fulfilled in play, can be spun out imaginatively in the form of conscious daydreams, a fantasy activity which may persist until adolescence, and far beyond it" (p. 83).

In the descriptions just given the nonmotoric, mental play is totally self-contained, all aspects of it initiated and controlled by the fantasizer. In a second, extremely common, form of Level IV play the motoric component (games), original fantasy (plays, movies, and books), or auditory and visual stimuli (music or dance) are provided by another or others. For example, the average American child and adult spends several hours each day in such activity when watching television.

### Spectator Play

The spectator of any age engaged in such play knows that he or she is involved in an activity which is without significant realistic consequences. For example, the baseball fan, be he 10 or 50, is using the game to resolve developmental conflict. Through identification with the players on the field, the latency-aged child may be dealing with phase-related issues such as competitiveness, exhibitionism, and sexual identity. The 50-year-old, also through identification, may be mourning for the lost body of youth and coming to terms with success or failure in various fields of endeavor; now that he no longer has the time or the opportunity for future success still available to the younger man on the field. These concerns may be addressed at both a conscious and unconscious level. When the game is over, its score soon forgotten, child and adult return to "real" activities. Books, movies, or plays serve the same function but offer the spectator more detailed fantasies which may be used in addressing real and intrapsychic issues and conflicts. Listening to music is another extremely common form of Level IV play. Highly evocative and capable of stimulating sexual and aggressive fantasies of all kinds, its ethereal, nontangible character is consistent with the make-believe, highly abstract nature of Level IV play. The endless variety from rock and roll to a Mahler symphony enhances the utilization of music by individuals of all ages. Music with words, song, is particularly effective in this regard. Teenagers endlessly "play" with the developmental tasks of adolescence, particularly the sexual ones, by enveloping themselves in the suggestive rhythms and words of the most popular groups. Peer group identification is solidified by this common interest as in psychological separation from parents whose musical tastes are usually different. The parents, in turn, nostalgically rework their own adolescent and young adult experiences by listening to the music of their generation. It is not surprising that older adults are more often attracted to the highly abstract aspects of classical music which often deal with more philosophical and serious preoccupations of the second half of life such as Handel's "Messiah" or Strauss's "Four Last Songs."

*Creativity and Play*

If play is considered to be a lifelong activity rather than a phenomenon of childhood, then much of the psychoanalytic literature on play and creativity can be conceptualized as an expression of Level IV play. Freud speaks to the essence of what I am calling Level IV play in "Creative Writers and Day-Dreaming" (1908): "a piece of creative writing, like a day-dream, is a continuation of, and a substitute for, what was once the play of childhood" (p. 152).

The child at play and the creative writer are alike in that both create a new world or rearrange aspects of their own experience in new ways. As the child grows, he exchanges play for fantasy and creates daydreams. I would suggest that this is not a cessation of play but an evolution from Levels II and III to Level IV. The adult also fantasizes (i.e., plays), but hides his fantasies because of their childlike quality or sexual and aggressive nature. This change in the nature of adult play is perfectly understandable when the higher level functions of the ego, such as enhanced reality testing and sensitivity to others' feelings and responses, and the superego, are taken into account.

The reader (of any age) can "play along" with the writer because, although the characters in the story may face danger and endure hardships, the reader is safe. He knows this form of mental play is make-believe. Freud (1908) addressed one of the functions of play when he noted that involvement with a piece of creative writing provides us with a "liberation of tensions in our minds" (p. 153). Greenacre (1959) agreed with and elaborated on Freud's ideas, concluding that "Play seems to be a rather general accompaniment of life" (p. 62) which adds to the creative imagination by "delivering the unconscious fantasy and harmonizing it with the external world" (p. 76).

*The Effect of Rules, Work, and Reality on Level IV Play*

Ostow (1987) observed that the author of a drama is not entirely free to elaborate his fantasies; he writes for others as well as himself and must comply with rules, regulations, and the expectations of his audience if his play (also called his work) is to be produced and seen by others.

Although Ostow is confining his remarks to the playrwright, I think they may be broadened to include all Level IV play activity. Anyone, be he playwright or spectator, who shares his daydreams with another, one or millions, must take into consideration the effect on his audience, filtering his daydream through the organizing and critical influences of the ego, superego, and ego ideal. The degree to which this occurs is a reflection of the level of maturation and sophistication of these psychic structures, thus explaining the greater effect of these influences on adult play and the greater tendency of adults, as Freud put it, to hide and disguise their fantasies.

Such a conceptualization blurs the boundaries between play and work in adulthood where many activities contain elements of both. Thus at Level IV there is not pure play, unaffected by thoughts or actions which have little or no real consequence. The playwright is both at work and at play when he writes; so is the analyst when he considers—and enjoys—his own fantasies which are stimulated by the patient's; they are useful in the work of understanding the patient, and also serve his own pleasure.

On the other hand, the playgoer, who sits in his seat and keeps his mental and emotional responses to himself; who is aware that he, like the actors on the stage, is pretending, is closer to pure play; experiencing a brief respite from the relentless pressures of work and reality, but still concealing his responses from others.

## A Developmental Line of Play in Adulthood

### THE LITERATURE

The psychoanalytic literature on adult games is very sparse, with two exceptions. The first, "Chess, Oedipus, and the Mater Dolorosa" by Reider (1959), gives a wonderful description of the complex dynamics of chess but does not conceptualize the insights in terms of either play or developmental theory. However, Reider does establish the principle that adult games are powerful expressions of the enormously complex dynamic unconscious.

The second, "On Play and the Psychopathology of Golf" by Adatto (1964), is more relevant to the subject matter of this paper. He demonstrates the importance of analyzing play material in adults. Using the information obtained from his patients, he concludes, "Instead of continuing to confine play to 'children's play', as is frequently found in the literature, or to limit adult play for the most part to a recreative activity in which leave is taken from reality and the superego, it is felt that *play should be considered a lifetime activity of the human being, and that its latent unconscious meanings rather than its manifest structure be used as a basis for understanding and comparison*" (p. 339f.).

## THE DEVELOPMENTAL LINE

Any attempt to describe the intrapsychic determinants of play at any point in the life cycle will be simplistic because of the complexity of conscious and unconscious thought processes and psychic structure. This is particularly true in adulthood where play expresses aspects of a multiplicity of developmental themes from the childhood past and the adult present. This developmental line is based on the idea that development is lifelong. Thus, in adulthood, as in childhood, play will be utilized as a mechanism for engaging and mastering current, phase-specific developmental tasks as well as those from the recent and distant past. This is so even when the external form of the play is the same as that utilized in earlier development phases; the difference is most evident in the conscious and unconscious fantasies which accompany the play. Adatto (1964) also recognized this principle, stating that singular games did not always have the same unconscious meaning, not even in the same patient. As a result, this developmental line is organized around some of the major themes which underline adult development, each treated chronologically according to the divisions of adulthood into young adulthood (20 to 40 years), middle adulthood (40 to 60 years), and late and late late adulthood (60 years and beyond).

## THE BODY AND ADULT PLAY

Thoughts and feelings about the body are a major conscious and unconscious dynamic theme underlying play throughout the adult years. In *young adulthood*, this somatic influence on play is expressed through two contradictory and dissonant themes: the enjoyment of the body at its peak of competence; and toward the second half of this phase the growing awareness of physical decline and the mourning process for the lost body of youth.

Because of the sense of self-esteem and narcissistic gratification connected with both physical and mental functioning in young adulthood, healthy players, as Ostow (1987) put it, "will therefore choose and contrive play-tasks that will really challenge them and that will be manageable, but just barely" (p. 201). Thereby they attempt to maintain the youthful illusion of personal invincibility and invulnerability.

In the 30s the gradual decline of physical prowess produces internal conflict between the need to accept the diminution in physical capability and the wish to deny the painful change. Based on the resolution of this internal conflict the healthy person will gradually move away from those sports such as football or soccer which tax the body beyond its current limitations and focus on less demanding activities which require less stamina and physical prowess.

In addition to mourning for the lost body of youth, individuals in the second half of young adulthood and in midlife must also relinquish their unrealized youthful fantasies of athletic fame and fortune. Because athletic heroes are now chronological contemporaries or younger, they are no longer comfortable subjects for identification, no longer bolstering fantasies of *future* success. In many adults these fantasies are zealously guarded, clung to, and expressed again through the identification with sons and daughters who have the precious gifts of a youthful body and a future athletic zenith.

The aging process in the body also forces a reengagement and a reworking of infantile themes, particularly the oedipus complex. As the body ages and they are defeated by younger competitors, men and women reexperience the infantile feelings of weakness and impotence, originally felt in relation to the oedipal parent. This mix of infantile and young adult themes is illustrated in the following clinical vignette. Like Adatto's (1964) article on golf, it illustrates the value of analyzing the play activities of adults.

R. came into analysis at age 35 because of sexual inhibitions and an inability to bring himself to marry. The victim of a verbally abusive father who was unsatisfied with his considerable academic achievement and uninterested in his outstanding athletic success, R. turned to sports as a source of narcissistic gratification and an outlet for his oedipally based rage. Exceptionally gifted in several sports, he was both admired and feared by his competitors, who inevitably ended up losing the competition. Now, for the first time, in his mid-30s, R. began to lose; particularly at tennis and basketball, his two favorite sports. His temper tantrums on the court and pervasive sense of gloom when he spoke of his losses during analytic hours became a major vehicle for the analysis of his unresolved conflicts from childhood, particularly about his abusive father; the phase-specific young adult issue about the aging body; and the inappropriate, but no longer successful, use of sports as a means of avoiding the young adult developmental tasks of sex, intimacy, and marriage.

In *middle adulthood* physical play is abandoned by many because of diminished ability and narcissistic injury. Others continue to use athletic play as a method of dealing with the aging process. To paraphrase

Peller (1954), they deal with the anxiety connected with the idea that "My body is not as competent as it used to be" with the compensatory fantasy "My body is as capable as it was when I was young." The illusion is furthered by the occasional great golf shot or tennis backhand which momentarily conquers age and time.

Healthy midlife players temper the intensity of their play in harmony with the body's capabilities—more doubles, fewer sets of singles in tennis, no more sandlot football—but others continue to push the body beyond its capabilities, resulting in unnecessary physical injury and sometimes the onset of psychopathology. For example, 44-year-old Mr. B. became depressed when he injured his knee in jogging. Anticipating surgery, he withdrew from family and friends and threatened to quit his job. Diagnostic evaluation revealed an obsessive character structure and an exaggerated reliance on physical as opposed to mental mechanisms for achieving narcissistic gratification.

In *late adulthood* physical forms of play continue to be a mechanism for coming to terms with the aging body, but most healthy individuals in late adulthood are more concerned with the maintenance of body integrity. Continued physical exercise obviously promotes that goal as well as providing a means of experiencing the body's intactness and the pleasure that comes from its use. Although an excellent performance may continue to be used to deny the aging process, play in late adulthood also stimulates the acceptance of physical aging because repeated imperfect attempts at accomplishing complicated physical acts such as hitting a baseball or putting a golf ball are constant reminders of the body's limitations.

THE EFFECT ON PLAY OF THE CONFLICT OVER THE ACCEPTANCE
OF TIME LIMITATION AND PERSONAL DEATH

Physical aging, marriage and parenthood, the death of parents, and acceptance of adult responsibilities gradually force the young adult to begin to recognize that he or she is growing old. As young adulthood shifts into midlife, each individual begins to focus on the monumental developmental task of midlife, the acceptance of time limitation and personal death. The internal preoccupation with and conflict over this painful realization affect every aspect of mental and physical life, including play, which becomes a major mechanism for the expression and mastery of the conflict.

All forms of mental and physical play are used for the same purpose. Among the physical games most commonly played by middle-aged and older individuals are tennis and golf. Both help in the engagement and mastery of this developmental task in the same way. Both are games which are not limited by time. Unlike life which has only one beginning, midpoint, and ending, these games are distinguished by their endless beginnings and endings, which allow the player symbolically to master time and imperfection—again and again. The dreaded loss of the self can be faced alone; or, like Peller's latency-age playmates sharing their apprehension of the superego, with a doubles partner or teammate.

Games in which time runs out, such as football and basketball, are usually played by the young, who have an abundant future and have not yet fully engaged the theme of time limitation. Midlife individuals participate in these sports as spectators. They face the prospect of time limitation narcissistically shielded from its sting by identification with the younger participants and spectator companions; and by the realization that even though time ended this particular contest in the make-believe world of play, another may be begun.

All forms of mental games also have the same rhythms and are played for the same conscious and unconscious reasons. Card games are a good example. They may be played without physical exertion, thus eliminating reliance on the aging body almost entirely. Like tennis and golf, they supply the player with an endless succession of beginnings and endings. Because these games rely on intelligence rather than physical prowess, they are narcissistically gratifying, emphasizing the adult's ability to think and reason.

Various forms of gambling are also utilized for the same dynamic purposes. The wish to get rich quickly, to get something for nothing, to rely on "chance" implies that one is lucky, favored, and singled out by the all-powerful forces which govern the universe and control human life and death. The absence of clocks in casinos in Las Vegas and Atlantic City also speaks to the "timelessness" of the activity. Despite these real and intrapsychic efforts, the impermanence of life and the awareness of the possibility of sudden death cannot be avoided, even in a casino, symbolized as they are by the silent slot machine, craps, and a bust in black jack.

The healthy elderly individual has accepted the idea that he or she will die and is more concerned with how death will come, with dignity surrounded by family and friends, or painfully and alone. The young adult and midlife themes do not disappear, as exemplified by the 80-year-old golfer who proudly announced that he shot his age, but they are muted.

The playfulness which Plaut (1979) describes in the works of elderly artists may be a reflection of the acceptance of personal death. Having mastered this primarily midlife struggle, the healthy older individual moves beyond the serious, contemplative creativity of that phase (Jacques, 1965) and joyfully reflects on the wonders of human experience with a greater sense of appreciation because of the acceptance of the realization that life is fragile and time is precious.

## PLAY AND OBJECT RELATIONSHIPS IN ADULTHOOD

> The healthy adult realizes, as part of his authentic appraisal of reality, the central position of change in his life. A basic aspect of that change is the shifting nature of significant emotional relationships. Adult involvement with loved ones such as children, parents, colleagues, and friends is in constant realignment. These too continue to shift in middle age— when healthy marriages deepen in significance (while others break up on the shoals of middle-age developmental issues); parents die or become dependent; children grow and leave; and friends increase in importance and in some instances leave or die themselves. As opposed to old age and in some respects to childhood as well, the task is to sort out, categorize, set priorities among relationships, and achieve a balance between internal pressures and external demands [Colarusso and Nemiroff, 1981, p. 90].

Play facilitates dealing with this developmental task of shifting object ties by (a) stimulating intrapsychic connectedness with objects from childhood; (b) facilitating closer ties with important objects in the present; and (c) providing a mechanism for the formation of meaningful relationships in the future. *Because it is a form of activity familiar to all human beings, from the youngest child to the oldest adult, play provides an important framework, a crucible in which human relationships can be forged and maintained.* When young children want to engage another human being, be it a familiar child or a stranger, they ask, "Do you want to play with me?" Although adults have other opportunities and settings in which to form relationships, they, too, utilize play situations as a means of forming and sustaining relationships.

Play is also an important activity for facilitating closer ties with important objects in the present. As Plaut (1979) noted, parents reexperience and rework their own infantile and childhood experiences by observing their own children at play and by playing with them. If the parents' needs are not extreme and their gratifications from the play are muted, the relationship between parents and children is enhanced and their healthy development stimulated. When the parents' needs are pathological and excessive, the opposite is true. For example, both analyst and adolescent patient had to contend with an overpowering father who pushed his son into football and wrestling, sports in which the boy had limited interest and ability. In addition to loudly criticizing his son's every move from the stands, the father would challenge him to compete. Even a recommendation for analysis for the father was turned into a contest. Yes, he would accept the "challenge," and he would finish before his son did.

Parents also attempt to master current adult and midlife themes, as well as infantile ones, through "play" with their children. Using the analogy of the corida and the "Moment of Truth," the point in the bull fight when the matador anticipates plunging his blade through the bull's aorta, Nemiroff and I (1981) described the moment in time in which both parent and child recognize, if not acknowledge, that the child is stronger or more physically capable than the parent. Often the realization occurs during a play situation. When his teenage son tauntingly challenged his father to a tennis match in which he boasted that he would defeat "the old man" 6-0, 6-0 for $20, the father readily accepted. Although he had lost an occasional set to the "young upstart," he had never lost a match and certainly not 6-0, 6-0. As he described it from the couch, my patient planned to win, pocket the $20, and teach his son a lesson. Instead of pounding the ball recklessly with each stroke, the boy methodically returned every ball, time after time, until his exhausted father quit in disgust at 4-0 in the second set. He refused to pay the debt, claiming that his son competed unfairly. The analysis of the episode eventually led the father to the realization of the depth of his envy of this son's youthful vigor and to a beginning understanding of his rage at "anyone under 20." Associations to the episodes occurred over and over again in the analysis as he worked through feelings about aging, oedipal rivalry, and the lost body of youth.

Play also helps adults deal with the death of parents, grandparents, and contemporaries through the various dynamics already described, particularly the identification with important objects through forms of play which are associated with them; and through the repeated "mastery" of time limitation and death by the symbolic renewal associated with the unlimited opportunity for new beginnings which are found in many games.

The sense of genetic immortality which grandparents experience through their grandchildren is heightened by playing with them or by watching them play. The conscious and unconscious fusion of memories from the grandparent's childhood and play activities in the present with the grandchild produce a profound sense of connectedness with the beginning of life rather than the end, providing an extremely narcissistically gratifying defense against the awareness of the physical limitations imposed by an aged body and the nearness of death.

SEXUAL PLAY

The development of various forms of play activity which are shared with one's partner or spouse can obviously enhance the couple's connectedness and enjoyment of each other. In this area Plaut's (1979) ideas on the relationship between play and adult sexuality and intimacy are enlightening. "Similarly, play must be an integral aspect of the sexual relationship. Otherwise, intercourse without foreplay depersonalizes the partner and foreplay without intercourse becomes teasing" (p. 227).

Sexual playfulness and games, including the acting out of fantasies, are important vehicles for the simultaneous reworking of infantile fantasies, recognition and acceptance of the different and complimentary nature of the male and female genitals, and the continued exploration and elaboration of the use of the body as a sexual instrument, as a plaything, so to speak. The playfulness of which Plaut speaks is an indicator of the mastery of infantile sexuality and of the readiness to engage current, phase-specific, sexual themes.

The failure to integrate sexual playfulness into the sexual repertoire in young adulthood may be an important factor in midlife pathology. A 50-year-old man left his "wonderful" wife of 30 years because of an incomprehensible sense of anger at her and the feeling that he had missed out on his youth by marrying too early. He entered treatment after he had separated from her in an attempt to understand his feelings and behavior. The early months of treatment were spent in the embarrassing elaboration of sexual wishes and fantasies which he had been unable to experience with his wife despite her sexual openness. Interpretation of the largely oedipal determinants of the fantasies gradually led to an inner freedom and acceptance. Eventually the patient began dating a much younger woman and acting on his fantasies, at first experiencing a sense of exhilaration and playfulness that was highly gratifying. But in time the realization that he had little in common with "somebody as young as my daughter who's dating me for what I can give her, and I don't mean sexually," led to the end of this relationship. Considerable interpretive work was also done on the attempt to deny the aging process and time limitation which were involved in the decision to leave his wife and become engaged with younger partners. After nearly two years of "playing around" on his own, the patient returned home.

### PLAY AS A RESPONSE TO WORK AND RESPONSIBILITY

For most healthy individuals, midlife is a time of immense responsibilities—for growing and grown children, grandchildren, and aging parents; for the demands of work; and for partner and self in the present and the future (retirement). Play provides an outlet for the powerful sexual and aggressive drives involved in these relationships and responsibilities. For example, in games which are played by individuals, the player is only responsible for himself or herself, not an extended family. In group games teammates participate as equals and helpers. Further, as in all play, the responsibilities accepted during the game and the outcome are usually without real consequences, unlike the obligations of everyday life.

Television, plays, and movies appeal to adults for similar reasons; through identification with the characters and plots in the make-believe situations, aspects of real pressures and responsibilities can be manipulated in fantasy without consequence.

Many individuals in midlife have reached their highest level of work achievement and will advance no further. This sometimes painful reality can be compensated for through play. In the world of make-believe, continued achievement is possible without concern for aging, obsolescence, and replacement by younger individuals.

### SUMMARY

In this paper the nature of play was explored. After reviewing psychoanalytic theory on the basic characteristics of play, I placed this enormously complex activity within a lifelong developmental context. Focusing on adulthood, I presented two developmental lines of play, the first conceptualizing play according to increasing levels of complexity, the second according to phase-specific developmental themes and tasks. I suggested that an increased understanding of the nature of play in adulthood has great clinical relevance, providing the analyst with a conceptual framework within which to explore the dynamically charged play material which is frequently presented by patients.

### BIBLIOGRAPHY

ADATTO, C. (1964). On play and the psychopathology of golf. *J. Amer. Psychoanal. Assn.*, 12:826–841.
BRUNSWICK, R. M. (1940). The preoedipal phase of libido development. *Psychoanal. Q.*, 9:293–405.
COHEN, M. (1987). Chimeric objects and playthings. *Psychoanal. Study Child*, 42:85–104.
COLARUSSO, C. A. & NEMIROFF, R. A. (1981). *Adult Development*. New York: Plenum.
ERIKSON, E. H. (1977). *Toys and Reason*. New York: Norton.
FREUD, A. (1965). Normality and pathology in childhood. *W.*, 6.

———— Nagera, H., & Freud, E. (1965). Metapsychological assessment of the adult personality. *Psychoanal. Study Child,* 29:9–41.

Freud, S. (1908). Creative writers and day-dreaming. *S.E.,* 9:141–153.

Greenacre, P. (1959). Play in relation to creative imagination. *Psychoanal. Study Child,* 14:61–80.

Jacques, E. (1965). Death and the midlife crisis. *Int. J. Psychoanal.,* 46:602–612.

Kleeman, J. A. (1967). The peek-a-boo game. *Pscyhoanal. Study Child,* 22:239–273.

Mahler, M. S., Pine, F., & Bergman, A. (1975). *The Psychological Birth of the Human Infant.* New York: Basic Books.

Moran, G. S. (1987). Some functions of play and playfulness. *Psychoanal. Study Child,* 42:11–29.

Neubauer, P. B. (1987). The many meanings of play. *Psychoanal. Study Child,* 42:3–10.

Ostow, M. (1987). Play and reality. *Psychoanal. Study Child,* 42:193–204.

Peller, L. E. (1954). Libidinal phases, ego development and play. *Pschoanal. Study Child,* 9:178–198.

Plaut, E. A. (1979). Play and adaptation. *Psychoanal. Study Child,* 34:217–232.

Reider, N. (1959). Chess, oedipus, and the mater dolorosa. *Int. J. Psychoanal.,* 40:320–333.

Solnit, A. J. (1987). A psychoanalytic view of play. *Psychoanal. Study Child,* 42:205–222.

Waelder, R. (1932). The psychoanalytic theory of play. In *Psychoanalysis,* ed. S. A. Guttman. New York: Int. Univ. Press, 1976, pp. 84–100.

Winnicott, D. W. (1953). Transitional objects and transitional phenomena. *Int. J. Psychoanal.,* 24:89–97.

# APPLICATIONS OF
# PSYCHOANALYSIS

# Preventive Intervention with the Children of Depressed Parents

## A Case Study

### WILLIAM R. BEARDSLEE, M.D., and
### HARRIET L. MacMILLAN, M.D.

*Children of parents with depression are at significant risk for impairment, but little is known about preventive intervention strategies prior to the onset of illness in the children. This paper discusses a preventive approach to assisting families in helping children cope with parental affective disorder. A case study is presented which demonstrates the compatibility of this family-based intervention with psychoanalytically oriented treatment for the parent. Key aspects of this work include the enhancement of self-understanding and resiliency in children.*

DEPRESSION IN ADULTS IS COMMON AND IS ASSOCIATED WITH SIGNIFICANT impairment. The National Institute of Mental Health estimates that a quarter of all Americans will experience a depression sometime during their lives (Lobel and Hirschfeld, 1984). Many of these are parents. Weissman et al. (1987) estimate that 8 percent of mothers are depressed. Children of parents with depression are at much greater risk for depression and other disorders over the course of adolescence than their counterparts in families where parents are not ill (Downey and Coyne, 1990; Beardslee and Wheelock, in press). The rates of depres-

William Beardslee is a Senior Psychiatrist at the Judge Baker Children's Center and was supported by a Faculty Scholar Award of the William T. Grant Foundation. Harriet MacMillan was a Visiting Fellow in the Department of Social Medicine, Harvard Medical School, supported by a Travelling Fellowship from the Ontario Mental Health Foundation during preparation of this manuscript.

Thanks to Dr. A. Kris for assistance with the manuscript and Dr. P. Grace for assessment of families.

sion are at least several times higher in children of parents with depression (Downey and Coyne, 1990). As many as 30 percent of youngsters in these families experience depression before they reach the age of 19 (Beardslee and Podorefsky, 1988). While there has been progress in treating childhood depression, there are almost no programs which have focused on the prevention of disorder in these youngsters.

This paper presents a case study of a preventive intervention with a family in which the mother had experienced a severe, longstanding depression. The work is part of a systematic endeavor to develop and assess the intervention strategy. By preventive intervention is meant that the focus of the work is to assist the family in developing strategies that, over time, will prevent the emergence of disorder in their youngsters and substantially enhance their resiliency. The intervention is strongly oriented toward the future of the family and the children. A psychoanalytic perspective was essential in the development of the intervention and in the treatment of this family. The case demonstrates the compatibility of this approach with psychoanalytically oriented treatment, but also illustrates that a related yet different therapeutic stance is useful in focusing on youngsters who are not ill.

The intervention involves the entire family and has a strong educational component, with an emphasis on the expression of feelings and interactions in the family about the mother's illness. Its main aim is to assist the family to develop a process through which the parents can help their children cope with parental illness and move forward with their own lives. Core elements of the intervention (Beardslee, 1990; Beardslee et al., 1993) involve clinical assessment of all family members, and education about what depression is, how it can be best understood, and about risks to and resiliencies of children. The educational material is linked to the individual life experiences of the family. Plans for the further enhancement of the children's capacities for resiliency are developed.

The intervention is conducted by a clinician who begins by meeting with the parents as a couple to obtain a history and an assessment of all family members. This is followed by educational discussions with the parents, and by individual interviews with the children. The clinician then works with the parents to help them decide which aspects of the experience of parental depression they wish to share with their children in a family meeting and then helps them during the meeting. This approach was designed with the idea that it could eventually be used by practitioners from a variety of disciplines because the number of children growing up in families where parents have serious affective disorder is so large.

The work of intervention highlights both the difficulties in and the value of an approach that is based in part on the enhancement of resiliency and understanding in youngsters (Beardslee and Podorefsky, 1988). In general, it is designed to address poor communication and misunderstanding among family members, described in previous empirical work on the functioning of such families (Keitner and Miller, 1990; Downey and Coyle, 1990; Beardslee and Wheelock, in press). It relies on the distinction between the diagnosis of disorder and the illness experience (Eisenberg, 1981) and focuses on the family's experience with illness. It is also based on the clinical observation that parents are generally committed to the well-being of their children's development, even in the midst of a painful and crippling mental illness, but often are without any source of help or advice about their children. They frequently turn to their own therapists for advice, support, education, and guidance for their children. This preventive intervention program has been developed to address those concerns in a manner that can complement and support individual therapeutic work.

Detailed descriptions of the general aspects of this approach have been presented. The safety and feasibility, crucial in the development of a new intervention, have been demonstrated. Families receiving this intervention were compared to families provided with the same information in a lecture format. Families receiving this intervention expressed greater satisfaction and showed more positive behavioral and attitude changes (Beardslee, 1990; Beardslee et al., 1992, 1993).

The case we present was one of the first conducted with an intervention. Insights from this case became guiding principles for the intervention techniques. The senior author, a psychoanalyst and child psychiatrist, undertook to explore whether it was possible to intervene with a family in which the children were not ill, but the mother suffered from a debilitating affective illness. Her treatment in psychoanalytic therapy and the interchange between the senior author conducting this intervention with her therapist, also a psychoanalyst, provided a unique opportunity to evaluate the compatibility of the two approaches.

## CASE PRESENTATION

Mrs. Elizabeth M. suffered from a profound depression which had required several hospitalizations. When first interviewed, she was receiving psychotropic medication and was in intensive psychoanalytic therapy three times a week. Both parents were anxious about whether their children had been harmed by the effects of depressive illness in the family, and what could be done to help the family understand the nature of depression. Independent assessment conducted prior to the intervention and at follow-up by an interviewer blind to the content and course of the intervention demonstrated that the parents believed the intervention was quite valuable to them. Independent assessment several years later again demonstrated that the youngsters were doing well and that the family believed the intervention was very valuable to them.

The intervention was audiotaped in its entirety and analysis of the transcriptions forms the basis for the case report. Because the work is presented in part as the process of developing the intervention and there is considerable emphasis on the clinician's (WRB's) experience at different points, it is presented in the first person.

*Mother's Story:* Mrs. M. was referred by a therapist at a local psychiatric hospital who described her as gradually recovering from a serious, incapacitating, depressive disorder which had extended over several years. Her disorder had been precipitated by an acute physical illness in one of her children and had required hospitalization. Shortly thereafter, she had experienced extremely disturbing flashbacks of being sexually molested in childhood. She then developed persistent feelings of worthlessness, thoughts of suicide, and profound changes in mood and activity level. Mrs. M. had been hospitalized for depression twice in the year prior to the intervention, and once several years before.

The referring therapist explained that Mrs. M. was chronically suicidal but was deeply concerned about the welfare of the children. During a preliminary meeting to discuss the format of the intervention, Mrs. M. repeatedly indicated her strong desire for help with concerns about her children and her wish to participate in the intervention. I was concerned that the severity of her depression might preclude Mrs. M. from directing her energies toward the children. Her therapist and I talked at length and agreed that we would work closely together. He indicated that he would continue to take responsibility for the care of her depression. We agreed that work with the family could also be helpful, but that the work would be postponed if Mrs. M.'s clinical condition worsened. While in some ways this was not the optimal time to offer this intervention, Mr. and Mrs. M. emphasized that the children were confused and frightened about her illness. It was evident that considerable misunderstanding existed in the family.

The main part of the intervention took place over six months and included eight sessions with the parents, one with each of the children, and one family session. Two additional follow-up sessions took place about six months later. The couple's sessions took place in my office. The sessions with the children and family took place in their home.

*November 5:* Mrs. M., in her 40s, was a tall, thin woman with greying hair. She appeared gaunt and pale, and her movements were slow, as if it took great effort just to sit and follow a conversation. There was little variation in the tone of her voice, even when she talked of painful and frightening matters. It was difficult to engage her in any sustained interchange. Mrs. M. described the history of her illness: a year and a half earlier, she had begun to experience painful, sudden, uncontrolled flashbacks of having been sexually molested as a child. These were deeply disturbing and only partially remembered. She became severely depressed and was hospitalized six months later because she "just couldn't go on any more." Over the next few months, she had been tried on a variety of antidepressants, but these had not relieved her symptoms. She had been hospitalized on two other occasions for exacerbation of depression with thoughts of suicide. Mrs. M. reported prior episodes of depression following the birth of two of her three children and during a physical illness which had required hospitalization.

In the first session, Mrs. M. spoke painfully about thoughts of killing herself. She stated that she would honor the agreement with her doctor not to harm herself. Mrs. M. expressed anger at her need for such an agreement, but acknowledged that she thought about suicide constantly. At one point, Mrs. M.'s thoughts of suicide were expressed in the following way: "I've begun to wonder about the future and to ask, 'What's the point?' I keep thinking things are bad. I slide. It's frustrating. 'Why doesn't my doctor just give me a good swift kick in the pants to end it?'" Indeed, Mrs. M. was at significant risk for suicide. I assessed this risk carefully in this session and at various points in the course of the intervention.

I was trying to understand not only what Mrs. M's experience had been, but also the experience of those around her, particularly what those around her shared at home. It was apparent that her pain, her wish to die, and her lack of energy had had an effect, not just on her, but on her ability to relate to and communicate with those around her. Similarly, her depression had profoundly affected her ability to perform many tasks. Mr. M. sat beside her, frightened by what she was saying, but not knowing how to help. I was acutely aware of the need to balance Mrs. M.'s desire to help her children with her immediate needs for psychiatric care. While it was crucial that the intervention not interfere with Mrs. M.'s recovery from her illness, her caring for and concerns about her children were very much a part of her will to recover.

The tension between my concern for her need to focus mainly on her own recovery and her worries about the children continued throughout the course of my work with the family.

I asked the parents to describe each of the three children: Thomas, 17, Lisa, 13, and Mary, 10. Mrs. M. spoke with warmth and enthusiasm about her children, in marked contrast to her affect at all other points during the interview. Thomas was characterized as outgoing and sensitive, easily frustrated, a good student, and a leader. Lisa was described by both parents as a nonstop talker with many friends, an athletic girl who enjoyed a good argument. Mary was quiet but had occasional outbursts of anger. During one outburst, she had said, "I wish I were dead." This comment had worried both parents. However, Mary had no symptoms of depression, no problems in school, and none in relationships or at home. Indeed, the children all showed considerable strengths. After discussion of how the children were functioning, I described what we would do together in the preventive intervention work. I emphasized the need for Mrs. M. to continue with her current therapy. Both she and her husband agreed.

*November 15:* After a review of events since the last meeting, Mrs. M. immediately launched into a discussion of the involvement of her extended family with her illness. There had been a great deal of family interference from her brothers and sisters, who gave unwelcome advice about her psychiatric care. Mrs. M. said they were all critical of her, her child rearing and her marriage. She described feeling out of control by the pressure from her family. She had felt overwhelmed on one occasion, and had rushed from the room because of a major altercation with one of her brothers. This had occurred in the presence of the children. After this encounter, Mrs. M. spoke with her son. "He was crying, upset, and really angry. Thomas was afraid we were going to divorce. I reassured him that this wasn't so, that we'd had a rough year but things would be all right. Then my husband reassured him too."

Mrs. M. reported Lisa's fear that she would commit suicide. Lisa had learned in health class at school that suicide occurred in people who were depressed. It was painful for Mrs. M. to describe how she had admitted to Lisa that the idea had crossed her mind when she felt really "low." She reassured her daughter that Lisa had not put the idea in her head. She commented that it must have been disappointing for Lisa that she could not reassure her that it was something that would never happen. Mrs. M.'s comments underscored how intensely the children were affected by their mother's illness. When Lisa desperately wanted her to say, "I will not commit suicide," she was unable to say this. From a broader perspective, this incident was an example of how the children could not deny her illness. These youngsters lived every day with the illness, i.e., they had witnessed the mother becoming angry and overwhelmed, sad and lethargic, withdrawn, frightened, and suicidal.

The parents asked for guidance about how to proceed with helping their children. I purposely chose an active, teaching role. I explained that they were making their children a priority and focusing on what was best for them. I discussed ways to explain depressive illness so that they could understand it and then help their children to understand it. I emphasized that Mrs. M. was not at fault or to blame for her illness. The analogy of a heart attack was developed. Society does not blame an individual who suffers a heart attack; it is accepted as an illness with a biological cause that requires a period of recovery, even though it may be affected by diet, exercise, and psychological variables. Depression should be understood in similar terms. It clearly causes biological changes; recovery is possible with treatment, but the person experiencing depression and her family must understand that recovery takes time. Mrs. M. said, "A heart attack is legal and depression is not. It feels so shameful. You should explain this to my parents and siblings."

Mr. and Mrs. M. asked how I thought the children were perceiving their mother's illness in light of work with other families. I said that the experience of a parent's depression is often very much on the children's minds. Children try to make sense of it in the best way they can. I indicated some of the characteristics of resilient children, and how these were relevant to their children.

At the close of the session, the parents again strongly expressed their desire to continue with the intervention, although Mrs. M. was clearly struggling with the symptoms of her illness. This motivation to be effective parents, despite impairment, made it both possible and necessary to continue. The parents appreciated that the children needed to understand what was happening.

*November 30:* We reviewed the need to help the children and the ways in which I would try to assist the parents come to a shared understanding of Mrs. M.'s illness. The parents would be able to decide what they wanted to communicate to the children about Mrs. M.'s experience of depression and about depression in general. I emphasized that youngsters growing up in families where there was depression in parents were at risk for experiencing depression and other disorders. If problems were present, they needed to be identified as early as possible. At the same time, I explained that many youngsters were resilient and did not develop problems (Beardslee and Podorefsky, 1988). What characterized such youngsters was the capacity to function independently and to pursue normal age-appropriate activities outside of the home.

Children identified as resilient did not feel responsible for the ill parent or guilt for the parent's disorder. The parents' description of their children suggested that they were doing well and had not experienced major psychiatric symptoms. I indicated that it was essential that the children continue to be active in school, with friends, and outside the home.

In response to this, Mr. M. asked very concrete questions about Mrs. M.'s depression. He was struggling to understand the nature of his wife's illness. I described various etiologic aspects of depression, specifically that there is both a genetic component in some families, and also psychosocial factors such as losses, post-traumatic experiences, and severe life stresses, which were linked with depression. Mrs. M. interjected that her extended family's view of depression was that it was something that she should snap out of and that she just simply kept perpetuating it herself.

Mr. and Mrs. M. were deeply concerned that her depression had been detrimental for the children. This issue posed a very real dilemma. On the one hand, if the youngsters were experiencing psychiatric disorder, it was essential to proceed with a referral for individual evaluation as soon as possible, even though identification of problems might be extremely disturbing to Mr. and Mrs. M. and might confirm Mrs. M.'s sense of failure about herself. On the other hand, if the children were not in distress, it was important to reassure the parents and relieve anxiety. According to their reports, there was no evidence of disorder in the children. Interviews with the children were scheduled and no referral for psychiatric services was made at this point.

As the session continued, Mrs. M. spoke of her fears about her relationship with Mr. M. and about her frustration in communicating with him. For example, she explained that she didn't want to hurt her husband, but she acted at times as though purposely trying to infuriate him and making him hate her so that he would just walk away. Mr. M. said he had also reached his limits. He knew what was going on but nevertheless was compelled to speak up at times. It was clear from Mrs. M.'s description of her therapy that this pattern was characteristic for her. Mrs. M. tried to force him away, both to spare him and to confirm a sense that she was bad and repulsive. Nonetheless, Mr. M. played a vital role with the children during her illness. He had taken over much of the parenting in those periods when Mrs. M. was impaired and was an essential support to the children.

The parents were becoming more acutely aware of the need to make a decision regarding discussion of Mrs. M.'s history of incest with the children. She made it clear that she saw her childhood victimization as causally related to her depressive illness, but was reluctant to discuss it with them, while Mr. M. thought it had to be discussed. Given the conflicting views, they needed to decide, together, what to discuss before the illness could be comprehensible to the children.

Mrs. M. painfully described her childhood experiences of victimization. She was 12 years old at the time. The perpetrator was her paternal grandfather who had since passed away. The experience itself had been deeply traumatic, as had the recovery of the memories. Furthermore, she had disclosed the experience to her parents and siblings who rejected her and offered no support. This reinforced her sense of betrayal and isolation. A psychiatrist she had seen one year ago had insisted that she talk to her family about the incest. She first spoke with her older brother who was "as cruel as could be" and said that she'd "gotten what she asked for." A second brother said it didn't surprise him and he also blamed her. She was devastated by his response. Mrs. M. said, "My mother screamed at me that neither one of them [father or mother] believed one word of it. My mother wanted to deny that it ever happened."

For Mrs. M., talking about the incest meant, to some extent, reliving it. Planning for the meeting in which she would tell her children about her childhood experiences aroused memories of painful encounters in previous family meetings. My approach was to help Mrs. M. explore what of this experience she wanted to share with her children. It was important to consider what the children had experienced, and what they were likely to encounter in the future. If the youngsters were eventually going to learn of their mother's traumatic history, it would be preferable for them to hear from their parents directly rather than from someone else. This was of particular concern since the incest had already been discussed with Mrs. M.'s siblings, and thus it was quite possible that the children would hear about it from one of their extended family members. I emphasized that when children have experienced and witnessed things that are disturbing, such issues are best discussed with them directly. This view has guided all my discussions with parents about what to tell their children about parental depression. Mrs. M. expressed relief after discussing the incest with her husband and me.

As Mrs. M. talked about her family, I gained a much clearer sense of the events surrounding the onset of her depression. It appeared that the extended family members were in fact a part of the problem; somehow they reinforced her sense of herself as ill and damaged.

It was essential to interview the children directly, to understand their individual perspectives of their mother's illness. The parents could only have faith in my judgment about how the children were doing, once they had been interviewed directly by me. I spent the remainder of the session discussing with the parents how I would talk with the children and hear their concerns. At their request, the interviews were scheduled in the family's home in surroundings familiar to the children. I raised my concern with the referring therapist that the intervention might be exacerbating her condition. Her therapist said that it was not, although her depression was not improving.

*Interview with Lisa, December 6:* I met first with the middle child, Lisa. An attractive, neatly dressed young girl, she was quickly at ease. She was relaxed, laughed easily, and displayed a full range of emotions. She spoke with a spontaneous, lively quality. I began by asking about areas of her life that were not threatening and then gradually moved to a discussion of her mother's illness.

Lisa talked about things as having gone "not too bad" in the preceding year. She described having numerous friends and being involved in many outside activities. I asked Lisa to talk about her mother. What worried her and what gave her hope? Lisa provided a clear, coherent description of her mother's depression over the prior year. With sadness, she described how her mother got progressively worse until she was hospitalized in the previous spring. Lisa clearly wanted to understand her mother's illness and didn't know much about it. Lisa's visits to the hospital had been few; she reported that it had been hard not seeing her mother. Lisa felt that there had been only limited explanations of what had gone on. I asked Lisa about her concept of her mother's illness. She said that her mother was depressed and that "depressed means being sad and upset." When asked what she thought saddened her mother, Lisa talked poignantly about her mother's struggles with extended family members.

Lisa denied any concerns about problems between her parents. She thought her mother's illness "had something to do with that she wasn't loved in her childhood." Lisa acknowledged that she had talked about this concern with her brother and sister and they had agreed. According to Lisa, the doctor didn't really tell the children much about what had happened. He just said it was something from the past and that her mother didn't want to tell them any more. She said that really didn't answer her questions, but she did feel that since then her parents had made more of an effort to respond to her questions. Her mother had told them that she had a lot of responsibility when she was a child and that it was just catching up with her.

I then asked Lisa in more detail about her understanding of the mother's depression. She said, "It's a chemical imbalance, I know that because I've heard that on the news. I think she's getting better, but she gets upset if we ask her how she's doing." When asked if she thought there were things that she hadn't been told, she replied, "I don't know, but my sister and brother think she's not telling us everything and that bothers us."

I asked Lisa whether she thought knowing what was going on was helpful to her. She nodded affirmatively. Did she worry that she or the family had caused her mother's illness? "No, at the hospital they had said very clearly we were not the cause." Most poignantly, Lisa said that she was worried that her mother would commit suicide. She remembered a particular day when her mother wanted to go shopping. "I wanted my father to go with her, because I had a feeling she would commit suicide. And then I spoke up, and since then she's let my father go with her. When I ask her questions about suicide, it makes her stop and think about all that she has, us, my father, and so she won't do it." The interview then turned to Lisa's concerns for her father. It was important to explore the experience of this adolescent as she thought about it from her father's perspective. "I think it's hard for him. Mom's family has been giving him a hard time and I think that's been difficult." Lisa said that she felt her father had taken good care of her mother.

Lisa talked about the reactions of her sister and brother. Lisa said her sister didn't think about it, while her brother had worried about the parents getting a divorce. Speaking about her mother, Lisa said, "I think it's terrible. She must have just had a terrible time."

I asked if Lisa herself had been depressed. She acknowledged feeling down during her mother's hospitalization but not in a persistent way. I asked about Lisa's questions and concerns for the family meeting. She responded with one word: "Suicide." Did she worry that talking about suicide might influence her mother? Lisa denied this as a concern and recounted a conversation with her mother, which indeed closely paralleled her mother's description of the same encounter.

*Interview with Thomas, December 6:* Thomas was a tall, handsome, athletic, and neatly dressed young man who spoke with energy and force. He provided only minimal information in response to questions and appeared eager to avoid talking in depth about his mother. His short, clipped answers were not uncharacteristic for youngsters of his age. His avoidance of talking at any length about events in the family was striking. As with Lisa, I began by asking him about school and activities. He talked about his courses and sports, including his favorite teams and about his membership in a leadership club. Thomas reported that he had good friends. When asked about problems in the family, Thomas replied simply, "Things are great." He denied any worries whatsoever.

About his mother's illness, Thomas stated in a matter-of-fact manner, "She went in the hospital and she just told us she was depressed and told us what happened. She thought her mother didn't like her or something." He said he had no warning that his mother was going into the hospital on either occasion. Thomas appeared acutely uncomfortable in talking about his mother.

Thomas and his siblings had a meeting with a psychiatrist during one of the mother's hospitalizations. He described it in the following way. "There were some things that they didn't tell us, but they're not really bothering me. We've picked up a pretty good idea from phone conversations and other things. It's that she had a hard time when she was a kid, her mother didn't love her, and now it's cleared up because her mom told her she loved her." When asked about his mother, Thomas said, "Things have been hard for my mother." Were there aspects to his mother's illness that Thomas didn't understand? "I don't care about those things. I wasn't told because I don't know. I don't want to know." I gently asked how Thomas was coping with this. "What I don't know won't harm me. I don't like all that stuff. I know it's weird. I like the basics. I don't want to know the fine details." Thomas said he thought his mom would get better and return to the "same old strict mom."

Thomas spoke of his concern for his father. He thought his maternal grandfather had been hardest on his dad and had really put the blame on him. When asked about his own difficulties, Thomas said it hadn't been too hard, but missing school to go to the doctor for the family meeting had been very difficult. Thomas expressed concerns about divorce and said that there were some questions that were unanswered. "I still don't know why she isn't acting better and why she can't do something about it. I don't buy that line that there's nothing she can do and time will heal it. Everything that can be done has been done and it's up to her now." Thomas talked about how frustrated he was with the length of his mother's illness. He denied any symptoms himself.

Despite his denial and firm resolve to avoid thinking about his mother's illness, it was clear that Thomas was deeply concerned for his mother. He desperately wanted some sign of hope, but he seemed almost driven to answer laconically in order to avoid thinking more about it. I had concerns about whether Thomas should be referred for therapy. Given the fact that both his parents felt strongly that he was functioning well, it made sense not to refer him at the time, but rather to follow closely what was happening with him.

*Interview with Mary, December 6:* Mary, the youngest child, was dressed neatly. She appeared somewhat cautious but anxious to please. She reported that she liked school and did reasonably well. She said she had good friends with whom she spent time and had no worries. When I asked about her mother, Mary said, "I worry that she won't get better. When she's on the phone, she cries a lot and that worries me, and I fear she'll go back to the hospital."

Like Lisa and Thomas, Mary said that the trouble had really begun the previous year. "Things were more hectic than usual. My mother didn't do as many things." Mary reported that her mother's first hospitalization had "come out of the blue," but the second time she and her sister had felt that it would happen because her mother had appeared somehow different. Her mother had been mad at the doctors because they hadn't been taking better care of her. Mary said that she had really missed her mother during the hospitalization. She indicated that there had been a good deal of conflict in the family. "Everyone" had been worried. Mary had been particularly scared because her mother had been losing weight. She denied concerns about her mother hurting herself but acknowledged worry about her parents getting a divorce. In response to an inquiry about the parents' explanations of mother's illness to her, she said she really didn't understand them. As the interview was ending, Mary spoke painfully about her fears for her mother. "I'm just worried about when she will get better because I don't know. I think it'll take a long time. Sometimes, in reaction to all this, I just get mad because she's not getting better as quickly as I want her to and I get mad sometimes, and I take it out on other people." She denied any symptoms herself.

In summary, all three youngsters were functioning reasonably well and yet all had been deeply affected by their mother's illness. There was a continuity across accounts provided by them and also some important differences. Thomas denied his mother's illness and wanted to make it her responsibility. Lisa was in some ways the most questioning, while Mary acknowledged that she was quite confused about the situation.

*December 15:* In this session with the parents alone, Mrs. M. reported she had discussed my interview with her son. He had said, "Since the depression was brought on because you didn't feel your parent's love, now that you know they love you, the depression should end." Thomas had told his mother "she was keeping the depression going." Mrs. M. was quite distraught on hearing this from her son. I took an active role in helping Mrs. M. understand that neither I nor Mr. M. shared Thomas's view but that this was Thomas's way of trying to make sense of her illness.

Mrs. M. was reporting this view of Thomas in part because it was a view that she had of herself at times. Mrs. M. believed that she should simply cure herself. I tried to show her that she was so bothered by what Thomas said because in part she agreed with it. I emphasized that her depression should be understood as an illness, not as a lack of will, not as something for which she should berate herself.

The parents turned to me for advice about what to discuss with the children. I reiterated that the children needed to know about events they had witnessed or feelings brought on by such events that were out of the ordinary or unusual and for which there was no explanation. Mr. M. said that he thought the issue of incest should be discussed because the youngsters might be worried that the mother's disorder had a genetic cause. He wondered if letting them know it was something to do with her childhood would relieve them. I emphasized that if the children were aware that something had been kept secret, it would be more harmful for them to hear about it from people other than the parents. It was obviously on the mother's mind and had been talked about by her extended family members. The children felt that something more was going on than they had been told. It seemed highly likely that they either knew of mother's victimization or would learn of it soon. While her extended family remained adamant in not discussing it with her, Mrs. M. wanted her children to know about the incest from herself and Mr. M. directly. She further reiterated that she was under pressure from her brothers and sisters to minimize her victimization, and she wanted to be frank with her children about what had happened.

The fact that she could not talk with or seek support from her extended family was extremely painful for her. This was indeed a repetition of the initial rejection that she had experienced by her mother. Her siblings continually found fault with her and her husband in a way that reinforced her sense of herself as unworthy of their affection. This made the need to have a discussion with her own children all the more important and yet added to the tension around the planning for the meeting.

Beyond the incest, however, there was much more to the mother's depression. This included her severe symptoms of loss of energy, agitation, irritability, blunted affect, and inability to perform normal tasks, as well as the ever-present thoughts of suicide. Furthermore, there were the circumstances of her treatment, the long drive from out of state for frequent meetings with the psychiatrist, and the medication changes that sometimes resulted in sudden shifts in mood and energy.

The process of my talking to the youngsters had already stimulated discussion between the parents and their children about the illness.

This was very much in line with two fundamental tenets of the intervention: (1) the experiences of the illness were real and important to the children and needed discussion because they were confusing and frightening; (2) it was clear that the occasion of talking with the parents and then with the children, in and of itself, stimulated important discussions among them outside of the meetings.

During the session, Mrs. M. appeared more pale and spoke with even less emotion than previously. She was becoming increasingly depressed and had more frequent thoughts of wanting to take her life. She was adamant that she would not be hospitalized and very much wanted to continue with the intervention. I spoke with her therapist following the session. He confirmed that Mrs. M.'s presentation was part of a general pattern of exacerbations in her depression. In his view, this was of great concern, but not related to the intervention. While it was paramount that Mrs. M.'s health not be jeopardized in any way, there were clearly areas of misunderstanding for this family that appeared to be causing distress for the children and the parents. After careful consideration and consultation with her therapist, I decided that the needs of Mrs. M. and her family could best be served by going ahead with another parent session, with the understanding that postponement of the family session might become necessary.

*December 20:* Despite her difficulties, Mrs. M. was very clear about her wishes for the family meeting. Mrs. M. wanted the children to be aware of what had happened but still be free to form their own opinions about their grandparents. On a deeper level, she wanted to be certain that they were healthy, and also that they would not reject her. The parents voiced their thoughts about how the children would react. Mr. M. thought that his son would definitely raise the issue of incest. Mrs. M. predicted that all three children would have a difficult time because they believed that "the whole truth" had been discussed at the time of mother's previous hospitalization. Mrs. M. described feeling "damned" if she revealed the incest to her children and "damned" if she didn't.

Mrs. M. discussed her traumatic experiences. The incest had occurred near a summer home on the ocean. The family had revisited that home for the first time the summer when Mrs. M. experienced the first symptoms of her depression. Mary had been on the beach, developed the acute onset of an asthmatic attack, and had been rushed to the hospital. Somehow this episode had triggered the flashbacks for Mrs. M. She felt physically ill, but could not understand the origin of her discomfort. Gradually she recalled riding with her grandfather in his big Mercedes. He stopped the car and sexually molested her. As I listened to Mrs. M. describe this scene, watched her painfully wrestle with these memories, and knew of her worsening depression, it became clear to me that more time was necessary before she could talk with the children.

The question remained: How could Mrs. M. and her family be helped, given her worsening depression? She appeared very downcast and saddened. Mr. M. reported being distant from her, as though he could not help her with her overwhelming feelings of despair. She was struggling with the need to be in control in the face of powerful and painful memories of victimization by her grandfather. Above all else, the discussion with her children should not be a repetition of the chaos and humiliation she had experienced in earlier discussions with her extended family members. Mrs. M.'s sense of self was closely tied to her parenting role; her parenting was one part of her life where she saw herself as being somewhat intact. If the children were unable to understand her victimization, there was the risk that such an experience would confirm her negative view of herself.

After much discussion with Mr. and Mrs. M., I suggested that the intervention be postponed until Mrs. M.'s worsening depression was in better control. Mrs. M. appeared disappointed but agreed with the decision. She understood the need to focus on her own recovery in order to help the children. There were several reasons for Mrs. M.'s increasing struggle with her illness at this point in time. Her medication was being changed, and her new antidepressant was not at therapeutic levels. It was the holiday season, and this was characteristically Mrs. M.'s most difficult time of the year.

I spoke frequently with her therapist during the weeks that followed. Despite her thoughts of suicide, Mrs. M. repeatedly indicated her desire to proceed with the intervention for the children. I spoke with Mr. and Mrs. M. regularly by telephone. After approximately six weeks, Mrs. M. began to recover. The parents returned for the next appointment three months later.

*March 10:* Mrs. M. appeared much improved, and both parents reported that the children had continued to function well. There was no evidence of a need for referral for the children, from the parents' point of view. Mrs. M. had made considerable progress in thinking about what she wanted to tell the children. One of the manifestations of her depressive illness was this constant fear that she did not have the respect of her children. She came to realize that this was not so, and that she had the ability to cope with her children. But it also pointed to the importance of her role as a mother in maintaining her stability. She stated that she regained some of her confidence as a mother.

Mr. and Mrs. M. returned to the issue of telling the children about their mother's history of victimization. Mrs. M. acknowledged that the children were already aware that she "had a rough childhood," but she felt they needed to understand the basis for her strained relationship with her parents. She was tremendously fearful of the children losing their relationship with their grandparents. Indeed this pointed out a central struggle for Mrs. M. in thinking about the family meeting. In her individual therapy, she was wrestling continually with the issues of her mother, of not wanting to lose her mother, and of the dilemma of her own parenting—how could she care for her children when it meant being so different from her own mother?

Mr. M. felt that the children needed to understand exactly what his wife had experienced, not only in terms of sexual abuse but emotional maltreatment as well. He was not advocating disclosure of specific details of the incest but felt that the children had a sense of something sinister in the past. Mrs. M. expressed the wish to give her children some idea of what she had been struggling with that had contributed to her feelings of sadness and thoughts of suicide, but did not want to go into the specifics of her abuse.

Mrs. M. was keenly aware of the association between her struggles as a parent and her own childhood experiences. At the same time, Mrs. M.'s anxiety about somehow harming the youngsters paralyzed her and kept her from enjoying time with the children. In the remainder of the session, the discussion focused on Mrs. M.'s fears of recapitulating her childhood and causing the same kinds of reactions in her children that she had experienced. While still depressed, Mrs. M. was able to focus on the goals of the family meeting. Mr. M. was supportive during the session but emphasized that she needed to tell the children as much as possible. Mrs. M.'s children were central to her understanding of herself. Finally, she lived with guilt that she hadn't told them the "whole truth" and she herself was increasingly aware of the cost of having been abused. We made the decision together to proceed with the family session.

*March 18:* I continued to work with Mr. and Mrs. M. in understanding the nature of her depression. Much of the session touched on themes from previous sessions. Both parents were trying to understand the illness experience sufficiently to be able to make sense of it to their children. Mrs. M. was terrified of having harmed her children because of her illness. She was deeply concerned that her affective illness inevitably would be passed on to them and had intense fears about something coming from her childhood that would get out of control and frighten her children. For Mrs. M. and the rest of the family, it was important to emphasize the difference between her life experience and that of the children.

*Family Session, March 31:* I met with the family in their home. I began by giving a brief history of how the family meeting had come to be. I focused the meeting on the children and asked about their concerns, with the aim of involving them early in the discussion. The three children denied any concerns. Mr. M. suggested that the children had decided beforehand to keep the meeting as brief as possible. Following the parents' request, I reviewed the basic teaching about depression. This gave the parents an opportunity to reflect on how their children were dealing with such information. The children sat silently. It was indeed evident that they had decided together to say nothing so that the meeting would be short. In fact, Thomas had specifically told Lisa and Mary not to speak. I first moved the discussion to an issue which had been of great concern to the children: their mother's hospitalization.

In some ways, the entire family wanted to deny or minimize Mrs. M.'s illness. I acknowledged their discomfort in coming together for such a meeting. While the children sat in silence, Mrs. M. challenged them about their concerns. The following vignette gives some sense of the discussion that ensued about suicide.

Mrs. M. said to the children, "You were really concerned. What about the time I left at night? Did you think I was never going to come back?" Lisa said, "Kind of." Thomas abruptly broke in and said, "Why are you asking that? You already know the answer." Mrs. M. said, "Do we?" I said, "I don't think they do." Thomas said angrily, "Yes you do. All you're doing is refreshing the memory of what happened. I just don't understand why you're doing this." Mary said, "But Mom, you're doing so well. Why do we have to possibly risk trouble with this meeting?" Thomas said, "We're not having any problems."

I reiterated the aim of the meeting. It was not to stir things up and make things worse but was a chance to understand things together. Thomas said, "I'd forgotten about all this." I suggested that people sometimes forget about things that are really painful when they don't want to deal with them. I emphasized that Mr. and Mrs. M. believed it was a good time to talk about the mother's illness and explained how talking about it now was more likely to prevent misunderstandings from coming up in the future that might cause harm.

Mrs. M. said, "I feel comfortable enough with the way things are going that I don't feel it will make things worse. I think it is another step forward. I love you very much. I'm going to tell you something today I've thought about for a long time. Because you're my children, I'm going to share it with you. I really want you to understand it and to know it so you're not going to be afraid of it and think it could happen. I think it's going to clarify things a whole lot for you."

Mrs. M. displayed courage in taking charge of the meeting. The youngsters continued to resist hearing about her victimization. Thomas said that he was afraid that he would break down in tears. Thomas said, "We've already been over what we're going to talk about. If not, then you lied to us all the time." Mrs. M. said, "What is it that you know?" Thomas said, "Something about when you were a child. You didn't think your mom loved you and that kind of stuff and then there was a little chemical stuff." Mrs. M. said, "There's a lot more to it. If you don't talk about things, they come back to haunt you. Well, Mommy had some pretty bad experiences as a child and I didn't talk to anyone about them because in my day and age no one did." Thomas said, "Maybe it has something to do with our grandparents." Mrs. M. said, "Do you think I want to dislike my parents? No, I don't. But there were some things left unsaid."

Mrs. M. then said, "I kept things unsaid too long and that's what happened. October a year ago it started. I went into a hospital. I was just having flashbacks like instant replays of things that happened when I was a little girl. After each of you were born, some of those flashbacks happened. I can remember one night, Daddy and I were sitting down eating a steak dinner and I started to cry. He couldn't understand why I was crying. I was crying because all of a sudden it was like I was at Mommy and Pappy's kitchen table eating dinner with all my brothers and sisters. A steak was put on the table, but I was not allowed to touch the platter until everyone else took theirs and then I took what was left. It all came back to me. It was an incident as a little girl that really hurt me. I was sexually abused by my grandfather. I'm not sure how old I was. He didn't hurt me physically, but he did hurt me. It's a hard thing to accept because it makes you wonder about yourself and what kind of person you are and why you were picked. I couldn't go to Mammy and Pappy and tell them. I just couldn't do it. It was Pappy's father. Who would believe me? I didn't share it with anyone.

"At the shore one summer we were driving around in my brother's Mercedes. Grandfather always drove a big Mercedes. Being there, in that car, I just started to feel very unsettled. I even felt sick. I didn't know what was happening, but things were coming back to me. We spent our summers down there on the shore. Some of what happened was coming back. I just didn't want to talk about it. Then I finally did. I told my brothers and sisters. Some of them accepted it, some of them denied it. The issue was the incest even though they wanted to deny it. My grandfather did it, but I also found out that my mother and I did not have a good relationship."

Thomas at this point said, "Let's get back to the steak here. Why couldn't you have the steak first?" Mrs. M. said, "That's the way it was. The boys had to have it first and whatever was left, I had." "Were there any other girls?" asked Thomas. "Just the one and she was a baby." "So you were the only girl?" "Yes, I was," said the mother. "It's almost like I was a single girl. I took care of all the kids. I did a damn good job. But it was just that I could never satisfy her the way I wanted to. I just never felt as loved as I could have felt from her. I felt it from my father but not from my mother. She had her own problems as a child. People have to deal with their own feelings. That's what I'm doing. I wanted you to know this because all my brothers and sisters know and you may overhear them talking. I didn't want you to hear it from anyone else."

Mr. M. said, "You know, when I first got married, her brothers would come and tell me how terrible her childhood was. Your mother never talked about it." Mrs. M. said, "I never went into the details of it with your father." Mr. M. said, "You can see what happens when you keep things inside. She was working so hard to keep the information inside because she didn't want to hurt anybody. We don't blame her parents. Your mother's father had been in the war. He was away when your mother was very small, and your grandmother's father had died when she was very young."

Mr. M. continued, "You know, one of the doctors said that a depression can be like a post-traumatic stress disorder. It's what you heard of with the Vietnam veterans. Some years later the cruelties and things that have happened come back to them." Thomas then said, "I wish she'd told us that earlier. We could have understood it better." He started to cry and said, "I really don't want to know this." Mrs. M. said, "Did you suspect it?" Thomas said no, but Mary said, "I did. Because I was watching the Oprah Winfrey Show and they had these people who were raped and sexually abused and a lot of them had depressions. So I thought maybe you were depressed because you'd been sexually abused." The mother then said, "You remember my telling you a long while ago if someone touched you and you felt uncomfortable, you should come and tell me?" Then the boy was sobbing and said, "I really didn't want to know that. I was having a grand old time and now I don't want to hear it. I'm mad at you for telling me." Mr. M. said, "It is better that you heard it from us than from one of the cousins," and Thomas said, "Maybe I could have lived my whole life without knowing." Then Lisa said, "I'm glad to know." Mrs. M. kept trying to tell Thomas that she told him because she loved Thomas and he said, "What you don't know won't hurt you. I didn't want to know that." Both parents tried to get him to talk, but he refused. "Your eyes are open now," said Mrs. M. Thomas said, "It doesn't put my mind at ease." Thomas asked to be left alone, and the mother said, "Maybe it won't be immediately helpful but in the long run."

I spoke up for Thomas and said I could see how he wished it had never happened, because things had been going well for him. I emphasized that the parents had chosen to talk about it partly so that it would no longer be a secret, and partly so the children wouldn't hear it from someone else. The girls said they were glad that the mother had told them. Mary said, "I wish she'd told us earlier because it all adds up." Mr. M. said, "I hope we can learn from this so that things won't get bottled up."

Mrs. M. reiterated her love, "The love that a parent has is completely different. It's the love that's leading me to tell you so that you'll understand, so that you won't be afraid for yourselves later on that maybe you'll get depressed because you didn't go through the childhood that I went through. I've always been honest with you kids and I don't want that to change."

I underscored that the main focus of the family session was not the incest but the children and their understanding of Mrs. M.'s depression. The mother then began to talk about how much better she had been. I was clear with the children that they could be angry with me and took responsibility in part for having the meeting. Mrs. M. interjected, "I had to bring out the incest, I had no choice. I didn't want you to know. Then finally I did." Mrs. M. said, "My mother and father did what they could. We don't dislike or blame them. We hope they're nice to you. We don't want what you know to affect how you feel about them. Now, you see that I felt like I was causing more pain to you people and to your father by just being there and I thought it would be easier if I wasn't here, if I went away for a while because I knew it was hard on you. Now I know that I would hurt you more by leaving and I couldn't leave because I love you too much. Even when I had thoughts of it, it wasn't to leave you forever. It was just to see if I could run away from myself."

I said that one of the main aims of the session was to take away the blame for Mrs. M's illness, to ensure that none of the children felt guilty. I turned to the children and asked if they had any questions. After it was clear that there were no further questions, I ended the family meeting and emphasized that I would be available as needed in the future.

*Follow-up:* After the family session, I spoke to the parents and met with them as a couple. Although Thomas had been upset in the meeting, he was calm and doing well by the next day. The other children were also well. In fact, the parents reported that Thomas was expressing anger toward the grandfather for his abuse of Mrs. M. The meeting had indeed been powerful and intense. Mrs. M. had revealed many more details of the incest in the meeting than either Mr. M. or I had anticipated. I had been very concerned about whether Thomas needed a referral because of his anxious avoidance during the family meeting. Both parents reported that Thomas had continued to function well and had not manifested any psychiatric symptoms. I also recognized that Thomas needed to separate from his mother. As a young man reaching adulthood, one of his developmental tasks was to relinquish the idea of his mother as perfect, and move on with his own life. Her illness was deeply troubling to him, in part because he was trying to separate from her in the face of feeling considerable guilt about her impairment. Furthermore, I also understood his behavior arising from his guilt about his rage at his mother, both because she had failed him and because he feared he had hurt her. A psychoanalytic framework was also helpful in understanding that he had a hostile transference to me. His reaction to me, in part, was derived from his reaction to his mother. Toward me he could express the anger and disappointment that were too dangerous to express toward her. Given these circumstances, his continued good functioning and his positive response to the discussion with his father one day after the meeting, it appeared best not to refer him for therapy at that time. I indicated that I would arrange a referral for any of the children should that become necessary in the future.

I stayed in regular touch with the family through the summer. Although there had been some tension between the children, they were doing well. Mrs. M. had suffered a relapse and was severely depressed. She underwent electroconvulsive therapy and had experienced some memory loss. Over the following months, the children continued to do well, despite further exacerbations of their mother's depressions. I remained available to them with some phone contact. I saw the girls and the parents approximately six months later when there was a question of a referral for family therapy. Several years later I also saw the couple. A colleague of mine had evaluated them independently with a semi-structured interview before the intervention, following the family session, and again two years later. The parents reported that the intervention had been helpful to them in understanding their children, and indeed what they had learned had started an ongoing process of understanding, There was no sign that the intervention caused additional trauma for Mrs. M. The course of her illness had been fulminant before the intervention began and continued to be so, unrelated to the relatively few sessions I had with the family. I had begun to see the family around winter holiday time, which had always been a particularly difficult time for Mrs. M. The parents commented on the value of reassurance from me and on my availability through their struggle.

## DISCUSSION

While there is an extensive literature about the psychoanalysis of both children and adults, few reports deal with directly advising parents regarding their children's needs when they are in psychoanalytic treatment. Nonetheless, as Kris (1981) has emphasized, "the analytic treatment of adult patients who are parents often comes upon problems in regard to their children" (p. 151). Kris has described clinical situations where an analyst may need to apply techniques, such as giving advice to parents during the course of analysis, that are closer to child guidance interventions than to psychoanalysis. His focus has been on situations in the analytic treatment of an adult patient, where crises or problems have arisen for the patient's children, and there has been an urgent need for action. Such intervention becomes necessary when a child is acutely at risk. Kris underscores the fact that the analyst may become aware of risks to the children of a patient long before such issues arise in the analytic process. An example of this situation is the treatment of a parent with a depressive disorder.

Fraiberg et al. (1975) described a psychoanalytically based approach in the treatment of impaired infant-mother relationships. The therapeutic work involved techniques that included an emphasis on support and developmental guidance through home visitation. While the intervention was based on psychoanalytic principles, the therapists used an approach that included psychoeducational aspects, similar in technique in many ways to this intervention with its emphasis on an active stance by the therapist and on developing and enhancing the adaptive strengths of children.

In the psychoanalytic tradition, there has long been interest in prevention. In 1952, Lindemann and Dawes highlighted the need for the analyst to "initiate efforts in preventive psychiatry" (p. 429). Despite this earlier literature, psychoanalytic therapy has traditionally centered on treatment rather than prevention. The analytic stance has concentrated on the individual patient and in particular on the powerful effects of early experience on current functioning. The focus of this intervention is on the future of the children and on the prevention of psychiatric disturbance. Based on psychoanalytic principles, the work reflects the conviction that consideration of the inner lives of children is vital to their well-being. The therapeutic work was informed by an awareness of the transference reactions. A psychoanalytic perspective was crucial in understanding Thomas's resistance to dealing with his mother, and in understanding her view of herself, and her conflicted inner life. While Mrs. M. demonstrated the capacity to have meaningful relationships, especially to care for her children (object love), she had relatively little capacity for self-love. Kris (1990) has emphasized the importance of attending to the patient's need for help with punitive, self-critical attitudes. This provided a useful framework for understanding the mother's conflicts about her own parents and her parenting. More generally, in Bibring's (1954) terms, the techniques of suggestion and clarification were employed in the intervention.

The therapeutic stance employed differed from the practice of psychoanalysis in several important respects. The work took place in the context of an ongoing therapy in which the clinician had a defined role to focus on the needs of the children, not to provide care for the mother's depression. Secondly, these individuals had not identified themselves as patient. Fostering their understanding and resiliency was the explicit goal, rather than analyzing resistance. The clinician functioned as a physician and teacher. Equally important was the stance of being a participant observer with the family, that is, listening to and learning about their lives, in part outside of a clearly defined theoretical framework. Use of narrative, of understanding the story of the mother's depression, as seen by the different family members, was central to the intervention. As both Mr. and Mrs. M., the children individually, and finally the family together talked about their own experiences, they developed an improved and shared understanding of the illness experience itself. Previous work on the connection between the ways in which people tell their stories and resiliency, in studies of civil rights workers, survivors of cancer, and children of parents with affective disorder (Beardslee, 1981, 1983, 1989) had demonstrated the value of the participant observer stance and the importance of self-understanding in allowing individuals to cope with difficult life circumstances.

As to the increasing severity of Mrs. M.'s depression, the delay between seeing the children and having the family meeting was somewhat unusual in our experience with families, as was the long time interval from beginning to end of the intervention. However, dealing with uncertainty about outcome and the course of parental depression is not uncommon in work with these families. In this particular case, there was a powerful signal event, a family secret around incest that needed to be discussed. Such a single powerful event has not always been present in work with other families, but the importance of the emphasis on the illness experience has been.

There were several healing principles in this case that have become evident in other cases as well. The family session occurred in the home, in the place that was most suitable from the family's point of view. The therapy was described by Fraiberg and her colleagues (1975) as "psychotherapy in the kitchen . . . familiar in its methods and unfamiliar in its setting" (p. 394). However, her use of home visits arose from the need for emergency treatment (there were no alternatives). In this intervention, the home was chosen as the best place for the meetings with the children and the family. The parents reported subsequently that this had been very important for the children. Perhaps Mrs. M.'s remarkable ability in talking with the children about the incest and her illness was related in part to meeting in her home.

A second factor was that the clinician emphasized that the material to be discussed during the family session was to be determined by the parents. They had to feel that they had mastered, individually and together, enough of the experience of Mrs. M.'s depression to be able to present it to their children, and that they were in control of what was expressed. The mother and father showed considerable courage in speaking about these very painful events in the face of the mother's struggle with her illness. The clinician provided a holding environment, a context in which they could speak to their children about her illness and childhood experiences.

A third factor that clearly enhanced the alliance and the work with the family was the availability of the clinician by telephone, at any point. While the parents used this avenue relatively infrequently, when they did so, it was often with great urgency. It is worth noting that immediately following intervention and two years later, the parents emphasized the availability of the clinician, their relationship with him, and the reassurance provided as central therapeutic factors.

Another important factor was that the family understood that the two clinicians were working together. When the clinician working with the family had concerns about suicide or depression, he communicated directly with the treating therapist, and always informed the parents of this communication. Likewise the mother's therapist communicated with the clinician working with the family. This may well have served as a model for the parents in developing and enhancing the communication with the children.

Finally, there was an ongoing need for discussion of the illness beyond the family meeting, both the time of intervention and during the ensuing years, as the mother continued to experience severe exacerbations of her depression. The perspective that the intervention could only start a process of discussion and the recognition of the need to encourage discussions over the ensuing years have become important guiding principles.

This was a family with considerable strengths. Both parents had a profound commitment to their children. Both had functioned as effective and good parents through the crucial early stages of development for these youngsters. Moreover, they were highly motivated for help with their children and were able to use the help effectively. The youngsters were functioning well in school and at home and had histories of good functioning before the onset of the mother's severe illness. Despite Mrs. M.'s strong commitment to the children, she did exhibit a distorted view of herself as a parent. The history of good parenting in the past was in part used to help her understand the distortions of the present. As an example, during an early session, Mrs. M. explained how she thought her presence was causing pain for the children and Mr. M., and that they might be better off without her, i.e., if she committed suicide. The clinician was very direct in his response by stating clearly that the family would not be better off without Mrs. M., and that her suicide would cause them great pain.

Much of this discussion has focused on Mrs. M. and her interactions with the children during the intervention. While Mr. M. was much less active in the family session, it was clear that he was a source of support for each of the children, and for Mrs. M. as well. Despite Mr. M.'s expressed frustration with the chronic nature of his wife's illness, as well as his anger toward her extended family members, he never lost sight of the main focus on parenting.

Mrs. M. emphasized that she did not want the children to learn of her victimization from anyone else. Mary reported that she first had this suspicion following an episode of the Oprah Winfrey show, during which the topic was depression associated with incest. Mary's account underscored the varied ways in which children may learn about different explanations for illness. These youngsters were exposed to much information about psychotropic medication (Prozac), depression, suicide and incest, on television, and in popular magazines. But such information was partial and incomplete; it was not aimed at providing comprehensive explanations of an ill parent's behavior to family members.

Understanding of countertransference issues was central to this intervention. The clinician had to grapple with feelings of helplessness and despair that he experienced in sitting with this mother, who was profoundly depressed. Perhaps, most importantly from the point of view of countertransference, she talked very often about suicide. Moreover, the clinician required an appreciation of the limits of the intervention. The intervention did not "cure" Mrs. M.'s depression, nor was it aimed at changes in character structure or personality function. It was an intervention primarily focused on the children. Reflection on the process of the intervention and awareness about the limits of what could be done were essential in dealing with the family.

In 1952, Lindemann and Dawes described the "development of the quest to find preventive methods in the field of psychiatry" (p. 429). This case history highlights the use of a preventive intervention in working with the children of parents with an affective disorder in psychoanalytically based treatment. Given the risk to children of parents with a depressive disorder, we emphasize the importance of focusing on prevention of disorder among children—even when they are not patients.

BIBLIOGRAPHY

BEARDSLEE, W. R. (1981). Self-understanding and coping with cancer. In *The Damocles Syndrome*, ed. G. P. Koocher & J. E. O'Malley. New York: McGraw-Hill, pp. 144–163.
——— (1983). *The Way Out Must Lead*. Westport, Conn.: Lawrence Hill, 2nd ed.
——— (1989). The role of self-understanding in resilient individuals. *Amer. J. J. Orthopsychiat.*, 59:266–278.
——— (1990). Development of a clinician-based preventive intervention for families with affective disorders. *J. Prevent. Psychiat. & Allied Disciplines*, 4:39–61.
——— HOKE, L., WHEELOCK, I. ET AL. (1992). Preventive intervention for families with parental affective disorders. *Amer. J. Psychiat.*, 149:1335–1340.
——— & PODOREFSKY, D. (1988). Resilient adolescents whose parents have serious affective and other psychiatric disorders. *Amer. J. Psychiat.*, 145:63–69.
——— SALT, P., PORTERFIELD, K. ET AL. (1993). Comparison of preventive interventions for families with parental affective disorder. *J. Amer. Acad. Child Adol. Psychiat.*, 32:254–263.
——— & WHEELOCK, I. (in press). Children of parents with affective disorders. In *Handbook of Depression in Children and Adolescents*, ed. W. R. Reynolds & H. F. Johnston. New York: Plenum.
BIBRING, E. (1954). Psychoanalysis and the dynamic psychotherapies. *J. Amer. Psychoanal. Assn.*, 2:745–770.

DOWNEY, G. & COYNE, J. C. (1990). Children of depressed parents. *Psychol. Bull.*, 108:50–76.

EISENBERG, L. (1981). A research framework for evaluating the promotion of mental health and prevention of mental illness. *Pub. Hlth. Reps.*, 96:3–19.

FRAIBERG, S., ADELSON, E., & SHAPIRO, V. (1975). Ghosts in the nursery. *J. Amer. Acad. Child Psychiat.*, 14:387–421.

KEITNER, G. I. & MILLER, I. W. (1990). Family functioning and major depression. *Amer. J. Psychiat.*, 147:1128–1137.

KRIS, A. O. (1981). On giving advice to parents in analysis. *Psychoanal. Study Child*, 36:151–162.

———— (1990). Helping patients by analyzing self-criticism. *J. Amer. Psychoanal. Assn.*, 38:605–636.

LINDEMANN, E. & DAWES, L. G. (1952). The use of psychoanalytic constructs in preventive psychiatry. *Psychoanal. Study Child*, 7:429–448.

LOBEL, B. & HIRSCHFELD, R. M. A. (1984). *Depression: What Do We Know?* Washington: U.S. Department of Health and Human Services and NIMH.

WEISSMAN, M. M., LEAF, P., & BRUCE, M. L. (1987). Single parent women. *Soc. Psychiat.*, 22:29–36.

# The Reaction of an Early Latency Boy to the Sudden Death of His Baby Brother

## JENNIFER DAVIDS, M.Sc.

*Surprisingly little has been written on the impact of the death of a baby on an older sibling. This paper describes how a narcissistically vulnerable latency boy grappled, in the course of his psychotherapy, with the painful loss of his baby brother. Emotional and cognitive aspects of his early confrontation with the reality of death are considered. The patient's six theories about the cot death are described. Attention is drawn to the value of the sibling relationship and to the narcissistic needs which this relationship fulfilled. The termination phase is discussed in the light of the dynamics of sudden loss. The safe therapeutic context provided the space in which this young, rather muddled latency boy could grieve and mourn this traumatic loss.*

SUDDEN INFANT DEATH SYNDROME[1] IS THE COMMONEST CAUSE OF DEATH between 28 days and 12 months, accounting for two-fifths of all postnatal deaths in the Western world (Milner and Rugg, 1989). The cause or, more likely, causes still elude medical researchers (Bacon and Bellman, 1983; Milner, 1987; Ponsonby et al., 1992).

This paper focuses on how a latency boy struggled to come to terms with the puzzle of his baby brother's sudden death at the age of 8 weeks. There were many other important dimensions of Alfredo's 2½-year twice-weekly psychotherapy, but they are outside the scope of this pa-

---

Staff member of the Anna Freud Centre, London, and Senior Child Psychotherapist, Departments of Child Psychiatry and Paediatrics, Middlesex Hospital, London.
1. The sudden death of unspecific cause in infancy (1987). British Paediatric Association Classification of Diseases compatible with 9th revision of the WHO International Classification of Diseases.

per. It should be noted that this psychodynamic psychotherapy did not focus on the theme of the sudden death, but issues relating to the death were taken up as they emerged in the material, alongside many other themes.

Alfredo was referred at 7 years 9 months by his parents for his lack of interest in schoolwork and his poor academic performance. For some months prior to his mother's pregnancy Alfredo had been wasting time during class and was easily distracted by and drawn to children who clowned. Faced with any academic task, he daydreamed. Pressured to focus and concentrate, he would produce work reluctantly at a snail's pace.

Alfredo and his sister, only 20 months his junior, were reported to fight like cat and dog. Rosa sailed through school at the top of her class. Alfredo experienced her as bossy, intrusive, and very competitive.

Alfredo clearly was a much-loved and treasured eldest and only son. Shortly after moving from Italy to England, Mrs. H. had become pregnant and Alfredo was delivered at full term with the help of forceps. He was a very easy, contented baby. Breast-feeding went well, but Mrs. H. was disappointed at not having the "instant mother feeling." Alfredo sat up and crawled early, but there was some delay in his learning to walk. When he was 10 months old, the mother became pregnant with Rosa.

Alfredo was a little late in talking, but "Once he started, he never stopped." Alfredo reacted strongly to his mother's one-week absence while she was in the hospital giving birth to Rosa. During this first separation Alfredo turned against his maternal grandmother who had come from Italy to look after him. To accommodate him, the maternal grandmother took over as much of Rosa's care as possible, leaving the mother free to attend to 20-month-old Alfredo, while feeling guilty that she was missing out on Rosa's baby days.

Alfredo tolerated separations from his mother at toddler groups. At 3 years he settled in well at nursery school. Toilet training was achieved just before his third birthday.

When Alfredo was 4, he was assessed by a psychologist who suggested he had visual perceptual difficulties and problems with visual sequencing.

Mrs. H. had two early miscarriages when Alfredo was 4½ and 5. We do not know how much he knew about them. The only material that hinted at some knowledge on Alfredo's part appeared early in the first months of treatment. Alfredo drew a machine which made wooden baby rabbits. A coffin was drawn next to the machine, and the wooden baby rabbits placed within it.

Mrs. H. recognized a tendency within herself to "spoon-feed" Alfredo. She described herself as an overanxious mother who found her children's growing up difficult. Her need to infantilize Alfredo may have been related to the two perinatal losses, especially in view of her wish for 12 sons, a dream she cherished since she was a young girl. Over the 2½ years of treatment, the psychiatric social worker and I both became aware of her depression. She was a highly intelligent, university-educated woman, who struggled to find expression for her ambitions and who clearly was frustrated by the traditional roles expected by her husband and extended family. Mr. H.'s work involved much international travel; his wife sometimes described him as a third child, unwilling to assume a paternal role.

At the time of the assessment Alfredo was described as immature for his age. Although he was friendly with children in the neighborhood, he did not have a large circle of friends. Four months before his eighth birthday, he was still clearly caught up with oedipal passions and rivalry. Alfredo became upset when he found his parents kissing and tried to pull them apart; on finding his father in bed late on New Year's day he demanded to know where he had been the previous night. When his dad replied he was tired and had been sleeping, Alfredo teased him, "I know where you were; you were with your girlfriend . . . with mummy."

## THE DEATH

Alfredo, at 6½ years, had shown much excitement at the prospect of having a baby brother with whom he hoped to play. During his mother's pregnancy he had become rather clingy and every morning inquired how the baby in her tummy was. Shortly after Mario was born, Alfredo's more negative emotions were revealed in his spraying baby powder all over the bathroom, afterward denying what he had done. He then settled down and developed a strong attachment to Mario, frequently saying that the two of them would play football together.

Alfredo, then 7 years 5 months, and his sister Rosa, 5 years 8 months, shared a bedroom. One night their 8-week-old baby brother slept in their room, as he had done from time to time previously. They woke up early and the next morning found Mario to be very still. As Alfredo described to me, many months later during treatment, "He didn't move, he just lay there." The two children watched their baby brother and when their concern became too much to bear, they called their parents to come and look. Things then moved very quickly. The ambulance was called, but Mario died before it arrived. Rosa reacted by crying and asking numerous questions. Alfredo responded with disbelief, "Are you joking me?" he said. The whole family was in shock. The parents telephoned the psychiatric social worker with whom they had established a relationship prior to the pregnancy, and she provided immediate support. The children attended the funeral and were told that Mario had gone to heaven.

The two children reacted differently to the loss. Alfredo was very silent, listened to his sister's many questions about Mario, but never asked directly himself. Immediately after the cot death, as the parents called it, Alfredo became greedy for chocolate, which he ate secretly and hid the wrappers behind the sofa. He requested a photograph of himself holding his baby brother. Apparently Mario had looked like him. As the months went on, he asked and said little about the bereavement. One day he heard his mother crying and came to comfort her, saying, "I'll be him for you." Four months after Mario's death, the parents, particularly the father, described their concern to me that Alfredo, whom they considered a sensitive boy, was bottling up his feelings. Mr. H. suspected Alfredo was preoccupied with thoughts of his baby brother, but keeping it all to himself. In the middle of a conversation about football, Alfredo had unexpectedly asked him various questions about the nature of God and the afterlife. Mr. H. had tried to answer them, according to the family's religious beliefs. The parents had refrained from questioning Alfredo, as they sensed that he felt they were prying. Yet, in the diagnostic interviews, five months after the funeral, Alfredo spontaneously communicated his concern about Mario's death. Asked about play interests at home, he said in a woebegone tone, "My baby brother died and I was really looking forward to playing with him." When the diagnostician said how very very sad this must be for him, he went on to say, "When my Mum told me I just didn't believe it." When the diagnostician responded that it was a difficult thing to understand, he said with appropriate affect, "No one did. Just not there . . . then there was the ambulance, but he was dead."

## THEORIES ABOUT THE DEATH AS THEY EMERGED IN TREATMENT

Alfredo seemed generally quite pleased about beginning therapy. Initially his primary mode of expressing himself was play. I was cast in the role of playmate in excited play scenarios. It was difficult to comprehend much of his rushed communications both because of his accent and his set of rather muddled and often indistinguishable ideas. There was frequently a primary process quality to his material and altogether his use of play, both expressive and defensive, reminded me of a much younger child.

During his second session he requested that we play a game he had played with the diagnostician. I was assigned the part of the daddy who goes out to buy chocolates, while baby and sister are fighting with each other. On Daddy's return, the baby snatches the chocolates and hides. Mummy then asks daddy where the baby has gone and the sister says that he has gone to Mars in a spaceship. Alfredo then zoomed the baby off in a Lego spacecraft which landed in his locker. The story became muddled at this point. The sister, riding on a tiger, and the brother frantically search for the baby brother, but he is not found.

I came to understand this dramatic play sequence not only as reflecting Alfredo's passionate wish to know *where* Mario was but also as expressing his yearning to be reunited with his lost baby brother. Interestingly, Parkes (1972) describes how several bereaved adults, although well aware that there is no point in searching for a dead person, experience a strong impulse to search. He writes of a widow, who a week after the death of her husband said, "I can't help looking for him everywhere. I walk around searching for him. I felt that if I could have come somewhere, I could have found him." She had thought of going to spiritualist meetings in the hope of getting in touch with her dead husband, but decided against it. Another widow described how she not only felt but even acted upon a restless need to search: "Everywhere I go I am searching for him. In crowds, in church, in the supermarket."

Mario's death clearly puzzled Alfredo. Over the course of several months Alfredo revealed different theories about the how and why of the death. Sandler (1975) cautions that the distinction between fantasies and theories is by no means clear-cut. A theory is a belief about the real world which the child has created, upon which he acts, and which structures his further thinking, fantasying, and behavior. The theory may be developed on the basis of imaginative constructions and may contain fantasy wish-fulfilling elements, but "nevertheless it develops *as an explanation of reality* in contrast to the conscious fantasy which is known to be a daydream" (p. 158) and which possesses the hallmark of unreality. Importantly, the reasonable explanations that a child creates, using all the facts at his disposal, are reasonable and rational for the developing child, but not necessarily for an adult. As Piaget has made us aware, a young child's logic differs enormously from that of an adult.

With the approach of the Easter vacation and our first short break, Alfredo brought memories about the very hot summer holiday they had spent in Italy the previous year. Mario had been very small then, only a few weeks old. In the midst of recalling and sharing the pleasures of the holiday activities and the joys of being together with his nuclear and extended family, he suddenly blurted out his *first theory:* perhaps Mario had got very hot and died. After all, Mario had been taken to the hospital and died soon after they returned to London. But equally Alfredo wondered whether a burglar might have crept into his room and killed him, but no, that could not be, because the burglar would have "got me" too.

The first theory was elaborated in a session later that fortnight. Alfredo painted a cave in which a baby dragon lived. A fire was coming out of the cave. The dragon's parents lived on the other side. The dragon had a big mouth and, if offended by bad language, could blow fire at you. As he continued to paint, Alfredo talked about Mario, recalling with affection how he used to pull amusing funny faces. As he drew different bands of color, Alfredo said, "If we'd given Mario a watermelon, he would not have been so hot." In the drawing, "the blue sky is trying to get to the fire." The mummy and daddy dragon were lazy, they did nothing, not even for themselves. I clarified that these parents did not seem to help or protect the little dragon. Alfredo then said the bands of colors resembled a rainbow; suggesting that the yellow color might be mustard, he quickly added that Mario never ate such burning mustard. I said I realized how often he had thoughts about his little brother and how, with the doctors and other grownups not knowing, he was left very puzzled and perhaps even worried. It seemed that he himself had many ideas about what had caused the very sad and really rather mysterious death.

Perhaps Alfredo deserves some credit for his theory of overheating. Bacon et al. (1979) presented evidence that the combination of excessive wrapping and mild infection could produce potentially fatal heat stroke in infancy. More recently, and this is since Alfredo ended his therapy, cot death has received much media attention. Parents have been encouraged to place their babies in supine positions in their cots. The rationale is that prone positioning may reduce heat loss and make a baby who is overwrapped more susceptible to hyperthermia. An advisable room temperature has also been suggested.

Work continued in the following weeks not so much on the question of why but of *where.* Alfredo frequently staged aeroplane searches. For example, a character called Samedy Sam flew off after a noticeably small Bugs Bunny who then turned into a white ghost in an aeroplane. Samedy used powerful binoculars for looking for the rabbit whom he could not catch up with. I said that perhaps he found himself wondering where his little brother might have disappeared to; maybe he wondered what kind of place he was hiding in now? Alfredo said immediately that he was probably in his grave in heaven in the sky. I said that might be one of the reasons why he played with aeroplanes and spacecraft and that at times when he was missing his brother badly, especially when he felt surrounded by the womenfolk at home in the absence of his father, he longed to zoom quickly across the world and the Milky Way to play once more with his little brother. Alfredo responded by nodding rather sadly and remained silent for the remainder of the hour.

For many months there was little material pertaining to Mario. Then with the approach of our first summer break, Alfredo's anxieties about the extended separation emerged slowly. The family was returning to their usual place of vacation. He talked again about his worry that baby Mario had died on account of the heat of the previous summer and now he had second thoughts about going on vacation because he too might become very hot. He expressed fantasies about his own skin peeling off and of having eczema. Interestingly, his mother told the psychiatric social worker that she was unaware of Alfredo having such a condition and thought he had perhaps heard about it at school. Previously Alfredo had delighted in air travel, now he shrank from the thought of flying. One day he fashioned a little plasticine man whose aeroplane flew too high and he got burned by the fiery sun in the sky. Alfredo recalled Mario crying on the return plane journey. I said it seemed that he felt flying had been dangerous and hurtful to Mario. Alfredo said, "Maybe he was crying because he was too hot." I said that he was very afraid that something disastrous would happen to him in Italy and that his baby brother's sudden death made him extra scared for his own safety, life, and health, so scared that he feared that he would suffer a similar fate to his brother. The summer holiday went better than he expected, although on his return Alfredo remarked with relief that he preferred London's rainy weather. When we explored further these fiery feelings, Alfredo complained of sweating and feeling hot when he played ball games during the session. Bodily excitement was quite dominant. When I talked about his experiencing his red-hot feelings as a little dangerous at times, he observed that he frequently got hot when he felt angry.

As the anniversary of Mario's death approached, Alfredo recalled holding infant Mario in his arms and boasted how he had stopped his crying. Sessions were spent playing many variations of hide-and-seek. At first he hid pieces of chalk in plasticine which he commissioned me to locate. While I searched for the concealed objects, Alfredo remarked that it was a very little piece of chalk, a baby piece. Each time I located the chalk infant, Alfredo beamed. There followed rather frenzied trips to space to search for Mario who, Alfredo suspected, had been captured. After many brave encounters with various space hippies, Alfredo, enacting a wish-fulfilling fantasy, finally "found" Mario playing safely and happily with his dead grandfather. Gradually, while acknowledging how Alfredo pined for Mario and how sadly he had to give up his many plans of playing with his little brother, I started to wonder whether, like many other boys, he might have felt his little brother to be a nuisance at times. Alfredo immediately said angrily that he wished his sister and not Mario was dead. But later that week he began to share how Mario had cried a lot at night, how this meant he could not sleep, and how he pleaded with his mother to feed the loud Mario. As he became more able to express and accept his jealousy of this rather idealized sibling, Alfredo began to enjoy outings with his mother, savoring not only the food they shared, but also her sole attention.

Further work on Alfredo's conflicts over aggression revealed that death was equated with hostile wishes in his mind. Believing in the power of his destructive impulses, Alfredo unconsciously believed that he had killed his baby brother. This hypothesis was confirmed in the material of the next four months. Alfredo's ambivalence toward his little brother became apparent. He began to make odd comments about noisy little children. He said he disliked Mario's screaming, although he had valued Mario as a playmate. Again he mused that somebody must have killed Mario, but no, this did not make sense, for surely that somebody would have killed him (Alfredo), too; after all he was in the same room (*second theory*). I talked about big brothers' wishes to get rid of, even murder, little brothers however much they loved them, but was unsure how much Alfredo heard me.

Again his curiosity about the question of *where* was pressing. After one of his first trips on the London Underground, which he had experienced as "all dark and exciting," Alfredo instigated yet another hide-and-seek game in our darkened room. While opening the curtains at the end of the game, he wondered aloud whether Mario might be hidden in some dark place. I asked, "Perhaps underground?" and he then talked about a recent visit to the grave. He claimed that he would not be scared of being underground, but he would, he thought, be frightened of one thing—seeing Mario's skull, he shuddered and pulled a face of horror. The following week he made a skull-and-crossbones keyring for his locker. His fascination with a film, *Back to the Future,* in which a young boy travels back in time to find his family as they were years before, seemed to communicate his wish to have his family all together, as they were one year before, and his longing to retrieve his dead sibling and bring him back to life.

To my surprise I heard of his struggle with a science project on a subject by which he had seemed much intrigued. He claimed to be distracted by the noise of the other children's chatter and could not concentrate on his project, resorting to chattering himself. I said that I wondered whether all our talk about Mario and space had got in the way of thinking about his project. "Funny I was thinking about those hippies," he said. When I interpreted his worry that his angry hot feelings might have killed Mario (*third theory*), he looked rather guilty and defensively said, "Rosa could have killed him too" (*fourth theory*). I took up his feeling I was accusing him and suggesting it was his fault. He nodded. I interpreted how very bad he felt about his angry thoughts and feelings. After a long pause while he played a flicking game with the plasticine, he said with slow deliberation, "I think it could happen to me, I might die." Later he blurted out, with tears gathering in his eyes, "I don't know why Mario died." I empathized with the painfulness of not knowing. Alfredo responded, "I do know that I was angry with him when he was screaming." It was very important for us to make clear distinctions between thoughts, wishes, and actions and disprove his theory that burning anger could cause death.

After a period of resistance, during which I was informed by Alfredo, hidden behind the curtains, that somebody had not wanted to come, guilt and blame reared their heads. A boy at school had accused Alfredo of murdering his baby brother and a few days later en route to the clinic when his mother stopped at the traffic lights outside the Hampstead tube station, Alfredo had paled and panicked on noticing a poster which read "Alfredo—Wanted for Murder." He had begged his mother to turn back, protesting his innocence. Wisely, she did not.

Alfredo had to face not only his own reaction to the loss of his little brother but also its effects on his parents. He was sensitive to his mother's sad moods and was also deprived of the usual emotional availability of his parents who were preoccupied with their own grief and mourning. The psychological absence of his parents constituted a second loss. For his ninth birthday present, Alfredo had set his heart on a dog. He was angry and disappointed when his father refused, saying that they had had a dog when Alfredo was small. This puppy had died after being knocked down by a car. Mr. H. doubted Alfredo's ability to control the dog and said he did not want to lose another dog. Fortunately the social worker was able to show the parents the displacement from babies to puppies, and some months later, the parents surprised Alfredo by buying him a dog.

In the course of the intense arguments about the dog and about the burial of the previous puppy, Alfredo began to wonder what had happened to Mario's bones. In contrast to his initial horror at the mere thought of Mario's skull a few months earlier, Alfredo could now express some of his fantasies about the change in Mario's body. He represented his ideas in a drawing of a rather large-eyed, endearing, but dead Mario. This "skeleton" was not frightening. I think it was a kind of self-constructed photograph, a concrete expression of Alfredo's memory of his responsive baby brother. It seemed that he was beginning to find the lost Mario within himself. He drew Mario without clothes and then said, touchingly, that he wondered whether he ever felt cold in his grave.

A few weeks later Alfredo's mother injured her back in a car accident. A visit to the same hospital where Mario had been taken by ambulance re-evoked memories for Alfredo. He had been feeling lonely during the half-term break and his desolation and sense of being bereft had reached a painful height. He burst out, "If I could choose whatever I wanted, I know just what I'd choose—Mario." We talked about how much more fun it would be to play with a live brother rather than a computer or one of his robot collections. Alfredo repeated my words, looked very sad, and then said tearfully that no one could bring him back. "Mummy can't, Daddy can't." I added, "I can't." Alfredo said he knew. "Only maybe God can and he hasn't." Alfredo was struggling with the painful realization of the finality of death and confronting the futility of wishes for life to be restored to the way it had been before the day when the ambulance had been called. He spoke with some interest about the doctors taking X-rays of mother's back. But his tone of admiration soon gave way to one of anger as he talked about the doctors not knowing what had happened to Mario. I reflected his sadness and anger, and said I guessed it must feel very confusing and muddling for him. He then made a paper aeroplane and, as he guided it onto the runway table, announced, "It's an emergency. It's coming in to land." As the plane came to safety, he pondered, "Maybe . . . I think he had AIDS. When we were in Italy, there was this baby girl. I think she gave it to him." This infant was not cute like Mario. He thought there was something funny about her; maybe she kissed Mario and gave him germs and Aids. This *fifth theory* was communicated at a time when oedipal material was prominent in treatment.

After several months of work on Alfredo's overly strict superego and issues of self-esteem, there was little mention of Mario, other than in a moment of exasperation with Rosa whom he viewed as encroaching on his fair share of time with his parents, when he cried out, "I'm glad I didn't have a brother as well as her!" There was no mention of his fears of the heat and of possible death which had worried him so the previous summer holiday. But the family faced a new upheaval around the time of the second anniversary of the death—a move to Australia, where Mr. H. had been offered an attractive job. And it was in the final nine months of the 2½-year treatment that issues pertaining to Mario re-emerged. At first Alfredo would not talk or think about leaving England. For once he and his sister agreed; they thought the idea of leaving their friends (Alfredo's circle had expanded) and school outrageous. Alfredo sorely missed his father who went ahead, leaving England six months before the rest of the family. He reproached his father for leaving Mario behind and could now accept my interpretation of his own wish to reproach his little brother for leaving him alone with his bossy mother and intrusive sister. But as time passed and departure became more of a reality, Alfredo began to express some excitement.

For Alfredo leaving England meant leaving Mario behind and this caused much conflict and pain. He had a recurrent nightmare about robbers digging up Mario's grave. The move seemed to revive feelings of losing his precious baby brother; once again he felt his own treasured baby was being stolen from him. He himself made inquiries about the possibility of taking along his dog to Australia and established that there would be no quarantine period and the dog could go with them. But only the memories of Mario could accompany him and awareness of this again confronted him with the finality of the loss. By contrast, his good-byes to friends were tempered by a mutual promise to write and visit.

In the transference I had often been cast in the role of his little brother and now in the termination phase Alfredo's anxieties intensified. Apart from the expectable anger over being replaced, the fears of being out of sight and out of mind, Alfredo worried that if I died after he stopped therapy, nobody would tell him and he would not even know. If his granny died, his grandpa would phone from Italy, but would anybody from the clinic think about contacting him? He doubted that they would. I said having lost someone in his family, he was terrified that being apart from people might become losing them forever.

During the termination phase Alfredo's *sixth theory* about Mario's death emerged. Alfredo was drawing a map indicating the location of a volcanic mountain. We had talked about his wish to drop lava on people he was feeling particularly annoyed with, including me. Scratching himself Alfredo continued to talk about the hot burning lava. I reminded him of his worry about eczema and his fear of dying from being too hot. He replied, "I thought that happened to Mario, but it didn't. I know what happened to him. Cop death." At first I thought he had said, "Cot death," but then I realized the mishearing. "What makes you say, 'cop death?'" I wondered. Alfredo answered matter-of-factly, "Because they were there." He was not quite sure where the cops were exactly, but they probably gave Mario food which was bad for him. He went on to share the rest of his theory. "He didn't swallow it straight away, but later that's what killed him." I talked about the world feeling like a very dangerous place, where cops whom one usually thought of as protecting and helping people became murderers plotting to poison helpless baby brothers.

It was interesting how Alfredo's own fantasies were already becoming woven around a new piece of information in an elaboration of this *sixth theory*. When I explained the phonetic muddle, Alfredo said, "Oh, a *cot* death" and became very thoughtful. "Does that mean he died in his bed?" He didn't wait for any answer, looked very worried, and then said, "I'm glad I haven't got a cot." I said his worry that something just as horrible could happen to him had suddenly come alive again, even though we both knew there was very little chance he would unexpectedly die in his own bed.

## Discussion

There is surprisingly little written about the impact of the death of a baby on an older sibling. Studies of sibling loss have focused on the intensification of guilt in the surviving child. Cain et al. (1964) point out that such guilt reactions form only part of the picture.

In recent years psychoanalytic authors have called attention to the value of the sibling relationship. Colonna and Newman (1983) and Provence and Solnit (1983) have emphasized that siblings are not only rivals but potential playmates, allies, teachers, and friends, fulfilling important object-related roles and narcissistic needs. Alfredo voiced his wish for Mario to be a playmate. He needed the responsiveness of and admiration by a baby brother. Also, he seemed to regard Mario as a potential male ally in a household where his father was often absent (and lived apart from the family for the last six months of treatment) and where the females were dominant and powerful. Oedipal wishes and conflicts were very much alive for Alfredo around the time of his brother's birth and it is possible that unconsciously Mario may have been experienced as Alfredo's oedipally created child. In terms of replacement dynamics, Alfredo, on hearing his mother crying, came to comfort her, saying, "I'll be him for you." He offered *himself* as a replacement. In time the parents decided against having a fourth child.

For some time, Alfredo idealized his dead baby brother, perceiving him to be something of an angel sibling while the live Rosa was hated. For many months she received much of the denigration which was really directed toward Mario.

Losing a younger brother entails losing a hoped-for relationship. Alfredo had to give up his dreams and plans for the future with his baby sibling around whom a twin fantasy seemed to be woven. Losing a baby brother so *suddenly* and without knowing the causals of the death served to increase Alfredo's sense of vulnerability. He developed intense fears of death, similar to those described by Cain et al. who wrote:

> The children were often convinced not only that they, too, would die, but that they would die either at precisely the same age or from the same cause or under the same circumstances as the dead sibling. The children, of course, had a generally heightened awareness and fear of death, feeling it could strike at any moment and at their siblings or parents as well as themselves. Notions of their parents' invulnerability, all-powerfulness and especially of their parents' strength as protectors, came crashing [p. 747].

Death became a serious consideration for Alfredo. I think his fear of death was partially an identification with the lost object. The lack of identified causes for Mario's death increased his fear for his own mortality and, in the termination phase, for mine. In the absence of an explanation, this young boy searched for his own ways of understanding in an attempt to establish some control over destiny and the unpredictable. It is interesting how some of these ways of understanding, these six cot death theories were more closely related to internal factors and conflicts, for example, his guilt over his hostility toward and rivalry with his baby brother, while others seemed closer to reality, albeit a distorted version, perhaps more influenced by what he had heard and misheard. Alfredo extrapolated from his own experience and knowledge of bodily illness, body functions, and baby care in a desperate attempt to explain an inexplicable loss.

Leon (1990) contends that before a child can mourn, he must acquire a concept of death. Research (Florian, 1985; Hoffman and Strauss, 1985; Kane, 1989; Landsdown and Benjamin, 1985) suggests that by age 8 to 10, most children are able to describe death as being *irreversible* (that is, permanent), *universal* (inevitably occurring to everyone, including oneself), and *characterized by nonfunctionality* (a total cessation of all bodily functions). Alfredo's struggle to attain such a cognitive comprehension of death was revealed in the course of his long psychotherapy, which he attended from age 8 to 10. Initially stunned by the sudden loss, he slowly confronted the difference between temporary absence and permanent loss. Alfredo certainly understood death to be universal, but what was heightened for him was the frightening notion of his own vulnerability: that he could die of unknown causes, as had his little brother. Although Alfredo knew on one level that Mario no longer moved, his emotional need to keep the image of his dead brother alive superseded his cognitive knowledge of nonfunctionality. One wonders how much Alfredo *knowingly* kept Mario alive—for example, playing games with Mario in the space flights—as a way of titrating the painful acknowledgment of reality with enjoyable fantasy.

This leads me to consider the controversial issue of the nature and form of childhood mourning. A brief review of the literature reveals that different authors disagree on the age at which children are capable of mourning. Bowlby (1960) believed that mourning (in the adult sense) is possible and can be observed from the sixth month of life onward, while Robert Furman (1964) and Erma Furman (1974) argue that mourning can be observed only from the third or fourth year onward. Anna Freud (1960) believed that prior to the maturation of the mental apparatus (in terms of reality testing, acceptance of the reality principle, partial control of id, readiness by the ego, achievement of object constancy), the child's reaction to loss is governed by the more primitive and direct dictates of the pleasure-pain principle. The nearer the child is to object constancy, "the longer the duration of grief reactions with corresponding approximation to the adult internal process of mourning" (p. 59). Wolfenstein (1965, 1966) believes that mourning becomes possible only with the resolution of the adolescent phase, after the appropriate detachment from the parental figures has occurred. Nagera (1970) holds the view that some aspects of the mourning process (as defined by Freud) of the adult mourner can be observed in children as a reaction to the loss of important objects, but he draws attention to the child's proclivity to use denial, inability to tolerate the prolonged painful affects of grieving, greater degree of ambivalence in object relations, and frequently distorted concept of death because of concrete and egocentric thinking.

In his discussion of the reactions of latency children, Nagera draws a distinction between two different aspects of the mourning process. The first one concerns the question: to what extent can the child experience and express the feeling of loss with the consequent signs of sadness and grief? Second, how far is it possible for the child to proceed with the slow withdrawal of the cathexis previously attached to the lost object, so that the freed energies are available for the cathexis of a new object? Nagera contends that the latter process is easier for adults than children. Latency children, in his study, strongly cathected a fantasy life where the lost object may be seen as alive and at times as ideal. Alfredo certainly seemed to have responded in a similar way, especially during the first year of treatment. Alfredo could make use of his psychotherapy to experience and express his feelings about his bereavement. For someone who initially presented as doing his schoolwork at a snail's pace and who struggled to focus and concentrate, Alfredo did much complex thinking about the death of his baby brother and did seem to achieve in time a detachment from this very significant internal sibling object. He did communicate his sadness and grief intermittently at times to me; perhaps it was safer to reveal his thoughts and feelings in the therapeutic context, rather than turn to his parents whose grief he sensed and whom at times he experienced as psychologically absent.

## BIBLIOGRAPHY

BACON, C. & BELLMAN, M. H. (1983). Heatstroke as a possible cause of encephalopathy in infants. *Brit. Med. J.*, 287:328–329.
——— SCOTT, D., & JONES, D. (1979). Heatstroke in well-wrapped infants. *Lancet*, 1:422–425.
BOWLBY, J. (1960). Grief and mourning in infancy and early childhood. *Psychoanal. Study Child*, 15:9–52.
———. (1961) Childhood mourning and its implications for psychiatry. *Amer. J. Psychiat.*, 118:481–498.
——— (1963). Pathological mourning and childhood mourning. *J. Amer. Psychoanal. Assn.*, 11:500–541.
CAIN, A., FAST, I., & ERICKSON, M. (1964). Childrens' disturbed reactions to the death of a sibling. *Amer. J. Orthopsychiat.*, 34:741–752.
COLONNA, C. & NEWMAN, L. (1983). The psychoanalytic literature on siblings. *Psychoanal. Study Child*, 38:285–309.
FREUD, A. (1960). Discussion of Dr. John Bowlby's paper. *Psychoanal. Study Child*, 15:53–62.
FLORIAN, V. (1985). Children's concept of death. *Death Studies*, 9:133–141.
FURMAN, E. (1974). *A Child's Parent Dies*. New Haven: Yale Univ. Press.
FURMAN, R. (1964). Death and the young child. *Psychoanal. Study Child*, 19:321–333.
HOFFMAN, S. I. & STRAUSS, S. (1985). The development of children's concepts of death. *Death Studies*, 9:469–482.
KANE, B. (1989). Children's concepts of death. *J. Genet. Psychol.*, 134:141–153.

Lansdown, R. & Benjamin, G. (1985). The development of the concept of death in children aged 5–9 years. *Child Care, Hlth, & Develpm.*, 11:13–20.

Leon, I. G. (1990). *When a Baby Dies.* New Haven: Yale Univ. Press.

Milner, A. D. (1987). Recent theories on the cause of cot death. *Brit. Med. J.*, 295:1366–1368.

———— & Rugg, N. (1989). Sudden infant death syndrome. *Brit. Med. J.*, 297:689–690.

Nagera, H. (1970). Children's reactions to the death of important objects. *Psychoanal. Study Child*, 25:360–400.

Parkes, C. M. (1972). *Bereavement.* New York: Int. Univ. Press.

Ponsonby, A.-L., Dwyer, T., Gibbons, L. E., Cochrane, J. A., Jones, M. E., & McCall, M. J. (1992). Thermal environment and sudden infant death syndrome. *Brit. Med. J.*, 304:277–282.

Provence, S. & Solnit, A. J. (1983). Development-promoting aspects of the sibling experience. *Psychoanal. Study Child*, 38:337–351.

Sandler, J. (1975). Sexual fantasies and sexual theories in childhood. In *Studies in Child Psychoanalysis.* New Haven: Yale Univ. Press, pp. 149–162.

Wolfenstein, M. (1965). Death of a parent and death of a president. In *Children and the Death of a President*, ed. M. Wolfenstein & G. N. Kilman. New York: Doubleday, pp. 62–69.

———— (1966). How is mourning possible? *Psychoanal. Study Child*, 21:93–123.

# Telling and Enacting Stories in Psychoanalysis and Psychotherapy

## Implications for Teaching Psychotherapy

## MARSHALL EDELSON, M.D., Ph.D.

*This paper is about teaching psychoanalytic psychotherapy. The approach to teaching is based on a view of the patient's plight or psychopathology, and on a way of listening to psychotherapeutic process, that focus on the stories a patient tells and enacts. The author relates how various experiences in his life led him to this narrative paradigm.*

I HAVE RECENTLY REALIZED THAT FOR SOME YEARS I HAVE BEEN TEACHING psychoanalytic psychotherapy in a different way than I had for many years previously. This paper describes the approach I now take. It is in three parts. First, I shall present a way of thinking about psychotherapeutic process that focuses on the stories a patient tells and enacts. Second, I shall try to identify what in my life has brought me to this way of thinking and the approach to teaching based on it. Third, I shall discuss my current approach to teaching psychoanalytic psychotherapy.

The paper is a personal account of some ideas and strategies I have come to find useful in my work as a psychotherapist and clinical

Professor of Psychiatry, Yale University School of Medicine; a practicing psychoanalyst, member of the Western New England Institute for Psychoanalysis and the Western New England Psychoanalytic Society, and educational consultant to the Institute.

Conversations with Daniel Levinson, who encouraged me, have helped me to write this paper. I am grateful to him for taking time from his own work to read painstakingly and to comment in detail on several editions of it. It is a revised version of a paper I presented at the Rapaport-Klein Study Group, Austen Riggs Center, Stockbridge, Massachusetts, June 13, 1992. Some material in it has appeared in different form or context in Edelson (1992a, 1992b).

teacher. It is the story of the evolution of my interest in the telling and enacting of stories. I have written informally and colloquially, as if I were having a conversation with you—an alert, somewhat skeptical, responsive reader. It would indeed feel odd to me to write formally or theoretically about an approach to teaching that includes suggesting to trainees that, in their psychotherapeutic work, they should pursue the particular and, especially in their interpretative interventions, avoid formality, universal generalizations, and reliance on theory. I think it desirable that form should match content. The way I write should exemplify what I write. It should provide an image of the way I teach and not simply a description of it, and convey how my thinking goes and not just the results of it. Previous practitioners of a similar mode of communication include, most notably, Plato, in the Socratic Dialogues, and Freud, especially in his *Introductory Lectures* (1916–17) and his paper on lay analysis (1926). One need not be a writer of equal mastery to attempt to write in this mode.

Throughout the paper, as in my teaching (for reasons that will soon become apparent), I eschew as much as possible the theoretical terms of psychoanalysis. I find it of great interest to notice how much the major discoveries and ideas of psychoanalysis can be discussed, without loss, in language about telling and enacting stories.

From knowledge of my previous work (1971, 1975, 1984, 1988, 1989, 1990, 1991, 1992a, 1992b), you may expect me to discuss something about problems of evidence and the case study, hermeneutic science versus natural science, or the structure and distinctive features of psychoanalytic theory. But in this paper I focus instead on the teaching of psychoanalytic psychotherapy.

I have previously suggested that, given the distinctive nature of psychoanalytic theory, the case study is especially appropriate to use in attempts to support claims about the scientific credibility of psychoanalytic explanation. I have described in detail the different arguments that a case study might use to support such claims; empirical data are an indispensable ingredient of these arguments (1984, 1988, 1989, 1991). I have also shown (1988, 1990, 1992a, 1992b) how an emphasis on the telling and enacting of stories in psychotherapy and psychoanalysis, and specifically an emphasis on fantasy, provides a way of identifying empirical data that are not biased by any of the theories currently debated by psychoanalysts. As prologue to the present paper on the implications for *teaching* of this focus on telling and enacting stories, I have considered its implications for *psychotherapy research* (1992a) and for *psychoanalytic theory* (1992b).

## TELLING AND ENACTING STORIES IN PSYCHOANALYTIC PSYCHOTHERAPY

The way I teach psychoanalytic psychotherapy is influenced by my conception of the *patient's plight* (his psychopathology, if you will) and influenced also by my conception of psychotherapy.[1]

I shall introduce my conception of the plight of some patients by telling a story. When I was a child I listened rapt to a radio program: *The Shadow.* Every episode began with an eerie hollow voice declaiming, "Who knows what evil lurks in the hearts of men? The Shadow knows!" In one episode, a criminal enemy of the Shadow invents a time machine in order to wreak vengeance on him. This enemy captures the Shadow and spends a 24-hour period visiting unspeakable tortures upon him. Then the time machine is set, dooming the Shadow to repeat this 24 hours throughout eternity. Unhappily, I can't remember how the Shadow got himself out of this fix!

Now I see patients who are trapped in scenarios of unslaked desire, relentless punishment, and horrifying dangers—and their suffering seems terrible to me. Their plight is that they are trapped in such scenarios ("trapped" is the operative word here). Their symptoms may be regarded as signs that they are caught in such a scenario, that they are compelled to participate in the scenario for time without end, and that they struggle to escape from the world of that scenario. This may not be the plight of all patients. So the question of the scope of the particular kind of psychotherapy I am discussing is a live question for me.

I see a patient then as in the grip of a scenario (usually more than one scenario). This scenario is more or less unconscious. (An unconscious fantasy exemplifies "unconscious scenario.") I hear the stories he tells or enacts as variants of the scenario in which he is trapped. That is, I understand these stories as part of his active attempt to shape or interpret his past and present life to conform to the scenario or to conscious fantasies that derive from the scenario. Sometimes the patient seems, more passively, to be simply reminded of the scenario by elements of experience; and then he imagines that he relives it.

The relation between a scenario and the conscious fantasy derived

1. I have just written "*his* psychopathology." I shall use "he," "his," and "him" generically except where it will be clear from the context that I refer to someone of a specific gender. I know this usage may alienate you. But communication is also hindered by awkward constructions such as "he or she," "his or hers," "him or her"; distracting constructions such as "s/he"; or nonstandard or ungrammatical constructions designed to avoid pronouns altogether.

from it is usually more or less disguised by means of such mental operations as condensation, displacement, iconic symbolization, and translation of verbal elements into imagery. In creating conscious fantasies, as in creating dreams, the patient may make use of the scenes and dramatic situations of his experience as materials. He transforms, combines, and embellishes these materials.

*A conception of psychoanalytic psychotherapy.* In recent years, I have found myself more and more focally aware of the stories patients tell me, and the stories they enact in which I am one of the characters. (Talking about enacted stories can be a way of talking about transference phenomena.) This increasing awareness has led me to a conception of psychotherapy for patients trapped in scenarios, a conception I shall also communicate in the form of a story—the story of Scheherazade.

Scheherazade tells stories nightly to her husband, the king, who has gotten into the cynical habit of beheading his queens after one night of love. That she tells these stories, and the way she tells them, are part of a story she does not tell but enacts. She tells these stories to achieve a certain purpose of her own, in a story she enacts with the king. She keeps him asking, "What will happen next? How does the story come out?" Each night she stops her story just at the moment of greatest suspense. Each night she avoids being beheaded at least one more time. She tells him wonderful stories for a thousand and one nights. Then their own story, the enacted story, has a happy ending.

Just so, a patient tells the psychotherapist stories about his current life outside the therapy hour, about his childhood, and about himself and the psychotherapist. Unlike Scheherazade, he is the hero of most of the stories he tells. And quite unlike the stories that Scheherazade tells, a patient is at the same time both the hero and the real adversary of the hero in most of the stories he tells. Often as adversary, he enters the story disguised as someone else. Through such cunning devices of the storyteller, an intrapersonal drama is converted into an interpersonal drama. A psychotherapist may fail to mark this conversion.

Like Scheherazade, the patient tells a story at a particular time for particular reasons, or to achieve particular ends. He may tell the story in a way that helps him to avoid, reject, or disown certain feelings or states. Or he may tell it to influence the psychotherapist. Just as we can differentiate the story of Scheherazade and her husband from the stories she tells, so what a patient hopes to accomplish by telling his story is part of another story, a story involving the patient and psychotherapist, which the patient is enacting rather than telling.

*What is a story?* No single simple definition will cover all the instances we might like to include in the category *story*. But a large family of instances have features characteristic of the classic Hollywood movie melodrama (Bordwell, 1985a, 1985b).

A protagonist has a wish and a problem in gratifying it. He wants to bring about, maintain, or avoid some state of affairs. By one means or another, he attempts to do so. But, in this attempt, he encounters opposition. An antagonist erects obstacles or imposes constraints that prevent—or threaten to prevent—the protagonist's attaining what he wants. The antagonist may be a person, Nature, or a social system. The protagonist overcomes, makes accommodative adjustments in response to, or fails to overcome the antagonist.

The story, from beginning to end, forms a trajectory from one state of affairs to another. There is a change in the protagonist's situation or in himself. The change may be for the better (happy ending). The change may be for the worse, or, despite the protagonist's efforts, there may be no change (unhappy ending). A change in the protagonist's situation may be a change in his environment, his body, or other persons important to him. A change in the protagonist himself may be a change in his feelings, his knowledge, or his moral character.

Especially characteristic of the scenarios in which patients are trapped is that the patient himself is at the same time both protagonist and antagonist, both hero and adversary, both the one striving to achieve a goal and the one acting as the chief obstacle to achieving that goal. The scenarios are, in this sense, intrapersonal. I have the impression, however, that psychotherapists and patients who favor interpersonal themes tend to neglect intrapersonal scenarios—for example, those that are about the patient's relation to his body and his attitudes toward and feelings about the wishes he has in that relation. Similarly, it is my impression that a patient's *own responses* to his wishes, feelings, and actions play a larger role in character and symptom pathology than might be guessed from the patient's (and sometimes the psychotherapist's) preference for telling stories in which the *responses of other persons* to him as well as his response to them are emphasized.

*Psychotherapeutic process.* A psychotherapist exhaustively inquires into the detailed particulars of each story told or enacted, and pays attention to just how a patient tells or enacts the story. He notices relations among the stories told or enacted. Some, although they have a different setting or occur in a different domain, are seen to be quite similar. Some are discovered to be different episodes, one perhaps leading to the other, to form a more complicated plot.

The psychotherapist pays careful attention to the circumstances that seem to trigger the telling or enactment of a particular story. What particular event, object, or feature of external reality on each occasion evokes the scenario or inspires the creation of some variant of it? How does a patient make use of the materials provided by external reality to act in such a way as to bring about an actualization of the scenario, more or less disguised? How does a patient exploit aspects of his experience to justify directing feelings belonging in a scenario to objects or persons in external reality?

As the patient comes to recognize the different versions of a "favorite" story, he increasingly realizes that he has a major hand in writing and directing it, and in assigning himself and others first one and then another part in the play. As he becomes able to identify what evokes his telling or enacting a story on each of many occasions, he increasingly understands its value to him—the purposes it serves.

Typically, he begins by viewing himself as passive victim. He attributes causation to the external situation. Eventually, he comes to see that what he has attributed to external reality stems from what he carries in his own mind, and from what he does, through imagination or action, to make external reality conform to it.

Gradually, the stories told and enacted take center stage in consciousness. They are sharpened and made explicit. The details are filled in. The twists and turns in the plot are tracked. A story comes to be recognized even as it appears in many revisions and disguises. The parallels among stories involving different characters or settings are observed. As part of this process, the patient begins to experience more fully what it feels like to have the wishes, beliefs, or emotions that belong to his stories. Of these he previously had only vague or transient hints. He has prevented them from coming into awareness at all or has paid them only peripheral attention. But they have continued to play a part, however disguised or transformed, in the stories he has told and enacted. As these stories are amplified, the patient acquires direct knowledge of what it feels like to have a certain wish, belief, or emotion. He becomes able to appreciate how it has disabled him, led him to form distorted images of himself or others, and caused him to act in ways that hitherto did not make sense to him. Fenichel (1941, p. 42), using the technical vocabulary of psychoanalysis, refers to "the task of reversing displacements, abolishing isolations, or guiding traces of affect to their proper relationships." "Unpacking condensations" also belongs in this list.

A patient may permit himself gradually to recover the more or less unconscious scenario from which his stories are derived, and to free himself from its grip. This does not mean that the scenario disappears from his mind or that he loses all interest in it. It means that the scenario no longer operates secretly and in the darkness to affect his experience of and response to reality. It means that he has become freer to ignore it, to alter its influence upon him, or to play with it.

It is my impression that in psychotherapy this kind of process is repeated over and over. The particular stories a patient tells or enacts may seem to change, but the task remains the same. Each go-around ("working through"?) is another brick laid. I use that metaphor rather than a metaphor about human development because it does not seem to me that, as one goes further and further in psychotherapy, one is doing something qualitatively different from what was done early on. That is why in my teaching, it does not seem to matter what selection is made of a set of sessions for discussion. The exercise is the same; but the trainee (like the patient) gets better and better at doing it.

It is also my impression that any instance or any number of instances of this kind of process has its effects, even when the unconscious scenario is not recovered. However, the sturdiness and persistence of changes in the patient does seem to increase with each go-around, just as the trainee's skill increases. If enough bricks are laid, the patient becomes capable of doing this kind of work on his own.

The risk, if the unconscious scenario is not recovered, is that the patient may remain in its grip. Perhaps he merely changes who takes what role, for example, but the stories he tells and enacts, even if somewhat altered in detail, continue to be variants—although I hope less pernicious variants—of the same scenario.

*An extended example viewing the process of psychotherapy in terms of stories told and enacted.* Let me tell you now a story that begins with a patient arriving late to a psychotherapy session, as she often does. The *content* of the story she tells has to do with the many difficulties that prevent her from completing a work assignment on time, and how her conscientious effort to overcome these difficulties made her late to the session. She describes herself as lazy, unorganized, uncreative, and stupid. She mutters how inflexible and callous her professor is. If she is late with the assignment, he will certainly be upset.

It is important to distinguish the content of a story from the *function* or purpose it serves on a particular occasion or for a particular patient. The same story may serve more than one function. The content of this patient's story focuses mainly on her dialogue with herself in which she blames and criticizes herself. But telling this story serves the function of countering the disapproval she imagines her psychotherapist feels in response to her coming late. She judges herself in the story she tells. But in the different story she enacts, she assigns the role of judge to her psychotherapist.

The *interpersonal* story here enacted with the psychotherapist enables her to escape or evade judgment. After all, she argues with him implicitly, she cannot be faulted for her conscientious efforts as a student to please her demanding professor. In addition, she only has to face the judgments of the psychotherapist during the sessions; between sessions she is free of him. Also, by criticizing herself, she beats the psychotherapist to the punch. These are some advantages the interpersonal story has over the intrapersonal story.

In the *intrapersonal* story she tells, she blames herself, taking the roles of both judge and judged. The judge is exceedingly harsh—and she cannot get away from herself. On the other hand, an advantage of the intrapersonal story is that now, identified with the role of judge, she takes on his power to hurt.

One heuristic in interpretation, here as in everyday life, is to infer motive from outcome, to suppose provisionally that the consequence of an action is what the action was intended to bring about. The content of the story she tells, then, suggests she may wish to defeat her professor by making him wait for assigned work.

The psychotherapist is reminded of stories the patient has told in other sessions: how her father dominated and criticized her and her secret strategies for defeating him. The psychotherapist notices thematic affinity among these stories about the past, the stories about what is going on currently in her work life, and the story that the patient seems to be enacting in the psychotherapy situation in which she defeats the psychotherapist by coming late.

The psychotherapist makes an interpretation, connecting the stories from three different domains of her life. The patient discusses the interpretation calmly and with great interest, expressing admiration and appreciation of the psychotherapist's ability to bring all these stories together. She adds some details, and remembers some other incidents which fit the narrative pattern the psychotherapist has detected.

In the next session, she tells a story about a fight she has just had with a younger brother. It is clear that even before the fight she had been irritable, belligerent, and provocative. And even now she is beside herself with rage toward her brother, a troublesome adversary who blocks her from achieving what she wants. In a screenplay, the brother would be the villain.

Another heuristic of interpretation: A patient's story may be a response to a recent event. The recent event may have reminded the patient of a story. A story may be his indirect answer to a comment or question by the psychotherapist. It may provide clues to the patient's reaction to an event within or outside of the treatment situation, or to something he himself has felt or said, perhaps a previous story he has told or a fantasy he has had. If this recent event can be identified, one may infer from it the function of the story the patient tells or enacts.

In this instance, "the psychotherapist offers an interpretation" turned out to be what someone writing a screenplay would call the triggering event (as in the movies when "a stranger rides into town"). A triggering event stirs things up, upsets a balance, gets a story going.

"Why," the psychotherapist wonders to himself, "does the fight story follow my giving an interpretation? Was 'giving the interpretation' a triggering event?" It is not immediately clear whether the "giving the interpretation" episode and the "fight with the brother" episode belong to the same story.

The psychotherapist reminds the patient of similar episodes in which she has been truculent and so provoked a fight. The patient complains bitterly that psychotherapy has done nothing to change her; she still acts as she always has. The psychotherapist notices that momentarily he feels defeated when the patient says this.

However, the patient soon settles down and becomes reflective. "Why do I get so angry? Why do I make life so difficult for myself by behaving this way with others? I know that there was no reason for acting so provocatively. I just defeat myself. I am my own adversary!" Now she is remorseful and wishes that there was some way to make up to her brother for her treatment of him. She thinks of ways to undo the bad effects of the quarrel.

The psychotherapist remembers the patient's reasonableness in the last session and contrasts it with the fulminations and irrationality with which this session began. He is reminded of a number of stories in which the patient became furious in situations in which, it turned out later, she felt denigrated. He wonders aloud whether she had felt humiliated in the previous session by his superior performance (making an interpretation). She then remembers being peripherally aware of such a feeling. "But, of course, I couldn't tell you that I envied you, or that I felt resentful because you are always the superior one, and I the inferior. After all, you were helping me. You would become offended. Then you would really send me away."

In my experience, this kind of response—in which a patient recovers a recent but mislaid conscious thought or feeling—is one of the most dependable indications that an interpretation is on target. I am surprised that the literature on the validity of interpretations rarely mentions this kind of response.

The psychotherapist, if he had been less involved in an attempt to follow and piece together a complicated story, might have relied instead on a theoretical formula. He might have thought, "The patient's rage was displaced from me to her brother." As you will see, this shortcut would miss some essential details of what turned out to be a more complex story.

The patient now tells an additional story—what a screenwriter would call a flashback. The psychotherapist hears it as an episode that connects the episode of the interpretation and the episode of the fight. The additional story: Later in the day following the previous session, the patient had had a conscious sexual fantasy. In it, scenes in which she was forcing someone to do what she commanded alternated with scenes in which she was submitting to another. A fantasy like this was a favorite of the patient's. It seemed always to lie ready in her mind, where it could be recruited for a variety of purposes in response to many different kinds of triggering events. It seemed especially likely to be evoked in circumstances she interpreted as humiliating. At this point in the psychotherapy, various versions of this favorite fantasy were relatively accessible to consciousness, although, embarrassed, she was always reluctant to tell these stories.

These sexual fantasies are cut off from any contact with her everyday life. They have as far as she is concerned nothing to do with her ordinary experiences. Why she has such fantasies is a mystery to her. They make no sense. The patient is not aware of any connection between her conscious sexual fantasy and her feelings in the previous session. She is not aware that the fantasy is the fulfillment of a wish stirred up in that session. The content of the psychotherapist's interventions frequently concerns the possibility of such a connection. Providing this kind of connection builds stories out of apparently unconnected episodes.

So the psychotherapist now wonders aloud whether, following the previous session, she had wished to be superior and powerful like the psychotherapist, and able to humiliate someone inferior as she felt she had been humiliated. Her fantasy seemed to gratify this wish, at least in imagination. The connection between the sexual fantasy and an actual event, which had triggered it, now becomes apparent to her. The purpose of the sexual fantasy was to counteract a painful experience.

Further details emerge in this session. Why couldn't she stay with a scene in which she tortured her victim? Uncomfortable with an image of herself as a cruel person, she softens the torture so it seems more like teasing. Then she reverses roles; as the director of this scene, she assigns herself the role of the character who is kind, gentle, and submissive, the one who is teased. She begins to recapture some details of the original scene, in which she was a torturer, and she is horrified by the details.

The psychotherapist realizes that she has omitted a piece of the story—how she felt about what she did in her own fantasy and how she gets rid of that feeling. For she habitually does not see any act or feeling that occurs in her everyday life or psychotherapy session as the result of what she more or less obscurely felt and thought as she observed herself playing a particular role in a sexual fantasy. (It is just this piece of the story the psychotherapist would have lost, had the story of the fight reminded him of a theoretical formula about "displacement.")

The psychotherapist wonders aloud: Had the patient been worried that the submissiveness she experienced in her fantasy might emerge in a real relationship? Seeing that she is submissive, someone might despise or take advantage of her. The patient then remembers that just before the fight she interpreted something that had happened as indicating that she had unwittingly invited her brother to treat her as an inferior. This was especially galling, because her brother is younger than she. It was her desire to cancel this invitation that she now believes compelled her, as it had on so many other occasions, to be obnoxious and domineering. Clearly, what is important here is her own response to herself as she is in her fantasy, and not what she imagines someone else's response would be.

Further details of this story about the fight between herself and her brother suggest its links to the sexual fantasy. I think it inaccurate, therefore, to regard this fight-with-the-brother story as *only* or even primarily a disguised expression of "the transference."

Finally, telling the story about her brother is part of an enactment in the psychotherapy of a story of vindictive attack and reparation. For telling this story makes it possible for her to take the psychotherapist down a peg or two by showing him that the psychotherapy is not working; she still behaves as she has always behaved. At the same time, by cooperating with him in doing the work of psychotherapy, she repairs the damage she fears she has done him, both by the acts of cruelty in her fantasy and by what she feels are ungrateful cruel reproaches about the inefficacy of the psychotherapy that she hurls at him because of her envy and resentment.

### My Own Story: How I Came to These Ideas

For many years, and increasingly it seems to me in recent years, a lot of people have been talking, although in quite different ways, about *narratives.* Lester Luborsky (1984) has written a manual for teaching psychoanalytic psychotherapy using an explicit narrative paradigm as a basis for the therapist's interventions. He has also reviewed research measures based on such a paradigm, in the context of his own use of such a measure in his research on transference (Luborsky and Crits-Christoph, 1990). The title of Roy Schafer's most recent book is *Retelling a Life: Narration and Dialogue in Psychoanalysis* (1992). Many other recent works in psychology and the humanities could also be cited. Maybe something is happening in our culture of which this talk about narratives is an expression.

Here, I have two alternatives, and for reasons that will be clear I choose the second. I might have written a review of the literature in which I engage in a strong polemic, showing how my ideas about stories are different from or similar to the ideas of others, and arguing of course with utmost rigor that mine are better. Some years ago, I would probably have made that choice. Now, however, I am mindful that I often exhort trainees to permit themselves to be reminded of their own life experience, not theory, as they listen to patients in psychotherapy. And consistently in making a point, I often tell stories to trainees about my own experiences, rather than expound rules of technique or give theoretical explanations. It is fitting then that in seeking here for the sources of my interest in stories and approach to teaching, I turn to my own life, rather than to philosophical doctrines or the technical, theoretical, or research literature of my profession. The particulars of where I'm coming from will differentiate the path I am taking from that of some others who, even though talking about narratives, are actually going in a quite different direction. In addition, there is a lesson implicit in these episodes from my life about what it may take to become, and what may interfere with becoming, a skillful psychotherapist and teacher.

*Early movies.* To my mother's dismay, when I was 7 years old I had to be taken screaming from a showing of the movie *David Copperfield.* The triggering events were scenes involving the cruel treatment of the hero by his wicked stepfather Mr. Murdstone (played by Basil Rathbone). At 8 I saw *The Prisoner of Shark Island.* The movie was about the physician who was unjustly imprisoned because he treated the assassin of Abraham Lincoln. He was pardoned because of his valor in coping with a plague on Shark Island. I felt what a fine thing it would be to be a doctor. At 9 I saw *London by Night.* The movie was about an Umbrella Man who, having been seen hobbling under an umbrella through the fog, was suspected of a series of murders. The movie featured a montage of close-ups of the terrified faces of citizens of London, with an image of the Umbrella Man hobbling through their large heads. As I remember it now, I could not sleep for months, kept awake by images of the terrified faces and the sinister figure superimposed on them; I was unable to get these images out of my mind.

So no one ever had to teach me or convince me that "merely" imagined stories could have profound effects! I began to imagine that I might become a writer of stories; during that same year, I had a little pocket notebook in which I wrote a jungle adventure about an intrepid explorer. By the age of 12, I was immersed in movies, going to downtown Chicago theatres to sit through as many as three triple features in one day. My life was, and in some important sense still is, in the movies.

When I was 14, I went fourteen times to sit through a movie called *Kings Row.* This movie tells a story of two friends, Parris and Drake. Parris, who was a good boy, goes to Vienna at the turn of the century, and becomes the first psychiatrist in America. He returns home because Drake needs him. Drake, who had been a young hellion, had awakened after an accident to find his legs had been amputated. Parris later discovers that the amputation had been performed unnecessarily by a sadistic surgeon to punish Drake for his sexual looseness with women. How would it affect Drake if Parris were to tell him what he had discovered? This movie, which portrayed father-figures as protectors and teachers but also as implacable cruel obstacles to relations with women, rang all sorts of changes on the theme of "father-son relations" and the related theme of "becoming a man."

Such movies provided me with one model for "the good story": the so-called classic Hollywood melodrama. They also taught me a lot about what one must do to be "a good audience" for such a story, namely, an active, involved, identifying-with-a-protagonist, expectant, questioning, waiting-for-an-answer, inference-making, hypothesis-forming, hypothesis-revising audience. Good training for a psychotherapist to be.

*College.* At 16 I became a student at the College of the University of Chicago. I participated in Socratic dialogues in small-group seminars, and favored this format when years later I became a teacher. I was exposed to the New Criticism, which imbued me with a sense of the autonomy of the study of cultural objects such as paintings, poetry, novels, and music. The study of such objects need not be dependent on knowledge of history, sociology, or the psychology of the creator. One can ask about such an object: How is it made? How do its parts relate to each other? What choices has the author or artist made? When do conventions, and what conventions, determine these choices? What reading or understanding of the work is best supported by the answers to these questions?

These are the questions I eventually asked about the stories a patient told or enacted in psychotherapy. Doing psychotherapy, I found it natural to be attentive to the choices patients make in telling and enacting stories. It was not difficult to recognize the devices, the defense mechanisms, and other strategies of representation and story-creation they used in making their stories. Or to be alert to the way a patient's story was told or enacted, not just to its content. Later, as a psychoanalyst in training, I read *The Interpretation of Dreams* through the lens of Freud's focus on how dreams are made—by what mental operations, using what materials.

This education in paying close attention to details and to the way in which a work of art was constructed made me suspicious of a relativistic view that the meaning of a work of art was whatever anyone made of it. How could people claim that one reading was just as good as another, and that the details of a work's construction were irrelevant to deciding among such claims! I was certainly influenced by I. A. Richards' work *Practical Criticism* (1929), which demonstrated that most readers were rather inept or careless readers, and showed where they went wrong. My reservations about relativism have reemerged in my current rather solitary belief that a close examination of the details of clinical materials can support one interpretation of those materials over a commensurate and incompatible rival interpretation. I find it difficult to accept the belief that differences among clinicians are unavoidable and unresolvable, and this disbelief is what I teach (see "Assessing the accuracy of interpretations" in part three of this paper).

But my antirelativism has been shaken from time to time. In the early 1960s, I was co-leader with Art Aronoff of a poetry study group at the Stockbridge Library. I didn't know what to make of the fact that everyone in the group seemed to understand the same poem differently. Either most of the readers were poor readers or something else had to be added to my thinking about such matters. What was eventually added is well represented by the work of Norman Holland (1968, 1973, 1988). He studied reading and readers. The same work, though it had discoverable intrinsic linguistic and organizational properties, might nevertheless evoke in each reader a very different unconscious fantasy, and so a different feeling and interpretation of the work.

It's the same with movies. Different people have very different responses to the same movie. The same person at different times has different responses to the same movie. Whenever we have this kind of situation, we assume that an internal structure mediates the relation between some aspect of reality and a person's response to it. David Rapaport (1960) made the point that observations such as "different responses to the same stimuli, the same response to different stimuli" indicate the necessity to postulate internal structures mediating relations between stimulus and response. An unconscious fantasy is such an internal structure.

*Spellbound.* At 17 I saw Ingrid Bergman and Michael Chekhov in Hitchcock's *Spellbound.* She was a psychoanalyst in love with her amnesic patient (played by Gregory Peck) and determined to rescue him from a murder charge by curing his "guilt complex." Chekhov, her wise former training analyst, tries to help her despite his qualms about the patient. Under the spell of this movie I came to a sudden decision, which from then on I never questioned. I would have a psychoanalysis and then become a psychoanalyst. Later I was convinced—a slight European accent was enough—that my psychoanalyst looked and talked like Ingrid Bergman. Another demonstration of the power of stories in our lives.

*The TAT.* I first came across the Thematic Apperception Test when I was a 19-year-old undergraduate major in psychology at Stanford University. I read about it in a book called *Explorations in Personality* by Henry Murray (1938), which described many methods for studying personality. For my senior project I put a classmate through all of them. It made immediate sense to me that one could learn a lot about people from the stories they made up, so much so that for this project I invented my own TAT, using pictures I cut out of magazines. (I was not impressed that the stimulus had to be ambiguous.)

I mention Murray's work again in what follows. I was not aware of the role his work had played in my own life until I wrote this paper; I feel I have reestablished a relationship that I had lost. His idea that you could use a variety of methods to study one person was a revelation. A person was a domain unto himself and one could make multiple observations in that domain. I set myself to notice repetitions and parallels in the subject's responses across methods. I noticed also when hypotheses to account for responses obtained from one method matched hypotheses to account for responses obtained from another method. These ideas and methods in turn came to influence how I listened, and taught others to listen, in the clinical situation.

*Graduate school.* At 21 I returned to the University of Chicago to do graduate work in psychology. Those were heady days. James Miller was Chairman of the Department and preoccupied with system theory. Hedda Bolgar, a Viennese psychoanalyst, taught me personality theory. I worked with Herb Thelen in his group dynamics laboratory. Carl Rogers, with whom I had little rapport, ran the Counseling Center. I thought, and still do, and now teach, that the psychotherapist should actively process what is communicated to him and do something with it. Rogers thought that, in my work with a young adolescent, which centered around the client's drawings and paintings, I talked too much.

William Stephenson, a red-headed Scotsman, conveyed a lot of enthusiasm for his method for obtaining quantitative data within a subjective frame of reference. I and a fellow graduate student used his method in a single-case study. In addition to a battery of methods for exploring personality mostly picked up from Murray, we arranged for the subject to participate in role-playing dramas we had invented. The situations to be enacted were chosen on the basis of what we had learned about the single subject. Involving the subject in these situations was designed to influence the subject's representations of himself and others in predicted ways. Apparently I already thought that the dramas in which people were involved in everyday life had the causal power to affect internal structures.

Mo Stein was my teacher in psychological testing. I thought his manual, *The Thematic Apperception Test* (1948), splendid in its rigor. What a combination: the richness of stories and disciplined thought! That integration became my ideal for myself as a professional, though all too often I was not to achieve it. Stein emphasized standard procedures of administration, reading the subject's responses without knowledge of the case history, and intraindividual comparison of stories. "Read the first story told by a subject," he taught, "and formulate hypotheses about that subject on the basis of that limited sample just as you would with any other sample of the subject's behavior. Then, check and revise these hypotheses according to the information in the next story; and iterate this procedure through the 20 stories. Notice parallels. Notice repetitions."

His conceptual scheme for analysis of the stories was one I already used at the movies. "Identify the hero. What are the characteristics of the setting? Who are the others in that setting? What objects (props) are important? What social pressures and ideologies impinge on the hero? What does the hero need? (The list of needs came from Murray.) How are these needs manifested in the actions the hero initiates toward objects, toward other people, or in the reactions the hero has to actions initiated by others? What attracts or repels the hero? What inner states, what feelings, does the hero experience? What modes—fantasy, planning, motor action—does the hero favor? Is the ending happy, unhappy, indefinite?"

Interpretation of the set of stories depended not only on picking up repeated themes but on careful observation across stories of the details of sequences. "What conditions precede the appearance of a particular need in different stories? What consequences follow the appearance of a particular need in different stories?"

All these questions continue to guide how I follow and process, and teach others to follow and process, the stories told and enacted in psychotherapy. I would like to attribute whatever confidence I have in teaching psychotherapy to what I have learned over many years, from psychoanalytic training, from doing different kinds of clinical work, and from whatever wisdom age confers. It is a bit disturbing to realize that the frame for much of what I teach today about psychotherapy was "in place" in me by age 21.

In graduate school, we had a year-long seminar on the philosophy of science and research methodology. (Psychology was self-conscious and defensive about its status as a science.) I am still drawing on that experience. Most of the issues about which I have written in this area were raised in that seminar. I wouldn't be surprised to find that many of the positions I have taken were explicit or foreshadowed in the papers I wrote for it. Again, it is a little disconcerting to think that I had most of the ideas I was ever going to have on the philosophy of science and research by age 21.

*Attempts at integration.* My work in psychotherapy and teaching psychotherapy is the better for my having wrestled with such issues as "the problems in establishing the credibility of an inference." But for many years following graduate school—through medical school, psychiatric residency, and eventually academic life—I had no particular success in integrating the side of me passionately interested in stories and the side taking great pleasure in the challenge of rigorous conceptualization and argument. The former, I knew, would no doubt be regarded as soft and was unlikely to impress anyone, the latter as tough-minded and likely to command respect. I became a member of a university faculty. I wanted to be promoted. I did what was required and enjoyed doing it. I gave myself up to the mastery and explication of difficult theories, such as Chomsky's in linguistics, Parsons' in sociology, Bertrand Russell's and other analytic philosophers' in the philosophy of science and formal logic, Fisher's in statistics and experimental design, and Freud's in psychoanalysis (especially his metapsychology). I wielded the weapons of indefatigable scholarship, trenchant criticism, and logical argument. I made implicit assumptions explicit. I examined the consequences for practice of holding one rather than another view. I did careful analyses of relations among theories. But the truth is, in doing all this, I left something important of myself behind, something I needed in doing and teaching psychotherapy.

Now and then, I tried to pull these two sides of myself together.

*Language and Interpretation in Psychoanalysis* (1975) is a peculiar hybrid. The conceptual tools I used in discussing interpretation were Chomsky's syntactic analysis and Roman Jakobson's phonemic analysis. But the objects subjected to interpretation include a Bach prelude and a poem by Wallace Stevens. In my mid-40s, I was much immersed in Stevens' poetry. It had a great deal to say about the effort of imagination to survive the pressure of too much reality.

Isn't it strange that psychoanalysis says so little about imagination? The word hardly appears in the psychoanalytic literature. Trainees continue to be uncomfortable when I encourage them to regard imagination as an indispensable aspect of clinical skill. It is as though I were encouraging them to do something disreputable.

Gradually, especially in doing and teaching psychotherapy, I found myself less interested in abstractions and a priori rules of technique. Lipton's (1977) paper on Freud's technique helped liberate me by taking a stand against dogma: No one can know a priori that an intervention is correct. One can only assess its validity by maintaining an attitude of inquiry and observing its impact and fate. Not everything the psychoanalyst does or says belongs to the domain of technique, although it is his job to discern the effects of everything he says or does.

There came a time when I could no longer read metapsychology, and I stopped teaching it. Merton Gill and Roy Schafer seemed to have gone through something similar, judging by their radical swerve from metapsychology after their brilliant studies of it. An account of psychoanalytic process in terms of telling and enacting stories, which takes narrative as a central concept, regards psychoanalysis as an extension of commonsense or folk psychology. Dramatistic concepts such as desires and beliefs play a central role in its explanations. It attributes causal powers to the semantic contents of mental states (Edelson, 1991; Hopkins, 1988). This characterization of psychoanalysis is not consonant with the aims or language of metapsychology.

Metapsychology is essentially an attempt to replace desire/belief explanation with a "nonsemantic" theory that describes contentless causal mechanisms or processes. Desire/belief explanation is especially exemplified in psychoanalysis by the explanatory use of unconscious fantasies as mediating between "stimuli" and responses to them. A nonsemantic theory, on the other hand, involves no reference to and assigns no causal role to mental contents (that is, internal symbolic representations of states of affairs that are part of, or the object of, desiring or believing). Metapsychology is, in this sense, like the learning theory that tries to formulate laws using concepts such as conditioning, reinforcement, and stimulus generalization without any reference to the content of what is learned. Metapsychology so conceived must fail as a psychoanalytic theory, if psychoanalysis is indeed trying to answer just those questions I have previously described it as trying to answer (Edelson, 1988, 1989). Stoller (1985, p. 105) makes the same point. My present conviction is that a science of psychology based on folk psychology is an explanatory apparatus that is quite good enough for the psychotherapist.

As my struggle for integration continued, I began to pay more attention to sensuous particulars than to conceptual labels. I think that a psychotherapist is the better for having a taste for nondestructive gossip. I like the highly personal particulars of an individual narrative, and I am leery even of theories about narrative or lists of general themes for classifying narratives.

I was supported in the direction I seemed to be moving, and in the belief that I did not have to abandon tough-minded empiricism and rigor altogether, by the work of several others. There were those few who saw fantasy as core to psychoanalysis: Arlow (1969a, 1969b), of course; Schafer (1968) who argued in a paper on the defense mechanisms that they were not contentless operations but fantasies; Reik (1941) who, in his fine work on masochism, showed beautifully how to lay out the details of the phenomena first before considering dynamics and etiology; and Stoller (1985) who studied sexuality, and so of course fantasies, at a time when psychoanalysis seemed to be losing its interest in sexuality. Theorists may lose their way, but any moviegoer knows how important sex is to a story.

Certain philosophers of mind and cognitive scientists were also helpful. Fodor (1981, 1983, 1987, 1990) argued persuasively that a science of psychology must be based on commonsense or folk psychology. Hopkins (1988) and Wollheim (1969, 1974, 1979) added that psychoanalysis was in fact an extension of folk psychology; and they also explicated the important role of fantasy in psychoanalysis. Some cognitive and computer scientists (Schank, 1982, 1990; Schank and Abelson, 1977), in the tradition of Piaget's *internal schema*, chose to work with *narrative, script, story,* and *scenario* as key concepts. Lakoff and Johnson (1980), Lakoff (1987), and Johnson (1987) focused on the role of imagination and metaphor in studies of reason and category formation. Lakoff (1987, pp. 380–415), an anthropologist and linguist, wrote a case study of anger. Examining metaphors used in expressing anger, he found that they seemed to "converge on a certain prototypical model of anger." Since that model had a temporal dimension and a number of stages, he formulated it as a prototypical *scenario*. Similarly, de Sousa (1987, pp. 181–184), in his cognitive theory of emotion, referred to how we learn the vocabulary of emotion from paradigm *scenarios* drawn from daily life in childhood and later reinforced by stories that are part of culture.

Do I list these formidable books, which it is true I did find stimulating and exhilarating, mainly to justify to scientific colleagues my interest in stories? Do I continue to be uneasy about owing knowledge and skill to the movies? For, if truth be told, despite this list, I do sound more like a moviegoer than a cognitive scientist when I am doing and teaching psychotherapy.

*An important observation.* The major shift in my thinking about psychotherapy took place when a few years ago I was struck by the difference between two kinds of sessions. In one, patients mainly told stories (usually but not always) eagerly and expressively. In the other, they repetitively described, catalogued, and generalized about their traits and states. Taking this kind of observation seriously has had felicitous effects on my work as a psychotherapist and teacher. That, despite some doubts, encourages me to persevere in drawing intuitively on my experiences of movies and in listening to and thinking about stories.

## TEACHING PSYCHOTHERAPY

I have found that many psychotherapists in training have already been "well taught." As anxious beginners, they cling to the theories and rules or precepts to which they have been exposed. Early in my teaching, I was struck by the fact that what seemed to pop into their heads when a patient said something was a theoretical idea about the patient, a generalization of some kind, a characterization of the patient, a diagnosis. What popped into my head was some other episode or story the patient had told; a story I knew from my own reading; a scene, event, or character from a movie; a scene involving the patient that the patient had somehow conveyed but not described; or an image such as a mother holding an infant.

A patient denigrates a psychotherapist who is about to go on vacation. A beginner is inclined to say, "You sound very angry." Perhaps, but less often, he may utter a generalization such as, "You devalue what you cannot have." However, I might ask the patient, "Have you ever heard the story of the fox and the sour grapes." If he says, "Yes," that may be enough. If he says, "No," I might continue, "Let me tell you the story. A fox saw some luscious-looking grapes. They were hanging too high for him to reach, so after a few futile jumps, he went off muttering, 'Who wants those grapes anyway! They're sour.'"

A patient comes into a session furious at his psychotherapist. He had been vividly imagining on his way to the session a scene in which the psychotherapist criticized him unreasonably for something he had done. A beginner is inclined to say, "You sound very angry." Perhaps, but less often, he may make what he considers to be a "transference interpretation," which again is in the form of a generalization: "You expect me to treat you like your father did." I might ask, "Have you ever heard the wrench story?" The patient will usually say, "No." I continue: "Let me tell you the story. A man's car broke down on a lonely stretch of highway in Nebraska. He needed a wrench to fix the car, and he didn't have one. So he set out on foot toward the one farm house in the distance he could see. As he walked, he thought to himself, 'I'll get to the farm house, and then the farmer will refuse to lend me a wrench.' He got madder and madder as he approached the house. When he got there, he knocked. When the farmer opened the door, he immediately shouted at him, 'Keep your god damned wrench!'"

A typical view psychotherapists in training seemed to have about interpretation was that it was a generalization about the patient that explained a lot. It was a general timeless truth, and rarely contained any indices of time or place or any reference to specific occasions. Most of them felt that the patient should come to these truths himself, so that they were hesitant to offer such explanations.

When they said anything to the patient at all, many asked a question, either about a fact or about why the patient had done something. It seemed to me that the request for a fact was not followed by any indication from the psychotherapist in training about what he intended to do with this information. The preference for asking questions seemed to have its origin in a disinclination to commit himself; he might make a mistake.

The why question seemed to me mostly to leave the patient at a loss, because his motives were in fact a mystery to him. But he felt he should know the answer, since otherwise the psychotherapist would not have asked him for it. The result was often a drop in self-esteem, an undesirable outcome to an intervention. Or he might make up an answer, which led both patient and psychotherapist down a path paved with rationalizations and surrounded by thickets of intellectualization.

I began to express some doubts about the notion that the patient should come to these truths by himself, and that the psychotherapist should stand by waiting for the patient to shout "Eureka!" Why pass the entire task of making sense of his experiences over to the patient, with the psychotherapist mainly providing empathy and acceptance? What might the contribution of the psychotherapist be? He was after all supposed to know something about how minds worked.

Another intervention preferred by psychotherapists in training was to comment about how a patient felt. Empathy was in, and a good thing for a psychotherapist to have. Since some inference seemed to be involved, however arrived at, the intervention could be counted as an interpretation.

However, I did not think that naming a feeling was the same as understanding how the patient felt. Understanding a feeling seemed to me to require knowing the contents of the feeling, knowing what was going on and who was involved when the feeling arose. What specifically did the patient imagine or remember that led him to feel as he did? The frequent comment, "You feel very angry," rarely included a statement of what it was, on a specific occasion, to which the patient responded with anger. I began to suggest that it might be useful when talking about feelings to mention in some detail particulars belonging to a time and place.

The various kinds of things a psychotherapist in training imagined saying to a patient often tended to be colorless, as in fact a number of texts recommend. Colloquial language was avoided, so much so that I could guess almost without mistake which patients had had previous psychotherapy and learned to talk "psychotherapese." People rarely use the word "angry" in everyday exchanges, talking instead about being mad, irritated, annoyed, pissed off. Furthermore, when the word "angry" is used by a psychotherapist, it almost always for most patients connotes a faintly negative evaluation. No matter what the justification, anger seems not to be a good thing to have, even where getting mad is okay.

But most prominently, the talk used with patients was vague and general. It rarely if ever evoked an image, described a particular scene, or narrated a series of specific events. An intervention having the following form hardly ever occurred: "Such and such happened on that particular occasion, and you reacted in this particular way, because it reminded you of the time that . . . , and you probably figured that the best way to prevent what happened then from happening again was to do such and such."

The beginning psychotherapist's talk was almost never vivid or dramatic. He rarely told the patient a story, retold the patient's story reordering or adding events to it, or suggested the links between a series of particular events, involving a specific cast of characters and occurring at a particular time and place. Pronouns, often ambiguous or of uncertain reference, were used instead of definite descriptions or names. Conceptual labels (usually in the form of noun phrases like "your sense of loss," "your terrible loneliness," "your dependency") were used to refer to feelings, motives, contentless defenses, and enduring traits as abstract entities.

What especially disturbed me was that the things said to a patient did not sound *personal*. I could imagine them being said to any number of patients and being accepted by all of them as true. I thought, on the contrary, that what a psychotherapist said to a patient should contain the particulars of the patient's experiences, so that it would be exceedingly unlikely that one would ever say exactly that to any other patient; it wouldn't make sense to anyone who had not had just those concrete experiences.

My experience was that if a psychotherapist made a timeless generalization, was somewhat vague, or dealt in abstractions, a patient's response was frequently in kind, or he simply ignored the statement and made no use of it. If a psychotherapist, making use of particulars imparted to him by a patient, told a good story, the patient was likely to feel listened to and to take in and use what the psychotherapist had said. Similarly, if a patient made a vague general statement about himself, it made a difference whether his psychotherapist got all interested in these timeless truths, or asked instead, "For example?"

Among other things, I tried language reform, repeatedly questioning a trainee's use of "it" and "that" wherever they occurred, for example. Since the user of a pronoun usually knew what its referent was, and was sure the patient knew, too, this was experienced as nitpicking and inducing self-consciousness. The use of "anger" and "angry" appeared to be ineradicable; I notice myself slipping into using such unnatural language to this day. These observations will come as no surprise to anyone familiar with the work of Roy Schafer (1976, 1983).

Helped by members of my seminar groups and the trainees I worked with individually, I began to develop a teaching strategy with three main objectives.

My first objective was to *loosen the stranglehold of theory*. I had previously given lengthy demanding reading assignments. I have now stopped assigning readings in my beginning and intermediate courses on psychotherapy. Beginners, having the notion that they are doing a very difficult job about which they know nothing, understandably cling to theory. Of course, beginners have to have something to draw upon when they listen to patients. I now tried to convince them that they knew a lot more than they thought they did, and that they could draw upon their own deeply entrenched knowledge and a well-honed body of skills. It was just that it had never occurred to them that this knowledge and those skills were relevant. The knowledge and skill I thought they probably had was about stories. They knew how to listen to, respond to, and tell a story.

I said, "When you are doing psychotherapy, and want to get your bearings, call to mind childhood experiences of wanting to be told a story, how you got your mother to tell you a story, memories of how you listened and responded to stories, what you liked and didn't like, what you wanted and especially enjoyed, what made you restless or turned you off, and what went on between you and the storyteller.

"Call to mind sitting with a friend at lunch, talking about what's been happening in your life, and your friend's life, asking and answering, 'What have you been doing? How has the week gone?' What kinds of things would each of you say and ask as the other told about various happenings? What did each of you do to arouse the interest of the other? How did each of you know when the other was not interested? How did that affect what was told?

"Call to mind watching a movie. Reflect on how a movie went about affecting you. What made you feel that it was a great, a good, a lousy movie?"

In attempting to free those I teach from the iron hand of theory, I might say something like the following—not all at once, of course, and always in response to some specific bit of clinical material: "Pay special attention to what comes into your mind as the patient talks, and include that in your account of the session." Then, when someone felt comfortable about including that in what he told me, I was often dumbfounded by the difference between what was going on in his mind and what he said to the patient. The former sounded so natural and on the mark, the latter so stilted and stereotyped. "Why didn't you say that!" I would cry. "Do you really think I could have? I wasn't sure that would be right. I thought it might be too much for the patient," he would answer.

"Don't make an effort to figure things out," I suggested. "Instead perk up when an image of any kind, a daydream, or some story you know pops into your head. Notice when the story the patient tells you, or something about the patient, how he looks or sounds, reminds you of a movie. Notice when you suddenly find yourself remembering some story the patient has told you maybe even months before so that you are surprised you remember it. These images, stories, and memories are comments about what the patient is saying, and may often lead you to something you might say to him in turn. Indeed, you may find that you use just what pops into your head in what you say to him."

A second and related objective was to get trainees *to eschew the vague and general, and instead to pursue the particular* (Levenson, 1988). "Out with conceptual labels summarizing or classifying experiences! Out with vagueness! Use pronouns sparingly. Repeat the particulars of the patient's story.

"Ask yourself as you listen to the patient: Can you see a scene in your mind, a particular time and place, particular characters? Can you see what they are doing? Hear what they are saying?

"If the patient speaks allusively, generally, although perhaps expressively, you provide the scene. Say things like 'What you convey to me, the image that comes to my mind, is a mother and child, and the child cries, and the mother knows instantly what the child feels and wants.'

"Where the patient has dropped a narrative line, ask, 'What happened next?'" In telling about a fight with his mother, a patient said in passing, "She tried to get my father on her side," and then went on to describe his mother's various demands and threats. The psychotherapist, as if he were watching this scene in the movie and there was a fade, found himself wanting to know whether the mother had succeeded in getting the father on her side. So when there was a pause in the descriptions of the mother's demands and threats, he asked, "How did your father respond to your mother's attempts to get him on her side?"

A third objective was to focus the trainee's attention on *the immediacy of the therapeutic moment* (Shapiro, 1989). I direct the trainee's attention to the moment-by-moment dynamics in a single session, the blips and perturbations, the minute changes of affect and emphasis. "Let's focus on the details of microprocess. Be a mole with your nose on the ground following the twists and turns in a barely discernible trail, not an eagle surveying a vast landscape, the valleys and peaks. Give your attention to the microprocess of this single session, not just to the macroprocess occurring over months and perhaps years of sessions." (I do not say that this is the only way to *do* psychotherapy, but rather one way to learn how to do psychotherapy.)

I say, "Try imagining that what the patient says is in some way a response to what you have just said, even though it does not seem to have anything to do with what you said." An example: Toward the end of psychotherapy, a patient told a psychotherapist how much she had gotten out of psychotherapy, the problems she felt she now had a handle on. The psychotherapist, ignoring her grateful comment about psychotherapy (and indirectly about him), asked for further explication of these problems. The patient became vague, and muttered some fragmentary phrases about "shame." The psychotherapist realized that he had been unable to accept her thanks and that she responded to the absence of an appropriate response by becoming ashamed of feeling grateful.

Another patient told a psychotherapist how much he meant to her, how important it was to her to have someone like him in her life. He wondered why, in that case, she made so little effort to make friends. Out of the blue, she began a furious argument about another matter. The psychotherapist said, "Did you feel pushed away from me when I talked about making friends." She said, "I was just thinking that. It reminded me of my mother, when I so much wanted to be with her, telling me to go out and play."

I say, "In a stream of communications by the patient, hear what the patient says at one moment as a reaction to, an assessment or correction of, what he himself has said at a previous moment. He may be saying, however indirectly, 'I don't like that I said that. . . . I didn't mean that. . . . I want to take it back. . . . I'm ashamed of what I just said. . . . I regret I made that hurtful comment.'"

*Interpretation.* What about interpretation? I suggest thinking of interpretation as storytelling. "The patient reports a series of events. You make a story out of these events. Show how they might be causally connected to each other. Where there appears to be a gap, where you cannot provide one of the causal links from what the patient has reported, inquire about the event that is missing.

"Tell the patient a story that answers the question, 'Why is the patient telling this story now? In response to what event? To accomplish what purpose, to deal with what feeling, to arouse what feeling in me?'"

It is striking to me that a psychotherapist will often give an interpretation when it is not clear to either him or the patient just what puzzling concrete particular, what question about a particular happening, that interpretation is intended to clarify or explain. I say, "Often the stories the patient tells belong to the genre 'mysteries.' Something has happened that puzzles or does not make sense to him. That is the ideal context in which to tell your story to the patient. Like the just-so stories that answer questions like 'How did the elephant get his trunk?' your story is one that answers a question the patient himself has raised. Because the patient is just at that moment curious and interested in the answer, he is most likely to listen to and take in your story."

Clearly the interpretations to which I refer stay close to the surface. They make use of the stories the patient is telling or has told. They draw the patient's attention not to what he has repressed (which is inaccessible as experience) but to what he has temporarily mislaid or recently forgotten, or from which he has withdrawn his attention.

I will occasionally cast my interpretation in the form of reminding the patient of a particular movie, saying a bit about the story of the movie, and asking—if the patient hasn't mentioned it—if he has seen it. It is very rare in my experience that the patient has not seen the movie. Often it turns out that the movie was important to him and aroused strong feelings in him.

A patient once reported a dream in which she was wearing a red dress. She said she would never wear such a dress out in the open. There was a rustling in the trees in the dream. This dream report reminded me of the scene involving Mammy's red petticoat in *Gone with the Wind*. My asking about the possibility that this scene was in the patient's mind led to the following revelations. The patient was deeply identified with Scarlet O'Hara, but disturbed by this identification. The particular scene was one she often remembered and had thought of recently. As I guessed and eventually asked about, she was menstruating. This discussion led to many more stories, including one in which, remembering how Scarlet tore down the green drapes to make a dress out of them, she imagined the pleasure she might have making bold colorful hats. This image, quite unlike how she thought of herself, came as a surprise, but it led to some gratifying developments in her life.

We underestimate the extent to which people in this culture are obsessed and affected by movies and movie-going. Patients rarely mention movies in their "associations" to dreams, for example, because they assume that the psychotherapist is probably not interested or that these are too trivial to bring up in such a serious setting. Often, a psychotherapist will not pick up an allusion to a movie that is not specifically mentioned, nor does the patient think of it spontaneously—unless it has become clear to him that the psychotherapist is in fact interested in such experiences. Movies that in my own work have been important to patients and provided them with narrative threads running through the stories they told and enacted in psychotherapy include: *Alien, Great Expectations,* and *Nicholas Nickleby.*

The troublesome possibility remains that the psychotherapist may introduce subject matter that has special meaning for him and no special meaning for the patient. Can we depend on the patient to ignore the intrusion of material that is "off target"? From my experience, my answer is a tentative "yes."

*Assessing the accuracy of interpretations.* In view of the inevitable degree of indeterminateness and ambiguity in clinical material, I encourage those I teach to generate more than one interpretation of the same material. It is a good idea to get out of the habit of thinking: "Obviously this patient is. . . . This patient's story is certainly . . . " and into the habit of thinking: "What is going on with this patient today, given what I have observed, could be this, *or* this. . . . The story the patient is telling or enacting today could be this, *or* this. . . . Given the stories the patient is telling or enacting, he may be in the world of this scenario, *or* in the world of that scenario."

Do you remember the report of four psychoanalytic sessions by M. Silverman (Pulver, 1987, pp. 147–165)? A structural theorist, two developmentalists, a self-psychologist, a Kleinian, an interpersonalist, an eclectic, and an object relations theorist responded to the report. Their commentaries were intended to clarify the way in which theory shapes technique.

In these sessions the patient alluded to three stories: the film *Now Voyager*, the novel *Don Quixote*, and the story of Helen Keller and her teacher Anne Sullivan. What do these stories have in common? They are stories in which someone rescues someone else from a bad situation or hurtful person. Does the patient wish to be rescued by the psychotherapist? Is she enacting a story of rescue? But the three stories also depict wondrous transformations. A person (not simply the situation she is in) changes. Does the patient wish to be transformed by the psychotherapist? Is she enacting a story of transformation?

Stories of rescue and stories of transformation are not incompatible. Both may be of interest to the patient. But surely one is closer to consciousness, or has a greater charge of feeling or sense of urgency attached to it. That is the one that is more appropriate as a basis for interpretation, on this particular day, in this particular session, here and now. The patient reports a fantasy in which a mad scientist does something to give her bigger breasts. This fantasy provides some evidential support, however weak, for the inference from the other three stories (which are not reported as fantasies) that a story of transformation, rather than a story of rescue, is most saliently on the patient's mind.

It is important that one cannot guess a psychotherapist's theoretical preference from his description of observations in terms of stories of rescue and transformation. In other words, observations so couched, while influenced by knowledge of narratives or stories, and of course then not *non*theoretical, are nevertheless and importantly uncontaminated by the very rival hypotheses about the clinical material or psychoanalytic theories that are in question. They can be used therefore to favor one of these rivals over another. If a trainee learns to observe at this level, he is unlikely to force what a patient says onto a procrustean theoretical bed, or to hear only what he expects to hear. He is more likely to be in touch with what the patient is experiencing here and now.

In the eight theory-driven commentaries on these four sessions, only two mention *Now Voyager*—although the psychoanalyst writes in an aside, "She repeatedly brings up *Now Voyager.* Is that the script for the analysis?" None considers the story of *Now Voyager* in any detail. One commentary mentions the allusion to Helen Keller. No commentary mentions the allusion to *Don Quixote.* Infatuation with theory, and with explicating theory, leads to ignoring details in the clinical material solely on the ground, as far as I can see, that they don't lend themselves to promoting a general theory. The mischievous witch, Theory, banishes what otherwise might be fascinating particulars clear out of the picture. See Pulver (1987) for the many other details to consider in constructing the story or stories most on the patient's mind in these particular sessions.

Most of all, I propose giving priority to a patient's actual subjective experience in assessing the credibility of an interpretative intervention a psychotherapist has communicated to him. An interpretative intervention is not about just any story that might in fact be somewhere in the patient's mind. It is about a story the psychotherapist believes is engaging the patient here and now.

Therefore, these are the kinds of responses that are important in concluding that a psychotherapist who has made an interpretation is on the right track: "Now, I remember an episode just like that which I forgot to tell you. On the way here today, I thought, or wondered, or imagined. . . . Just yesterday, this morning, right after the last session, I. . . . That reminds me of something that happened with my mother."

These new events are of a time or place. They complicate, enrich, or complete the story, add a missing piece to it, provide a clarifying flashback to an earlier event, give some necessary background. The patient's response may include other stories that are similar to, or constitute an attempt to counteract, the story he has told or enacted, and about which the psychotherapist has commented. The patient may deepen a mood evident in the story commented on, or may give more details about its setting. The patient may burst through to an emotional state that is clearly appropriate to the unfolding story and therefore, no matter how embarrassing or painful, makes sense.

I am inclined to think I am on the right track if the patient's response to my communication tells me more than I knew before, surprises me, adds a new twist to a story, carries the story further, or involves an intense expression of feeling—as I may begin to laugh or cry, sometimes quite unexpectedly, when something about a movie, I am not always sure what it is, touches me.

I am inclined to think I am on the wrong track if the patient convincingly challenges what I say by pointing out particulars that are inconsistent with it or not encompassed by it, if the patient ignores what I say, or if what I say has no impact on him or the story he is telling or enacting.

Mere assent or dissent is evidentially irrelevant. So are timeless generalizations or generalities, no matter how eagerly or enthusiastically the patient offers them.

*A ready-made set of stories.* Wouldn't it be useful in teaching psychotherapy to a beginner just to give him a set of stories often told or enacted by patients so that he would recognize what story he is hearing or caught up with the patient in enacting? Psychotherapy research might come up then with a set of stories from its empirical studies that a psychotherapist should have ready at hand when listening to patients. Maybe psychotherapy research can even show that patients with different personality or character disorders, for example, are partial to particular kinds of stories. Indeed, psychoanalytic theory itself might be regarded as an effort to provide a set of common or typical scenarios.

A set of stories ready at hand? I don't think so, for a variety of reasons. I am, as you can tell from what I have said so far, leery of anything that promotes reliance on formulas, even if these be archetypal narratives rather than abstract or general concepts. I would recoil from the prospect of stretching the patient's material on still another procrustean theoretical bed instead of focusing on the particulars in what the patient tells.

But mainly, I don't think that there is a finite list of stories any more than I think there is a finite list of sentences in a natural language. Narrative competence can generate an infinite set of stories, including completely new never-before-created stories, just as linguistic competence can generate an infinite set of sentences, including completely novel sentences, from a finite set of components. For example, see the computer program "for the writer of novels, short stories, plays, screenplays and television episodes" called *Plots Unlimited* (Sawyer and Weingarten, 1990)—"a creative source for generating a virtually limitless number and variety of story plots and outlines."

*The next chapter.* Further development of the narrative frame for studying psychotherapeutic process and for teaching psychotherapy requires a consideration of the differences among such concepts as *scene, dramatic situation, story,* and *plot.* Under what circumstances and why does a patient primarily convey that a scene (such as the "primal scene"?) is on his mind? When and why does a patient depict primarily a dramatic situation (such as "an oedipal configuration") without unfolding its consequences? When and why is a patient ready to tell, or to enact, an actual story (a chronological series of events, causally linked)? When is it necessary for the psychotherapist to become aware of the plot of a story (the order in which events are actually and not necessarily chronologically presented)? Do these differences make a difference? What about the role of different props and settings in the patient's tellings and enactments? What is the patient's subjective relation to the characters in his imagined scenarios? These are questions for the next chapter of my story.

## BIBLIOGRAPHY

ARLOW, J. A. (1969a). Unconscious fantasy and disturbances of conscious experience. *Psychoanal. Q.*, 38:1–27.

——— (1969b). Fantasy, memory, and reality testing. *Psychoanal. Q.*, 38:28–51.

BORDWELL, D. (1985a). *Narration in the Fiction Film*. Madison, Wis.: Univ. Wisconsin Press.

——— (1985b). The classical Hollywood style, 1917–60. In *The Classical Hollywood Cinema*, by D. Bordwell, J. Staiger, & K. Thompson. New York: Columbia Univ. Press, pp. 1–84.

DE SOUSA, R. (1987). *The Rationality of Emotion*. Cambridge, Mass.: MIT Press.

EDELSON, M. (1971). *The Idea of a Mental Illness*. New Haven: Yale Univ. Press.

——— (1975). *Language and Interpretation in Psychoanalysis*. Chicago: Univ. Chicago Press, 1984.

——— (1984). *Hypothesis and Evidence in Psychoanalysis*. Chicago: Univ. Chicago Press, 1986.

——— (1988). *Psychoanalysis: A Theory in Crisis*. Chicago: Univ. Chicago Press, 1990.

——— (1989). The nature of psychoanalytic theory. *Psychoanal. Inq.* 9:169–192.

——— (1990). Defense in psychoanalytic theory. Computation or fantasy? In *Repression or Dissociation*, ed. J. L. Singer. Chicago: Univ. Chicago Press, pp. 33–60.

——— (1991). Review of *Mind, Psychoanalysis and Science*, ed. P. Clark & C. Wright. *Psychoanal. Q.*, 60:101–108.

——— (1992a). Can psychotherapy research answer this psychotherapist's questions? *Contemp. Psychoanal.* 28:118–151.

——— (1992b). Telling and enacting stories in psychoanalysis. In *Interface of Psychoanalysis and Psychology*, ed. J. Barron, M. Eagle, & D. Wolitzky. Washington, D.C.: American Psychological Association Press, pp. 99–124.

FENICHEL, O. (1941). *Problems of Psychoanalytic Technique*. New York: Psychoanalytic Quarterly.

FODOR, J. (1975). *The Language of Thought*. New York: Crowell. Harvard University Press reprint, 1979.

——— (1981). *Representations*. Cambridge, Mass.: MIT Press.

——— (1983). *The Modularity of Mind*. Cambridge, Mass.: MIT Press.

——— (1987). *Psychosemantics*. Cambridge, Mass.: MIT Press.

——— (1990). *A Theory of Content*. Cambridge, Mass.: MIT Press.

FREUD, S. (1916–17). Introductory lectures on psycho-analysis. *S.E.*, 15 & 16.
——— (1926). The question of lay analysis. *S.E.*, 20:183–258.
HOLLAND, N. (1968). *The Dynamics of Literary Response*. New York: Columbia Univ. Press, 1989.
——— (1973). *Poems in Persons*. New York: Columbia Univ. Press, 1989.
——— (1988). *The Brain of Robert Frost*. New York: Routledge.
HOPKINS, J. (1988). Epistemology and depth psychology. In *Mind, Psychoanalysis and Science*, ed. P. Clark & C. Wright. New York: Basil Blackwell, pp. 33–60.
JOHNSON, M. (1987). *The Body in the Mind*. Chicago: Univ. Chicago Press.
LAKOFF, G. (1987). *Women, Fire, and Dangerous Things*. Chicago: Univ. Chicago Press.
——— & JOHNSON, M. (1980). *Metaphors We Live By*. Chicago: Univ. Chicago Press.
LEVENSON, E. (1988). The pursuit of the particular. *Contemp. Psychoanal.*, 24:1–16.
LIPTON, S. (1977). The advantages of Freud's technique as shown in his analysis of the Rat Man. *Int. J. Psychoanal.*, 58:255–273.
LUBORSKY, L. (1984). *Principles of Psychoanalytic Psychotherapy*. New York: Basic Books.
——— & CRITS-CHRISTOPH, P. (1990). *Understanding Transference*. New York: Basic Books.
MURRAY, H. (1938). *Explorations in Personality*. New York: Oxford Univ. Press.
PULVER, S. (1987). How theory shapes technique. *Psychoanal. Inq.*, 7:141–299.
RAPAPORT, D. (1960). On the psychoanalytic theory of motivation. In *The Collected Papers of David Rapaport*, ed. M. M. Gill. New York: Basic Books, pp. 853–915.
REIK, T. (1941). *Masochism in Modern Man*. New York: Farrar, Straus.
RICHARDS, I. (1929). *Practical Criticism*. New York: Harcourt, Brace, & World.
SAWYER, T. & WEINGARTEN, A. (1990). *Plots Unlimited*. Malibu, Calif.: Ashleywilde.
SCHAFER, R. (1968). The mechanisms of defence. *Int. J. Psychoanal.*, 8:175–202.
——— (1976). *A New Language for Psychoanalysis*. New Haven: Yale Univ. Press.
——— (1983). *The Analytic Stance*. New York: Basic Books.
——— (1992). *Retelling a Life*. New York: Basic Books.
SCHANK, R. (1982). *Dynamic Memory*. New York: Cambridge Univ. Press.
——— (1990). *Tell Me a Story*. New York: Charles Scribner's Sons.
——— & ABELSON, R. (1977). *Scripts Plans Goals and Understanding*. Hillsdale, N.J.: Lawrence Erlbaum.
SHAPIRO, D. (1989). *Psychotherapy of Neurotic Character*. New York: Basic Books.
STEIN, M. (1948). *The Thematic Apperception Test*. Cambridge, Mass.: Addison-Wesley Press.
STOLLER, R. (1985). *Observing the Erotic Imagination*. New Haven: Yale Univ. Press.

WOLLHEIM, R. (1969). The mind and the mind's image of itself. In *On Art and the Mind*. Cambridge, Mass.: Harvard Univ. Press, 1974, pp. 31–53.

———— (1974). Identification and Imagination. In *Freud: A Collection of Critical Essays*, ed. R. Wollheim. New York: Anchor Press, pp. 172–195.

———— (1979). Wish-fulfilment. In *Rational Action*, ed. R. Harrison. Cambridge: Cambridge Univ. Press, pp. 47–60.

# Portraits of Survival

## A Twenty-year Follow-up of the Children of Buffalo Creek

RICHARD G. HONIG, M.D.,
MARY C. GRACE, M.Ed., M.S.,
JACOB D. LINDY, M.D.,
C. JANET NEWMAN, M.D.,
and JAMES L. TITCHENER, M.D.

*This study is a follow-up of the children of Buffalo Creek "hollow" who survived the dam collapse and flood of 1972. It was conceived as a complement to the 1988 NIMH-funded follow-up investigation of the children of Buffalo Creek conducted by the University of Cincinnati Traumatic Stress Study Center.[1] That 1988 study utilized standardized methodology to assess levels of psychopathology present among those who were children at the time of the 1972 flood. Among the original child subjects, results demonstrated that the rates of both posttraumatic stress disorder (PTSD) and levels of other psychopathology had sharply declined as the children moved to adulthood. Several questions remained unanswered: the long-term meaning which the flood had in the survivors' lives and its impact on their adaptation as they progressed through the subsequent stages of emotional development. For these reasons, we, as*

Drs. Honig, Lindy, Newman, and Titchener are on the faculty of the Cincinnati Psychoanalytic Institute and the Department of Psychiatry, University of Cincinnati, College of Medicine. Ms. Grace is Co-Director of the University of Cincinnati Traumatic Stress Study Center and serves as research consultant to the Cincinnati Psychoanalytic Institute. This project was supported by the Research Fund of the Cincinnati Psychoanalytic Institute. The authors would like to thank MelaDee Cunningham, Administrator of the Cincinnati Psychoanalytic Institute, for her invaluable assistance on this project.

1. NIMH Grant #MH42644, B. L. Green, Principal Investigator.

*psychoanalytic investigators who had been members of the original clini-
cal assessment team, planned an interview of child and adolescent survivors as a follow-up to our interviews in 1974 with a particular focus
on meaning and adaptation.*

## BLACK WATER, BLACK MUD, BLACK SUN

ANY ATTEMPT TO KNOW THE CHILDREN OF BUFFALO CREEK REQUIRES SOME
familiarity with the events of February 1972. But could anyone ever
know all that happened in that valley on that cold, wet, bleak Saturday?
We have a patchwork, a collage of reports of people who witnessed
portions of the disaster from different perspectives. Some of these
scenes were overwhelming and unimaginable before they actually occurred. Real knowledge of all that happened would require that a
helicopter with foreknowledge would be hovering low over the Buffalo
Mining Company's tipple at 7:45 A.M. on February 26, 1972. About 15
minutes later it began.

Pittston, a huge conglomerate, was the major stockholder of Buffalo
Creek Mining Company. The mine was at the top of the 17-mile-long
valley where three smaller streams united to form Buffalo Creek. A
tipple is a towering structure built to separate various grades of coal
from slate and other forms of waste brought by conveyor to the tipple
top to fall to lower levels assisted by large amounts of water. The waste
or "slag" is usually piled nearby where spontaneous combustion ignites
it to burn forever. In this case the waste was piled to form a dam upon
Buffalo Creek. This lake was also replenished by water pumped
out from the depths of the mine. Immediately below the mine was
Saunders, a settlement with a church and a dozen houses. From there a
single-track railroad, the creek, and a narrow paved road for buses,
cars, and trucks formed a braid as they crossed and recrossed each
other all the way down to the end of the creek at the Guyandotte River.
Natives had talked for years of the possibility that the dam could give
way and then, well, "God only knows!"

It had been raining for several days. Some experts had been inspect-
ing the dam as it grew increasingly boggy and "unstable," which seems
now to be a world-class euphemistic understatement.

A clock found later from Saunders showed 8:01 A.M. It must have
been a brief moment between breakthrough and total destruction as
Saunders was carried away by the tremendous wall of black mud esti-
mated to have been 30 to 40 feet high over the creek bed. The speeding

wall theory accounts for the variability of destruction of homes and property in the upper third of the 21-mile length of Buffalo Creek.

At several points along the course of the black mud-water there were areas of complete devastation opposite remarkably preserved areas where the houses stood, wet and soiled but not carried away to the next bridge where dams were created out of houses, trailers, autos, and out of anything one might imagine, including human bodies. This peculiar course resulted from the force of the water-mud actually caroming its way through the steeper walls of the valley in its upper third. In a few days, when all was quiet, when the families were able to return, a new phase of the disaster began.

In those times it was a struggle, sometimes an ordeal, to reach Buffalo Creek valley from the outside world. Yet the survivors needed everything. Four thousand people were homeless. The National Guard were a force for order.

Religious and other service groups sent in volunteers. It required more than one year to get three trailer camps (perhaps more accurately, trailer slums) established. One well-known incident illustrates the tension between angry survivors and well-intended relief planners. An electrician and foreman in a mine, who had performed with high grades for leadership and strength in the early days, stepped into the highway with a rifle when he saw a HUD trailer on its way. With the rifle he directed the trailer to his houseless property, where he and his family resided for several years.

One version of the legend, told by children now when visitors ask, ends with the memory of tumbled, falling-apart houses bearing black Xs signifying those to be burned where they were found. Cries of outrage and sorrow are remindful of the same sort of catastrophe in the 1930s in the Dustbowl when families saw the X on their houses. Heavy smoke darkened the sun. "Psychic impairment," the phrase lawyer Jerry Stern used for later legal action, commenced.

There is a grave in a small park halfway down or up the valley. It reads:

THIS TINY TRIO
Boy Girl Boy
*Who were the victims of the Feb. 26, 1972*
*Buffalo Creek Disaster are unknown to us*
*by name but to Our Heavenly Father*
*they are known as three little angels.*

Just as in other man-made catastrophes, unknown soldiers who have lost everything commit us to mourning. Those children who survived commit us to study.

## LITERATURE REVIEW

The first description of the impact of the flood on the community can be found in Kai Erikson's classic, *Everything in Its Path* (1976). As the Buffalo Creek litigation proceeded, a wealth of clinical information was gathered on both the adult and child survivors and formed the basis for the earliest Buffalo Creek research. This initial exploration (Newman, 1976; Titchener and Kapp, 1976; Titchener et al., 1976) described phenomenologically, from an intrapsychic viewpoint, a population of child and adult survivors. Eighty percent of the adults were seen to have developed postdisaster impairment. Subsequent empirical research on Buffalo Creek adults utilized data from psychiatric reports on both sides of the litigation and examined individual differences in response to stress with a multivariate statistical approach (Gleser et al., 1978, 1981; Green et al., 1983). In that project, two psychiatric evaluations were available on the 381 adult survivors and the 207 child survivors who were litigants in the lawsuit brought against the coal company. The study was notable for the amount of impairment found. In the adult sample at least minimal impairment was noted in 70 percent to 80 percent of the group.

Later studies explored changes in the level of impairment over time in the Buffalo Creek adult survivor group. Changes were found on most of the outcome measures of psychiatric impairment and distress, whether clinically rated or self-reported. Proportions of PTSD diagnosis decreased significantly as well (Green et al., 1990). Among adults, however, a residual elevation in psychopathology was present two decades later when compared to a nearby valley and the survivors continued to show a rate of PTSD of 23–28 percent.

Several recent reviews of the literature on child trauma or disaster experience have been organized along the PTSD framework (Lyons, 1987; McNally, 1992; Pynoos, 1990; Terr, 1985), including an investigation of types of stressors which are likely to produce PTSD (McNally) and specific symptoms of PTSD in children (Pynoos, 1990; Terr, 1985, 1991). Green et al. (1991) used a developmental perspective to review the child disaster research regarding children who had experienced collective natural and man-made disasters.

Empirical studies of the children of Buffalo Creek by the Traumatic Stress Center found probable PTSD present in 37 percent of the children seen in the 1974 investigation[2] (Green et al., 1991). Psychopathology in the children was shown to be significantly related to parental psychopathology. That study also found age positively and significantly related to level of psychopathology (Gleser et al., 1981). Newman's (1976) observation of the children indicated that developmental level, the reaction of the immediate family, and exposure to the flood all contributed to the child's level of impairment.

In 1988, the National Institute of Mental Health funded a follow-up investigation of the children of Buffalo Creek who were then young adults.[3] Using a standardized methodology, 99 of the original 207 children were interviewed to determine levels of current adjustment. Rates of PTSD declined from 37 percent to 5 percent. Levels of psychopathology also declined and were not significantly different from control sample scores.

What remains to be commented upon in the literature dealing with short-term and long-term effects of the Buffalo Creek flood is a clinical perspective which describes the impact of the flood on the course of development and adaptation of these children. This is the focus of our investigation. Prior work in this area indicates that adaptation in children to traumatic circumstances appears to be distinguishable in certain respects from the responses of adults. This appears to arise not only because of the developmentally specific cognitive and affective structures in place at the time, but also because of an increasing ego flexibility. The sudden alterations in family constellations as well as the direct impact of trauma on the child tended to result in developmental psychopathology at the time of traumatization (Newman, 1976).

The long-term characterological impact of traumatic events occurring during childhood has long been a central tenet in psychoanalytic thinking. More recently, observations by analysts of children in the midst of traumatic events point out longitudinally that hypertrophy of certain defenses active in coping with trauma may occur (Pynoos, 1989). Directly relevant to our own clinical longitudinal study are Lenore Terr's observations regarding trauma-precipitated personality change (1979). Terr (1991) describes such change as either representing traumatic reenactments occurring so frequently as to lead to personality alteration or, alternatively, as representing a defense that went into operation at the time of the trauma to protect the psyche.

2. Although PTSD was not an official diagnosis in 1974, mental health professionals were looking for symptoms of traumatic neurosis. These symptoms were used as a basis for a diagnosis of PTSD. For a comprehensive description of these procedures, see Green et al. (1991).

3. NIMH Grant #MH42644, B. L. Green, principal investigator.

METHODOLOGY

In March of 1990 our interview team of seven psychiatrists was formed. Of these, six were analysts and four were child psychiatrists. Six of our members had been part of the 1974 and 1975 lawsuit assessment teams. Four of us had been involved in the publication of earlier Buffalo Creek research findings. Throughout our current endeavor, we had the logistical support and consultation of the University of Cincinnati Traumatic Stress Study Center.

Initially, our team spent several brainstorming sessions pondering how best to approach our subjects. Our desire was to conduct as unstructured an interview as possible so that our subjects' own associations might lead us to discover the various meanings the flood experience had come to have for them as their lives unfolded. At the same time, we wished our technique to be sufficiently standardized so that our interviews could be compared.

Ultimately, we delineated the content areas we wished to explore and certain standard questions we would ask. For all subjects, the interview would begin with their available conscious memories of the flood. During this segment, the interviewers agreed to be as unobtrusive as possible. Upon the completion of their spontaneous flood accounts, the subjects would be more actively questioned about specific aspects of their flood experience, such as decisions made at the time, the immediate aftermath, family responses, etc.

We then questioned our subjects about their subsequent life trajectories, with particular attention to such developmental markers as progress in school, negotiation through adolescence and autonomy in late adolescence, and the evolution of intimate relationships and career decisions. We also reviewed the subjects' current life situations and any contemporary emotional symptoms including sleep problems, nightmares, anxiety, startle or panic attacks, depression, and substance abuse. A sleep history was taken with the subjects being asked to recall dreams that occurred during the years immediately following the flood as well as recent dreams.

We asked the subjects to describe a highly stressful event that had occurred in the last five years and to compare it with the stress of the flood. We asked how they coped with this stress and about its resolution. We also elicited their reaction to a recent "hassle."

At the conclusion of our interview, we asked the subjects to repeat two activities they had performed when interviewed as children or adolescents in 1974. The first was to complete the Bird Fable, a standard child psychiatric projective technique. The second was to draw a picture of the flood as they now recalled it. As we anticipated having access to the 1974 child and adolescent studies for many of our subjects, these last two items were included to provide an opportunity for direct comparison with those data.

With our protocol thus prepared, our interview trip took place on the weekend of April 20, 1990. Ironically, it rained heavily throughout our stay in the valley. We wondered how this might sharpen our subjects' reminiscences about that other "rainy time." In the week prior to our arrival 40 individuals had been contacted by members of the Traumatic Stress Study Center who were familiar to these subjects through the previously completed NIMH study. Of those contacted, 19 subjects had agreed to be interviewed either in their homes (13) or at our motel headquarters (6). All subjects were financially compensated for their participation.

Of those 6 subjects who had agreed to be interviewed at the motel, only 2 actually arrived for their interviews, even though for most of them only a 10-minute drive was involved. We were more successful with those seen in their own homes where all 13 scheduled interviews were completed.

As part of our methodology, each of our interviews lasted between 60 and 90 minutes and was either audio or video recorded with the permission of our subjects. When video tapes were made, two team members were often involved, with one operating the equipment. A valuable offshoot of this arrangement was having an outside observer to the interview process.

Of those subjects who kept their appointments with us, all were cooperative with our purposes and many eager to talk about the flood. The experience was often recalled vividly and with affect. In a number of instances, we were impressed with the additional detail and affect that emerged at the end of our interviews when people were asked to draw their memories of the flood. We had earlier debated whether to include this exercise as we were concerned lest many adults would feel too self-conscious to cooperate. This seemed never to be the case, however, and the results were so productive that we wondered whether this should be included in any trauma assessment regardless of the victim's age.[4]

Immediately upon our return to Cincinnati, our research team began weekly meetings to begin reviewing our tapes. As we proceeded, we were struck that despite the NIMH study findings of so little residual PTSD in these same subjects, we seemed to have elicited evidence in

4. In this regard see Terr's comments (1990) about positional memory.

many of our interviews that the flood experience indeed had had an enduring influence on the subsequent lives and development of these persons.

As we further reviewed our tapes with this impression in mind, it occurred to us that the presence or absence of residual PTSD might not be the only or perhaps even the most valid measure of the long-term impact of a traumatic event. Rather, we began to suspect that the long-term impact might be best discerned in persistent "patterns of adaptation" which may have originated as coping responses to the trauma. These patterns, which might evolve into characterological mechanisms of defense, appeared to be more or less adaptational from the perspective of the individual's subsequent emotional development and from the perspective of the individual's capacity to confront other stressful events.

With these ideas as our guide, we attempted further to elucidate the flood's impact on subsequent adaptation by a more intensive review of the interviews with a number of our subjects for whom we had access to the 1974 child or adolescent diagnostic studies. For each subject, we attempted to categorize, on the basis of the 1974 study, the coping style that was then evident and which appeared to have arisen or been reinforced in response to the flood trauma. When possible, the subject's immediate patterns before and after the flood were compared. Next, we turned to our 1990 interview to explore to what extent the adaptive pattern had persisted or changed as the person moved from childhood and adolescence into their adulthood. We also attempted to explore to what extent the flood-related adaptive pattern was limiting or enhancing overall adult development and to what extent the particular pattern appeared fragile or resilient in the event of new pressures. Finally, by examining our findings against the backdrop of those of the University of Cincinnati Study, we explored the question of what factors within the individual or family might have favored the emergence and persistence of a person's particular pattern of adaptation and whether that particular pattern seemed to mitigate or exacerbate the subsequent persistence of PTSD or other emotional symptoms.

## CASE STUDIES

### HELEN

During her interview in 1974 Helen, who had just turned 15, was described as shy, lacking in spontaneity, and "impoverished" in her thinking. She spoke of herself as more shaky, nauseous, nervous, and restless at night than before the flood. She was now less able to sustain friendships than before.

Two special aspects of Helen's experience of the flood included (1) her being carried up the mountain by her grandfather (in some narratives, this is uncle; most likely it is grandmother's husband) because she had a cast on her broken ankle; and (2) the sight of a dead baby compressed by two boards. She also saw many dying people pass in the water torrent beneath her. She was saddened by the deaths and struck by the fact of her survival while others in the same situation died.

In the two years since the flood Helen had shown several adaptive behavior patterns of note. She had demonstrated *compensation through industry* by turning from a C student into a hardworking A to B student. The interviewer thought of her as managing her depression by this overcompensation.

She also tried to manage her sadness within the interview by calling to mind pleasant things. Despite the current symptoms her earliest memory was "having fun." Her wish was that there never had been a flood and her hope was for peace and love. This *turning negative into positive* seemed to have both a conscious and unconscious (reaction formation) component.

She also seemed to sequester or *loculate negative affect*. While acknowledging sadness and guilt that others died, she did not dwell on this emotion, but rather moved quickly to "I guess I lived and they died" (let's get on with it).

As she described the event itself, other coping mechanisms were striking, both in herself, and in her immediate family.

*Positive narcissism:* Helen never doubted that she was loved and that some way of overcoming her inability to manage in her foot cast would be found. She sought from the people around her the help that would save her. In a more reflective stance she admitted she could have died, yet at the same time she seemed never to give it a second thought.

*Preparedness:* Helen's family anticipated the flood, had provisions ready, and dealt with the crisis in an orderly manner.

*Decisiveness, self-sufficiency:* Helen's family took decisive action in the flood and did not hesitate, turn back, or become confused. Reflecting this confidence two years later, Helen responded to the fallen baby Bird Fable with "The little bird flew away and had her own family."

There was a curious paradox here between a tendency toward *Pollyanna denial* (e.g., wishing there was no flood, that her parents would reunite, and wanting to remember only fun), and a *pragmatic reality testing* decisiveness (e.g., in the Bird Fable, while the little bird flies successfully, she knows she will not get help from the mother and father birds who will fly off in different directions—an accurate assessment of the disunity of mother and father and their divorce).

In 1990, Helen was a 31-year-old woman. She was interviewed in Columbus, Ohio where she had moved in her early 30s. She was attractively dressed, engaging, and almost effervescent. Her handshake was warm and her eyes engaged readily and in a friendly manner. She said she almost immediately recognized the interviewer as one of the doctors who had interviewed her (this was not in fact the case). She seemed to find in the interviewer and the interview process a way of connecting to the people of Buffalo Creek, to ties in her childhood which were largely fond ones. It was almost as if we (in the project) were extended family.

She described her current circumstances as quite good with regard to work where she had held an industrial position as a machine operator for some 13 years. She was pleased about the development of her children and with her parenting and, although divorced, was dating and seemed actively engaged in a rather full life. She lamented about not having many close friends, which seemed in part to be a function of her separation from the people of Buffalo Creek. Nonetheless, she was happy about her move to Columbus and certainly would not trade it. She largely denied current emotional difficulties.

When Helen discussed her memories of the dam collapse and flood in 1972, several factors were striking. The family was alerted for the possibility of a flood, were up early that morning, and were dressed. Grandfather monitored the creek and informed people when the water began to rise. All the children were out of the house and up the hill in ample time. While both mother and father were not in the house (the children were staying with grandparents over the weekend and mother was out of the valley having separated from father), there was within the family that was in the house a sense of order and close bonding. Helen had broken her ankle and was in a cast. She was carried by her uncle up the side of the mountain. When confronted with the grotesque image of an infant's body severed between two boards, grandmother had shielded Helen's eyes from the sight with her body. Helen's internal method of handling the grotesqueness by saying to herself, "That's not a baby, it's a doll," was striking. The family displayed spontaneous and open weeping and grief. They returned to the site of the house after the flood.

Helen saw in her immediate family competence, preparedness, care, and concern for her, along with an open expression of emotion. Helen's account of the reunion with father who had trudged several miles through the mud to find her was moving almost to tears, as was the excitement of mother learning that her supposedly dead daughter was alive. The aftermath, although disruptive to the family unit, provided in terms of Helen's subjective experience an opportunity to "have fun" with other kids all sleeping under a single roof.

Helen's life trajectory involved moving away from the valley, finding good work in Columbus, Ohio, marrying, using the $9,000 payment of the court case as a down payment for a new house, and developing some stability for her new family. When her husband was unable to contain his objectionable alcoholic behavior, she instructed him to leave and with some self-confidence she went about building a life as a single parent.

Management of the divorce was a major life event which Helen handled as related in the interview with dispatch and firm action. When asked to respond to a current hassle, she described a recent flood in her basement. She reacted to this by waiting until a neighbor was able to help, which he did rather competently. Her role was to engage the neighbor in a friendly manner and to offer a sense of confidence to the children and to those who were anxious, including herself. The matter was settled without undue alarm.

Another hassle involved an interaction with her daughter who violated one of the rules for her own safekeeping during an afternoon when she was home alone. Helen handled this openly and directly, expressing her anger and instructing her child as to the correct behavior. Although Helen denied remembering recent dreams, she did recall a dream some years ago connected with the death of her grandfather and involving the carrying of his coffin on the side of the mountain. She is one of the four people carrying the coffin. It falls and tumbles down the mountainside with grandfather falling out. She is terrified. We thought this to be a reference to Helen's having been saved by grandfather during the flood and to the terrifying potential of damage to herself having been activated through grandfather's death.

In her current drawing of the flood, Helen depicted all of the major events which she saw within a single confined space drawn almost as a view from a helicopter. There was considerable emotion as she described the images of the houses and the people floating by, of the bodies, and of her fear. It was our view that these images were contained within well-constructed boundaries. An interesting contrast was offered when compared to the drawings she made as a child in which only fragments of the scene were depicted as though she were under water viewing them.

Helen appeared to have *loculated* her Buffalo Creek trauma. She maintained an adaptive, assertive view regarding herself and was generally trusting regarding others and their ability to help in crisis. The positive traits she exhibited in her current roles and conflicts (single parent, setting limits, job planning for the future, reactions to adverse happenings, ex-husband's drinking, and recent "flood" in basement) had their antecedents in the Buffalo Creek dam experience.

Eighteen years later, *compensation through industry* had served Helen well in her stable and substantial work as supervisor in a manufacturing plant. *Planfulness* had allowed her to invest in a house, build her assets, and maintain her family as a single parent. When it came time to bid farewell to her alcoholic husband, she acknowledged the pain but booted him out of the house *decisively* and *forcefully* and never looked back. She was pragmatic when push came to shove.

In a current hassle, when her basement was flooded she never doubted that the neighbor would help, much as her uncle had carried her up the mountain. Her *positive narcissism* was fully intact. Helen's preflood gregariousness had returned and the shyness observed at age 15 appeared to be absent.

Most striking as she described the actual flood and the trauma of the severed infant was how she had loculated the painful affect through the denial mechanism of "It's a doll." Helen surrounded her trauma in a "balloon" of denial which floated unobtrusively overhead until some life event by chance punctured it.[5]

HENRY

In 1974, Henry was 16, the fifth child of seven children with one older brother, three older sisters, and a younger brother and sister. His father was a coal miner. In his 1974 interview two years after the flood, he appeared tired and apathetic. Although he tried to laugh and smile, these emotions seemed restricted. He felt sorry for people who had lost family members. Two of his friends had died in the flood. He imagined these people had gone through a lot of torture.

Henry's experience of the flood included anxiously watching the creek which was close to their house and hearing his father exclaim that the water was black. This confirmed his fear that the dam had broken. The family ran up the mountain to safety. Henry's 26-year-old brother

5. Metaphor of balloon suggested by Terr (personal communication, 1991).

who was living across the creek left the very day of the disaster and did not return for several years. The entire family appeared to have been depressed.

In the two years since the flood, Henry had shown several patterns of adaptive behavior. He *assumed major responsibility* for his family. This was a word he used several times. He felt an increased need to care for his brothers and sisters, to tell them what to do, and to supervise their being home at the right time. He became angry if he was not obeyed. He felt responsible for the family whenever it rained or father was not in the house. He was anxious and worried about another flood. Some ambivalence about his responsibility was suggested in 1974 when he said he looked forward to having a family of his own in the future, but one not as large as his original family "because of the responsibility."

Another theme in the 1974 assessment was a sense of loss, sadness, and social withdrawal because many of his friends moved away or died, so there were fewer people available for friendship. This may also have been an allusion to the loss of his older brother which he did not discuss directly in the 1974 interviews. The loss of peers and a brother was also related to his assumption of a responsible role in the family.

Another adaptation, somewhat depressive and sacrificial, involved the *shift in vocational motivation*. Before the flood his school motivation was minimal. After the flood he tried very hard to do better and did so for a time, but the following year his grades fell again. His hopes at the time were to go into the service and gain training as an electrician or a mechanic. In 1974 he wanted to graduate as quickly as possible so as to get out of the valley, and he wished to be a professional basketball player. The intensity of the conflict between family responsibility and desire to leave the valley was reflected in his 1974 answer into the Bird Fable: Henry hesitated between the little bird staying in the nest or flying away, but he finally decided to stay in the nest.

In the 1974 interview Henry was moderately depressed, anxious, socially isolated, and caught in a conflict between responsibility for family versus urges to leave his home and the valley. He had feelings of loss with friends and his older brother leaving the valley. The intensity of his feelings and conflicts only became evident in the 1990 follow-up interview.

In 1990, Henry was a 33-year-old coal miner, who had built his home a stone's throw away from the ancestral home his father had rebuilt after the flood. He was married and had a 7-year-old daughter. Two older daughters from a previous relationship visited him on weekends. He was involved in the current massive strike on the Pittston Company, his employer, and was actively reliving memories of the flood in the context of the strike, as some strikers carried signs saying "Remember 1972." Current symptomatology involved chronic mild depression with anxiety dreams and insomnia, worry about money and alcohol abuse. He was recovering with the help of his church. He also experienced instability due to the vicissitudes of his relationship to the Pittston Company. He was often angry at the company for failing to provide sickness insurance and benefits for his parents as they aged and died. He had endured a number of subsequent traumas which had put the flood into some perspective.

Overall the outstanding adaptive pattern which persisted from the 1974 interview was a *strong sense of responsibility* which continued unabated. In the absence of his brother and identifying with his strong father, he had carried on and rebuilt the homestead of the family. He had become a leader in the coal-mining community.

As he described his memories of the flood, Henry often pointed toward a nearby house closer to the creek where he had lived at the time of the flood. He now lived in a house a little higher on the hill. It seemed he spoke much more vividly than in 1974: "I remember the water, the real black water. Me and Dad were at the side of the road and saw the big water come around that curve. Seeing bodies, parts of bodies. . . . It was real muddy. Dad went back home the night after the flood. He didn't want to leave the house. Later I saw the house was mud and water up to my knees, it looked awful. I figured Dad would move. The house was so twisted. But my Dad decided no one would tear down this house. It was his father's house. Later Dad would drink and talk about his house. Dad was responsible. I believe the hardest part was seeing his house move off its foundations. The house was everything he had worked for. And it was his father's house. He worked so hard and he had to remodel it."

When asked if he remembered any emotional problems at the time of the flood, he said, "No, not at 15, 16. I don't recall. At 15, there's no responsibilities."

The sense of growing responsibility pervaded his responses to questions concerning his adaptations to the new stresses in his life, which have been numerous. The one he rated as far worse than the flood was his third daughter's near death from meningitis at the age of 3 months. This was the greatest mental suffering he had ever experienced. For several months he constantly drove to the hospital in Huntington. Another tragedy in his late teens was the loss of his younger brother in a car wreck. He coped by sleeping in his brother's bed.

Subsequent stresses accentuating his intensely ambivalent relationship to his employer, the Pittston Company, involved their fighting against health benefits for both his parents in their terminal illnesses. Father had cancer and black lung and mother had heart surgery. There was no health coverage or compensation. Henry's rage against the company was carried out in *responsible ways as a major leader* in the union which had been picketing for 11 months. He said that picketing was much harder than working in the mines. Picketing was his example of a recent "hassle."

His 1974 symptoms of loneliness and wistfulness about not leaving the valley had persisted. "If the flood hadn't happened, there would be more people here. A lot of people left. If they stayed, this would be a better place to live. My brother, he left the same day. Lots of friends moved to other states." Asked if he had wished to move, he said, "It was up to my parents. I was 14, my brother was 26." Later he added that he had tried briefly to leave the valley and attend college, but he had been increasingly and intensely homesick and returned home evermore frequently. The conflict which was reflected in Henry's 1974 answer to the Bird Fable continued to perturb him. Perhaps his weekend drinking, which also was identical with his father's pattern, was an attempt to attenuate the conflict. For a year, he had been in a state of recovery with the help of his church.

Henry's answer to the Bird Fable in 1990 was definitive; the baby bird flew to his mother's pine tree. It was unclear whether, as an adult, this answer reflected a dependent need or a mature nurturant need in caring for his family and parents. But it was clearly staying home.

Henry's current drawing of his memories of the flood was remarkable for his mastery of the scope of the disaster, his perceptual perspective from a distance, the extent of the graphic detail about homes, location of key family members and other people on the edge of the flood, and a body and wreckage caught up in the flood. As he drew the picture, he associated to the flood in vivid detail.

In summary, the major adaptive theme in Henry's experience of the flood and his subsequent life involved important vicissitudes in a strong sense of responsibility and his assertion of a growing leadership role in his family and community.

*Responsibility* is already the major adaptation visible in the 1974 interview, with strong identification with his stalwart father and replacement of his disappearing older brother.

In conflict with the assertion of responsibility were two other themes, one of sadness and isolation, the other of wishing to leave the valley, which he made a failed attempt to do in his late teens. Feelings of homesickness and vocational insecurity interfered. This conflict was reflected in both 1974 and 1990 versions of his response to the Bird

Fable, the outcome of which was to stay home. Following in the footsteps of his father, he drank heavily on weekends, but he had been in recovery for a year at the time of the 1990 interview.

It was interesting that in 1990, when he looked back at his teenage self after the flood, he reflected that at that age "there's no responsibilities" (in 1974, however, he was already immersed in responsible activities for his family).

His adult view of his adult role was certainly clear and powerful. He conveyed pride in continuing the line of home-keeping and work in the valley started by his grandfather and carried on through the flood devastation by his father.

The costs of Henry's assumption of responsibility, in terms of conflicts about social isolation and the sacrifice of not leaving the valley, are manifested in symptoms of anxiety and depression. These were not trivial, but neither were they incapacitating. He had maintained his manly, fatherly, and leadership roles with great dignity.

## MARTHA

In her 1974 assessment at age 16, Martha was described as "anxious, quivering, and tearful." Her flood experience then recounted was first of a feeling of "numbness" as she heard the news of the flood. She recalled seeing floating bodies, cars, and shoes, and a man holding on to a post being washed downstream. No other details were reported. She did comment that her family had 70 relatives in the valley and that none of them had died in the flood.

Prior to the flood, Martha had struggled somewhat successfully to overcome a lifelong sense of shyness and being a "mother's girl." These efforts had led to her becoming a majorette and vice president of her homeroom.

Subsequent to the flood, Martha described feelings of anger, restlessness, and being less tidy. She also reported having less energy and fears of the rain. She developed sleep problems that led to her sleeping with her mother the 5 out of 7 nights a week that her father worked the owl shift. She said her social life had constricted since the flood and was limited to her boyfriend who had lost his mother to suicide around the time of the flood. Martha felt she was mothering this boy but was too guilty to stop.

Most striking was Martha's tendency to ruminate about death. In addition to the ruminations, she dreamed once or twice a month of her own death. One such dream reported was: "I think I am dead, my hands won't move. I try to open my eyes and they won't open."

Upon awakening, she was afraid to go back to sleep: "I am afraid of dying."

Martha's major modes of adaptation which seemed to have arisen in response to the flood experience as described in 1974 could be categorized as follows.

*Being a hard worker:* Martha said she was working harder at school and that this helped her forget the horrors of the flood and to feel less depressed. At the time of the interview she was receiving straight As, a better performance than prior to the flood.

*Assuming an adult role:* Martha's parents were described as depressed since the flood. Martha said she was trying to make more adultlike decisions on her own because of this. In relationship to her boyfriend, Martha had become a caretaker but was ambivalent about the burden this presented.

*Preoccupation with death as an attempt to overcome the fear of death:* Although Martha's fear of death was near-phobic, it also could be described adaptively as an attempt magically to overcome the fear of death through constant vigilance.

Dynamically, Martha's premorbid flood development suggested a rather dependent, insecure child who had been struggling consciously and successfully to achieve a more outgoing and independent status. Following the flood, Martha's life and world constricted and assumed an aura of danger and uncertainty as her community and family supports crumbled. Also, considerable survivor guilt was occasioned by the remarkable lack of injury to the 70 family members present in the valley. A religious explanation was sought for this.

Martha's being a hard worker and keeping busy seemed to be an attempt to keep the depression, anxiety, and fears of death at bay. Her assumption of the caretaking role seemed to assuage the survivor guilt and also to combat the regressive pull occasioned by her feelings of helplessness and vulnerability caused by both the immediate flood experience and the subsequent lack of availability of her depressed and shaken parents. Most impressive was the pervasive fear of death seen in both conscious preoccupation and in repetitive dreams. This seemed overdetermined and to represent the reliving of the death exposure before and after the flood, an expression of survivor guilt, and the fear of uncontained regression in the face of the crumbling of Martha's usual community and family support systems. These various coping strategies appeared to provide only brittle protection. At the time of the 1974 assessment Martha was judged to be very symptomatic.

Returning to interview Martha in 1990, we found her a 3-years-married, 30-year-old woman eagerly awaiting us on her front porch. Upon entering Martha's home, we were immediately struck by the meticuously executed, extremely fancy Victorian style of decoration. Exquisite attention and planning had gone into every detail of her furnishings, creating the impression of a life-sized doll house. When we complimented Martha on the decoration of her home, she acknowledged it was her hobby and consumed much of her free time. She commented that she had started collecting things for her house during her late teenage years. She said she was a person who never threw anything out, but "We use things, never letting anything die."

When we asked Martha to tell us some things about herself and her current life, she stated that she was much calmer and happier since her marriage to her truck driver husband. Previously she had been moody and noted a tendency to drift from thing to thing. Boredom had set in after five years as a teacher and she was now back in school taking courses preparatory to entering pharmacy school. Martha mentioned that she had periods of depression and still became quite anxious when it rained.

When we asked Martha for her memories of the flood, considerable more detail emerged than was elicited during her 1974 interview. Martha herself was surprised about how much affect surfaced as she spoke with us. She commented that she never talked about the flood with anybody, although her parents and grandmother still talked about it frequently. She explained that she did not say anything to them about the flood because she felt that everybody else's stories were so much worse than hers. She still considered it strange that so many people died when her entire family survived. She wondered if her grandmother's continual praying led God to look out for their family.

When Martha thought about the flood, she mainly remembered the bodies of people floating by and her feelings of helplessness. She stated that as they lived far up the valley, they were not as involved in the flood as most other people. Her mother for years had feared that there would be a flood and because of this several years prior had moved the family from their house, which was close to the dam. At the time of the flood, this house was rented to another family, the mother of whom was killed in the flood.

Martha said that on the morning of the flood she had gone out by herself walking. She saw some cars moving in the water and went home and told her parents. This allowed them to save their own car. Afterward someone called their house and told them the dam had burst and that 80 percent of the people in that part of the valley were dead.

Martha had many relatives up the valley, including her grandmother and aunt who lived close to the dam. She and her parents anxiously waited for many hours with the fear that their own relatives had been killed.

Martha said that the worst thing she remembered seeing that day was a woman floating by holding a baby. She screamed for someone to help the woman, but no one did. Further downstream the woman was rescued, but the baby was dead. Martha especially remembered her helplessness at hearing the lady screaming for help and her not being able to do anything.

The day after the flood, Martha's father went up a route no one else knew about looking for people who might have been hurt. At the time she feared her father would not return. She also remembered the radio announcing the dead day after day following the flood. She kept learning of friends who had died.

At the conclusion of our interview Martha executed her flood drawing and tearfully recalled additional details. After the flood it had bothered her for several years that they were always finding body parts such as "hands and things" that had been lodged in different places. She remembered again the lady with the baby floating by and her shouting for people to get her out.

If we look at the modes of adaptation that were described in the 1974 interview and which seemed to be at least partially a response to the flood experience, our observations appear to indicate not only a persistence but a further consolidation of these mechanisms.

*Being a hard worker:* Martha described a chronic sense of boredom and restlessness. She tended to become depressed if she did not keep busy. The enormous energy that had so obviously gone into the details of the decoration of her home attested to her compulsivity. Notable in this regard was that the care in decorating seemed to be cosmetic and limited to the surface. The underlying structure of the house seemed to be in ill repair, "papered over."

*Assuming an adult role, taking care of others:* In a manner very reminiscent of her descriptions of her relationship with her boyfriend at age 16, Martha told us that her current husband of 3 years had a crippled leg. She said she only agreed to go out with him initially because he was crippled.

Reminiscent of her 1974 descriptions of herself as trying to make more adultlike decisions in response to the distress of her parents, Martha stated that several years previously her father after years of illness had an operation during which a tumor was discovered. While he was lying open on the operating table, the family had to decide whether to remove the tumor which would then necessitate a colostomy or to leave it alone which would likely have meant his death. Martha's mother and two sisters "went to pieces" while she was the one able to remain calm and make the decision to remove the tumor. She commented that she had always had less rapport with her father than her sisters because he resented her being "mother's little baby."

Martha's persistent ambivalence about the caretaking role surfaced when she was asked to describe a recent hassle in her life. She said she had taken in her brother-in-law who was an immature person and who wanted her to do everything for him as though she was his mother. This was hard because Martha was going to school at the time. She was able to tell him that he needed to take care of himself. She commented additionally that she had similar problems with her husband because of his handicap and the fact that his mother had previously done everything for him.

Further indication of Martha's caretaking was evident in her handling of the $10,000 flood settlement which she personally received. She stated that she gave this money to her parents to help them replace the home which had been lost in Man.

*Preoccupation with death as an attempt to overcome the fear of death:* At the time of her 1990 interview Martha remained preoccupied with death and admitted that she worried all the time about the people she cared about dying. She had had this worry about all her boyfriends after the flood and now had it about her husband being killed when he was out driving his truck.

Of the three patterns of coping described in 1974, it was this preoccupation with death which seemed to have undergone the most elaboration. Martha appeared to deal with these fears through merging them with religious beliefs in an afterlife and by cultivating what she described as her powers of premonition, "bad feelings" which "come over me." Martha seemed more reliant on this magic than she did in 1974, to the point where we felt her reality testing might be impaired.

For example, Martha described that three or four years ago she heard a car wreck and then saw a car go into the river. She was overcome by a feeling that she was "supposed to go over to the car" and said that she saw in her mind a visual image of a man drowning with his head caught under a rock. She felt that she was being sent by God to save him. She claimed that she searched and searched and finally did find a man who was caught under a rock and held his head above the water and saved him from drowning until other rescuers came along. Such premonitions were described to be fairly frequent.[6]

In Martha's dreams, a transformation of the death fear into a yearning for paradise emerged. She commented that in her recent dreams she is always happy and that whatever happens there is always a way out. She said she frequently dreamed about God. In one such dream he just appears to her as a light and says her name. She is very frightened and feels very small. She runs from him. He knows he is frightening her and so he pulls back and the light becomes much dimmer. She has the urge to run after him but fears that when she gets to him, she is going to die.

As regards the fragility or resilience of the adaptational styles in response to subsequent stresses, Martha reported being prone to the breakthrough of bouts of depression whenever she did not keep herself busy. She also commented that when it rained for three or four days in a row, she began to remember the flood and "fear doom."

In spite of these symptoms and Martha's occasional reliance on magical thinking, it appeared that the coping mechanisms described do by and large protect Martha from many of the symptoms of residual posttraumatic stress disorder. She was judged to be not significantly symptomatic on the U.C. protocol. Relying only on Martha's results on the U.C. study, we might have been tempted to conclude that the flood had indeed only had a minor and passing impact on the subsequent course of Martha's life. The impression we were left with from our experience in interviewing Martha was far different. Our data suggested that the flood had a powerful impact on the subsequent course of Martha's adolescent and adult development and had significantly contributed to the consolidation of her brittle characterological defensive patterns.

### ROSE

In 1974 Rose appeared to be a "quiet, expressionless, deadpan" 12-year-old who cried during the interview, especially in relation to her losing friends as a result of the flood (it is not clear whether this was as a result of relocation, death of sister's friend Mary Jane, other deaths, or all of these sources). She was frightened of the creek rising and anxious when "pictures" of the flood came to her unbidden.

Rose was the second of five siblings and the eldest girl living in a

---

6. As regards posttraumatic omens and prescience, see Terr (1984).

rented five-room house with mother at the time of the flood. The family's income in 1974 was $200 a week. When she was 8 years old, her father had moved away. Prior to the flood family functioning was marginal, with her older brother taking on some absent father functioning.

The flood experience itself had several terrifying features. When she first looked out the window, there was a "wall of water coming out of the stream." No one was prepared and the exit disorderly. When mother returned to the house for blankets, she fell and became trapped and older brother Tony pulled her away as she was sinking below the water level.

In the 1974 interview Rose dwelt on a dead baby being carried by a mother on her shoulders; and in the 1990 interview she dwelt on a dead baby caked with mud whom she saw at the temporary shelter. At the time of the flood, Rose did not feel protected by the adults. Subsequently, adults made no effort to explain what transpired or to share the meaning of the experience. Her anger and disgust with adults' responses were displaced onto the way adults were treating Tony. He was being threatened with legal charges for "stealing" rope to save lives in the rescue operation. Prominent in her response to the flood were themes of *regression, interrupted nurturance,* and *staying close to avoid harm.*

When asked about her wishes in 1974, she wished "to stay with mother," and "for mother to be better." When asked about her favorite animal, she spoke of being mother's "Persian cat whom mother could pet." In the Bird Fable she saw the baby bird as "able to fly so she would return to the tree where the mother bird was and help her build a new nest." In terms of career, she wanted to be a nurse or a teacher.

Rose's 1990 interview took place in her modest apartment in Man, West Virginia. As she sat by the open window of her kitchen and rocked and recounted her memories of Buffalo Creek, a sadness about her past and her present life was omnipresent. Rose kept the interviewer at some distance in terms of trust throughout. Nonetheless, she was sufficiently cooperative and in fact surprised both herself and us with the openness of some of her accounts.

In 1990, Rose was divorced and her two children, aged approximately 9 and 8, were her major focus of attention and life gratification. Phyllis, her daughter, was in the adjacent room as we talked. Rose's full-time occupation was looking after her children. She said that she spent most of her time in her kitchen where she was a good cook; but she often found herself just sitting and rocking and looking out of the window. She cried easily and heavily and thought of herself as being depressed. We agreed. She was actively troubled by sleeplessness and nightmares and specifically bothered by dark rainy days and by thunder, all of which preceded the dam collapse and flood.

The memory traces were of the flood beginning without warning. By then the flood had already reached a considerable height. Her image was of a mountain of water which was about to engulf them. Father was away from the home; mother and the six children left the house as best they could. While trying to gather blankets, mother was struck down by some object as she tried to leave the house. She was pulled from the house by her son and barely escaped. That first image of the rising waters was associated with absolute terror and the conviction that she was about to die. This conviction stayed with her even after the family was relocated in the junior high school where she described water seeping in through the edges of the building. She imagined that outside of the building the wall of water would still rise and that the walls would collapse and kill all inside. Rose and the rest of her family finally left in their pajamas without shoes. The next image which had stayed with her was that of a 2-year-old baby brought out of the flood, covered with mud and dead. The baby was later cleaned off and returned, carried like a sack of potatoes over the back of the man who had brought it in. That man and others were weeping and Rose, thinking in terms of the present, spoke of why was it that an innocent child was dead, how could people have done such a thing as to have created a dam which had broken and killed so many people. In fact, she had no idea what had caused the flood, and the thought passed through her mind that up the valley everyone must have turned on their faucets and created this huge mass of destruction. The single image of this 2-year-old infant who had died in the flood seemed to be a lifelong emblazoned mental scar which in retrospect she felt strongly influenced her subsequent life. This influence had something to do with her wish to become a school teacher. While it was a little difficult to establish the logical links here, two possibilities were suggested. (1) Teachers could somehow produce a generation of people who would build dams which would not collapse and cause such destruction. (2) Educated people might learn to find the words to describe the nature of their experiences and their emotions. What was so striking in this woman, even in this interview 17 years later, was the absence of the ability to put into words the emotional states that she felt or to understand the actual connections and causation of how one particular event led to another.

In describing her own mental mechanisms, Rose said that she buried things. These things were deep inside her and they never came out, neither the words nor the emotions, and these connected with deep sorrow and deep rage. Rose's was a grief that lacked words.

Rose's life trajectory did not move as she had anticipated. She did not become a teacher. In fact she dropped out of school in the 10th grade when she became pregnant. Fourteen months after the birth of Phyllis, she had her second child. Shortly thereafter the premature marriage ended badly. She now had a boyfriend who made a number of ventures into the area in which we were conducting the interview, I think largely to check to see if she was okay.

Rose remembered dreaming about the flood for a number of years and then the dreams began to dissipate. More recently, a remembered dream was that her little boy had gone out of the house and walked down the street where he was shot. Rose ran out and hurled herself on his body in an effort to contain the damage, although he was probably dead. (There was a hovering attentiveness to her children which was more than apparent in the interview and the interactions around the house.)

Rose's drawing was rather neat and schematic, almost serene; but she explained that the wavy lines at the top of the drawing which looked like mountain tops were the top of the wall of water. Floating on and beneath the water were two bodies, the faces drawn in with downturned frowns which she described as "dead bodies floating by." The two houses, her own and that of a relative, had water up to the roof line. Although drawn from the hillside perspective, the picture conveyed no sense of safety. The danger was not bounded or contained. The response to the Bird Fable was that the mother bird flew down to the baby bird, then provided safety for her (a reversal of her response in 1974).

The general impression was of a depressed 29-year-old divorced woman with little to look forward to in her life save for her mothering activities. She was overtly depressed in the interview and had neither processed successfully nor contained successfully the traumatic images of the dam collapse and flood of 1972.

Rose had sought to make something positive out of the flood, to become a school teacher and help children to understand about words. Instead her life had been one in which she more passively moved with events (pregnancy, marriage), committed her time and energy to maintaining a safe home, but drove away those who were close by her excessive hovering. She was unable to put the court settlement money to a permanent use.

In the flood experience, Rose was also carried away by events and became the recipient of somewhat ineffective care (mother was overwhelmed; brother not up to the task; kids on their own). The completion of the Bird Fable still reflected unfulfilled longings of the child as paramount.

Life had remained for Rose a permanent anticipation of the flood's return. She stared out her kitchen window as though surveying the landscape for a rising creek; she hovered over her children, dreaming that her son would be shot if he went out of her sight. Those whose job it was to protect her (current boyfriend) appeared interested but perhaps not quite up to the task like her older sibling in the flood.

In 1991 as well as 1974, the themes of *regression, interrupted nurturance,* and *staying close to avoid harm* were dominant. Rose remained symptomatic in connection with the flood. She was frightened by rain, looked out her window listlessly, and continued to have sad and frightful memories.

Her current boyfriend hovered about the building as her interview proceeded and as she hovered over her children. A current dream repeated anxiety over separation, with death as the price for straying too far. Most strikingly, her drawing continued to depict her as beneath the water level of the flood.

## DISCUSSION

As we trace the fate of the flood-related coping responses recognized in our 1974 explorations as these responses consolidate into more enduring patterns of adaptation and perhaps even stable character traits, we can begin to discern a spectrum of "adaptational possibilities." The particular way in which the individual's coping response to the trauma consolidates or does not consolidate appears to influence the ultimate resiliency or rigidity of the adult personality, the response to subsequent trauma, and the sense of meaning or purpose derived from life. The failure to elaborate stable, trauma-related, adaptive patterns would appear to leave the individual vulnerable to subsequent chronic PTSD. From another perspective, the absence of PTSD at long-term follow-up, far from indicating that the trauma did not have a significant lasting impact, may rather imply that highly significant and idiosyncratic effects need be sought, not in the review of symptoms, but through exploration of the enduring patterns of adaptation and their origins.

For Helen, the trauma appears to have been largely *digested.* Her "death dream" suggests still active remnants, but, as observed, these are well contained. What is more striking is her overall self-confidence, decisiveness, and resiliency played out against a background of trust that people will and do provide and protect in times of exigency. For

Helen, the experience of the flood, although having left clear evidence of its traumatic impact at the time of the 1972 interview, appears ultimately to have presented an opportunity for consolidating adaptive traits of compensation through industry and loculating negative affect as well as to have reinforced the positive narcissism derived from feelings of being loved and well protected by her family.

At the other extreme from Helen on our spectrum is Rose, who evidences *no effective coping responses* to the flood trauma either in 1972 or in the follow-up in 1992. Indeed, of our four subjects, Rose was the only one who had significant residual PTSD symptomatology in the University of Cincinnati 1988 study. Unlike Helen, Rose felt totally unprotected at the time of the flood. Family functioning appeared marginal before the flood, and during the flood her mother fell, was trapped, and required rescuing. In both 1972 and 1990 assessments, we see persistent themes of regression, interrupted nurturance, and anxious hovering, all a seeming perpetuation of the traumatic state itself. Dramatic in Rose's 1990 drawing is her depiction of herself as beneath the water level of the flood, the position occupied by her mother in her 1972 description.

Intermediate stations in our adaptive spectrum are occupied by Henry and Martha. For Henry, the most prominent theme emerging in both 1972 and 1990 assessments is his observation of and *identification* with his father's response to the flood, both at the time and in the ensuing years. Like his father, he copes by assuming the mantle of male responsibility as it was presented to him. This cloak weighs heavily upon him and imposes burdens of anxiety, depression, and restriction of choice, but he also gains through it a sense of pride, strength, and fulfillment through his ability to assume his station in the multigenerational male tradition. Subsequent traumatic events, of which there are many, are borne in a similar spirit which further reflects this sense of endurance and community, as evidenced by his response to the many strikes and layoffs he has weathered.

For Martha, such a sense of evident purpose and historical continuity is lacking in the presence of an even more *rigid character structure*. Interviewers were immediately struck by her compulsivity, which seemingly represents a further ossification of the "being a hard worker" mechanism that allowed her to push away the horrors and the depression after the flood. In her memories of the event, she is a caretaker, guarding the family. This trait too only solidifies as she now worries over her parents, her husband, and sometimes his relatives. Anxiety is poorly contained and death imagery is ever present in her dreams. Martha's watchfulness for the next disaster assumes near-psychotic proportions in her visions and premonitions which seem clearly to recapitulate fragments of the flood experience. By and large, however, the extreme rigidity does safeguard the integrity of Martha's personality, with no overt breakdowns and only occasional breakthroughs of more intense anxiety and depression. Of note is Martha's eagerness to talk to the interviewers about the flood and the freshness of the associated affect. Her unfortunate guilt has for years kept her isolated from other family members during their frequent discussions of the flood and perhaps thereby precluded her potential for better integrating the experience.

For all four of these survivors, the family's response to the flood and its aftermath as reflected in their 1990 narrative accounts appear closely tied to the evolution of the adaptive patterns which subsequently emerged. Helen felt protected; she now feels trusting and secure. Henry watched his father, both his grief and his determination, and he identified. Martha's parents were remote; she was the look-out then and still is. Rose's family nearly drowned, and now she barely treads water. These findings would seem to correlate with earlier Buffalo Creek studies that demonstrated psychopathology in the children to be significantly related to parental psychopathology (Gleser et al., 1981).

In addition, we might consider viewing our subjects' 1990 descriptions of their family's 1972 flood responses as "early memories" in the clinical sense. From this perspective, these memories as well as the entire 90-minute interviews from which they are drawn would be seen as condensations, the unraveling of which might reveal rich information about the children's experience of their family throughout their early development and the internalizations that took place. We might even wonder how often a family's response to trauma as experienced and later remembered might serve as a "psychodynamic snapshot" which captures crucial aspects of the family's influence on the child's development and internalizations. Further elucidation of the significance of these memories of the family's trauma response and of the other "clinical impressions" gleaned from our interviews would require a much more intense, psychoanalytically informed investigation than was possible within the scope of this study.

A final note in our considerations of the evolution of our subject's coping responses into stable character structures: all of the subjects that we have described were adolescents at the time of the flood (except for Rose who was 10). We might question whether the adolescent period of development is a particularly sensitive time for such transformation from coping response to character structure. Such questions are consistent with Peter Blos's observations that the central developmental task of the late adolescent period is character consolidation, which includes the automatization of idiosyncratic ways of dealing with stress (1962, p. 129). Blos points out not only that the role of trauma in character formation is central but also that it is important to look beyond posttraumatic symptoms to posttraumatic meaning:

> A character trait which forms slowly at the end of adolescence owes its special quality to a fixation on a particular trauma or component of a trauma . . . focal traumata furnish a relentless force which propels the young adult towards a certain way of life which he comes to feel as his very own. . . . Remnants of trauma relate the present to a dynamic past and establish that historical continuity in the ego which accounts for a sense of certainty, direction, and harmony between feeling and action [1962, p. 134].

Such observations are consistent with our findings in the children of Buffalo Creek.

## BIBLIOGRAPHY

BLOS, P. (1962). *On Adolescence.* New York: Free Press.
ERIKSON, K. (1976). *Everything in Its Path.* New York: Simon & Schuster.
GLESER, G. C., GREEN, B. L., & WINGET, C. N. (1978). Quantifying interview data on psychic impairment of disaster survivors. *J. Nerv. Ment. Dis.,* 166:209–216.
——— ——— ——— (1981). *Prolonged Psychosocial Effects of Disaster.* New York: Academic Press.
GREEN, B. L., GRACE, M. C., CRESPO DA SILVA, L., & GLESER, G. C. (1983). Use of the psychiatric evaluation form to quantify children's interview data. *J. Consult. Clin. Psychol.,* 51:353–359.
——— KOROL, M. S., GRACE, M. C., VARY, M. G., LEONARD, A. C., GLESER, G. C., & SMITSON-COHEN, S. (1991). Children and disaster. *J. Acad. Child Adol. Psychiat.,* 30:945–951.
——— LINDY, J. D., GRACE, M. C., GLESER, G. C., LEONARD, A. C., KOROL, M. S., & WINGET, C. (1990). Buffalo Creek survivors in the second decade. *Amer. J. Orthopsychiat.,* 60:40–54.
LYONS, J. A. (1987). Post-traumatic stress disorder in children and adolescents. *Develpm. Behav. Ped.,* 8:349–356.
MCNALLY, R. J. (1992). What stressors produce DSM III-R post-traumatic stress disorder in children? In *Post Traumatic Stress Disorder in Review,* ed. J. Davidson & E. Foa. Washington, D.C.: American Psychiatric Press.
——— (1993). Assessment of PTSD in children. *J. Consul. Clin. Psychol.* (in press).
NEWMAN, C. J. (1976). Children of disaster. *Amer. J. Psychiat.,* 133:306–312.

PYNOOS, R. S. (1989). Personal communication.

————— (1990). Post-traumatic stress disorder in children and adolescents. In *Psychiatric Disorders in Children and Adolescents,* ed. B. D. Garfinkel, G. A. Carlson, & E. B. Welber. Philadelphia: Saunders, pp. 48–63.

TERR, L. C. (1979). Children of Chowchilla. *Psychoanal. Study Child,* 34:600– 603.

————— (1984). Time and trauma. *Psychoanal. Study Child,* 39:633–665.

————— (1985). Psychic-trauma in children and adolescents. *Psychiat. Clin. North America,* 8:815–835.

————— (1990). *Too Scared to Cry.* New York: Harper & Row.

————— (1991). Childhood traumas. *Amer. J. Psychiat.,* 148:10–20.

TITCHENER, J. L. & KAPP, F. T. (1976). Family and character change at Buffalo Creek. *Amer. J. Psychiat.,* 133:295–299.

————— ————— & WINGET, C. N. (1976). The Buffalo Creek syndrome. In *Emergency and Disaster Management.* Bowie, Maryland: Charles Press Publishers.

# Reflections on a Year's Psychotherapy with a Psychotic Man

## JENIFER A. NIELDS, M.D.

*A year's psychotherapy with a psychotic man during the author's residency training is described in detail. Fundamental questions regarding the patient's potential for therapeutic change are raised. These questions concerning this specific patient are then generalized to broader research questions regarding the efficacy of treatment for the severely and persistently mentally ill.*

WHAT FIRST INTERESTED ME ABOUT MR. B. WAS THE FACT THAT HE WAS intensely purposeful, keenly intelligent, and at the same time flagrantly delusional. He was committed to the work, and there were things he desperately wanted to accomplish. He was also terrified: terrified of me, of starting with a new doctor, of what the work would uncover. I, too, was anxious, being new to my role as a psychotherapist, and was a bit overwhelmed by the patient's intensity and craziness.

This paper describes the progress of our work: how my understanding of him developed and how he changed or seemed to change over the course of the year. The first section offers a portrayal of this imaginative and wildly psychotic man: the ironies, frustrations, and private tragedies that constituted his life and the perceptiveness and tenderness that were buried in and behind his florid delusions. The second section raises some questions about the work: how and whether it helped—or did not help—and what sort of therapeutic gains this patient might have achieved under optimal circumstances. In the con-

---

Dr. Nields is in private practice.

I would like to thank Sidney Phillips for his encouragement, thoughtful suggestions, and careful readings of many drafts of this paper.

cluding remarks, this case study is used to raise more general questions about psychoanalytic research into the efficacy of the institutional treatment of the severely and persistently mentally ill.

## The Clinical Work

### EARLY PHASE

Before I met Mr. B., I was informed by my supervisor that he was an interesting patient, very intelligent but chronically delusional, and that this year they were trying something new regarding his treatment. For the prior several years, Mr. B. had requested a female therapist; his request had been denied because it was felt that his transference to a woman tended to become too intense: the last time he had been with a female therapist, he had been hospitalized several times. The previous year, with a male therapist, had been a relatively stable one for Mr. B., and since he remained adamant that he wanted and needed to work with a woman, his request was granted.

A further introduction to Mr. B. took the form of an elaborate off-service note by his former therapist. From it I learned that Mr. B. was a veteran in his 40s diagnosed with chronic paranoid schizophrenia. He had had his first psychotic break while in the military. He had been first in his class in high school, had been on the hockey team, and had had three years of college where he was a straight A student in science. His mother had died when he was 7 years old, and his father only a few years ago. He lived alone and audited science courses at a local university. Though he had few social contacts, he did have a supportive brother who lived out of state and whom he saw occasionally. He spent most of his time at home alone, working on his studies insofar as he was able. His studies consisted of constructing and writing voluminously about various theories relating to science and medicine. His theories were elaborate, intrinsically logical, even ingenious, and markedly delusional. They had, however, caught his therapist's interest enough to have been reported in some detail in the off-service note. Many pages of his writing had also been included in the chart. In addition, there were copies of correspondence between Mr. B. and the *Physics Quarterly,* a scientific journal to which Mr. B. had submitted some of his papers. These letters consisted mainly of Mr. B.'s reproaches of the journal for its unwillingness to publish his work or for its lack of response to his letters. The early letters from the journal were polite refusals but the later ones were ominous, forbidding him ever to be seen on their property. Mr. B. had been arrested for trespassing in his effort to get the journal to heed his requests for publication.

One of Mr. B.'s ideas involved a proposed form of chemotherapy in which lecithin would be used to link polar and nonpolar agents, thereby enabling penetration of the drug into both water-based and fatty tissue, such as breast. Other ideas included the effects of mescaline on brain chemistry, the uses of nitrous oxide in psychotherapy, the effects of particle spin on planetary motion, and various ways to save the world, which he felt to be in imminent danger of being blown up.

It was clear that Mr. B.'s former therapist had liked him and that Mr. B. had been satisfied with the year's experience. In fact, he had stayed out of the hospital entirely for the first time in many years. Despite this progress, two issues remained sources of dissatisfaction: one was that Mr. B. wanted a female therapist, and the other was that he wanted a therapist who would get his ideas published.

At our first meeting, Mr. B. introduced himself to me in a way that was in keeping with what I had read about him. He told me he had seen Dr. A. for one year, and that experience had been good. He reiterated that he needed a woman therapist. He explained that his mother had died of breast cancer when he was 7 years old. Consequently, he had grown up with his father, brother, and many male cousins. He had had a fiancée before his stint in the military, but had had a psychotic break there when she stopped answering his letters. He reported that he lived alone, and spent a great deal of time talking on TV and radio call-in shows. He told me what medications he was taking, that he had a tremor of the head and hands, and that he had wires in his brain. When I asked him what he wanted from therapy, he replied that he wanted help for himself and for mankind and that he wanted hope. Asked how I could help, he said, "I want you to write articles on double-dating, nitrous oxide, mescaline and heroin."

We talked about his hopes and fears for the upcoming year, and he mentioned some issues that proved prominent in our year's work. One was the question of whether or not I would understand him and his concern about his capacity to communicate. His struggle with this latter issue was to take many forms. His calling in to radio and TV shows, for instance, was an attempt to communicate, to break his isolation. Even his careful and extensive elucidation of his theories to me in sessions and his efforts toward getting them published were, at least in part, efforts at communication. He wanted this to be a good first session. When I asked if he had felt understood in the past, he replied, "Seldom." I inquired when, and he said, "When the physics professor talked about time and motion." I wondered aloud if Dr. A. had understood him, and he replied, "He didn't write the articles. Heaven is for 4's, Paradise is for 2's," and then said that he got very down when he feared no one would publish his work, and that he could use some nitrous oxide right now.

His responses in this first session indicated a fear of losing control, of being overwhelmed by his feelings, of exploding and being destroyed. He suggested that these fears might turn out to be specifically related to me, but that on the other hand I might be able to help him with them in a way that would turn out to be very beneficial. He said he thought I was "very sane, very in control." When I asked whether or not this was helpful, he said, "It's partly helpful: that you're in control . . . and partly not helpful: that you make me feel out of control." He said, "I might have to be strapped down and given mescaline because I have a lot of feelings that I haven't expressed in a long time. I have fears of being used to trigger a nuclear war in some way." His persistent request for a female therapist who would be the catalyst for the release of feeling also expressed his hope that bringing out his feelings would do him good. He hoped that I would help him become "less bionic, more biological."

An excerpt from our third session gives a sense of what our early dialogue was like and the manner in which Mr. B. introduced, in delusional or quasi-delusional language, clues regarding the issues that concerned him. His responses to my interpretations tended to be oblique, sometimes suggesting that I was on the right track, but at other times his comments were entirely obscure to me, suggesting that I had been off-base. At this point in the therapy, we spoke like children engaged in parallel play: we were conscious of one another's presence while not fully relating to each other. We interacted in a way that was indirect and seemingly uninvolved, as if to disavow the intensity of the issues at hand.

Early in the session, for example, Mr. B. began ruminating aloud about the "four options"—his thoughts as to how the present crisis in world affairs might be handled. At this time, I was still only marginally acquainted with this theory. He opened the session by saying,

Mr. B.: I've been bionic since '76 [when he had his breakdown] and since then there have been electronic sounds in my head. They've been softer recently, since I started seeing you. I don't want to be bionic. The Fourth Option is to Do Nothing. There are four options. The Third is Thermonuclear Holocaust.

Dr. N.: Sounds scary.

Mr. B.: Less so if you keep it abstract.

Dr. N.: Is that why you talk so much about physics: because feelings are scary?

Mr. B.: Do you know why I chose physics over medicine? Because particles don't feel [clearly I was on track, but then his meaning became obscure to me; perhaps he wanted to keep both me and his feelings at a manageable distance]. The Second Option is Conquest. The Western world destroys the Third World by crucifixion. The First Option is the U.N. The Fourth Option, Do Nothing, is the same as the Third, Thermonuclear Holocaust.

Dr. N.: So you have to work very hard to keep things from falling apart.

Mr. B.: But the Third World might not cooperate. Hence we have to threaten them with conquest. The U.N. solution would probably work if we just threaten. What makes me angry is rendezvous with mistresses. Why not double-date, like the Gorbachevs and the Reagans?

Later in the session, he spoke about his first psychotic break: "You know I saw God: male and female, a couple, and their eyes were like the setting sun, the optic nerve emitting light. I walked away in shock. I think the higher Gods come in foursomes. After I saw them, I was crucified; the transducers in my head were turned on, and my brain was coming out of my skull." Following this experience, he said, he became "bionic" and subject to the mind and will of higher powers: "They are the scientists; I'm just a technician. I get all my ideas from them."

Thus, early in our work, Mr. B. seemed quite strange to me. He was intense, hard to follow, and there was much he wanted to convey. But the rapid pacing of his ideas, linked by obscure logic, left me not knowing how to respond. His way of speaking gave him a disconnected, machinelike quality. This quality was intensified by the fact that his head shook as he spoke, and he tended to stare until the whites of his eyes showed when he was anxious.

Gradually, however, it struck me how certain of his theories (three in particular) related to aspects of his life history and were efforts to provide solutions to his most pressing life problems. Although he set them forth in the language of science or politics and expressed them as generalizations, I began to glimpse the intensely personal origins of his ratiocinations and thereby became able to respond and interpret in a way that felt more direct, less disconnected. I began to see how the sheer logic of the way he put his theories together would seem to him irrefutable, and how the intensity of the experiences they were based on explained why his theories were so vitally important to him. The urgency with which he explicated them became understandable, no longer off-putting.

The most prominent theory involved an invention, "milk pills," which, used properly, could save the world. These were to be made of oxytocin, prolactin, and human chorionic gonadotropin. He wanted me, being a doctor, to help manufacture and market them. The combination of hormones was designed to induce lactation in women, all of whom should take them. The lactation, in turn, would provide a form of birth control, thereby solving the population problem. Ideally, each woman would have just one child. Milk pills would be protective against breast cancer, the incidence of which was lower in women with a history of breast-feeding. At the same time, these pills would bring out loving, maternal feelings in women. Such a transformation would be most beneficial since the world, given all the warfare that existed, was clearly suffering from a lack of tender feelings. Furthermore, so his theory went, the women, when they weren't nursing their babies, could nurse their husbands. This would help counteract the husbands' jealousy of their children. And, of course, he added, female doctors could nurse their patients.

Mr. B.'s mother, as mentioned above, had died of breast cancer. She seemed to have been distant and uninvolved with him. He did not recall physical tenderness from her and, much later in our work, Mr. B. said, "I don't know if I was breast-fed, but somehow I feel sure I wasn't." The second of two boys, Mr. B. was born at a time when his mother was clearly ill-equipped to deal with another child. The world, he later said, was in need of the "milk of human kindness." And Mr. B. wanted my help to become less bionic, more biological, that is, to seem less under the control of mechanistic forces outside of himself, more integrated in his sense of himself and his feelings. He wanted me to love him. Later on he would say that our therapy was good because we could talk about things as important as *milk*, and given that, and my understanding of that, why in the world wouldn't I go ahead and get his ideas *published?*

Another of Mr. B.'s theories was about double-dating. This one was not as fully developed as the one about milk pills, but was nevertheless of great importance to him. Double-dating was to be adopted as a general practice in order to dispel the threat of nuclear war and thereby save the world. The prototype of such a practice was the Gorbachevs and the Reagans, whose friendly meetings were already advancing the cause of world peace. Double-dating as a solution to the world's problems was often the subject of his calls to radio talk shows. On a more personal level, double-dating would make the world a safer place by minimizing harmful jealousies while maximizing the potential for satisfying encounters. He and I, for instance, could double-date without threatening my marriage or arousing my husband's anger against him. His fiancée could, perhaps, have seen someone else while he was in the service and still have included him in her life when he returned.

The third of the theories with which he was most preoccupied had to do with "Pairing of the children." He thought the world would be much better off if boys and girls were paired off, as "little couples," from the age of 5. Each couple would have one child, and then double-date and share the children of other couples. The significance in his life of this theory he made quite clear. He had had a very painful and lonely adolescence and thought people would be better off not having to go through such experiences—*ever!* Furthermore, aside from the loss of his mother, the most painful experiences of his life had been those times when he was rejected by a girlfriend: first, by his high school girlfriend, Lucy, and then, in the service, by his fiancée Carla, after which he had had his psychotic break. If he and Lucy had been paired up from childhood, then he wouldn't have had to lose her and perhaps would never have gone psychotic.

As I began to see in his delusional theories the personal concerns that motivated them, he began to seem more human to me. For all his craziness and, at times, grandiosity, he also had a certain perspective and humor about himself. He related various incidents that indicated his awareness of how strange he must seem and how he put people off. There was a tragic side as well to this awareness. He had said, on one occasion, "My intelligence makes my illness more sharp." And, I suppose, his insight and awareness of his potential made it seem more tragic. He noticed how people generally responded when he tried to explain himself to them: "One word out of my mouth and they think I'm crazy." He described an occasion when he had felt with particular poignancy the self-defeating effects of his craziness: he had been invited to dinner (a very rare event) by a young couple who had recently had a baby. The wife was a nursing mother. Everything had been going along smoothly; they had had a sumptuous three-course meal; he had enjoyed himself. "But then," he exclaimed in extreme frustration, "I had to open my big mouth and ask her for some *milk!*" It went without saying that the young mother had not taken kindly to the request and that it had put a damper on the evening. He could see in retrospect what he had done: how he had sabotaged himself; but his longing at the time, like his regret now, must have been overwhelming.

## MIDPOINT

Exactly halfway through the year, a crisis occurred that proved to be a turning point in our work and the beginning of a new mode of relating that was to characterize our interactions during the second half of the year. What came up in the therapy was the prospect of the ending of our work together six months later. At a deeper level, this raised the issue of abandonment by a central female figure in his current life as well as recalling abandonments by women at crucial junctures in the past. These past abandonments, including, prototypically, the loss of his mother, had been so traumatic to him that he had been prone to lose touch with reality. Recall that his first psychotic break had occurred in the context of his fiancée not responding to his letters. The result of our work subsequent to this crisis was that he was able to negotiate my vacation in March and the ending of our work together in June without decompensating or losing touch with his feelings. He was also able to anticipate with hopefulness his relationship to a new female therapist the following year. What emerged during and subsequent to the crisis was a change in our communication patterns from the parallel-play type in which we interacted only obliquely and each spoke his or her own language, to one that was often very direct, clear, coherent, and intense, and in which he spoke in an undisguised way about his feelings and life experiences.

The crisis was set off by my mentioning, in late January, that we had reached the midpoint of our work, and that in June our work together would be ending; he would have a new doctor in July. He responded by saying that June seemed a trillion years away and that my mind worked strangely. The next session, however, he spent talking anxiously about thermonuclear holocaust and euthanasia. In the middle of the next week, he called me in a panic. Voices were telling him to tell me he had faked his army records, and that if I believed that, he would lose an eye (I?). He was terrified lest he be called a fake or used as a football to set off a nuclear war. He was feeling suicidal. We spoke back and forth over the telephone in the manner that characterized our dialogues at that point in the therapy: indirectly, as if in different languages, but with at least a rudimentary awareness of one another's meaning. I remarked that his panic over nuclear war had arisen when I mentioned the prospect of our being split apart in June. I wondered aloud whether he feared that he was being toyed with and passed along—like a football— from doctor to doctor, as if our interactions held no personal meaning, as if he were unimportant. I wondered if he thought that I regarded the pain he had gone through in the service in the course of his break-down as insubstantial. I asked him if he felt he needed to be in the hospital. He responded with reiterations of his fears, but his urgency abated over the course of the conversation. At first he thought he might need hospitalization, but later he was able to assure me of his safety and agreed to increase the dosage of his antipsychotic medication for the next few days, until our next appointment.

He came in to his next session reporting that he had felt better after composing a paper. He brought me a copy of what he had written, which consisted of an outline of his "Soviet American Plan for Peace" and his "United Nations Plan." He had typed his thoughts out neatly, in outline form:

Soviet American Plan for Peace

To encourage large scale peaceful Soviet American trade:
1. Large-scale cultural trade
2. Large-scale industrial trade
3. Large-scale scientific trade
4. Large-scale technological trade
5. Large-scale medical trade
6. Large-scale educational trade
7. Tourism

and: Have U.S. government agents double-date their Soviet counterparts. Unify Nato and Warsaw Pact Nations into one organization.

The second part of Mr. B.'s paper, the "United Nations Plan," included meticulously stipulated reallocations of funds currently spent on weapons, to be used instead for things such as "chemical defense," "biochemistry," and "automation"; it also included a system for selling votes: "fifty million dollars per vote per year and five billion dollars per veto as a flat rate per veto," with profits going to the U.N. He concluded by saying, "The only way to not only prevent the extinction of the human species, but also bring wealth, peace, good health, and long life to us all is to start by having the superpowers love each other and thus maintain a lasting, persistent, and true peace with each other and globally as well."

He affirmed, in response to my questioning, that putting his thoughts onto paper, organizing them and typing them up, made the world seem more "orderly" and helped him to feel more safe. In this case, he had been worrying about thermonuclear holocaust, that the world might be blown up, but felt better after typing up plans for a solution. This took the edge off his panic and averted his suicidal despair.

We continued our parallel-play type dialogue, but eventually, in the course of this session, he began to respond more directly to my questions, to speak more explicitly about feelings and life events. This constituted a striking change. In the past, although he could speak quite coherently about science, about things that were emotionally neutral, and could recite aspects of his history, whenever he was feeling threatened or upset about something he would resort to delusional language.

After this crisis, he seemed to have developed greater flexibility. He continued to revert to delusional thinking when he felt overwhelmed or seriously misunderstood, but this came to be, to an increasing degree, the exception rather than the rule.

I again related his worry about the world being blown up to the announcement of my leaving in June. He reiterated his concern that he not be considered a fake and that I not think his military records had been faked. I acknowledged that the breakdown he had experienced while in the service had been very real and very painful, to which he assented. I asked him if that had been the most painful experience of his life, and he said no: the most painful experience had been losing his high school girlfriend. He then went on to reflect that this had been like losing his mother twice. I mentioned that he would be losing me in June, but getting a new doctor. He requested that his new doctor be a woman, stating again that June seemed a long way away, and then lapsed into his less direct mode of interacting, musing to himself at the end of the session: "I think I'm the Eighth Christ."

Mr. B. arrived for his next session, again having found relief after gathering his thoughts and typing them up. The paper he brought in, this time untitled, was unlike anything he had shown me in the past. It was only marginally delusional, and was for the most part clearly connected to reality, to his feelings, and to his present situation. Whereas the others referred to world affairs and were addressed to no one in particular, this paper was about him and was addressed, specifically, to me. The writing of it, instead of externalizing and projecting his feelings, seemed to involve an active remembering and reliving of past traumatic experiences in the light of his present, threatened loss. This second paper was, in a sense, a formulation and clarification of the themes we had touched on in the previous session.

> Why losing Lucy *is worse*. Losing Lucy *wasn't* worse.
> I *want* to remember Lucy.
> I *Don't* want to remember the service. I *Don't* want to remember the torture [Arizona State Hos.]. I *Don't* want to remember the (bionic) psychological warfare. You experienced a taste of the (bionic) psychological warfare.
> *I was very strong when I lost Lucy.*
> *I wasn't as strong when I went into basic training. I lost Carla when I went into basic training. She ignored my letters.* I went absolutely crazy in Basic Training. I thereafter in the military hospital thought I was sane and everyone else in the service crazy. This included my psychiatrist. I did have a severe nervous breakdown in basic training which I believe was a natural reaction to being forced to learn to murder other human beings.

*I don't want to be a bionic toy.*

I need your help and I need psychiatry for psychotherapy as well as for medication.

*Please don't pull your love out on me.* I AM REAL.

During this session, Mr. B. talked for the first time about his mother as he remembered her when she was alive. He went on to say, "It was very lonely growing up without a mother. I basically had to bring myself up." We talked about what he had written. When I asked him, in reference to the last line of his paper, what pulling my love out might mean, he said, for example, believing the voices that told him to tell me he'd faked his military records. Although I did not know what he meant by this at the time, it was clear that something about his experience of me enabled him to feel "real" and to reject his psychotic version of reality. This point is complex and crucial and will be addressed below, along with other points relevant to these two pieces of Mr. B.'s writing.

Over the subsequent months, Mr. B. spoke with increasing directness about issues that were prominent in his life, both past and present. He talked about his mother: how even before she became ill, she had been remote, had not shown physical tenderness, had not shown affection. Mr. B. related more of the details of his relationship with his high school girlfriend, their physical relationship, his concern that there was something not right about him, even back then. He told about his current "girlfriend," Susan, whom he had met in a mental hospital and who was hospitalized and hallucinating, and about being made angry when the father of someone he had met at school forbade her ever to see him. He talked about his feelings for me. We talked together about how he would cope when I went away for three weeks, and how this would be a kind of rehearsal for when I left for good in June.

ENDING

As the June transition approached, we talked about the ending of our work together and about his hopes for his new doctor. We spoke about how my leaving would be similar in some ways to his past losses of Lucy and Carla, but how it would also be different. He asked me details about where I would be going. He then reflected that he had been devastated when he lost Lucy and could not afford to be devastated again. He asserted that he loved me, but that he would be able to cope when I left because he was "more mature" now than when he lost Lucy. Asked what that meant, he said, "Able to deal with pain." The parting was indeed painful, but, the January crisis past, he did not lose hold of reality in anticipating the parting in June. The talk of thermonuclear holocaust had, for the most part, abated, and there were no more instances when he feared he might need to go into the hospital. He continued, at times, to speak in global terms, but easily made the transition to more personal expressions. In general he expressed satisfaction with what he had accomplished over the year, having successfully weathered some difficult times and having been vindicated in his insistence on being assigned to a female doctor.

There was one issue, however, which remained unresolved between us until sometime during the last month of our work. This was the issue of the publishing of his ideas—specifically that I should aid him in such publication. The resolution of this issue required my understanding more fully what it represented to him and, as in the case of any of his delusional ideas, conveying this understanding in such a way that he knew he had been heard. This took me a long time. In general, I was direct with Mr. B., but when he asked me point-blank whether I would publish his writings or write about his ideas, I became evasive. Early on, I told him that I had my hands full with the job I had. As the year wore on and he became more insistent, I became more and more ill at ease about the issue. There was a lot I could honor in what he said, yet I dreaded having to articulate the plain, hard facts of the situation: that the idea, for instance, that milk pills could save the world was nonsense. His theories, while eloquently expressive of his experience, while logical and ingenious in their own way, were invalid as science, useless as medicine. His intelligence was conveyed in them, but so also were his lack of medical education and his flagrantly delusional thinking. No scientific or medical journal would print them. No one would take them seriously. Such a disclosure would, I thought, have been devastating to him and our relationship, in that it would have suggested that what he was or what I thought him to be, ultimately, was a mere crazy man, his ideas useless, senseless, delusional ravings. It might have made all my affirmation and interest seem like pretense or condescension. Yet I felt there was some genuine but as yet unarticulated purpose to his insistence on this issue. What, then, I wondered, made the act of writing and the hope of publication so critical to Mr. B.?

Put quite simply, the writing and hoped-for publishing of his papers were a way, partly real and partly metaphorical, of achieving what he needed in order to survive. He needed to find order in his inner world, and he needed to find a way to connect with other people. To a large degree, the act of writing served the former function, and the hope of publishing his ideas was expressive of the latter.[1]

At times, Mr. B.'s thoughts and feelings constituted a terrifying jumble. The act of organizing his thoughts and writing them down served to make the underlying chaos of his feelings seem more manageable. A paper such as the "Soviet American Plan for Peace" provided a solution, in a metaphorical realm, for the problem he faced, a fear of annihilation, and therefore gave him a temporary feeling of relief and stability. Mr. B. himself emphasized that his writing helped in that it created "order"; through his writing he achieved coherence: his ideas as set forth in his papers were intrinsically logical, even though they were also largely delusional.

The issue of communication, of connectedness, was a life-and-death issue for him. It seemed most often to have been a feeling of isolation: of being cut off, disconnected from the world and from reality—and, by corollary, from himself—that caused him to become suicidal. He would feel better when he succeeded in making contact: with a radio show host, with me or, through his writing, with an imagined readership. He wrote to the *Physics Quarterly* once, after they had rejected one of his papers, "Publish or perish." They, understandably, took this as a threat and called in the FBI to see whether or not Mr. B. was a dangerous person. He explained that what he had meant was: "If no one will publish my work, *I* shall perish." Hence, the whole issue of publication became understandable as a metaphor for his need to find a way to communicate coherently, to connect with the world; his requests to therapists to get his ideas published became understandable as a metaphor for his need for them to help him in this task. Without this connection to the world—to reality, to other people—and without something of himself or his meaning being accepted, validated, and reflected back to him from the outside world, he would cease to feel real or human and would become, he feared, bionic or a fake, without a life or a will to call his own.

Mr. B. knew, on some level, that his papers were not serviceable to others as they were; as he put it: "I can do *part* of the job, but I need you to *complete* the job." This statement could be taken both in the literal

---

1. This is, of course, a simplification. Publication also related, among other things, to feelings of self-worth and potency. My discussion here relates to those issues that figured most prominently in the transference to me; there were other themes: oedipal issues, castration fears that came up and were expressed in his battles, for instance, with the *Physics Quarterly* and in their mutual threats, but these themes receded as our work progressed; concerns relating to nurturance and being understood took their place.

sense in which he meant it, referring specifically to getting his papers published, and in a metaphorical sense, referring to the fact that he needed me to help him psychologically: to hold onto his subjective reality, organize his experience, and communicate it coherently. He spoke about needing me because of my training and the more respected position in society that my sanity and my degree conferred. He had said, on one occasion, "Who would believe a schizophrenic?" and on another occasion, "I know I'm not crazy because I can be understood by people such as yourself."[2] He also needed my help in order to relate effectively to the world; he needed me because my mind worked differently from his, because I wasn't crazy.

On one occasion I had remarked that there would, of course, be times when I would fail to understand him. His response was to say, with evident panic, "*When*—when have you *ever* not understood me?" The suggestion that I might not at all times be fully cognizant of the workings of his mind constituted an unbearable threat. He had said, on more than one occasion, quite cheerfully and nonchalantly, "You just read my mind." It would seem, therefore, that he assumed a kind of fusion of our minds: he could not tolerate the idea of their separateness because he felt he, or his mind, was incomplete, nonviable. Indeed he often spoke about some missing part, something cut out of him or unformed, misplaced or artificial, about his brain having been transplanted or his heart cut out, about wires in his head, transducers in his head or his brain coming out of his skull. He needed me to understand him not just in the usual sense of the word, but to supply the missing parts, to make the missing connections in his mental functioning and in his psyche.

There was also a basis for his wish for publication and for my help toward that end that was less metaphorical, more closely linked to reality. Mr. B.'s papers were, after all, his best efforts at making sense of things and ensuring his survival, and he wanted to get across something of the fruits of his efforts to the world at large. Specifically, he wanted to

---

2. This is an interesting statement. At first blush, it seemed to me poignantly ironic because he was, indeed, so crazy. Yet in a sense, to be crazy *means* to have a reality that is different from and unintelligible to the people around one ("delusions" become "beliefs" if they are shared by, for instance, a cultural or religious community), and, conversely, if one's reality were intelligible to a significant other person, then one would feel, or become, not so crazy. For Mr. B., the experience of being understood contributed to a feeling of authenticity; that his inner experience was recognized helped him to hold onto it and to feel "real." This assuredness of his own subjective reality, in turn, helped him to express it more directly, fully, and coherently and thereby to sound—and, in effect, be— less crazy. See also Stolorow et al. (1987).

convey something of what he understood to parents and doctors who might be charged with the care of people like him or who might be caring for him in the future. He said, "It's good I can communicate with you, but I want to be able to communicate with the whole world." As expressed in his milk-pills theory, he wanted to make public a way to prevent breast cancer and to ensure that mothers bonded with their babies; he wanted me to learn from him how to care for people like him, and he wanted me to make that knowledge known. As he put it once, "You're my therapist, but I also consider you my student." I replied, "Because I listen to you?" and he said, "Yes; but I also hope that if something moves you, you'll write about it: about milk pills, or pairing of the children."

The clue for what I ultimately said that seemed to resolve the issue came in a session shortly after the midpoint of our work. He had been expressing concern about Susan, his friend who was in the hospital and hearing voices. He said, "I know it's because there's a microphone in her head. Right now there's no microphone in my head, just thoughts." Later in the session, the dialogue continued as follows:

Mr. B.: I didn't love Carla as much as Lucy, or Susan as much as Carla.

Dr. N.: Because you couldn't afford to be devastated again?

Mr. B.: Yes. But I *do* love Susan and I love you [slowly, thoughtfully]. When you're in the new place, if you meet anyone who hears voices, you can tell them it's because there's a microphone in their head.

Dr. N.: I think you're saying to me that you hope we'll each have learned something from the other: that you'll have learned something from me and I'll have learned something from you that we each won't forget, even when we're not meeting together anymore.

Mr. B.: Yes. That's it. That's exactly it.

As June approached, Mr. B. became ever more insistent about the issue of my publishing his ideas. He found out I had been an English major, from which he concluded, "God put us together for a reason. You have no excuse!" On another occasion, he appealed to me, distraught, uncomprehending, "What in what I've said doesn't make sense?" Later, he raised the issue yet again, and I knew we had to come to some kind of resolution, painful as that might be. What I found myself saying was, "No. I will not try to get your papers published, but I will remember our work together and will remember you. Our time together will inform my work with other patients in the future and my teaching of other doctors and, one day, I may try to write something about it—about you and about your ideas." His reply was, "That's good enough." He did not raise the issue again until he once more alluded to it during our final session. He had been saying, among other things, that he felt we had accomplished a lot. "But," he said, "I do wish you'd write those papers." I said we'd talked about that, and I reiterated my position as described above; he responded, "I think you're better than a Beverley Hills psychiatrist because you don't tell me what I want to hear; you tell me the truth."

It seems, therefore, that although my answer was not exactly what he wanted to hear, he valued it, and in some way it brought him relief. Not only did it leave him undamaged and our relationship intact, but it may indeed have been crucial to both him and our relationship. My prior evasiveness, my inability to be clear and frank with him about this issue, could be seen as both a collusion with his delusional thinking and a form of disrespect. I suspect he took my ultimate refusal at least in part as an affirmation of reality and a form of confidence in him. Perhaps the work we had done over the year was necessary as groundwork to enable him to respond as he did; his response shows a genuine tolerance for differences both between the two of us and between his wishes and external reality that had not been evident earlier in our work.

## DISCUSSION

What can be understood from a fragment of work such as this, lacking the opportunity to follow it to its natural conclusion? There appeared in the year's work some intriguing beginnings of change: in this man's ability to communicate, in his relationship to external reality, and in his relationship to me. How did these changes come about, what underlay them, and what might they have led to in the future? Could they ever, for instance, have amounted to something that could aptly be called a "resumption of development" or "structural change"? Or would psychotherapy for this man serve, at best, a "holding function," supplying some structure and some support, helping him to maintain a psychological equilibrium? Perhaps it could have offered more. Would this man have been capable of more, given the chance to pursue psychotherapeutic work uninterruptedly, with the same person? Would it be therapeutically grandiose to wonder if he could have achieved a firmer sense of self and of external reality that would have left him less vulnerable to psychosis? Could a sustained, continuous psychotherapy have offered him some practice at being emotionally intimate with another person, including all that this can teach about what one feels, how one impacts on the outside world, and how one reacts to it?

I shall take a closer look at the change and offer some speculations about the dynamics of it—not with the aim of answering these questions, but rather to provide a more substantial basis for raising them. I will use Mr. B.'s two papers written during the crisis to exemplify the nature of these changes and will begin by raising some further questions.

What, for instance, underlay the changes in communication patterns? What caused or enabled Mr. B. to speak directly to me during the second half of our work and to revert less often to global issues and delusional concerns? The progress of our year's work was in keeping with a formulation by Stolorow et al. (1987) regarding the treatment of psychotic patients:

> Essential to the psychoanalytic treatment of psychotic patients is that the therapist strive to comprehend the core of subjective truth symbolically encoded in the patient's delusional ideas, and to communicate this understanding in a form that the patient can use. Consistent empathic decoding of the patient's subjective truth gradually establishes the therapeutic bond as an archaic intersubjective context in which his belief in his own personal reality can become more firmly consolidated. Concomitantly, we have found, the delusional concretizations become less necessary, recede, and eventually even disappear, only to return again if the therapeutic bond or its subjective validating function becomes seriously disrupted [p. 134f.].

What, then, happened during the crisis at the midpoint of our work to catalyze such a change in our communication patterns at that particular time? The threat of my leaving served, for one thing, as the vehicle for the transference of feelings and memories associated with past abandonments. Those experiences of loss and abandonment had been devastating to him and had tended to plunge him into psychosis. The repetition of this theme in our work enabled him to relive those past abandonments in a way that afforded him some mastery, and left him feeling, for the time being, less terrified, helpless, and confused. Indeed his first response to the threat of my leaving was to become panicked over the prospect of thermonuclear holocaust, without any awareness of what had prompted his terror. His panic was temporarily assuaged, first by our conversation over the phone, and then by the composing of his paper, "Soviet American Plan for Peace," which provided a solution, within his delusional system, for what threatened him. The next week, he brought in an entirely different sort of paper, one that constituted a more direct response to my interpretations. As noted previously, the content of the paper represented a new mode of relating to the past traumatic experiences. His experiences, for example, of losing Lucy, losing Carla, and going crazy were recalled and expressed directly in the light of his present experience of needing me, or my "love," and being threatened with the idea of losing it. To underscore

the function of this recollection: could the importance of his relationships with these women reside in his hopes for a nurturant, loving
relationship that he never had but desperately wanted with his mother?
These relationships were meant not only to give solace in the present
but also to repair structural rents of the past, and his relationship with
me provided one further such opportunity for repair. The paper
served to give coherence and order, in a nondelusional way, to both his
feeling states and his experience of the outside world at that time of
threatened loss. In some sense, it continued a process that had been
initiated by me when, over the phone, I had linked his present terror
over nuclear war to the threat of my leaving and when, later on, our
discussions broadened to include past abandonments. But this is only a
partial explanation of what happened.

What Mr. B. said, in reference to this time, was:

> Mr. B.: I've learned what I consider to be traumatic experiences are not
> all that traumatic. Like when I thought I was going to be a football, used in
> a nuclear war, and I called you up. I think that was a crisis in our time
> together, and you helped me through it.
>
> Dr. N.: Can you tell me more about that crisis?
>
> Mr. B.: I think it was tied together with the very nature of my disease. I
> was being told that all my symptoms were fake. The voices said, "Tell your
> psychiatrist you're faking it." You dealt with that very well. The voices were
> telling me I was faking it, and you turned that around.
>
> Dr. N.: And how do you think I did that?
>
> Mr. B.: I think you neutralized it.
>
> Dr. N.: How so?
>
> Mr. B.: By being you: by not changing from T1 to T2 to T3. The crisis
> was at T1 and you retained a constant composure through those times.
> The voices were telling me I wasn't real, but you stayed the same.
>
> Dr. N.: Let me see if I'm understanding you right. The voices were
> telling you you weren't real; you called me up, and because I didn't change,
> you knew I was real, and I reassured you that you hadn't changed, either;
> that you were real.
>
> Mr. B.: Yes, exactly. So what it boils down to is that you're real and I'm
> real. But I almost lost it.

What was it about my response, then, that was so important to him,
and what did it mean for him to feel "real"? Perhaps the simple fact that
I was still there—not destroyed by his rage or his imagined peril, not
changed by his projections—called his psychotic view of the world into
question. The fact that I was not put off by his craziness and urgency
must have been reassuring to him. It must also have been reassuring that
I could offer him a consistent view of reality that he could relate to but

that did not change, as his own did, with the changes in his feeling states. That I could empathize with him made him feel, somehow, more substantial and helped him to experience his feelings directly rather than projecting them diffusely onto the external world. At the end of his second paper composed during this time he had written: "Please don't pull your love out on me. I AM REAL." When I asked him what he had meant by this, he replied, "Don't believe what the bionic voices said to me. By telling you about that, I felt I was going against myself." I asked, "And you didn't want me to believe that version of you: that you were a fake?" He replied, "No I *am* real. And bionic." Something about my response "neutralized" the part of him that was "going against [him]self," and kept the "real," "biological" part of him from being overwhelmed by the "bionic," psychotic part.

It seems, then, that I served a dual function: I presented him with a coherent, consistent version of external reality and I empathized with and helped him to articulate his inner experience. My role was, in many ways, like that of a mother in the context of whose responses a child's experiences of himself and of external reality become organized and take on meaning. Loewald (1956–57) writes about some of the ways a mother's responses make possible the psychological development of her infant in a way that can be related to my work with Mr. B.:

> The understanding recognition of the infant's needs on the part of the mother represents a gathering together of as yet undifferentiated urges of the infant, urges that in the acts of recognition and fulfilment by the mother undergo a first organization into some directed drive. . . . These acts are not merely necessary for the physical survival of the infant but necessary at the same time for its psychological development insofar as they organize, in successive steps, the infant's relatively uncoordinated urges [p. 237].

In some sense, Mr. B.'s delusions reflected "undifferentiated," or not fully differentiated, "urges." The function I performed when he called me in terror over the fear of thermonuclear holocaust and being a football was analogous to that performed by a mother in interpreting a baby's crying as due to hunger vs. fatigue vs. cold; the child may raise a cry of fear or discomfort but not know what brought on the discomfort or what, in the real world, he is afraid of. Mr. B., too, was unaware of the cause of his panic. My comments (e.g., "You began talking this way when I spoke of our separation; did you feel this way when Lucy left you?") were attempts to clarify both the immediate and the underlying sources of his sudden, intense foreboding. Put another way, Mr. B.

confused internal and external worlds, did not know what he felt or why he felt it. He projected his feelings outside and tried to assuage them by affecting the external world (via his publications, his pronouncements, such as the "Soviet American Plan for Peace"). My comments were attempts to help him sort out his feelings and distinguish them from external reality so that each made sense and each could be addressed appropriately.

Through my responses, Mr. B. began to know his feelings, to differentiate them, and to understand their causes. He began to be able to modify his reactions to the things that happened to him. To give another example: once, after being rejected by a female classmate, he wrote on the college blackboard threats about impending nuclear disaster. By this action, he was expressing an aggressive urge the true source and target of which he was unaware of at the time. He was frightened and alarmed by his own behavior. After talking about it in therapy, the specifics of the situation became clearer to him; his behavior made sense, although he continued to see it as maladaptive. Instead of feeling diffusely and needing to broadcast intimations of danger, he later said, "I guess I was angry," and it was clear to him why this was the case.

The progress of our work depended on some degree of "understanding recognition" on my part of the origins and nature of previously split-off feelings and urges on Mr. B.'s part. My articulation of this recognition helped him to own and name his feelings and to render them more manageable and less terrifying. This process involved the localization of his feelings within himself and the identification of what had aroused them outside himself; hence it involved a differentiation between and a reorganization of his internal world and external reality which previously had seemed, paradoxically, both fused and unrelated.

One may examine this point further by looking at the therapy relationship as expressed in the two papers he wrote around the crisis time. The second paper was explicitly addressed to me. It affirmed a connection between us and requested that I not sever it: "Please do not pull your love out on me; I am real." This represented a relatively highly developed response to the threat of my leaving: he articulated his need for me and what it was about me that he needed, and he asked that I not take it away. The first paper, on first glance, would seem not to reflect the therapy relationship in any form whatsoever. It contained no explicit mention either of him or of me. It was impersonal, and seemed to be speaking, in general terms, about world affairs. It was, nevertheless, written in response to the threat of an impending separation from me.

He had expressed his panic over this separation by talking, loudly and anxiously, about the prospect of "thermonuclear holocaust." In outlining a plan for peace, the paper functioned metaphorically to avert this threat which, to examine the concept of thermonuclear holocaust more closely, consisted of the splitting apart of an atom, of an essential unity, causing heat and total destruction. The suggestion, then, was that he experienced us, psychologically, as one, as inseparable, and that our separation would be fatal to him. In this context, his fear of thermonuclear holocaust suggested a developmental stage prior to his existence as a separate individual (similar to that suggested by his response: "When have you ever not understood me"), and one in which our relationship, at least on some level, was one of fusion, of essential unity, in which his separate self was as yet inconceivable and nonviable.

The second paper, then, reflects the beginnings of a distillation of self and other out of an unarticulated, psychotic unity (the "world" as represented in the first paper). The second paper affirmed our connectedness and at the same time began to define his individuality, hence also his separateness from me and from the external world. It began to articulate his subjective experience and thereby to affirm his existence as a "real," viable, thinking, feeling, separate person. The experiences that he described in this paper—of the service, of losing Lucy, of losing Carla, of going crazy—were unique to him. The paper detailed important aspects of a unique personal history, hence affirming his existence as a separate individual. The experience alluded to in the first paper, by contrast, was generalized, externalized, common to all people, and conveyed no suggestion of individuality. It would seem, furthermore, that this fledgling experience of psychological separateness was what enabled him to react to my leaving, when it actually occurred, in terms of loss, rather than of annihilation.

Similarly, during the second half of the year, he began to talk more explicitly about himself: his personal experiences and his personal reactions to them. Previously he had tended to fill his sessions with proclamations and explications of his theories, laid forth with urgency, but in a way that tended to create distance and to disguise their personal import. As part of what "changed" during the second half of the year, he began, less ambiguously and more successfully, to communicate: to speak directly and with feeling, in a way that both conveyed his meaning and served to create a genuine connection with another person. Reversing the paradox of a self that seemed both fused with and unrelated to the external world, it seemed that he had begun to develop a separateness—a consolidation, perhaps, of his "real" self—that made intimacy possible.

## Conclusion

At the end of the year, Mr. B. expressed his disappointment: "It's taken about a year to really get to know each other. It really has. I've been learning what 'normal' is. I don't want a repeat of this year in the sense that I've had a lot of overwhelming feelings. Starting with a new doctor will be like starting from scratch."

The glimmer of developmental change in this man, occurring in the context of hard-won, mutual efforts to communicate, raises serious questions about the effect of annual shifts in therapist for the chronically mentally ill. Especially since the therapeutic terrain is that of self and object constancy, does the yearly change in therapist offer safe ground to "practice" separations and reconnections in the context of the constant "institutional object"? Or do these treatment interruptions merely reopen old structural fault lines again and again? Put another way, do such interruptions undermine or even destroy the fragile psychological structures that can emerge in the course of treatment so that the potential for development seems lost? Since these fundamental questions about the efficacy of psychotherapeutic treatment for the severely and persistently mentally ill would fit into a simple, feasible clinical research paradigm, we must ask ourselves why this research has not been done. Is "chronicity" partly iatrogenic? In the end my work with Mr. B. raised more questions than it answered. But they are important questions to articulate, and they point to a fertile area for future investigation. It is perhaps ironic that, in an era when molecular and neurochemical research into severe mental illness is ascendant, these questions could best be answered by psychoanalytically informed researchers.

### BIBLIOGRAPHY

Loewald, H. W. (1949). Ego and reality. In *Papers on Psychoanalysis*. New Haven: Yale Univ. Press, 1980, pp. 3–20.
—— (1956–57). On the therapeutic action of psychoanalysis. In *Papers on Psychoanalysis*. New Haven: Yale Univ. Press, 1980, pp. 221–256.
Stolorow, R. D., Brandchaft, D., & Atwood, G. E. (1987). *Psychoanalytic Treatment*. Hillsdale, N.J.: Analytic Press.

# Family Romance Fantasy Resolution in George Eliot's *Daniel Deronda*

LYLE L. WARNER, Ph.D.

*A nineteenth-century novel explores the effect of family romance fantasies on an adopted young man's search for identity and on his eventual life-goal and love-object choices.*

THE CURRENTLY POPULAR ADOPTEE SEARCH FOR BIRTH PARENTS, AS A WAY to resolve identity conflicts and confusions, proceeds with the manifest purpose of ending the mystery of unknown origins. The latent source of the motivation to search is the enduring hope of finding an ideal parent and recapturing an ideal self. Family romance fantasies accompany the adoptee's quest, bringing a collision of fantasy and reality when a search is successful and a meeting with a birth parent occurs. The inevitable experience of disillusionment ultimately can free the adoptee to reintegrate the identifications with the adoptive parents and can reaffirm the adoptive attachments. In view of the fact that the adoptive relationships are the primary psychological roots of the development of the adoptee's self, a good search is one that also clarifies the meaning of the adoptive relationships. "They are my *real* parents," says the adoptee for whom the search has served to clear away confusions and to answer those existential questions, "Who am I? Where did I come from? Who do I belong to?"

George Eliot's nineteenth-century novel *Daniel Deronda* explores an adoptee's search for identity and proposes a resolution that invites psychoanalytic exploration. Daniel Deronda is a Jew raised by an adop-

---

Clinical social worker, in private practice in Boston, Mass.

The wisdom and encouragement of Frederick Ehrlich, M.D., and Margaret Frank, M.S.S.W., are gratefully acknowledged.

tive father who is an English baronet. He only discovers his Jewish roots in young manhood, after he has acquired the culture, confidence, and polish of an aristocrat. During his search for identity, he becomes the disciple of a Jewish scholar, Mordecai, who imagines that Deronda is the man who can fulfill his Zionist dream. Deronda's upbringing among the ruling class has fitted him for a leadership role. His story is entwined with that of Gwendolen Harleth, the heroine whose sufferings attract his sympathies. Gwendolen is a beautiful, desirable woman who begins her adult life with the immoral decision to marry a man with a prior obligation to another woman because she needs to secure her own and her mother's financial futures. Murderous wishes toward her arrogant, cruel husband prevent her from attempting to save him when he is drowning. Deronda, her confidant and moral adviser, resists her sexual allure. Deronda also becomes attached to Mirah, the sweetly chaste sister of his Jewish mentor.

Eliot imagines the events of childhood, adolescence, and young adulthood that form the character of her hero and the nature of his search. The discoveries of his search lead him to undertake the visionary goal of establishing a Jewish homeland in Palestine and to marry Mirah who will share his goal. In the end, Daniel Deronda arrives at a solution to the loss of the fantasies of his adoptive and natal parents that preserves his valued sense of self while at the same time it contains his anger toward these parents.

Eliot's rich though fictional "case" material offers an unusual opportunity to examine perplexing questions about the meaning of adoption and the potential of a search to promote a workable integration of the self and object representations that have their basis for an adoptee in real and imagined connections to two sets of parents. "I don't feel adopted anymore," said one contemporary adoptee after her successful search for her birth parents had resulted in the undoing of previous feelings of alienation from her adoptive parents.

The ego mastery of family romance fantasies is central to the development and denouement of the novel and to the reader's satisfaction with the resolution of disillusionment that the novel offers. Family romance fantasies are an influential source of the hero's character and motivations and of the hopes and expectations that Daniel Deronda brings to his real relationships. His fantasies of his mother are for the most part unconscious until the moment when he meets her; until then they are revealed in their transference manifestations. Two versions of these fantasies, idealizing and devaluing, attract him to two very different women, one struggling for a moral life, the other firmly set on a virtuous path. Fantasies about his adoptive father are both conscious and unconscious, ideal and disappointed. The repressed fantasy that owes its origins to the childhood idealization of his adoptive father, perhaps encapsulating as well his feelings about the loving birth father whom he lost, is transferred to the prophetic stranger who imagines a destiny for him that reverberates with his adolescent dreams of himself as a great leader, "like Pericles or Washington." The conscious fantasy is that the beloved and essential adoptive father is his "real" father. He imagines himself an illegitimate son who, one day, will be acknowledged.

Many readers have argued with the plausibility of Eliot's denouement which also disappoints their romantic wishes for the hero. Her resolution of his losses through the projection of his hopes onto a grand, seemingly illusory life mission, and the renunciation of his attraction to the woman who has aroused his passion can seem inexplicable. To the psychoanalytically informed reader, however, these choices seem not to be a whim of the author's but to embody her understanding of neurotic compromise.

Clinical observations of the family romance fantasies of adopted children have described them as tenacious. The paradigmatic family romance fantasy (Freud, 1909), rooted in infantile illusions about the parents, serves the needs of the latency child struggling to maintain a positive sense of self despite disappointments in the objects. The fantasy may continue to exist and to find expression (Frosch, 1959; Greenacre, 1958; Kris, 1956), but the need for the fantasy is expected to wane with adolescent resolution of earlier conflicts. As Clothier (1943), Nickman (1985), and Wieder (1977), among others, have observed, the fact that other parents exist makes these fantasies harder to master; they remain an obstacle to the resolution of ambivalences about the adoptive parents.

In latency feelings about the adoptive realities merge with the occurrence of the family romance (A. Freud, 1965); for the adopted child these fantasies have disparate origins. They take off from the infant experience with the adoptive parents; from the feelings about the self and the other parents that have been derived from shards of information about the biological parents; and from the feelings of the adoptive parents about the other parents as they convey their versions of the story of abandonment and rescue (Warner, 1985; Rosenberg and Horner, 1991). In adopted children, the content of these fantasies is considerably modified. In contrast to the exalted, idealized images that characterize the family romance fantasies of children raised by their natal parents, adopted children in treatment reveal devalued images. These are connected to the damaged narcissism that is the result of traumatic revelations of the rejection of the first parents and the too early disillusionment of the child's belief in an unassailable attachment to the adoptive parents (Brinich, 1980; Wieder, 1977). However, there is both treatment and research evidence that adopted children develop both kinds of fantasies, romantic as well as devalued (Sherick, 1983; Warner, 1985).

Family romance fantasies that function to protect narcissistic equilibrium for other children often fail to do so for adopted children. Like Deronda's, the adopted child's wish, sometimes expressed in a restitutive fantasy, is of a blood tie to the adoptive parents which would remove the humiliation of being adopted. It is suggested that having older adopted children and adults learn the reality behind their fantasies by meeting their birth parents can enhance identity formation (Colarusso, 1987). Such a meeting can clear away fantasy images of these parents that interfere with the integration of the images of the adoptive parents and of the self images that have derived from connections to two sets of parents. The resolution of the family romance fantasies depends upon this integration of biological origins and adoptive experience, however it is achieved (Rosenberg and Horner, 1991).

Psychoanalytically informed research into the intrapsychic experience of the adoptee's search has revealed that the function and content of family romance fantasies changes with changing developmental needs and as cognitive capacities and the understanding of adoption develop (Warner, 1985). In most cases, the adoptee who decides upon a search has recovered idealized fantasies of the birth parent, having reordered the devalued fantasies that haunted adolescent musings. These latter fantasies, in turn, have been superimposed upon earlier paradigmatic family romance fantasies of the idealized type that derived from a gratifying early experience with the adoptive parents.

The action involved in the search is an externalization of multiple levels of conflict resolution. In the course of a search and as a result of the encounter with a birth parent, most significantly with a birth mother in this research sample of women (Warner, 1985), some adoptees were successful in using the search to de-romanticize their images of their birth parents; to disentangle their self-images from their fantasy images of these parents; and to reintegrate their self-images on the basis of a more positive understanding of their identifications with their adoptive parents and more reality-based identifications with the birth parents. In so doing they achieved a foundation that gave room for oedipal ambitions. The often-repeated description of how the search had changed them was a sense of a new freedom to get on with their lives (see also Schechter and Bertocci, 1990). In the original and in follow-up interviews a number of women reported an enhanced capacity for intimate relationships, readiness for marriage, and both the birth and adoption of children.

Adoptees who had been able to use the search developmentally had had a good enough adoptive experience, and they brought to the search a fairly mature understanding of the separateness of others and a readiness to imagine a comfortable separateness from the parents that did not destroy the feelings of connection. The key to a growth-enhancing search result is the capacity to forgive the self and both sets of parents for the losses that adoption has inflicted and to derive a life-enhancing result from the disillusionment that is inevitable when fantasy meets reality.

The search theme, with its corollary exploration of core fantasies, is established in the opening paragraph of *Daniel Deronda* as the 25-year-old hero muses about his compelled but conflicted attraction to the heroine, Gwendolen Harleth. Later we will understand that his attraction to Gwendolen is a transference of fantasies of a lost mother that pervade his perceptions of women. Daniel himself remains unaware of the dynamic motivating power of these fantasies for a longer time—until the moment when a meeting with his mother is imminent: "The tender yearning after a being whose life might have been the worse for not having his care and love, the image of a mother who had not had all her dues whether of reverence or compassion, had long been secretly present with him in his observation of all the women he had come near" (p. 681).

Conflicting wishes impede the way to a focused search. As the story begins, the young hero, who has been raised by a loving adoptive father, is in a period of identity moratorium. While the authorial voice condemns the secrecy that causes shame, Deronda, although suffering from the secrecy, also relies on it for his own denial of his truths. His predominantly stronger wish is to preserve the vulnerable conviction that his adoptive father, Sir Hugo Mallinger, is his "real" father. The protection of fantasies that connect, alternately, to a good and feared self-image inhibits his search. Beneath the open secret of his clouded origins is the internal, problematic secret of his ambitions. The novel's action can be seen as Deronda's acquisition of self-knowledge and knowledge of the world sufficient to accept his truth when it is revealed; to discover a valued self-image that is separate from the image of his adoptive father; and to move his oedipal conflicts to a higher level.

Eliot portrays Deronda's shame about his secret past as the mainspring of his character, comparing his shame to Byron's feelings about his deformed foot, never quite hidden in its shoe, a "sore" that never heals. His secret shame is the conviction that he is a bastard son whose putative father, the "uncle" whom he loves, does not acknowledge his paternity. A premature reserve develops, hiding the dread of his secret origins and of what others may know about him: "His ears were open now to words which before . . . would have passed by him unnoted; and round every trivial incident which imagination could connect with his suspicions, a newly-roused set of feelings were ready to cluster themselves" (p. 207).

Distress and anger, however, are transformed by this uncommon young man. Deronda's awareness of his own suffering becomes an unusual capacity for empathy: his "inexorable sorrow takes the form of fellowship and makes the imagination tender" (p. 215). To understand the motives of others as springing from their unique histories and sensitivities, to comprehend rather than to blame, becomes his guiding quest.

As Eliot's story opens, her hero is ready to cope at a new developmental level with the conflicts that are embodied in his search. Perhaps it is for this reason that a fantasy of his mother is aroused by the sight of Gwendolen Harleth. A chance rescue from drowning of a forlorn young woman has opened him to a confrontation with his own truths, loosening his compromise solution for dealing with the uncertainty of his origins and his bonds of attachment. Until this moment, Deronda had protected himself from reading any of the clues at hand; his denial begins to break down at a developmentally appropriate time.

In a flashback, Eliot describes the psychology of the boy whose most urgent need is to belong to the only father he can remember, the "uncle" whose loving care has won his deepest affections—his "primary psychological parent" (Goldstein et al., 1973). We see Daniel at the age of 13, when his childish resolution of his ambiguous relationship to his father/uncle fails to serve his wish for connection. Until then he had been unquestioning, satisfied that "uncle" was his special name for his father; despite evidence to the contrary, he has believed that the father of his heart is the father of his being. Emotional consistency has not required logical consistency. A new view of their connection has emerged from application of his adolescent acquisition of a capacity for logical thought and of adolescent sexual enlightenment.

"How was it that the popes and cardinals always had so many nephews?" (p. 203) he asks his tutor, who explains that "nephew" is a euphemism for an illegitimate son. To the adolescent Daniel, being the "pope's nephew" is preferable to the loss of the fantasy of a blood tie to his uncle. In this bond Daniel has found security, love, and a model of manhood that is his guide to his future. Sir Hugo Mallinger had never claimed to be Daniel's father, but Daniel, like many young children who are told about their adoption, had disavowed the information about other parents which threatened his reliance on a secure bond with his adoptive parent.

Eliot describes this moment of disillusionment with his parent as an epoch of great sorrow for the young Daniel. Events of this kind, she tells us, have more influence on the formation of character than the formal educational experience to which adults give their attention. Eliot imagines, perhaps because this disillusionment has come late in his childhood, that Daniel's ego is capable of containing his ambivalence; his disillusionment does not extinguish his love for his father. Nevertheless, we miss an expression of the anger that such a boy must surely feel; sadness is the feeling that predominates. The seeds of his emergence into a separate person have been sown, though it will take time and experience before this new insight can be translated into growth.

An immediate consequence of Daniel's compromise interpretation of his tie to his uncle is that, to safeguard his security, Daniel must suppress his questions. His solution is an ambivalent one. It protects the bond that is the source of his well-being, but it also reinforces a sense of shameful secrets. The illegitimate circumstances of his birth, his mother's disappearance or abandonment of him—these thoughts provoke questions that he dare not ask lest he reveal his anger and confirm the stain of evil in his origins. His uncle/father has done him a great wrong, and his mother too has been wronged.

Fantasies about his lost birth mother begin to surface in his attraction to certain women. Like many another child seeking a new level of integration of self and object representations, Daniel has protected his image of a good self by constructing rewarding fantasies of his parents. The fantasy constructs of his adolescence and postadolescence cast him in the role of rescuer, a role that becomes the linchpin of his masculine character. Accordingly, his sympathy is drawn to lives liable to difficulty and struggle. Devised to serve defensive needs aroused by his suspicion that a terrible flaw in himself is the cause of his loss of his mother, and of his secret shame, the role of rescuer begins to serve multiple functions in the organization of his character.

His self-image as a rescuer both counteracts and assuages the guilt that attaches to his loss. He imagines restoring his mother to a loving relationship and to a virtuous life; fantasies of her and of himself as her rescuer are the template for his real relationships with women. The rescuer image allows him to deny his anger, to undo hostile and sexual wishes, and to counter his stained self-image. The role of rescuer allows an expression of his masculine strivings that is benign rather than dangerous.

One image of his lost mother, now summoned up by this view of Gwendolen Harleth in the despicable attitude of a gambler, is of a woman gone astray whom Daniel imagines rescuing from her own self-destructiveness. This fantasy bears the stamp of Daniel's adolescent conflicts: to a judgmental adolescent adoptee wrestling for control of his sexual impulses and digesting a new understanding of illegitimate birth, the mother who appears to have violated sexual morality is a harlot.

Freud (1910) describes the women who are the objects of rescue fantasies as being of the type of Gwendolen Harleth: they are flirtatious women, even harlots, who belong to another man. Freud found rescue fantasies to be "derived from the infantile fixation of tender feelings on the mother" (p. 168f.). Like Daniel's, "the libido has remained attached to the mother for so long, even after the onset of puberty, that the maternal characteristics remain stamped on the love-objects that are chosen later" (p. 169).

The other fantasy mother image is revealed when Daniel first contemplates Mirah, whom he rescues from drowning herself in the Thames. The joining of artistic and scientific insight may be found once again in comparing Eliot's plot construction to Freud's interpretation of a dream symbol: "A man rescuing a woman from the water in a dream means that he makes her a mother, which . . . amounts to making her his own mother" (1910, p. 174).

In the plot denouement, after his mother rejects his love, Daniel will choose Mirah to be his wife. As he watches Mirah, the fantasy becomes momentarily conscious: "The agitating impression this forsaken girl was making on him stirred a fibre that lay close to his deepest interest in the fates of women—'perhaps my mother was like this one.' The old thought had come now" (p. 231). This image of a "forsaken girl," a victim of terrible circumstances, unable to prevent her own self-destruction, has perhaps been less available during adolescence. More mature and more worldly now, Daniel is ready to entertain a sympathetic view of his mother's circumstances.

More than most young men, Daniel may need a moratorium period in order to bring together the conflicting sources of his identity. Interestingly, Erik Erikson (1975), who formulated the concept of the identity moratorium in recalling his own process of identity formation, was, like Deronda, an adopted son. The wider world that Daniel has experienced at Eton and Cambridge has given impetus to new questions about his future. When he went away to school, he declared an ambition to become an English gentleman and to sit for Parliament, to follow in his uncle's footsteps. Now those goals are not appealing; perhaps he hopes to find a less conflictual arena for the expression of his competitiveness and ambition. He preserves his affectionate feelings for his uncle, however, even as he separates from him and differentiates his ambition for himself from the model of his easygoing parent.

Daniel is drifting in a boat on the Thames when two important meetings occur: his discovery of the suicidally despairing Mirah; and his meeting with the visionary Jew, Mordecai, who declares his belief that Daniel is designated for a special destiny. Daniel is not ready to make any sense of Mordecai's greeting, "I expected you to come down the river. I have been waiting for you these five years" (p. 550). In Daniel Mordecai envisions a new Moses.

The receptivity of an aristocratic young Englishman to Mordecai and his Zionist dream requires explanation. Daniel muses that his uncle would call Mordecai's zeal fanaticism, but his own speculative nature and his capacity to imagine himself as a historical figure permit his attraction to the man and his ideas. Awareness of his own feelings of alienation, based on his equivocal familial connections, can be imagined to open him to a sympathetic view of a man who belongs to an outcast group.

Here again, a derivative of his idealized childhood fantasies, inspired by the early, gratifying relationships both with his Jewish birth father and his adoptive father, may be operative, finding a transference object in Mordecai. Does his attraction to Mordecai contain a buried memory of the father of his infancy and has this memory become entwined with early memories of his adoptive father? Once he imagined his uncle/father as playing a large role on the world stage and dreamed of a proud future as his son. Eliot connects Daniel's receptivity to Mordecai's vision to his habitual reliance on fantasy to anchor his affections.

Daniel's search crystallizes when he meets Jews for the first time and is taken for a Jew. At the outset, he has only the typical English gentleman's prejudices about Jewish values, customs, and manners. In a Jewish synagogue in Frankfurt he experiences his receptiveness to Jewish ritual and we wonder whether he is awakening to a resonance that has been prepared by an unacknowledged awareness of his history. Before Daniel learns the truth of his genetic and historic roots, he has lost his conviction that he could not possibly be Jewish; uncertainty gradually has replaced outright denial and aversion. Daniel's preparation to know the truth of his origins is a quest for a positive Jewish identity. In developmental terms this is an essential part of his psychic separating process. He has been searching for a positive sense of the self that is separate from his uncle/father and to reclaim a part of the self that has been devalued.

This casting of the adoptee as a Jew, the stranger, the other, the person born into a low status, devalued group who is masquerading respectability is a creative correlative that well expresses the adoptee's sense of a stigmatized identity. Eliot provides a number of clues that suggest that Daniel has known of his Jewish roots and taken refuge in denial. Noting that he must have been circumcised, several critics have asked, "Did he never look down?" (David, 1981). His denial has been supported by studied unconcern about his background on the part of his social group allowing them to preserve their stereotype of the despicable Jew, so unlike this admired friend.

The shame of illegitimate birth and of abandonment by his mother have been borne by Daniel with the assistance of fantasies that protect a good sense of self, but the terrible shame of Jewish origins has been hidden from himself. We wonder whether Daniel's attraction to a tattered, sick, sallow-faced Jew reminiscent of an Old Testament prophet has been prepared for by a lifting of repression that grows out of the process of separating from his uncle/father and a wish to find a new, sympathetic view of his otherness.

Deronda's search has begun, as do those of modern adoptees, with the overcoming of fear of confirming unsavory origins. He has recovered a compassionate fantasy representation of his mother, and he has found inspiring models of Jewish character, but still he resists initiating a search for his mother. If, as Mordecai believes, his mother is Jewish, then presumably he will embrace the heroic task that has been put before him. He cannot end the mystery of his mother because he must hold onto the fantasy of belonging by birth to his uncle. The fear of discovering that this unbreakable connection does not exist can be interpreted as the external representation of the fear of losing the bond with his uncle/father if he frees his oedipal ambitions.

Daniel's relationships with Gwendolen and Mirah during his period of identity search are testing grounds for self-discovery. In having him decide between them, Eliot once more portrays internal conflicts on the interpersonal level. We may read in his attraction to two very different women, the one promising sexual fulfillment and the other an uncompetitive support for great ambition, a representation of his internal conflicts. He imagines that he must choose between the two ambitions; he cannot integrate both.

When he meets the compelling Gwendolen, he tries to put aside his attraction to her because "he felt himself in no sense free" (p. 202). A man who has not found his spiritual destiny is not free to choose a wife. But in another way he is not free. Not until he has exorcised the shame of his mother's desertion of him can he imagine himself worthy of a woman's love. Conflict seems to impair his freedom to accept his sexual passion for a woman whose image is joined with that of his mother in his fantasies.

Events move toward their climax when Daniel learns that his mother is alive and wishes to see him. His uncle delivers her letter, a cold forewarning of the moments to come, commanding him to meet her in Genoa. Deronda courageously seizes the initiative: "And Deronda's whole soul was possessed by a question which was the hardest in the world to utter. . . . But at last Deronda looked at Sir Hugo and said, with a tremulous reverence in his voice—dreading to convey indirectly the reproach that affection had for years been stifling—'Is my father also living?'" (p. 676). Thus he accepts that the father of his heart is not the father of his being.

There is a tremendous sense of English reserve in this momentous scene. There is silence; there is Sir Hugo's tentative confession of guilt for withholding knowledge about Daniel's mother from him. After Daniel offers his forgiveness and a testament of his great affection for his uncle, "the two men clasp each other's hand for a moment" (p. 676). Deronda has reached the limit of his control of his feelings. He has ventured the hardest question and has received an answer that over-turns his belief in a blood connection to his adoptive father. Fear in the expectation of a meeting with his mother must follow when he has lost his indwelling hope of being claimed as a true son. He cannot ask about her.

As Deronda awaits his meeting with his mother, whose very name— the Princess Halm-Eberstein—might discourage thoughts of Jewish birth, he imagines himself as part of Jewish history, as one of those "Spanish Jews centuries ago driven destitute from their Spanish homes. . . . Inevitably, dreamy constructions of a possible ancestry for himself would weave themselves with historic memories which had begun to have a new interest for him with the discovery of Mirah, and now, under the influence of Mordecai, had become irresistibly domi-nant" (p. 682). Here Eliot foreshadows the resolution that he will find when his discovery of the limitations of his intense parental attach-ments leads to a displacement of his tender feelings onto his ancestral group (Sants, 1964).

In their momentous first meeting Eliot gives us havoc where we ex-pect outpourings of love, a scene of cold formality, more of an audience than a reunion until the heat of anger sets it on fire. Anticipating this encounter, we remember the previous scene of reunion, between the long-separated Mordecai and his sister Mirah, their joy at being re-united and their sadness for time lost. The reader's own archaic wish to believe that a mother forever loves any child to whom she has given birth makes the meeting a ruin rather than a reunion.

Daniel's mother was a famous Jewish singer. She begged her admirer/ lover, Daniel's "uncle" Sir Hugo Mallinger, to take her son when he was 2 years old. She had married her cousin and borne a child in fear of denying her father's wishes; her father had died soon after her mar-riage. Daniel's father had been the loving parent; he too had died. She has sent for her son because now she is dying.

Every adoptee approaches the mother whose loss has created a sear-ing narcissistic injury with one supreme wish: to learn that he or she was wanted at birth, while part of the mother's body, or at the moment of conception. This is the existential wish to know that one's birth was meaningful, that one was not a mere accident or inconvenience. Many do not discover the importance of this wish until it is denied, or, in happier circumstances, granted. The defeat of this deepest longing must be a shattering blow to his narcissism. Rare is the person who could, as Deronda does in this depriving encounter, give so unyielding a mother so many offers of love.

The Princess tells Daniel that she never loved him and never wanted him. She has even told her father's friend that her son was dead; "I meant you to be dead to all the world of my childhood" (p. 700). And to his wish to believe her capable of love, she responds, "I am not a loving woman" (p. 730). She has sought this meeting not for the pleasure of seeing him but because she is afraid to die without discharging her father's commission to deliver his family papers to the grandson, not yet born, who could carry on his goals. A learned Jew, Daniel's grand-father had devoted his life's thought to the destiny of the Jewish people; he had held a vision of "separateness with communication" as the key to their place in the world.

It had been his mother's purpose to defy her father's wishes and to sever her son from his Jewish identity, but in fear of death she has called for him. She experiences the demands of love as an encroach-ment on her freedom to develop her own talent and individuality. Love is fetters; love is submission to the will of another; love brings terrible disillusionment. As these scenes unfold, the reader contemplates the Princess's hatred of her father who had wanted a son. Has her oedipal defeat left her unable to love her son or to accept his love? A dying woman now, she wishes that she could have found room for love, but she is too proud to recant the choices of a lifetime. Like an ancient heroine, she permits her son only the filial duty of remembering her with his prayers when she is dead.

The scene between Deronda and his mother derives its force from his disappointment in the gulf between fantasies and reality. "He had lived through so many ideal meetings with his mother," Eliot tells us (p. 535). Deronda's first words to her, "I have thought of you more than of any other being in the world" (p. 536), confirm the reader's insight into his preoccupation with her image. At the second meeting, still hoping for an expression of motherly love, Deronda again compares the fantasies he has lived by to the cruel reality of the moment: "It made the filial yearning of his life a disappointed pilgrimage to a shrine where there were no longer the symbols of sacredness" (p. 566).

In this ego-filtered metaphor of his disappointment the reader finds reassurance of Deronda's ability to withstand his disillusionment of his mother's love and of the power of his own love to reunite them after a long separation. His protected development in a loving adoptive relationship has given him this strength. Daniel's capacity to understand another's motivations again has been put to a test he could not have envisioned; he accepts this test and remains true to his ideal for himself. Nevertheless, in regaining his empathic stance, he is evading anger that will still find expression.

Deronda has discovered a legacy that can give new meaning to his life. He has a meaningful past. He has lost the fulfillment of his heart's wishes, but he has gained a patrimony. Had Deronda not prepared himself for the possibility of Jewish roots, he would have encountered both a cold, denying mother and a legacy he would have had to refuse, discoveries that followed the recent disillusionment of his fantasy about his uncle. Restitutive comfort could be found in learning that his birth father had wanted and loved him and that a grandson was his grandfather's hope for the perpetuation of the dream that had illuminated his life. Thus does an adoptee find solace for the loss of his fantasies of origins that have become "an autobiographical screen," the basis of his personal myth (Kris, 1956).

When he finally meets his mother, he can say, "It is no shame to have Jewish parents—the shame is to disown it" (p. 698). We can compare Deronda's experience to that of the person who has borne adoption as a stigma and who, in the course of a search, learns to use the new term *adoptee* to signify self-acceptance. George Eliot and her hero Deronda share an important conviction: that secrecy is destructive and creates shame. And Eliot's story dramatizes another truth that is equally relevant to the modern adoptee who chooses to search: that the prize is to be won by the searcher who can separate images of the self from the images of the parents, who can maintain a loving self-image despite a disillusioning experience with the real parents, and who can forgive both self and parents for the limitations that are a real part of life. Those who cannot reintegrate the images of self and object in a harmonious concept of personal identity after the loss of fantasy idealizations will remain stuck in the past.

A sadder man emerges from the final meeting with his mother: "Deronda did not know how he got out of the room. He felt an older man. All his boyish yearnings and anxieties about his mother had vanished. He had gone through a tragic experience which must for ever solemnize his life, and deepen the significance of the acts by which he bound himself to others" (p. 571).

Eliot tells us that the proper goal of a journey into the past in search of one's origins is the discovery of the self and its future. She shows us the seductive pull backward, to reclaim lost love and lost sources of narcissistic gratification, then she pulls us forward to the essential quest for the choice of a path for the future that is grounded in an acceptance of the past.

The process that Deronda undergoes destroys illusions about his parents that have been central to his image of a good self, yet it also promotes some forward development. In reintegrating his self and object representations, he preserves a loving image of himself. However, the search for himself is not fully realized and he remains unable to resolve his oedipal conflicts in ways that are satisfying to the reader or predictive of his own future satisfaction.

With the conclusion of the climactic scenes between Deronda and the Princess Halm-Eberstein, the novel's denouement is prepared. Deronda has taken possession of essential knowledge about his origins; he believes he has found his place in history. He has overcome the sense of shame that caused him to hide the sources of his most characteristic motivations. His search has operated on two levels—as a search for new mastery of old conflicts as well as a search for information. It has given rise to compromise resolutions in the realms of sexual desire and ambition.

To many readers, it has seemed a defeat for Deronda and for Eliot that she was unable to imagine an ending that could unite the destinies of Deronda and Gwendolen. It is she who has excited his passion, although he has suppressed his erotic interest in her. He marries; he will have an intimate, affectionate conjugal bond. Like every good Jew, he will "rear his family as if he hoped that a Deliverer might spring from it" (p. 726). But in this union the expression of his full sexuality seems unlikely. The result of his discoveries about his parents is the renunciation of sexual passion.

Would his choice have been different if his encounters with his mother had given him time and scope to relinquish his fantasies? He has been denied his deepest wish; his disappointment is decisive in his choice of a wife. An affirmation of his mother's love—a warm physical embrace at the moment of meeting, a loving response to his offering of love—might have inspired him to open himself to love's sensual pleasures. His rescue fantasy has been defeated. Now he chooses the woman who does not need further rescue. Before his attraction to Gwendolen had felt compelling yet dangerous. Now he renounces these wishes as incompatible with the sense of self and destiny that are leading him forward. His wrenching and evasive departure from Gwendolen is marked by a feeling that he is mourning a lost image of himself.

How shall we interpret Deronda's acceptance of the spiritual destiny prepared for him by Mordecai and by his Moses-like upbringing as "an accomplished Egyptian" (p. 721)? We cannot be surprised when, in answer to the question of the old Jew who delivers his grandfather's trunk of papers, Deronda announces: "I hold that my first duty is to my own people, and if there is anything to be done towards restoring or perfecting their common life, I shall make that my vocation" (p. 792). To this large extent he has embraced the identity that has its source in his blood ties and accepted the duty imposed by his patrimony from his grandfather.

His need to effect personal rescues has become a sublimated desire to transform the state of a large group, the Jews, forming an idealistic goal. After the failure of his wish to rescue his mother, he reaches a more mature acceptance of the limitations of what can be done to alleviate the suffering of another; this change in him is recorded in the difference in the way that he responds to Gwendolen's guilt and fears for herself after the drowning of her husband. In dedicating himself to work on behalf of his ancestral group, Deronda makes a choice that meets the urgent need of the moment. When the confrontation of his separateness from his primary parental objects threatens his sense of a good self, characteristically he finds reparation for his losses in imagining himself in a new rescuer role.

The complexity of Deronda's understanding of what he will bring to his work suggests awareness that his identifications are also rooted in his adoptive experience and that he has the task of integrating two, disparate streams of origin. To Mordecai he insists: "'Don't ask me to deny my spiritual parentage, when I am finding the clues of my life in the recognition of my natural parentage'" (p. 821). His adoptive, English, Christian upbringing is a permanent influence, but his chosen goal must take him far from home.

Deronda's solution for his disillusionments, despite the constancy of his affections, alienates him from the attachment to his uncle. His wise father understands that his beloved son needs time away in order to reinvent—on new terms of greater separateness and in the light of new acceptance of his ambition—the affectionate relationship with his parent that has been his bedrock. Not yet ready for an expression of his oedipal ambitions that can be contained within that relationship, he is more comfortable in allowing himself to surpass his father in aspiring to be a leader of a denigrated group. However, the Zionist goal as presented is without a basis in political realities. Deronda appears once again to be chasing an illusion.

Shortly after his last farewell to his mother, Deronda makes precipitate life choices. Given Eliot's great capacity for empathy, we wonder whether she felt that the pain of her hero's disillusionments would keep him forever seeking new illusions. Or did she, too, imagine that we leave him midstream in his adult developmental course? In the last chapter of *Middlemarch* Eliot asks, "Who can quit young lives after being long in company with them, and not desire to know what befell them in their after-years?" The events that bring *Daniel Deronda* to a close may be the end of the novel, but not the end of the story.

*Daniel Deronda* uses the metaphor of adoption to highlight the universal struggle to find a balance between the need for the freedom to pursue one's own goals and the need to maintain sustaining connections. In the perspective of this analysis, it is a story of the reworking, beginning in adolescence, of separation-individuation issues that blend developmentally into appropriate oedipal strivings. Adoption gives a special twist to this task as it does to the developmental tasks of real-life adoptees. Deronda undertakes this task as a young adult; when adoption is added to the picture, the burdening of separation issues may delay developmental readiness to address them (Brinich, 1990; Schechter and Bertocci, 1990). What we observe in Eliot's hero is a compromise formation that is part of an ongoing process. The life issues that have emerged from his history cannot be imagined to end with youthful identity consolidation. Like Eliot who renounced the marriage-is-the-happy-ending conclusion for her novels, we know that the story continues to develop in adult life (see, for example, Lord and Cox, 1991). When Deronda says that the effects of the secrecy will never be undone, we take Eliot's meaning to be, more profoundly, that Deronda's future problems and choices must forever bear the burdens (and the gifts) of his unique experiences. Inevitably scars have been inflicted, and compromises with ideal hopes must follow.

Nevertheless, out of his adoptive experience has come an admirable, loving young man with an appetite for life's greatest challenges. A good enough adoptive experience has influenced the quality of his search and made his a good one with a growth-enhancing result, although it has not permitted the full resolution of his developmental conflicts.

Interestingly, literary critics have registered disappointment with Eliot's depiction of her hero; to some Eliot's characterization has seemed not quite "rounded," not quite real, not quite a fully realized portrait of a man. He is "namby-pamby." In part these judgments appear to miss the windows into internal dilemmas that Eliot provides even while she focuses on external developments. Nevertheless, a deeper analysis of his character and of his identity resolutions suggests that the flaws that critics ascribe to the realization of the character in fact derive from the author's complex understanding of her hero. One wonders whether he shares a decisive flaw with his creator.

Fear of anger is the flaw or issue that stops the resolution of Deronda's fantasies that would free his oedipal strivings without threatening to destroy his connections. He remains stuck in the childish position of believing that hostile wishes bring destruction. His high ideal of respect for otherness, an ideal that is connection-preserving, has not been integrated into a parallel tolerance of his own feelings and motivations.

For George Eliot herself, the family romance fantasy was a central theme as we may conclude from the number of her novels in which it finds expression. In *Daniel Deronda*, her last novel, her last try at imagining the full integration of these fantasies, she came much further than she had in the earlier *Silas Marner*. In that story, revelations of the truths of the lives of Silas and Eppie, his adopted daughter, do not lead forward. Silas and Eppie find a lifelong paradise in the garden that they have created together.

Eliot's great achievements were accompanied both by large personal suffering and unusual personal rewards in the middle of her life. The effects of Eliot's compromise resolutions of her core fantasies were both positive and negative. They provided freedom for the reach of great ambition; freedom for the muse that allowed her to make her woman's voice heard; and freedom to give and receive unusually sustaining love and companionship. At the same time, unhappily, her compromise resolutions did not arm her against the losses and ambiguities that she endured in familial and social relationships. Although we must not underestimate the effects of the hostility of her world to a woman of her ambition, the suffering that she expressed in endless mental anguish and physical affliction are evidence that her intrapsychic balance remained uncertain (Redinger, 1975). Nevertheless her incomparable literary achievement is a testimony to the creativity that can be inspired by an enduring fantasy that never fully yields to reality.

We do not imagine that Deronda will achieve his Zionist dream and yet Eliot's dream—of "separation with connection"—the goal that exceeded her grasp, has been achieved in our time both for women and for the Jews.

## BIBLIOGRAPHY

BRINICH, P. M. (1980). Some potential effects of adoption on self and object representations. *Psychoanal. Study Child,* 35:107–133.

———— (1990). Adoption from the inside out. In *The Psychology of Adoption,* ed. D. M. Brodzinsky & M. D. Schechter. New York: Oxford Univ. Press, pp. 42–61.

CLOTHIER, F. (1943). The psychology of the adopted child. *Ment. Hyg.,* 27:222–230.

COLARUSSO, C. A. (1987). Mother is that you? *Psychoanal. Study Child,* 42:223–237.

DAVID, D. (1981). *Fictions of Resolution in Three Victorian Novels.* New York: Columbia Univ. Press.

ELIOT, G. (1876). *Daniel Deronda.* London: Penguin, 1967.

ERIKSON, E. H. (1975). Identity crisis in autobiographic perspective. In *Life History and the Historical Moment.* New York: Norton, pp. 17–47.

FREUD, A. (1965). *Normality and Pathology in Childhood.* New York: Int. Univ. Press.

FREUD, S. (1909). Family romances. *S.E.,* 9:237–241.

———— (1910). A special type of choice of object made by men. *S.E.,* 11:165–175.

FROSCH, J. (1959). Transference derivatives of the family romance. *J. Amer. Psychoanal. Assn.,* 7:503–522.

GOLDSTEIN, J., FREUD, A., & SOLNIT, A. J. (1973). *Beyond the Best Interests of the Child.* New York: Free Press.

GREENACRE, P. (1958). The family romance of the artist. *Psychoanal. Study Child,* 13:9–43.

KRIS, E. (1956). The personal myth. *J. Amer. Psychoanal. Assn.,* 4:653–681.

LORD, R. & COX, C. E. (1991). Adoption and identity. *Psychoanal. Study Child,* 46:355–367.

NICKMAN, S. L. (1985). Losses in adoption. *Psychoanal. Study Child,* 40:165–198.

REDINGER, R. (1975). *George Eliot.* New York: Knopf.

ROSENBERG, E. & HORNER, T. (1991). Birthparent romances and identity formation in adopted children. *Amer. J. Orthopsychiat.,* 61:70–77.

SANTS, H. J. (1964). Genealogical bewilderment in children with substitute parents. *Brit. J. Med. Psychol.*, 37:133–141.

SCHECHTER, M. D. & BERTOCCI, D. (1990). The meaning of the search. In *The Psychology of Adoption*, ed. D. M. Brodzinsky & M. D. Schechter. New York: Oxford Univ. Press, pp. 62–90.

SHERICK, I. (1983). Adoption and disturbed narcissism. *J. Amer. Psychoanal. Assn.*, 31:487–513.

WARNER, L. L. (1985). *Adopted Women's Search for the Biological Mother.* Unpublished doctoral dissertation, Smith College School Social Work, Northampton, Mass.

WIEDER, H. (1977). The family romance fantasies of adopted children. *Psychoanal. Q.*, 46:185–200.

# Index